RECENTLY...?

BRING BRING

NO, IT'S ACTUALLY YOUR FAULT.

和 月 伸 宏

NOBUHIRO WATSUKI

HER NAME IS GINRIN 3

THE PAIN IN MY BUTT HAS GONE AWAY
(REFERRING TO THE PREVIOUS VOLUME),
SO I AM CYCLING ONCE AGAIN. YAY! YAY!
WHENEVER I AM NOT WRITING, I RIDE AT
LEAST 20 TO 30 MINUTES EACH DAY. IT'S
FAR FROM ADEQUATE EXERCISE, BUT
MOVING MY BODY MAKES ME FEEL AS
THOUGH MY PHYSICAL CONDITION IS GET-
TING BETTER. THE OTHER DAY I GOT
CARRIED AWAY AND TRIED TO REACH MACH
SPEED, FELL OVER, SCRAPED MY KNEE,
AND BLED. I'M LIKE...A KINDERGARTNER?!

Rurouni Kenshin, which has found
fans not only in Japan but around
the world, first made its appearance
in 1992, as an original short story in
Weekly Shonen Jump Special. Later
rewritten and published as a regular,
continuing *Jump* series in 1994,
Rurouni Kenshin ended serialization
in 1999 but continued in popularity,
as evidenced by the 2000 publication
of *Yahiko no Sakabatô* ("Yahiko's
Reversed-Edge Sword") in *Weekly
Shonen Jump*. His most current work,
Busô Renkin ("Armored Alchemist"),
began publication in June 2003, also
in *Jump*.

RUROUNI KENSHIN
VOL. 21: AND SO, TIME PASSED
The SHONEN JUMP Graphic Novel Edition

STORY AND ART BY
NOBUHIRO WATSUKI

English Adaptation/Pancha Diaz
Translation/Kenichiro Yagi
Touch-Up Art & Lettering/Steve Dutro
Design/Matt Hinrichs
Editor/Kit Fox

Managing Editor/Elizabeth Kawasaki
Director of Production/Noboru Watanabe
Vice President of Publishing/Alvin Lu
Vice President & Editor in Chief/Yumi Hoashi
Sr. Director of Acquisitions/Rika Inouye
Vice President of Sales & Marketing/Liza Coppola
Publisher/Hyoe Narita

Printed in the U.S.A.

Published by VIZ Media, LLC
P.O. Box 77010
San Francisco, CA 94107

SHONEN JUMP Graphic Novel Edition
10 9 8 7 6 5 4 3 2 1
First printing, November 2005

www.viz.com

PARENTAL ADVISORY
RUROUNI KENSHIN is rated T+ for Older Teen and is recommended for ages 16 and up. This volume contains realistic violence and alcohol and tobacco use.

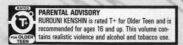

SHONEN JUMP GRAPHIC NOVEL

Rurouni Kenshin™

STORY & ART BY NOBUHIRO WATSUKI

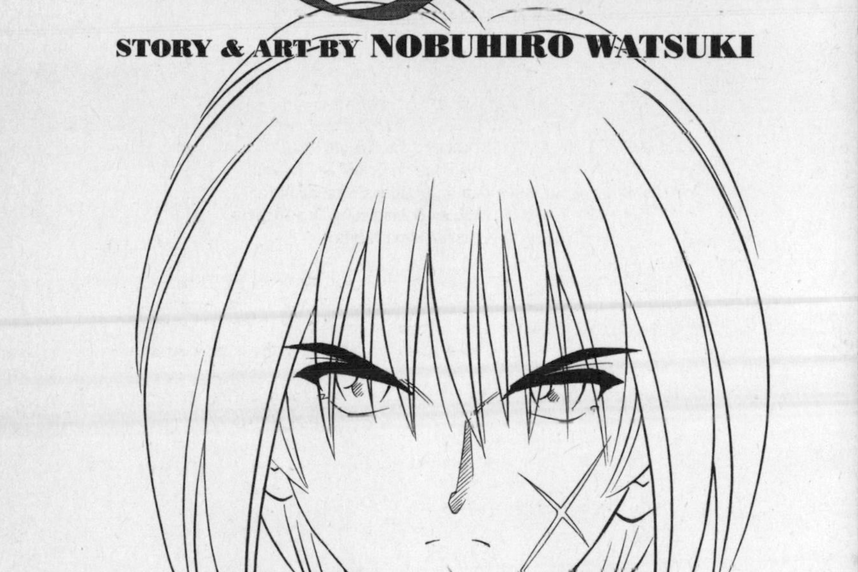

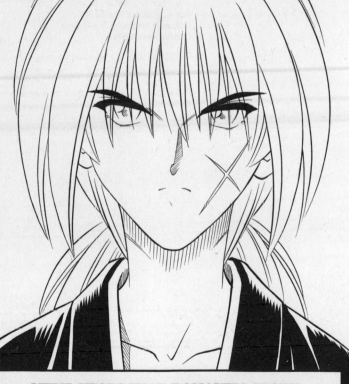

MEIJI SWORDSMAN ROMANTIC STORY

Vol. 21: AND SO, TIME PASSED

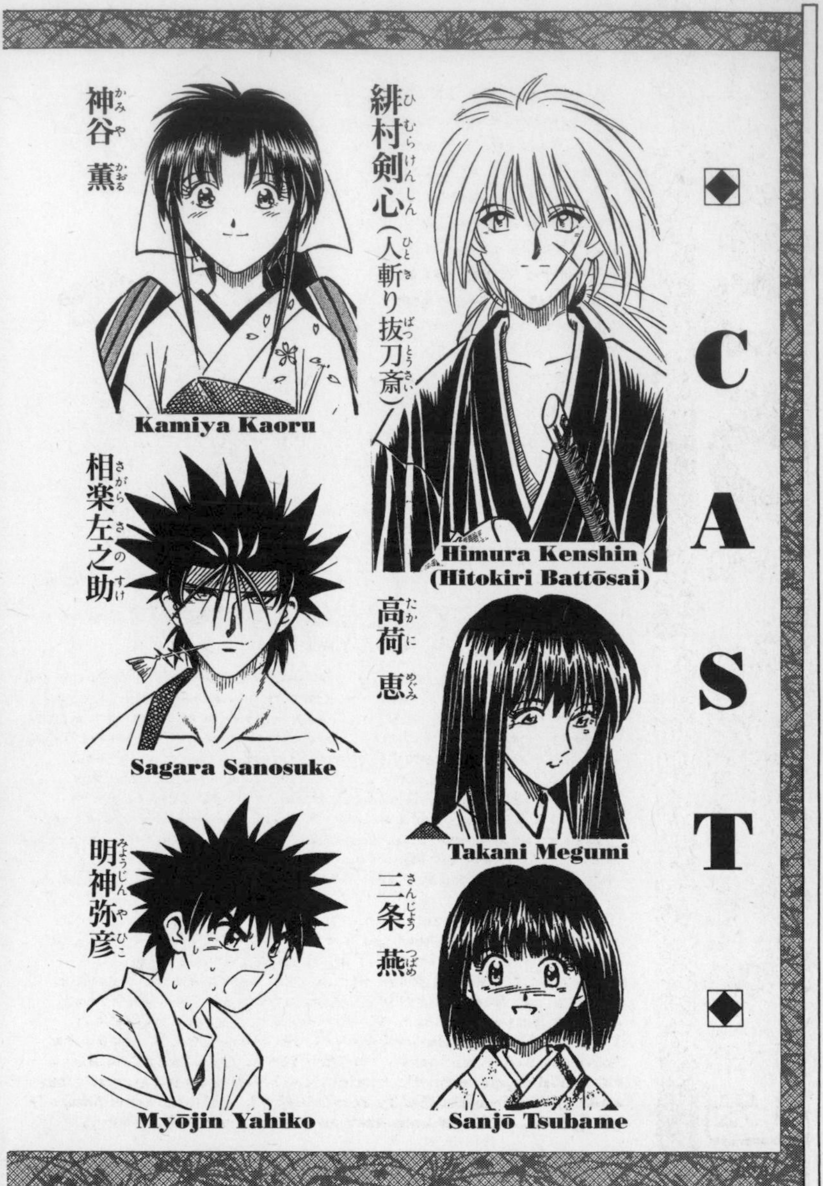
CAST
緋村剣心（人斬り抜刀斎）
Himura Kenshin (Hitokiri Battōsai)
神谷薫
Kamiya Kaoru
高荷恵
Takani Megumi
相楽左之助
Sagara Sanosuke
三条燕
Sanjō Tsubame
明神弥彦
Myōjin Yahiko

Once he was *hitokiri*, an assassin, called Battōsai. His name was legend among the pro-Imperialist or "patriot" warriors who launched the Meiji Era. Now, Himura Kenshin is *rurouni*, a wanderer, and carries a reversed-edge *sakabatō* to prohibit himself from killing.

雪代 縁
(ゆきしろ)(えにし)

Yukishiro Enishi

雪代（緋村）巴
(ゆきしろ)(ひむら)(ともえ)

Yukishiro (Himura) Tomoe

T H U S F A R

Kenshin and his friends return to Tokyo after a deadly battle to defeat Shishio Makoto and his ambitions of conquering Japan. However, their peace is short lived as those with grudges against Battōsai gather for revenge, attacking Akabeko, Maekawa Dojo, and police chief Uramura's house. To make matters worse, Kenshin finds out that the mastermind of this new attack is Enishi, the brother of Kenshin's deceased wife Tomoe. Enishi confronts Kenshin and declares that he will lead an assault on Kamiya Dojo in ten days. Kenshin decides that although he can never fully atone for his crimes, he will fight to protect the present, and begins by telling the story of his past to his friends.

The time is Bakumatsu. Kenshin is wielding his sword for the "New Era." Tomoe, who got her fiancé killed by Kenshin, joins the "Yaminobu" and approaches Kenshin to uncover his weakness. To her surprise, Tomoe comes to care for Kenshin. But the Yaminobu, who had this in mind from the beginning, capture Tomoe in order to lure Kenshin into the "Binding Forest." Although the evil forest dulls his senses, Kenshin continues to defeat his opponents—but not without consequences. Before his opponents die, explosions damage Kenshin's hearing and vision. Kenshin finally reaches the location where Tomoe is being held, and now faces the last of the Yaminobu. But...?!

CONTENTS

RUROUNI KENSHIN
Meiji Swordsman Romantic Story
BOOK TWENTY-ONE: AND SO, TIME PASSED

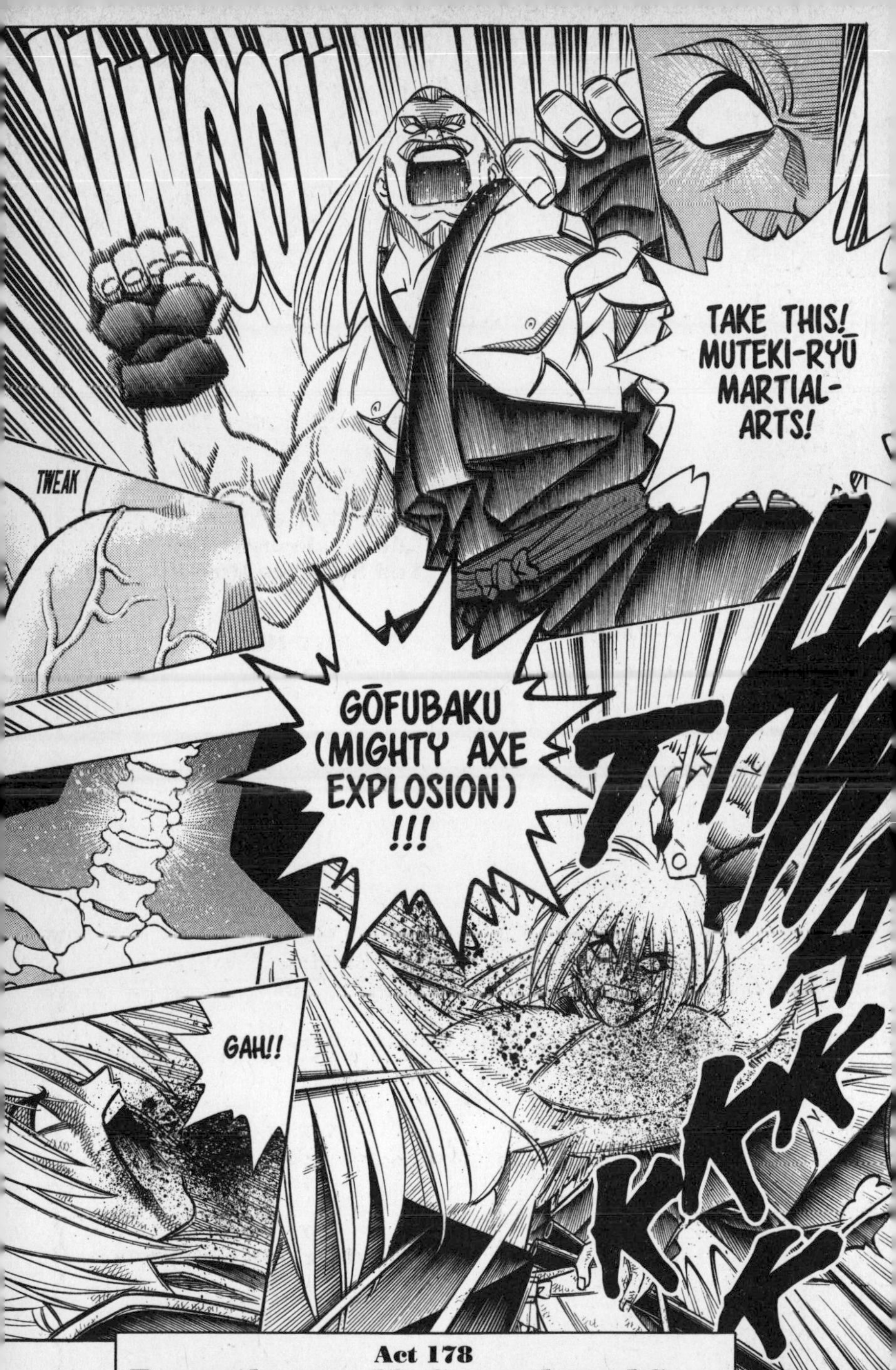
TAKE THIS! MUTEKI-RYŪ MARTIAL-ARTS!
TWEAK
GŌFUBAKU (MIGHTY AXE EXPLOSION) !!!
GAH!!

Act 178
Remembrance 13: Cross-shaped Scar

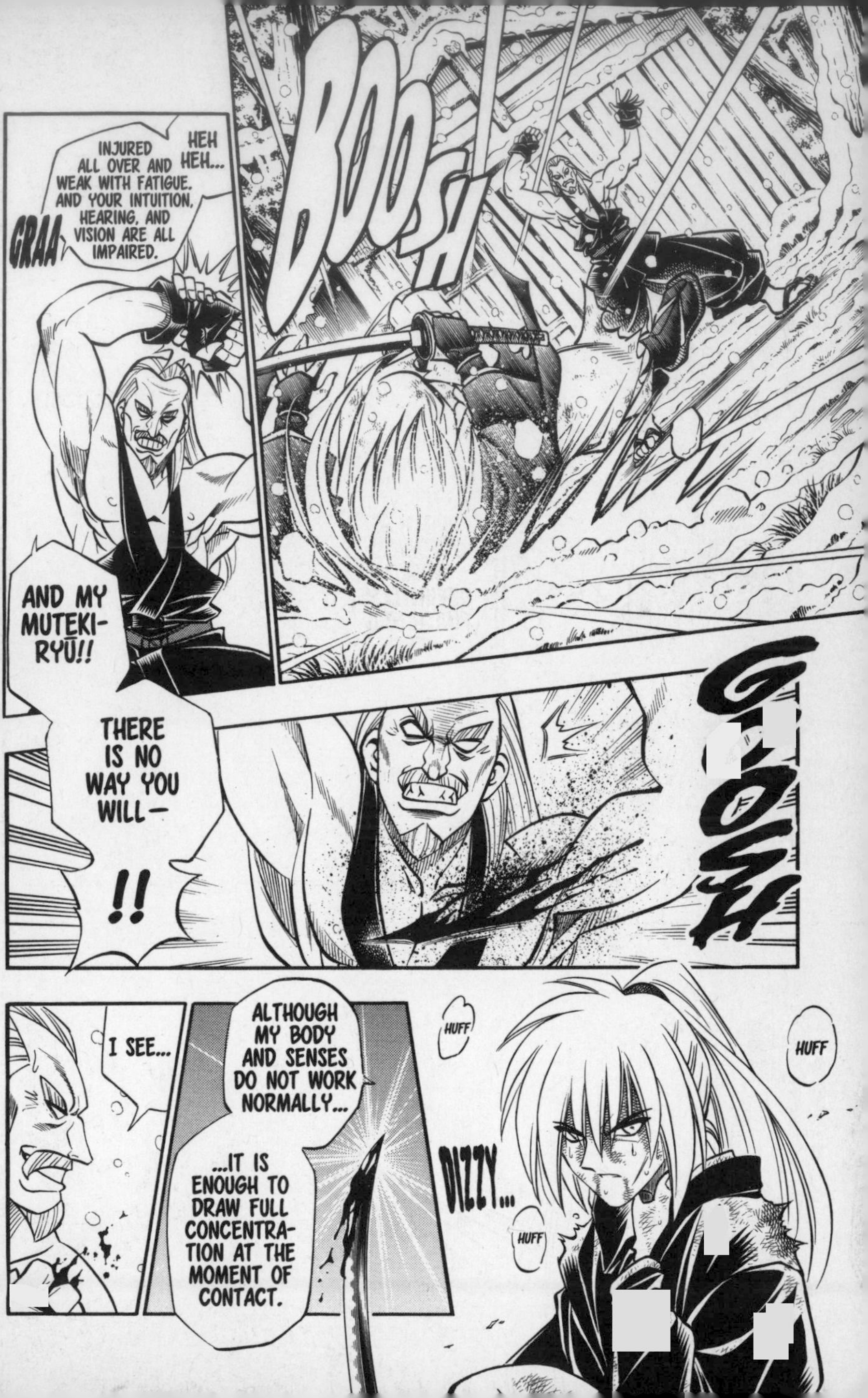
BOOSH
HEH HEH...
INJURED ALL OVER AND WEAK WITH FATIGUE. AND YOUR INTUITION, HEARING, AND VISION ARE ALL IMPAIRED.
GRAA
AND MY MUTEKI-RYŪ!!
THERE IS NO WAY YOU WILL—
!!
HUFF
HUFF
DIZZY...
HUFF
ALTHOUGH MY BODY AND SENSES DO NOT WORK NORMALLY...
...IT IS ENOUGH TO DRAW FULL CONCENTRATION AT THE MOMENT OF CONTACT.
I SEE...

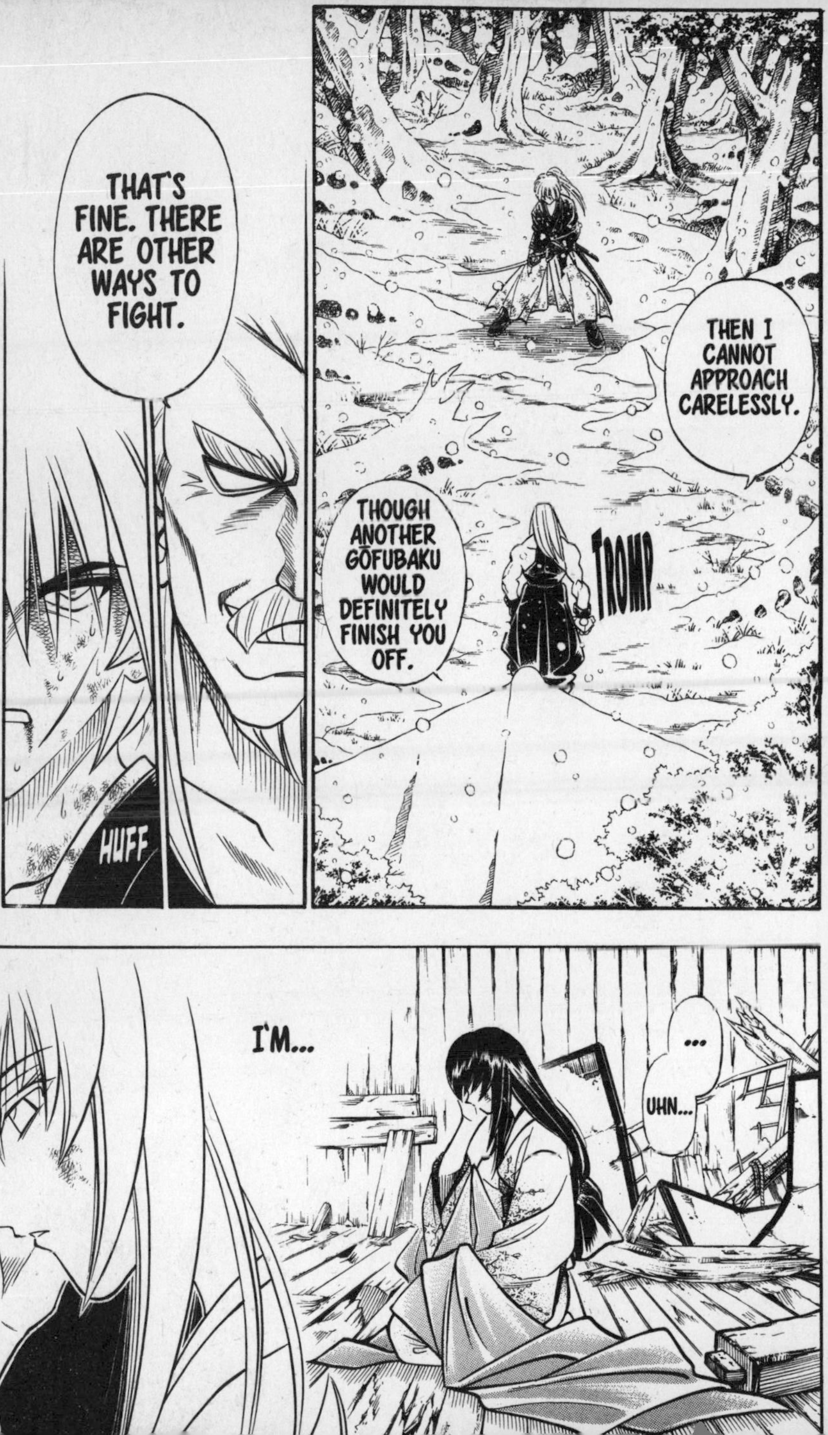
THEN I CANNOT APPROACH CARELESSLY.
TROMP
THOUGH ANOTHER GŌFUBAKU WOULD DEFINITELY FINISH YOU OFF.
THAT'S FINE. THERE ARE OTHER WAYS TO FIGHT.
HUFF
...
UHN...
I'M...

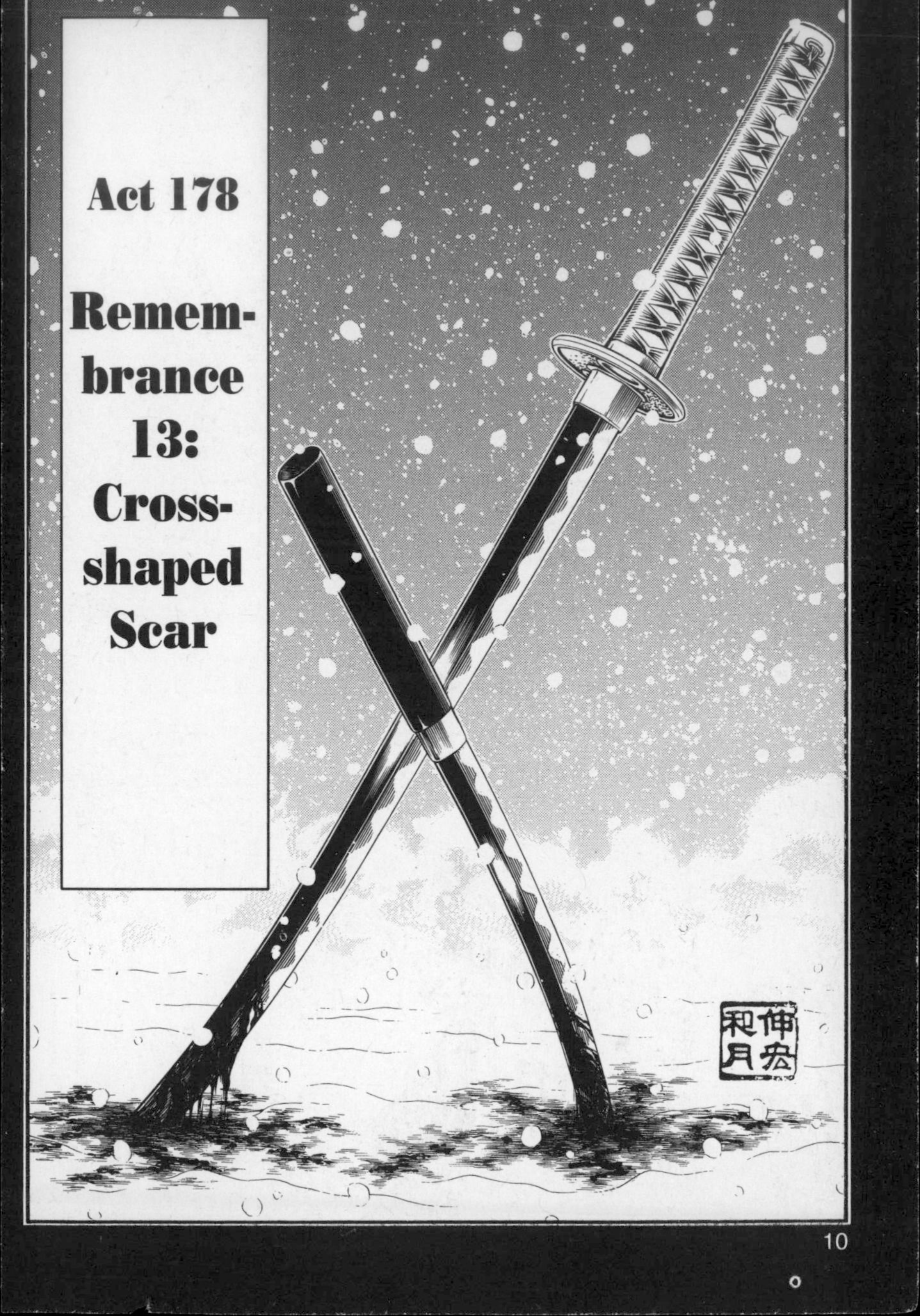
Act 178
Remem-brance 13: Cross-shaped Scar

READ THIS WAY

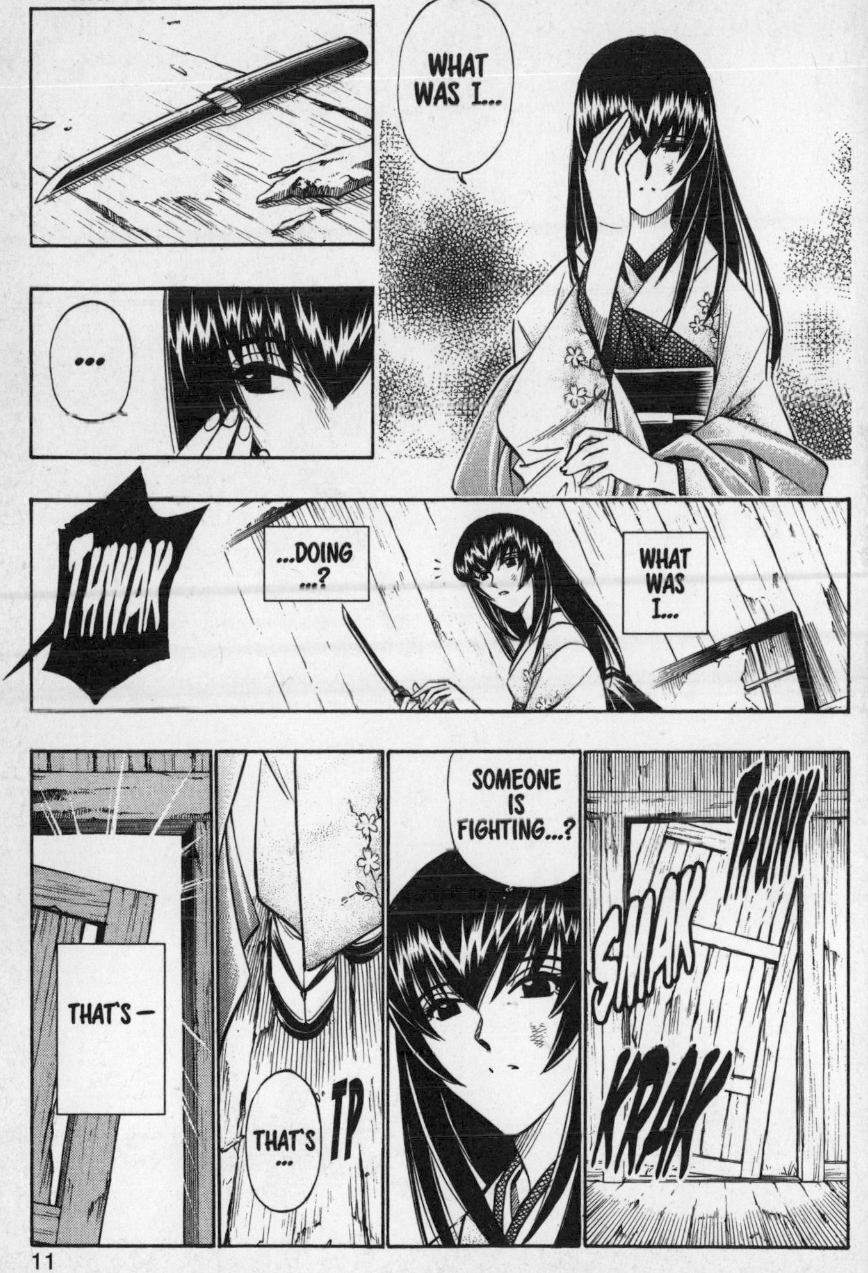
WHAT WAS I...
...
WHAT WAS I...
...DOING ...?
THWAK
THUNK
SMAK
KRAK
SOMEONE IS FIGHTING...?
THAT'S ...
TP
THAT'S —

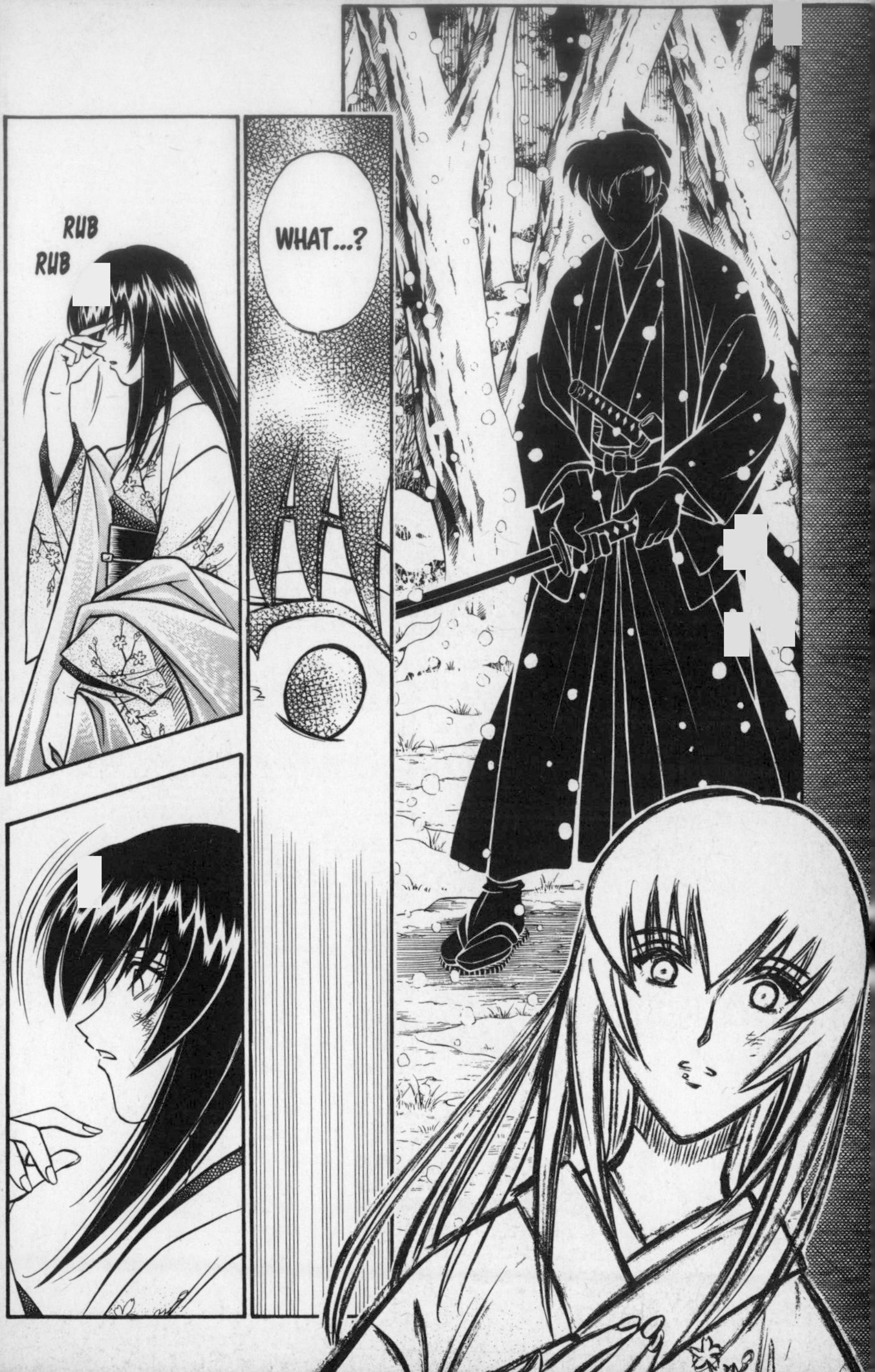
WHAT...?
RUB RUB

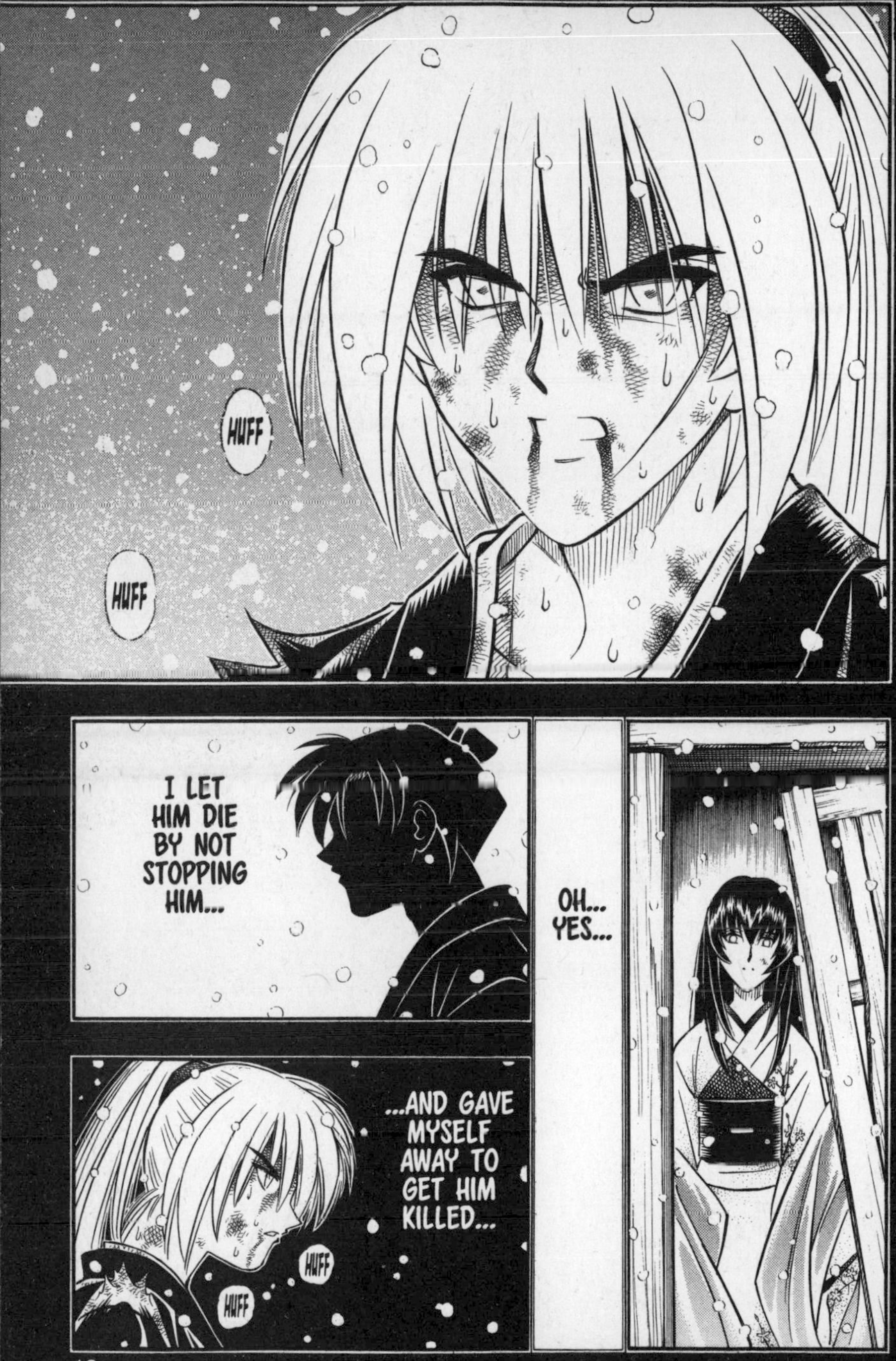
HUFF
HUFF
OH... YES...
I LET HIM DIE BY NOT STOPPING HIM...
...AND GAVE MYSELF AWAY TO GET HIM KILLED...
HUFF
HUFF

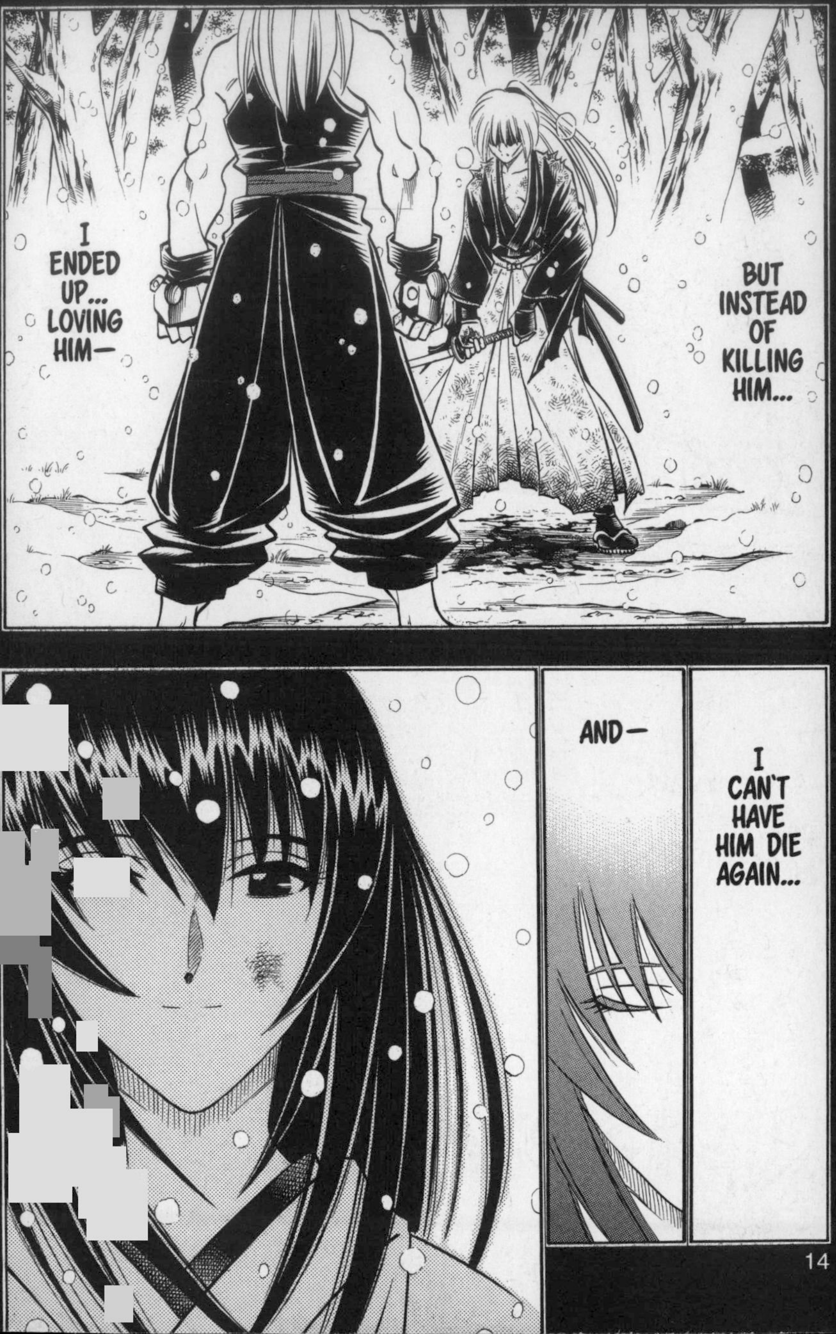
BUT INSTEAD OF KILLING HIM...
I ENDED UP... LOVING HIM—
I CAN'T HAVE HIM DIE AGAIN...
AND—

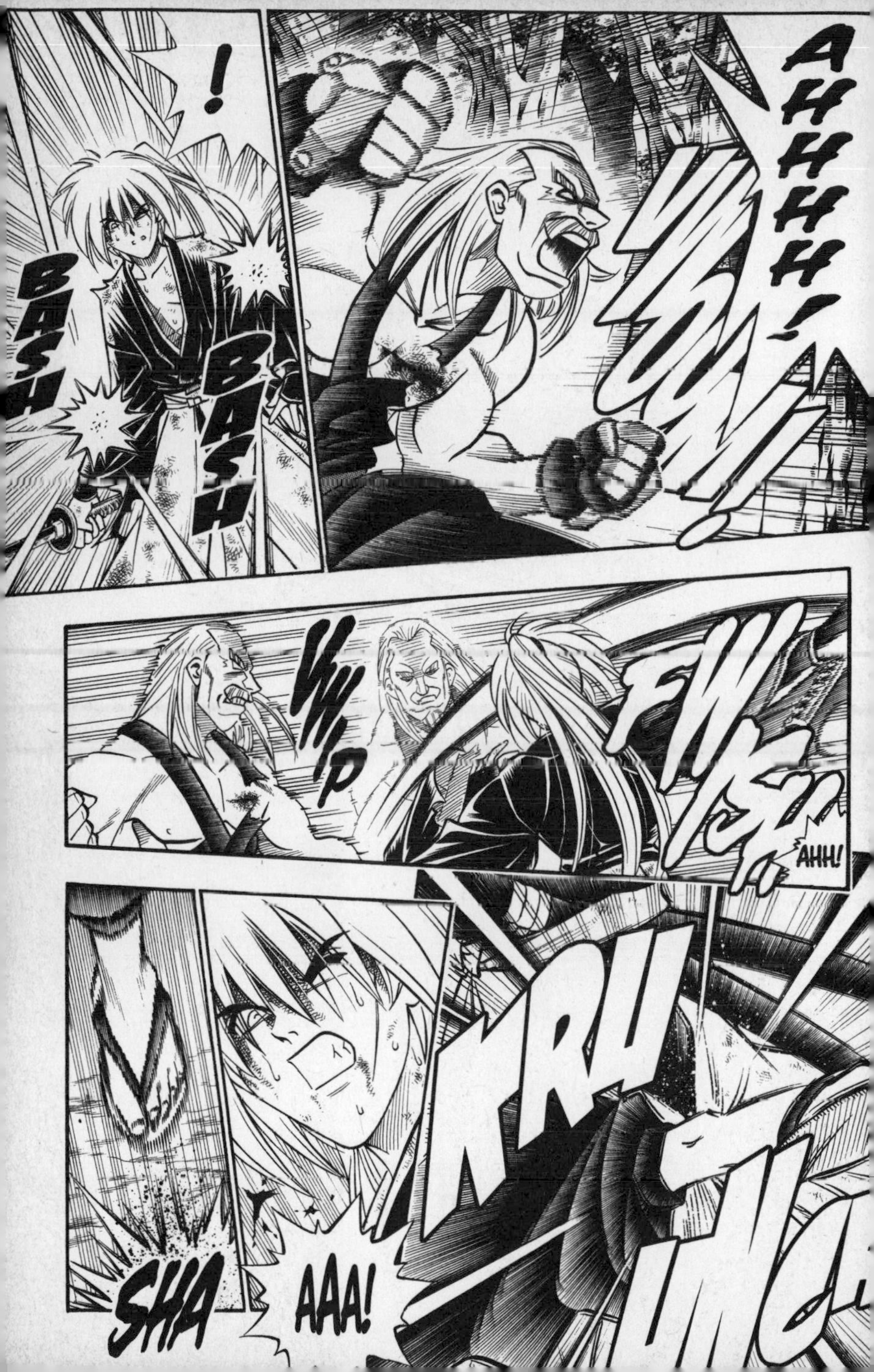
AHHHHH!
!
BASH
BASH
WHIP
AHH!
AAA!
SHA

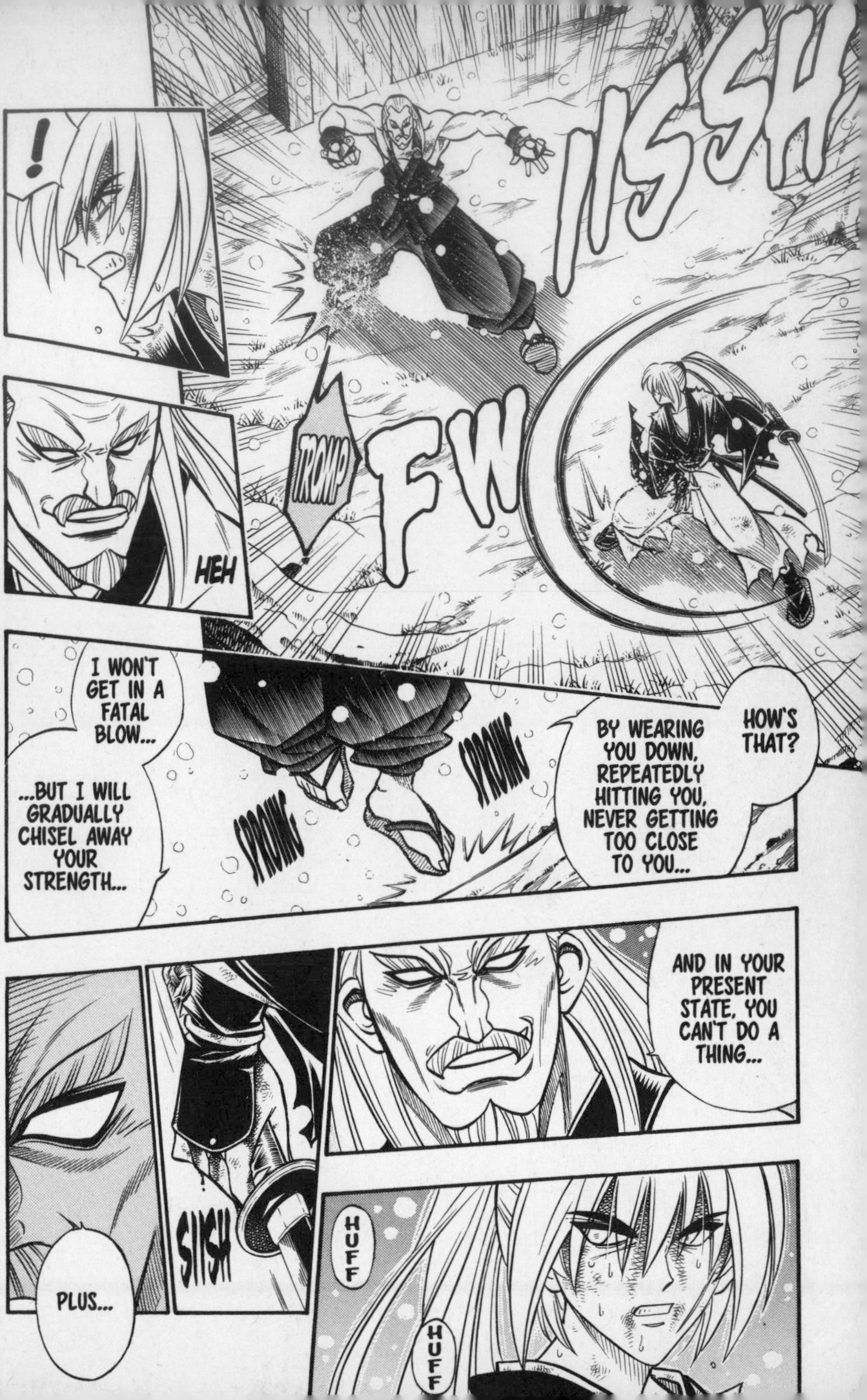
ISSH
FW
TROMP
!
HEH
HOW'S THAT?
BY WEARING YOU DOWN, REPEATEDLY HITTING YOU, NEVER GETTING TOO CLOSE TO YOU...
SPRONG
SPRONG
I WON'T GET IN A FATAL BLOW...
...BUT I WILL GRADUALLY CHISEL AWAY YOUR STRENGTH...
AND IN YOUR PRESENT STATE, YOU CAN'T DO A THING...
HUFF
HUFF
SIISH
PLUS...

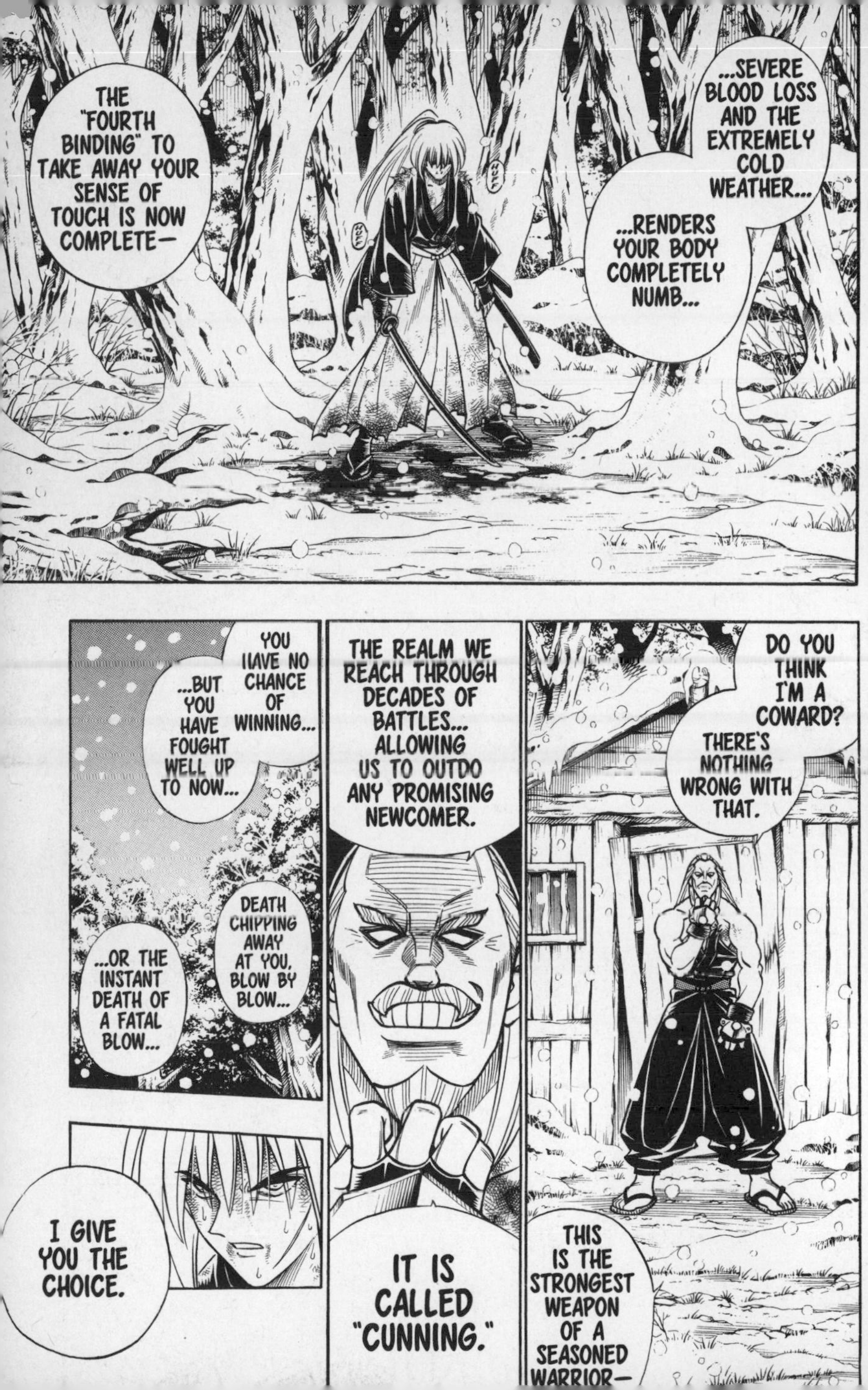
...SEVERE BLOOD LOSS AND THE EXTREMELY COLD WEATHER...
...RENDERS YOUR BODY COMPLETELY NUMB...
HUFF
HUFF
THE "FOURTH BINDING" TO TAKE AWAY YOUR SENSE OF TOUCH IS NOW COMPLETE—
DO YOU THINK I'M A COWARD?
THERE'S NOTHING WRONG WITH THAT.
THIS IS THE STRONGEST WEAPON OF A SEASONED WARRIOR—
THE REALM WE REACH THROUGH DECADES OF BATTLES... ALLOWING US TO OUTDO ANY PROMISING NEWCOMER.
IT IS CALLED "CUNNING."
YOU HAVE NO CHANCE OF WINNING...
...BUT YOU HAVE FOUGHT WELL UP TO NOW...
DEATH CHIPPING AWAY AT YOU, BLOW BY BLOW...
...OR THE INSTANT DEATH OF A FATAL BLOW...
I GIVE YOU THE CHOICE.

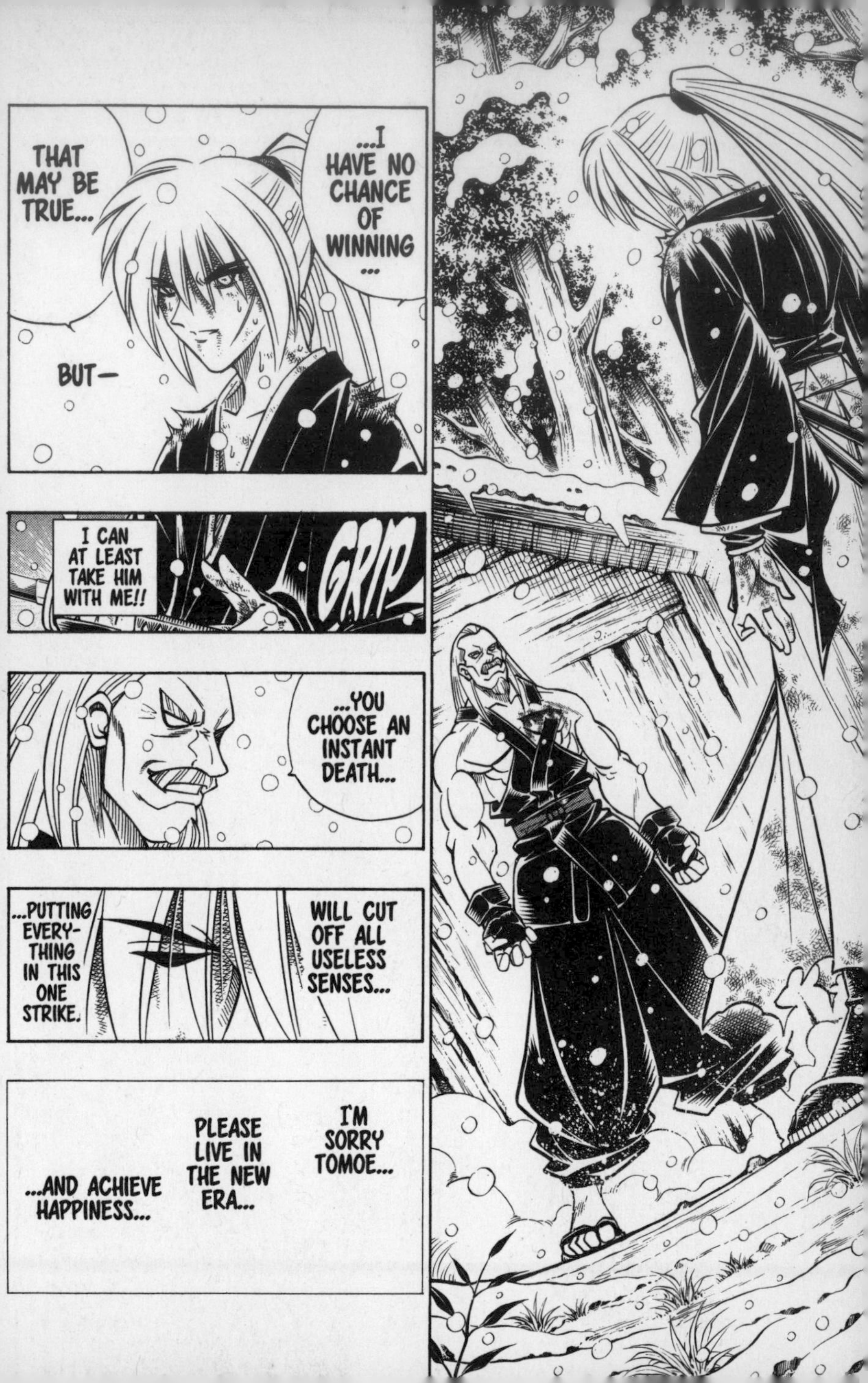
...I HAVE NO CHANCE OF WINNING ...
THAT MAY BE TRUE...
BUT—
GRIP
I CAN AT LEAST TAKE HIM WITH ME!!
...YOU CHOOSE AN INSTANT DEATH...
WILL CUT OFF ALL USELESS SENSES...
...PUTTING EVERYTHING IN THIS ONE STRIKE.
I'M SORRY TOMOE...
PLEASE LIVE IN THE NEW ERA...
...AND ACHIEVE HAPPINESS...

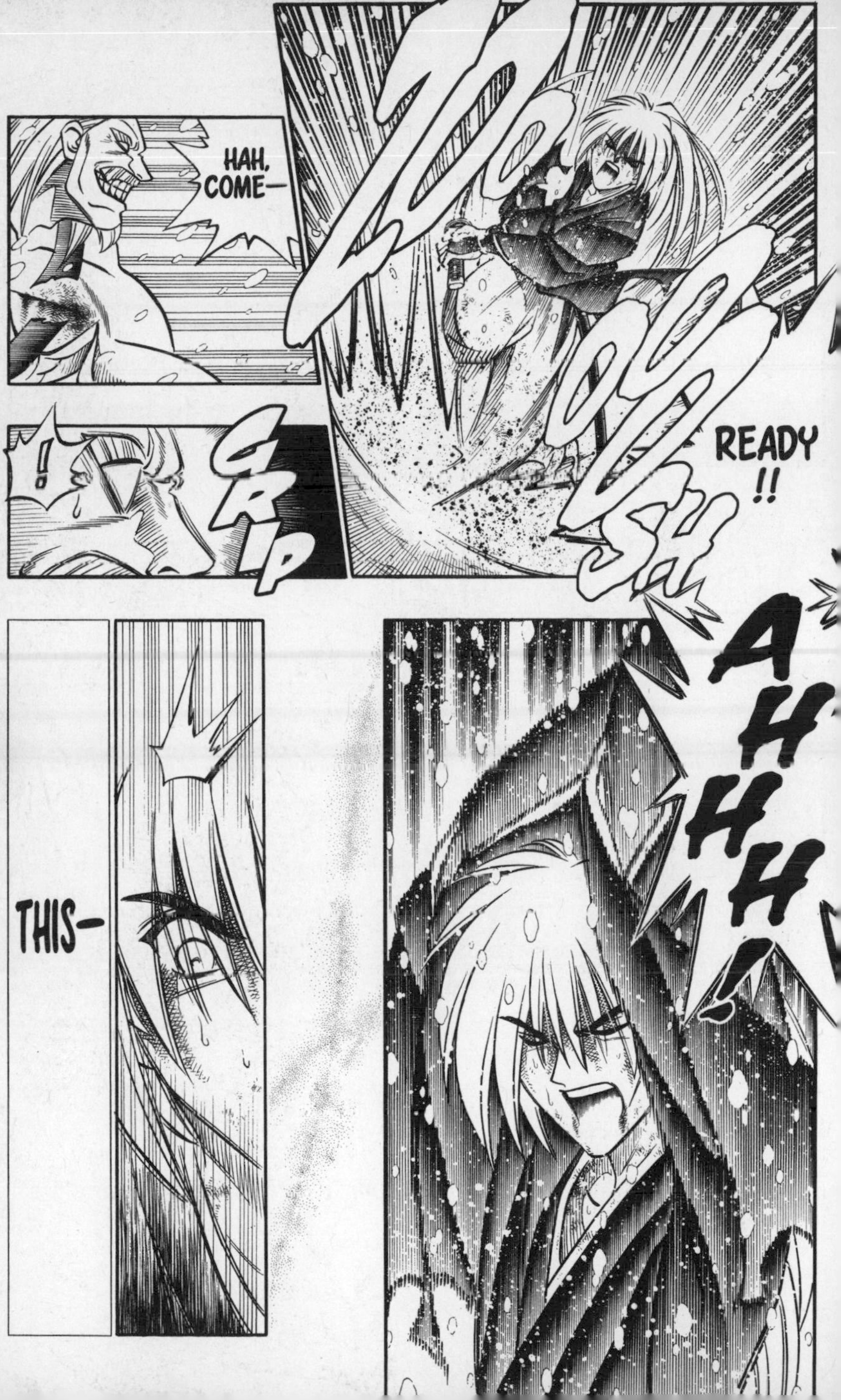
READY !!
HAH, COME-
!
GRIP
AHHHH!
THIS-

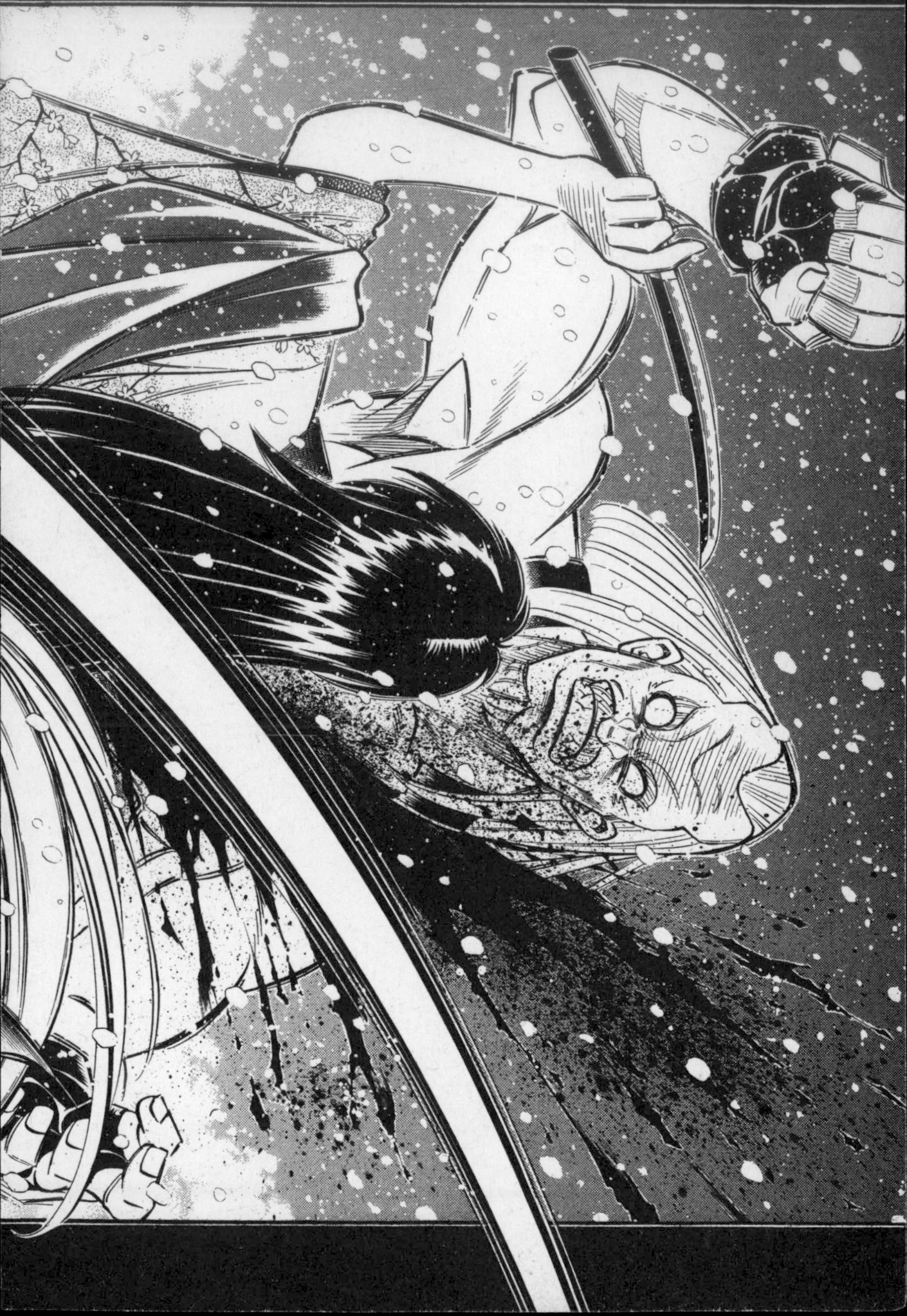

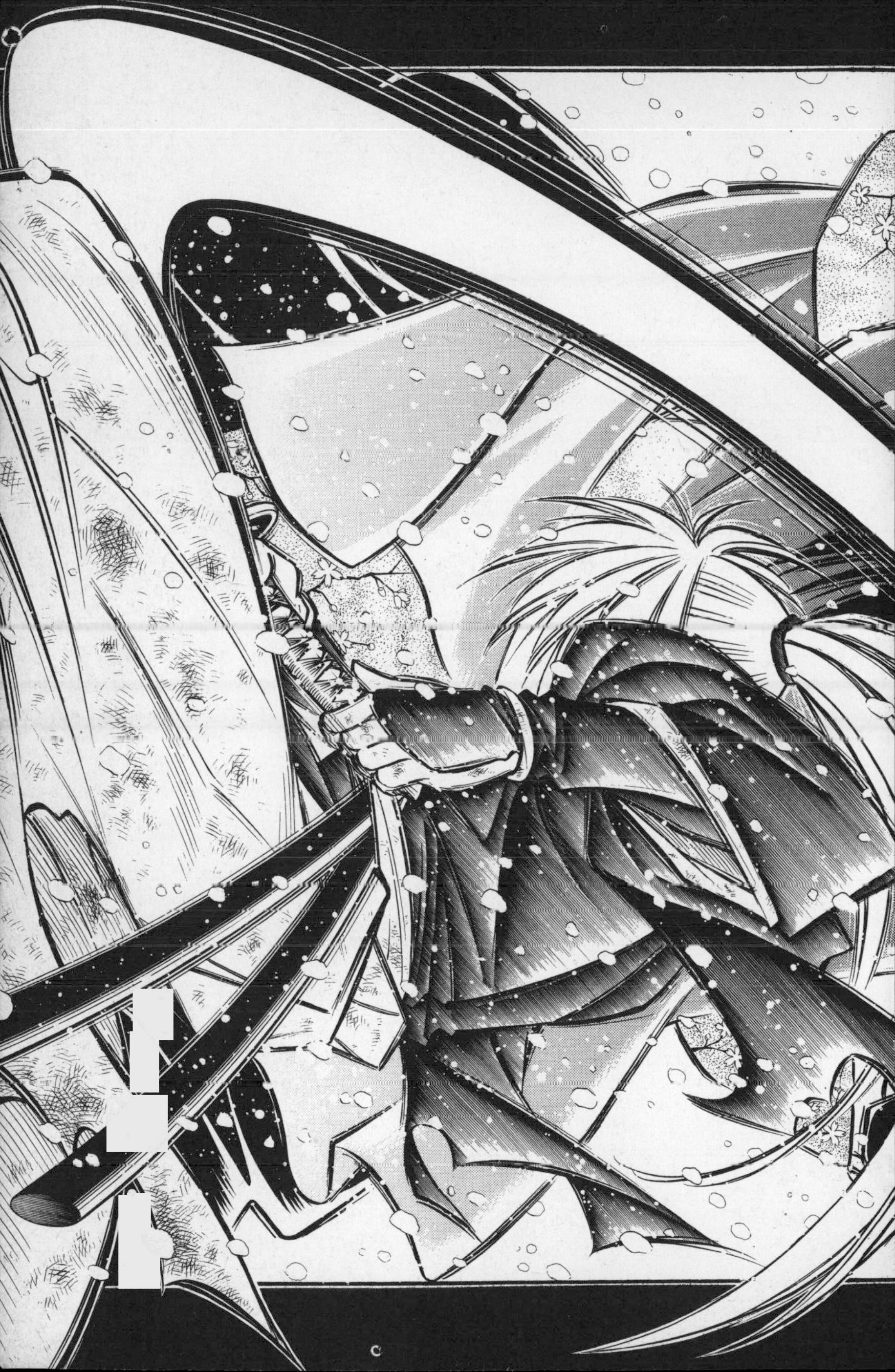

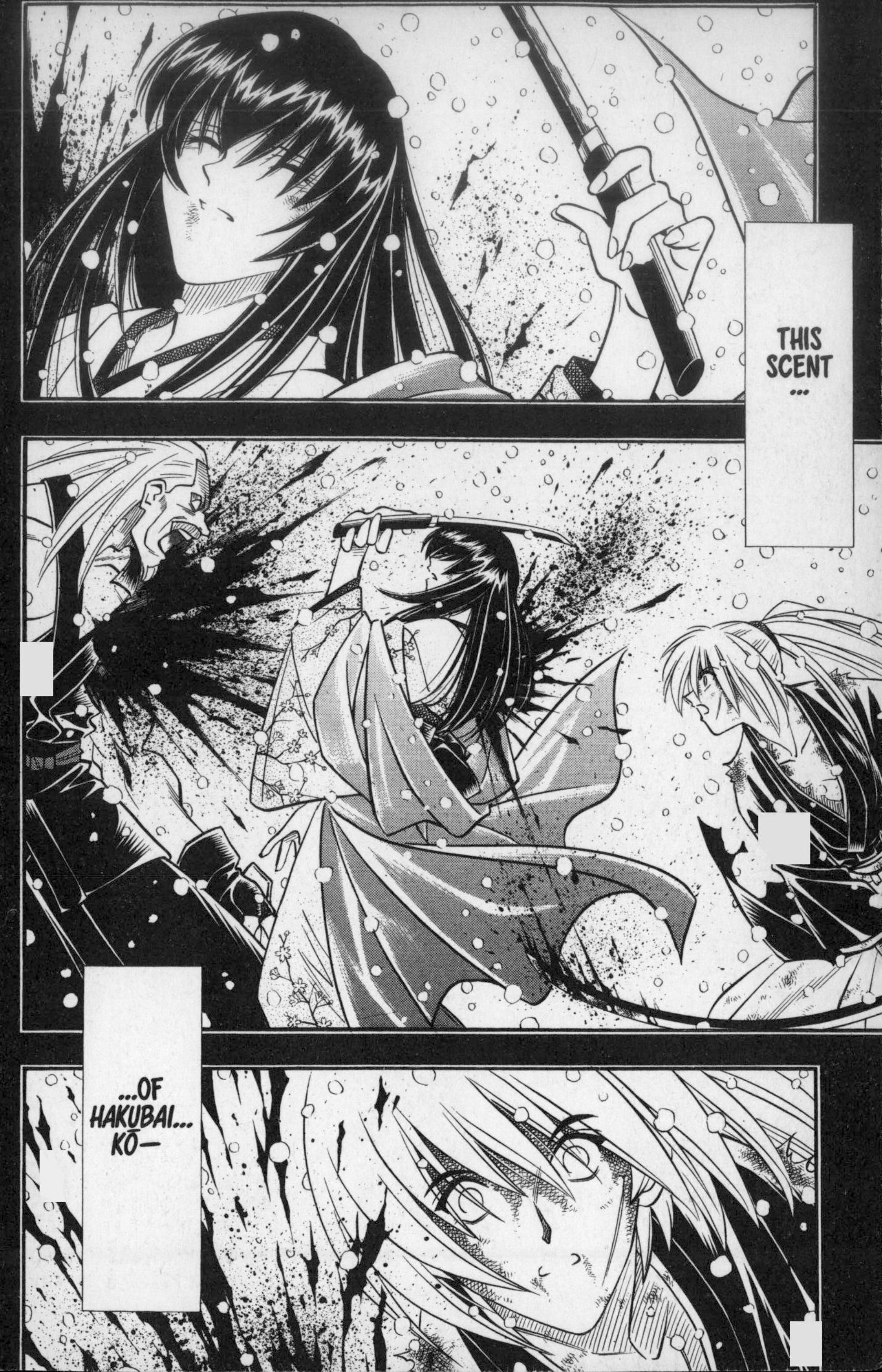
THIS SCENT
...
...OF HAKUBAI... KŌ—

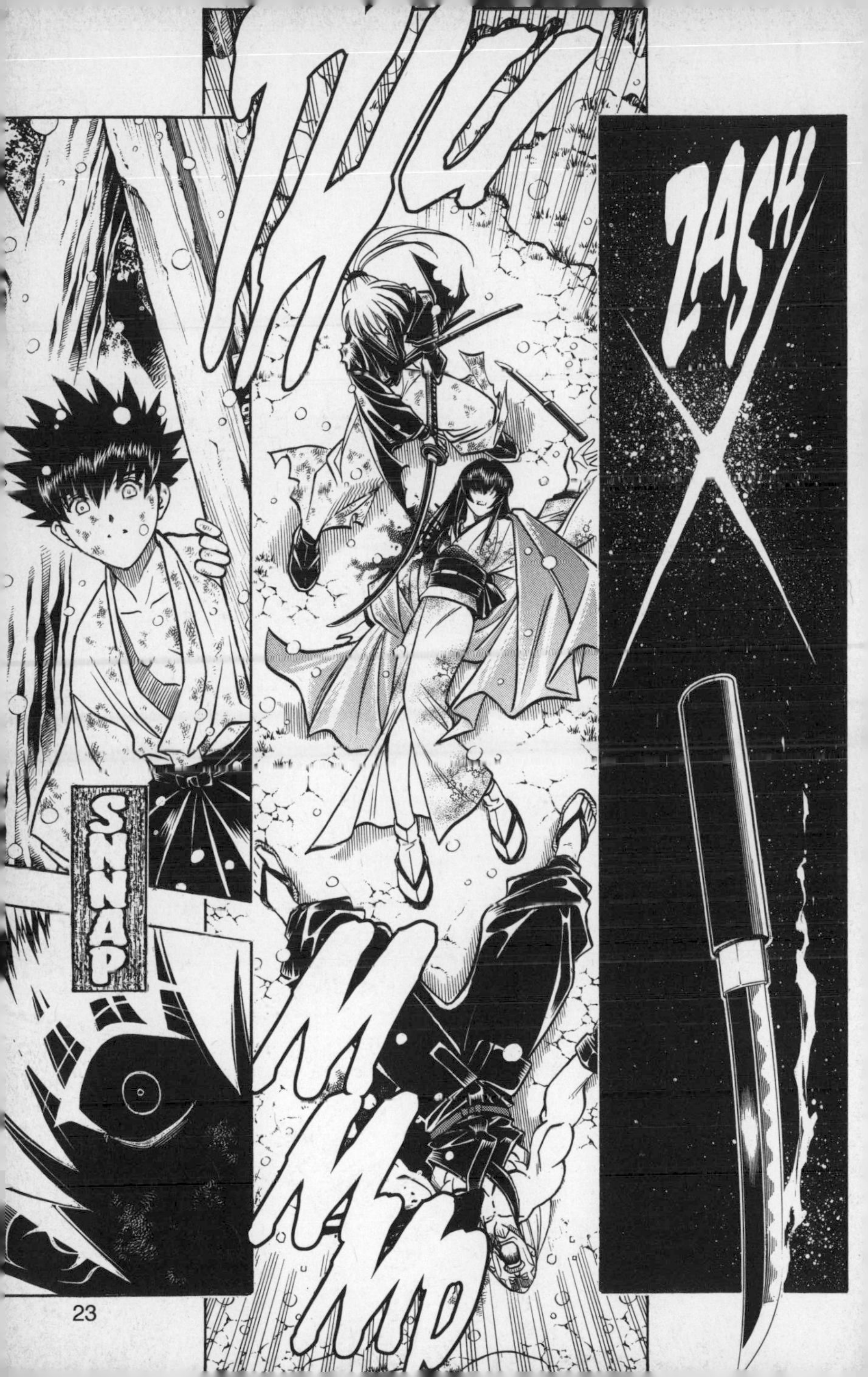
ZASH
SNNAP

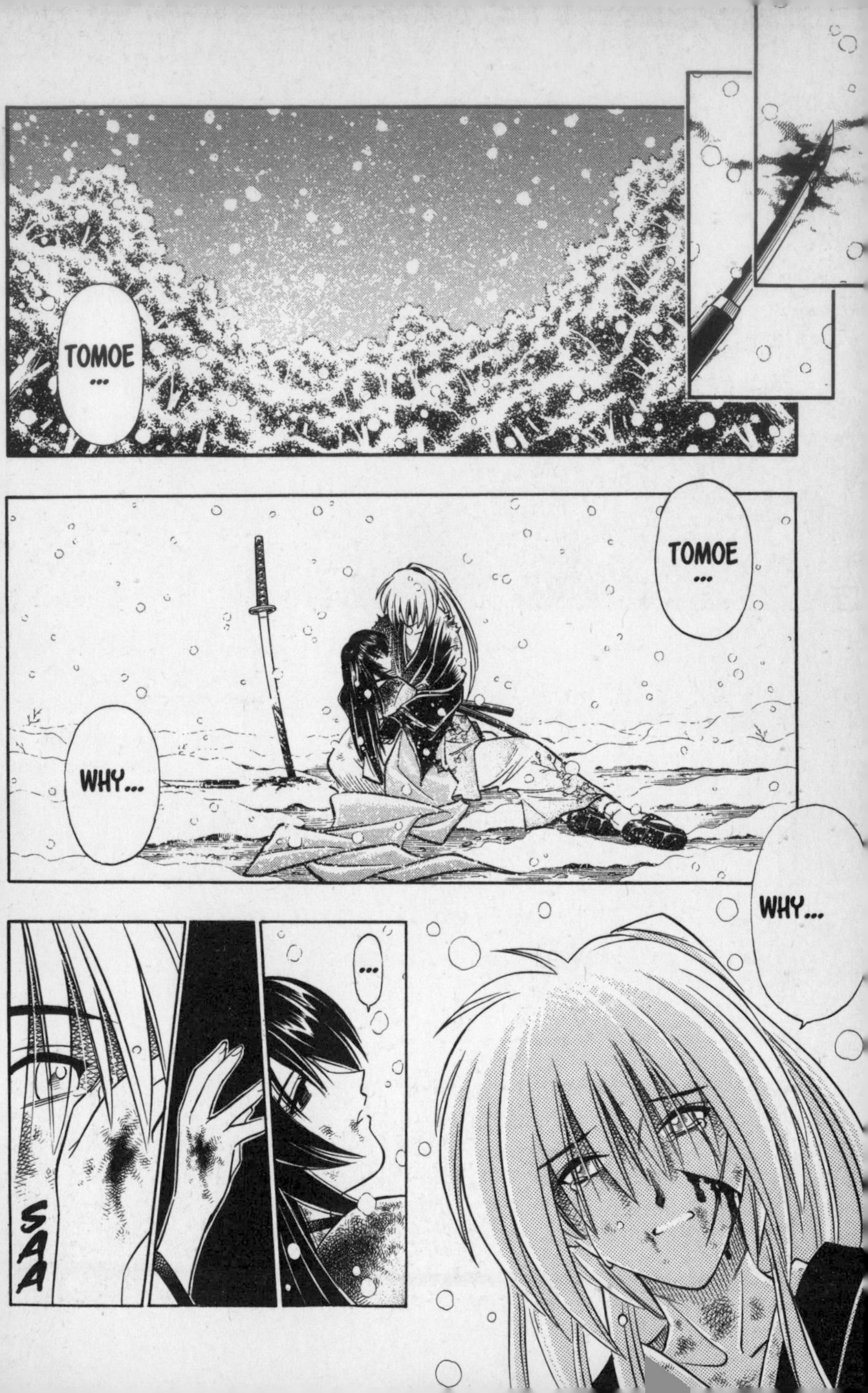
TOMOE ...
TOMOE ...
WHY...
WHY...
...
SAA

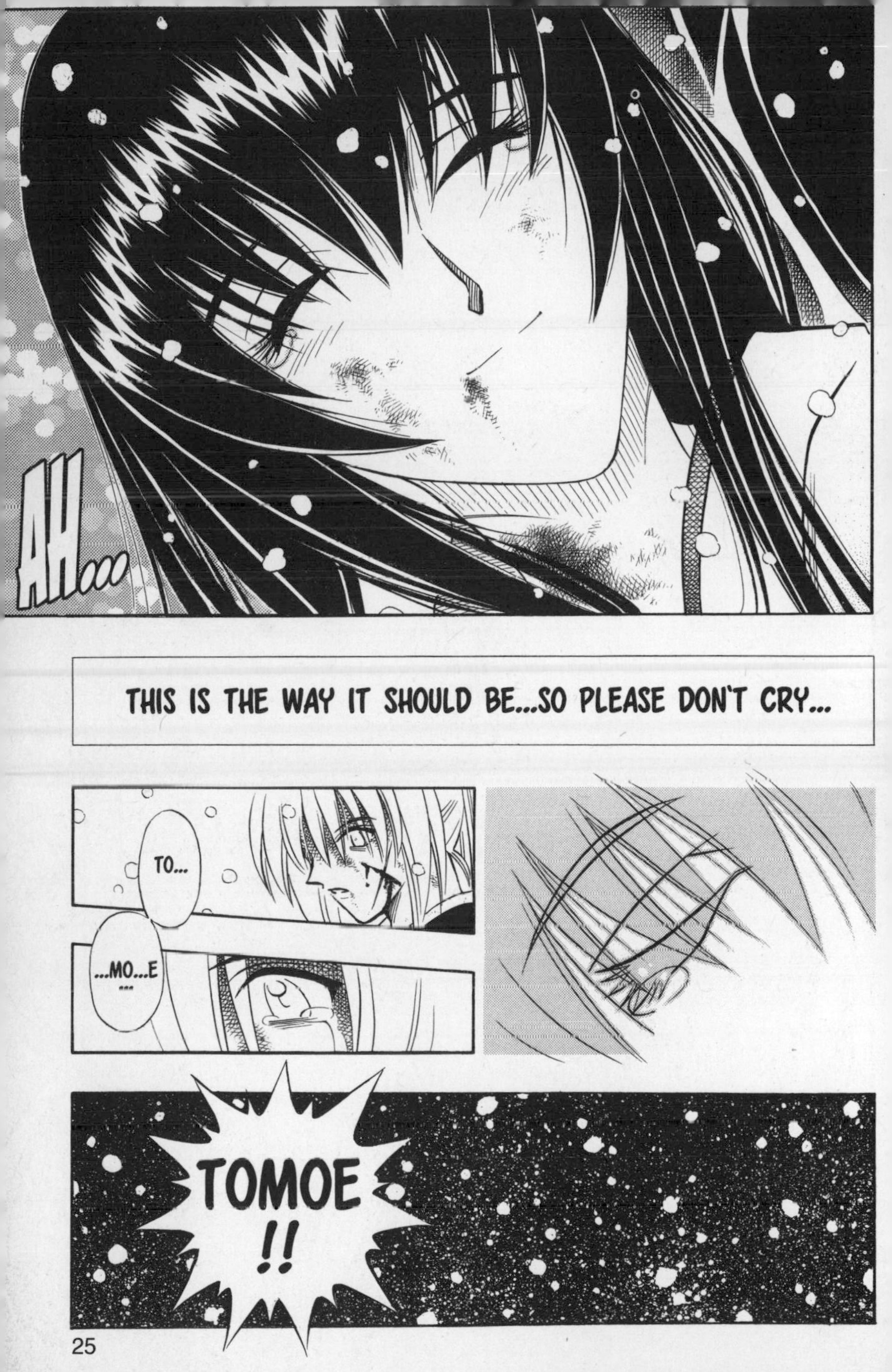
AH...
THIS IS THE WAY IT SHOULD BE...SO PLEASE DON'T CRY...
TO...
...MO...E ...
TOMOE !!

Rurouni Kenshin

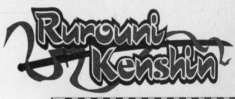

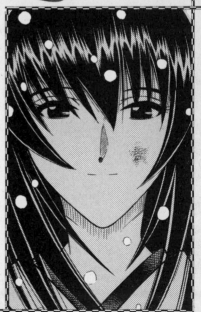

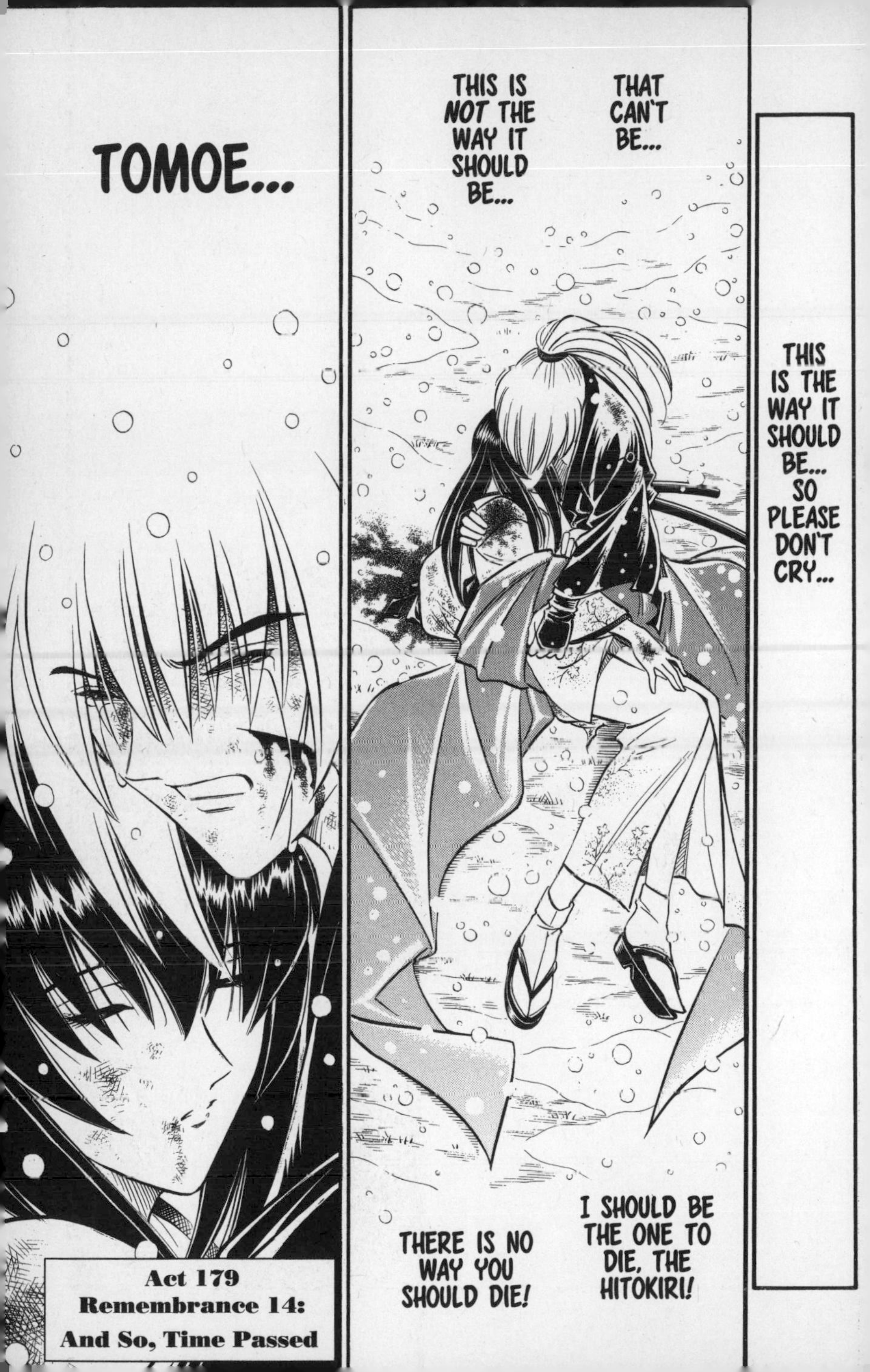
THIS IS THE WAY IT SHOULD BE... SO PLEASE DON'T CRY...
THAT CAN'T BE...
THIS IS *NOT* THE WAY IT SHOULD BE...
I SHOULD BE THE ONE TO DIE, THE HITOKIRI!
THERE IS NO WAY YOU SHOULD DIE!
TOMOE...
Act 179
Remembrance 14:
And So, Time Passed

Act 179

Remembrance 14: And So, Time Passed

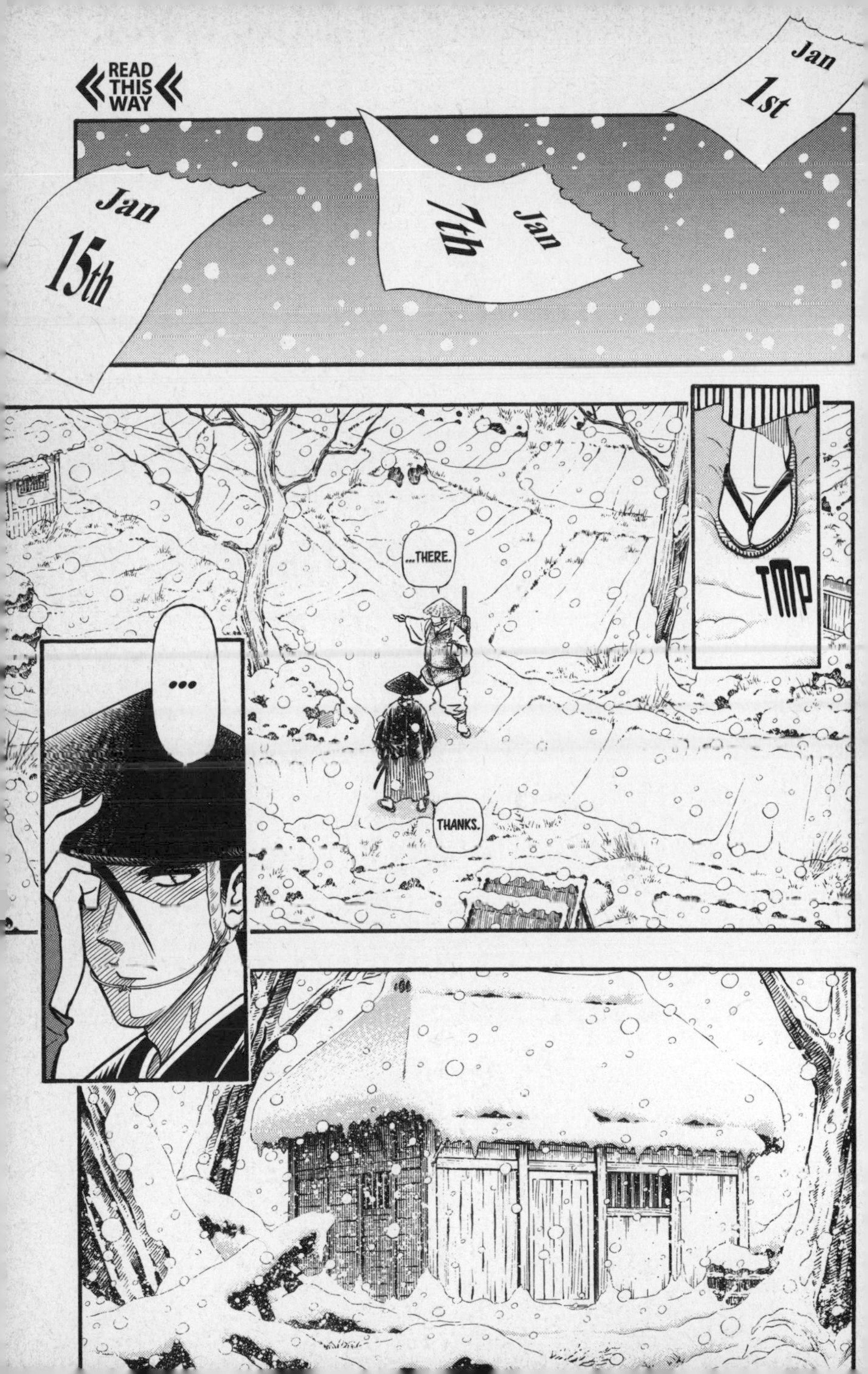
READ THIS WAY
Jan 1st
Jan 7th
Jan 15th
TMP
...THERE.
THANKS.
...

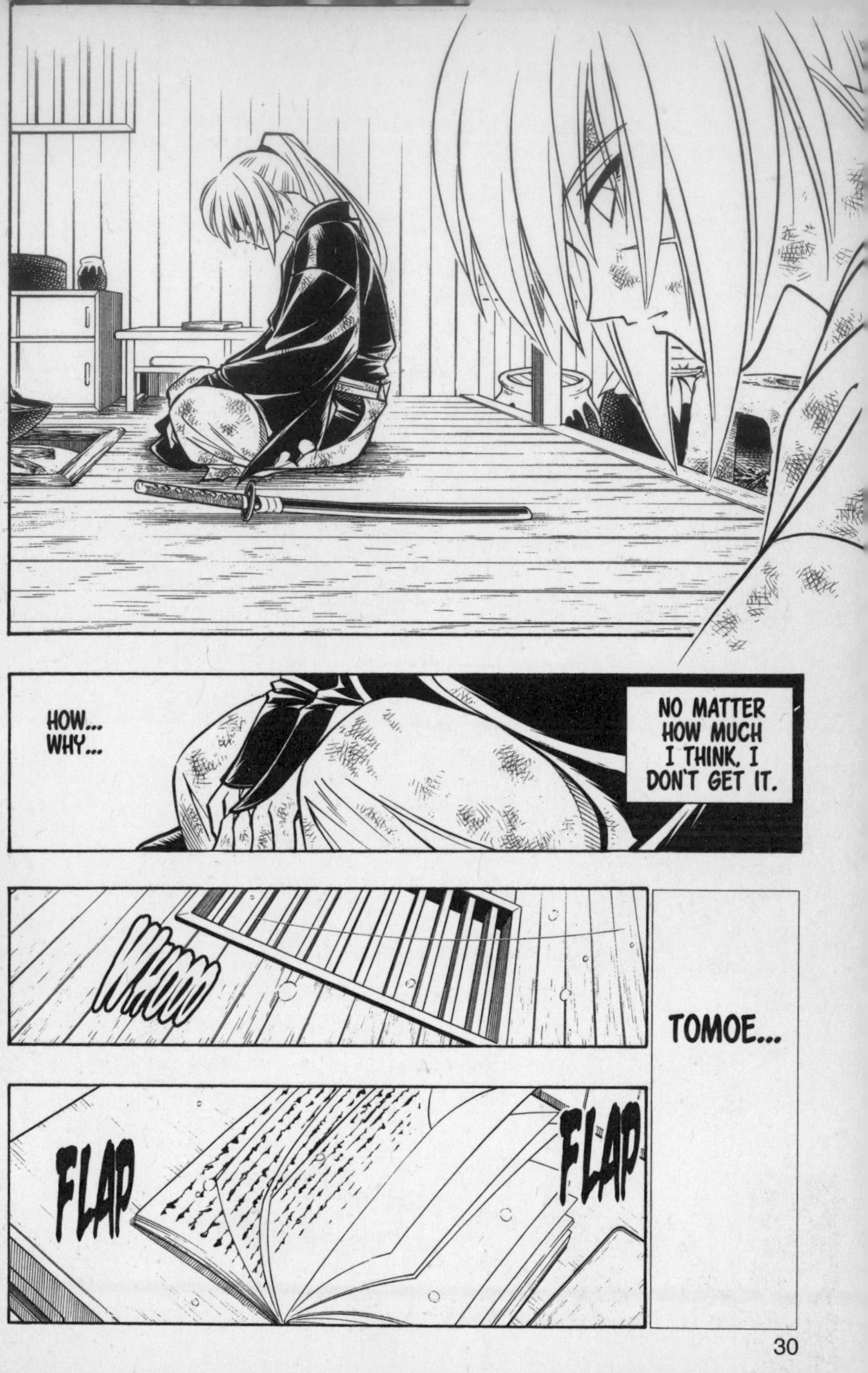
NO MATTER HOW MUCH I THINK, I DON'T GET IT.
HOW... WHY...
TOMOE...
FLAP
FLAP

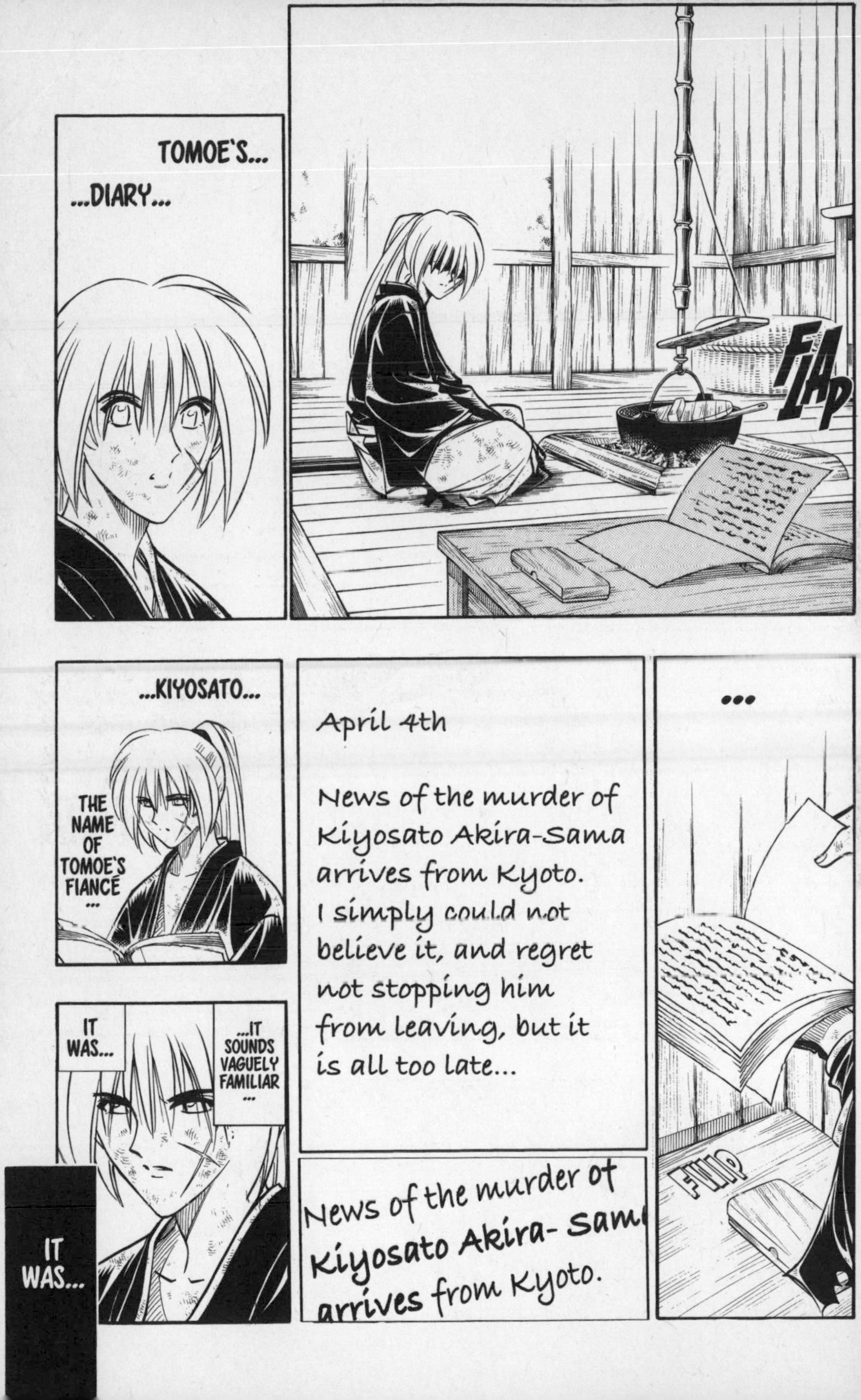
FLAP
TOMOE'S...
...DIARY...
...
FLIP
April 4th
News of the murder of Kiyosato Akira-Sama arrives from Kyoto. I simply could not believe it, and regret not stopping him from leaving, but it is all too late...
News of the murder of Kiyosato Akira-Sama arrives from Kyoto.
...KIYOSATO...
THE NAME OF TOMOE'S FIANCÉ ...
...IT SOUNDS VAGUELY FAMILIAR ...
IT WAS...
IT WAS...

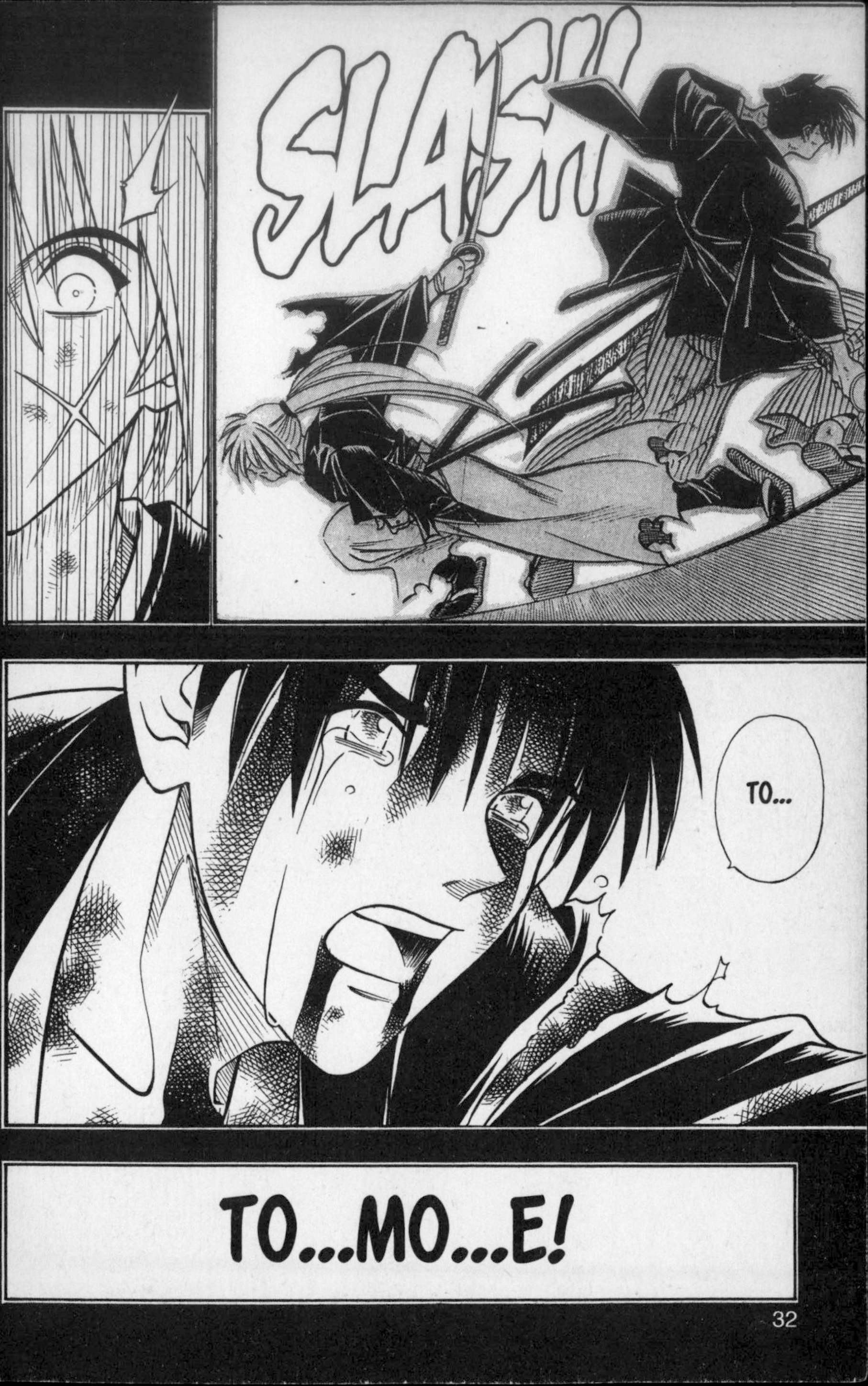
SLASH
TO...
TO...MO...E!

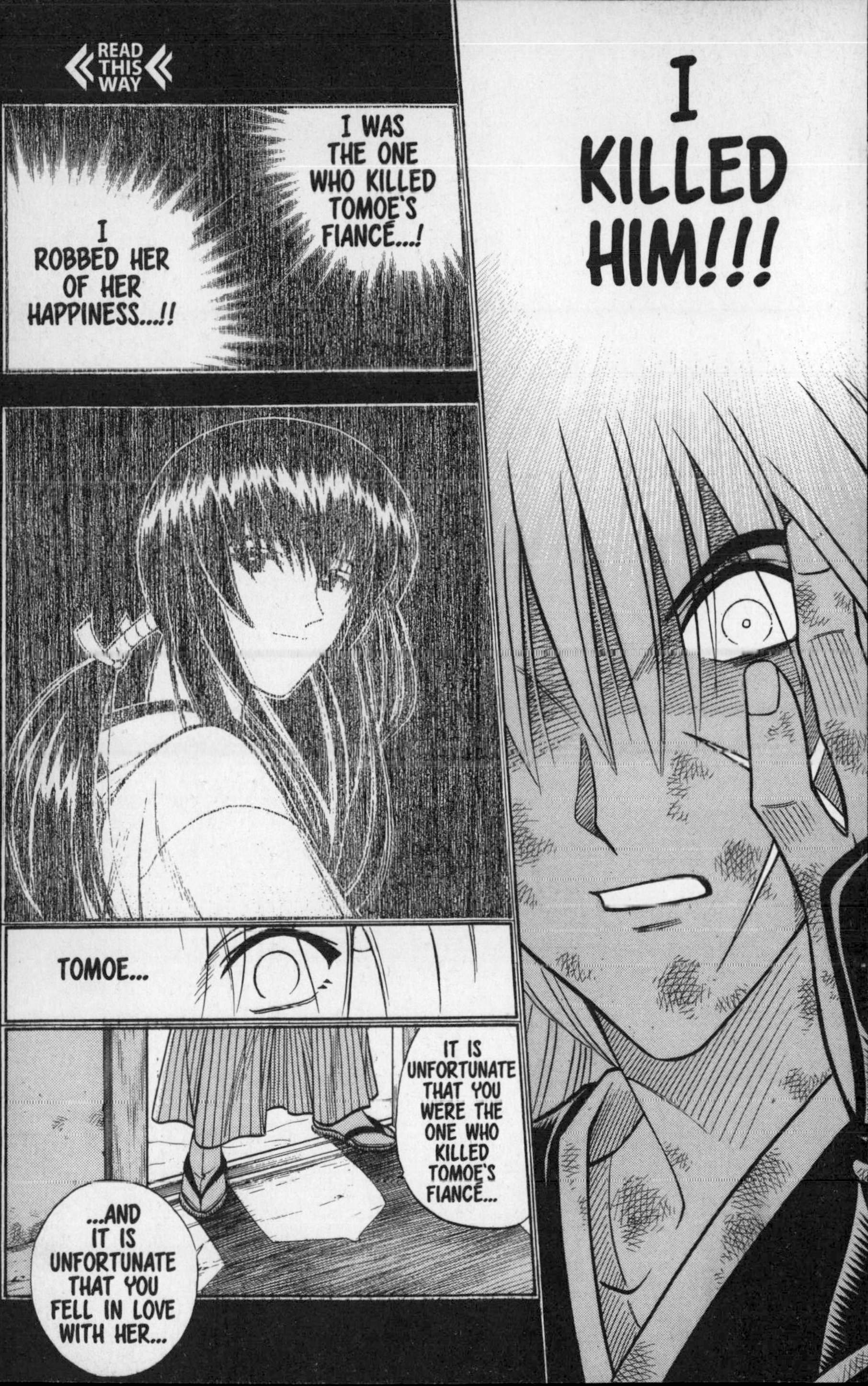
READ THIS WAY
I KILLED HIM!!!
I WAS THE ONE WHO KILLED TOMOE'S FIANCÉ...!
I ROBBED HER OF HER HAPPINESS...!!
TOMOE...
IT IS UNFORTUNATE THAT YOU WERE THE ONE WHO KILLED TOMOE'S FIANCÉ...
...AND IT IS UNFORTUNATE THAT YOU FELL IN LOVE WITH HER...

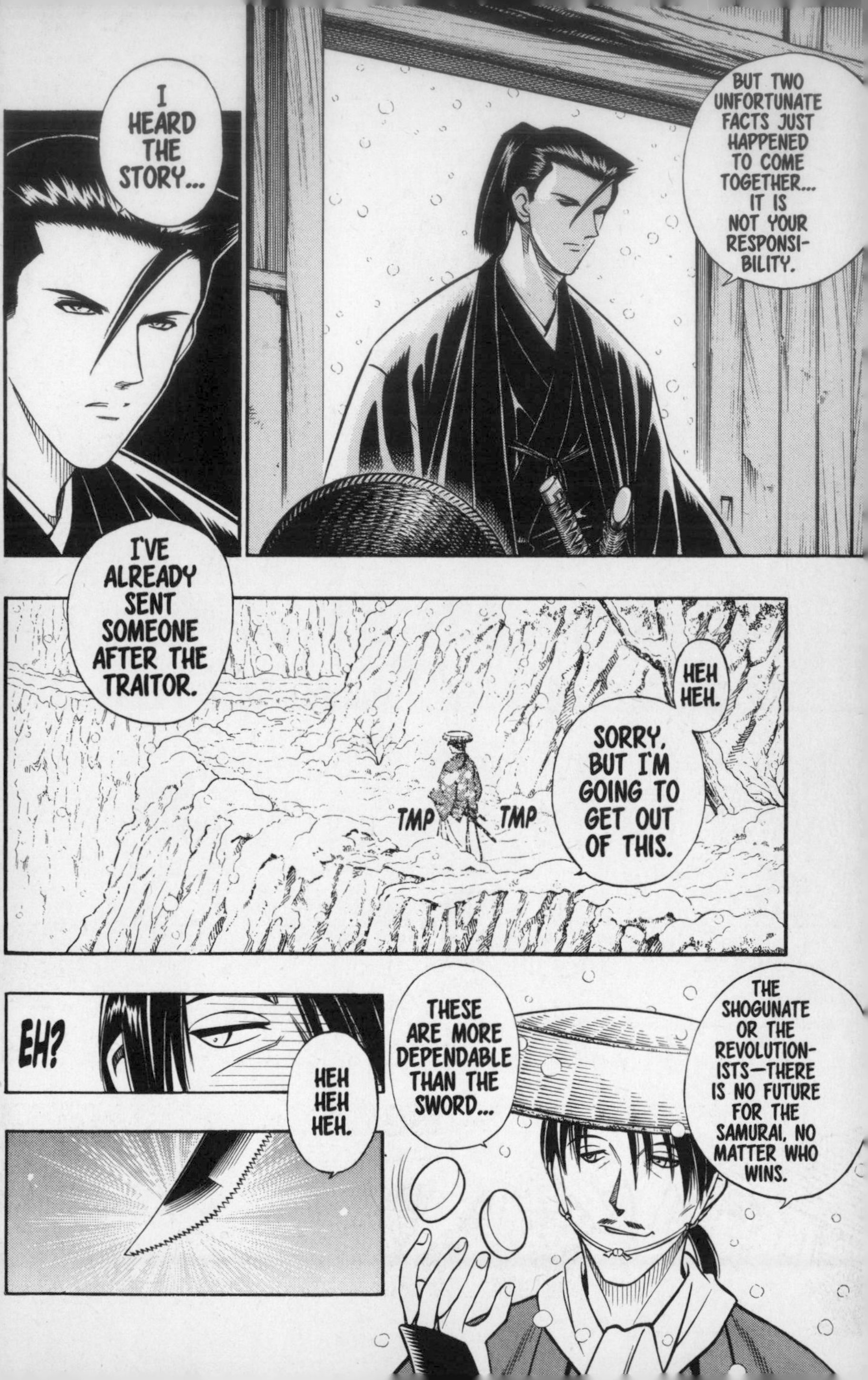
BUT TWO UNFORTUNATE FACTS JUST HAPPENED TO COME TOGETHER... IT IS NOT YOUR RESPONSI-BILITY.
I HEARD THE STORY...
I'VE ALREADY SENT SOMEONE AFTER THE TRAITOR.
HEH HEH.
SORRY, BUT I'M GOING TO GET OUT OF THIS.
TMP
TMP
THE SHOGUNATE OR THE REVOLUTION-ISTS—THERE IS NO FUTURE FOR THE SAMURAI, NO MATTER WHO WINS.
THESE ARE MORE DEPENDABLE THAN THE SWORD...
EH?
HEH HEH HEH.

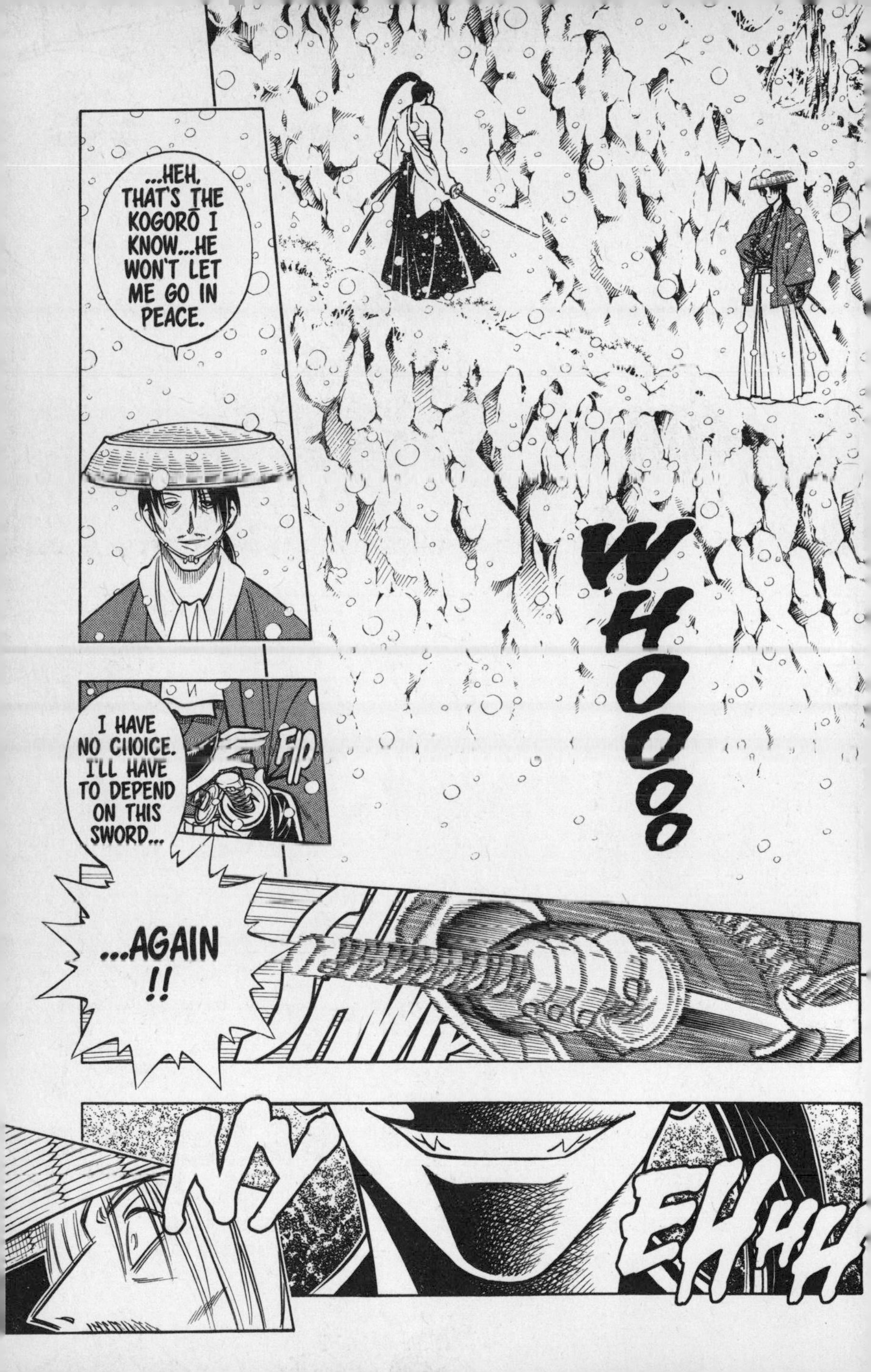
WHOOO
...HEH, THAT'S THE KOGORŌ I KNOW...HE WON'T LET ME GO IN PEACE.
FIP
I HAVE NO CHOICE. I'LL HAVE TO DEPEND ON THIS SWORD...
...AGAIN !!
NYEHHH

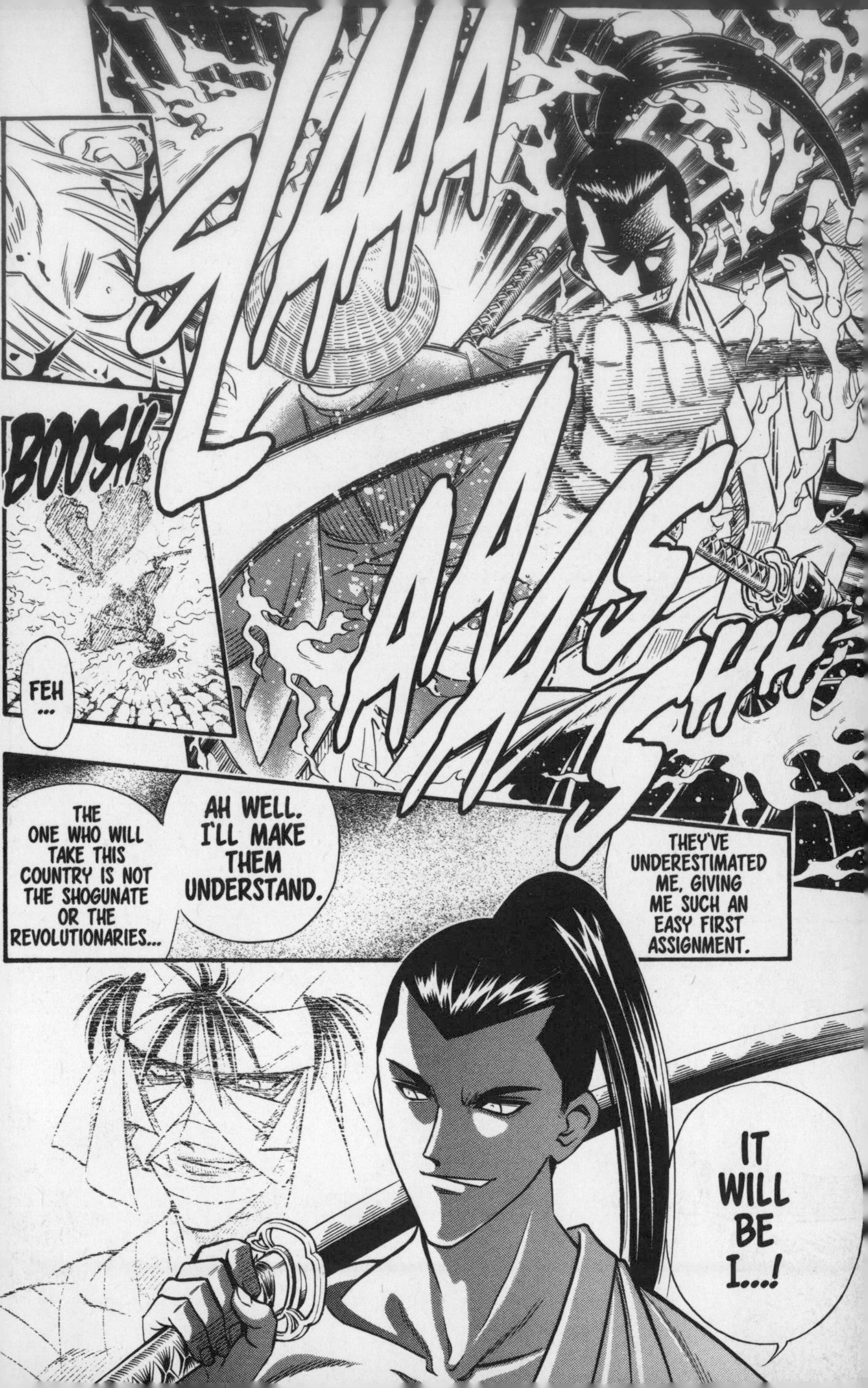
BOOSH
FEH...
THEY'VE UNDERESTIMATED ME, GIVING ME SUCH AN EASY FIRST ASSIGNMENT.
AH WELL. I'LL MAKE THEM UNDERSTAND.
THE ONE WHO WILL TAKE THIS COUNTRY IS NOT THE SHOGUNATE OR THE REVOLUTIONARIES...
IT WILL BE I...!

READ THIS WAY

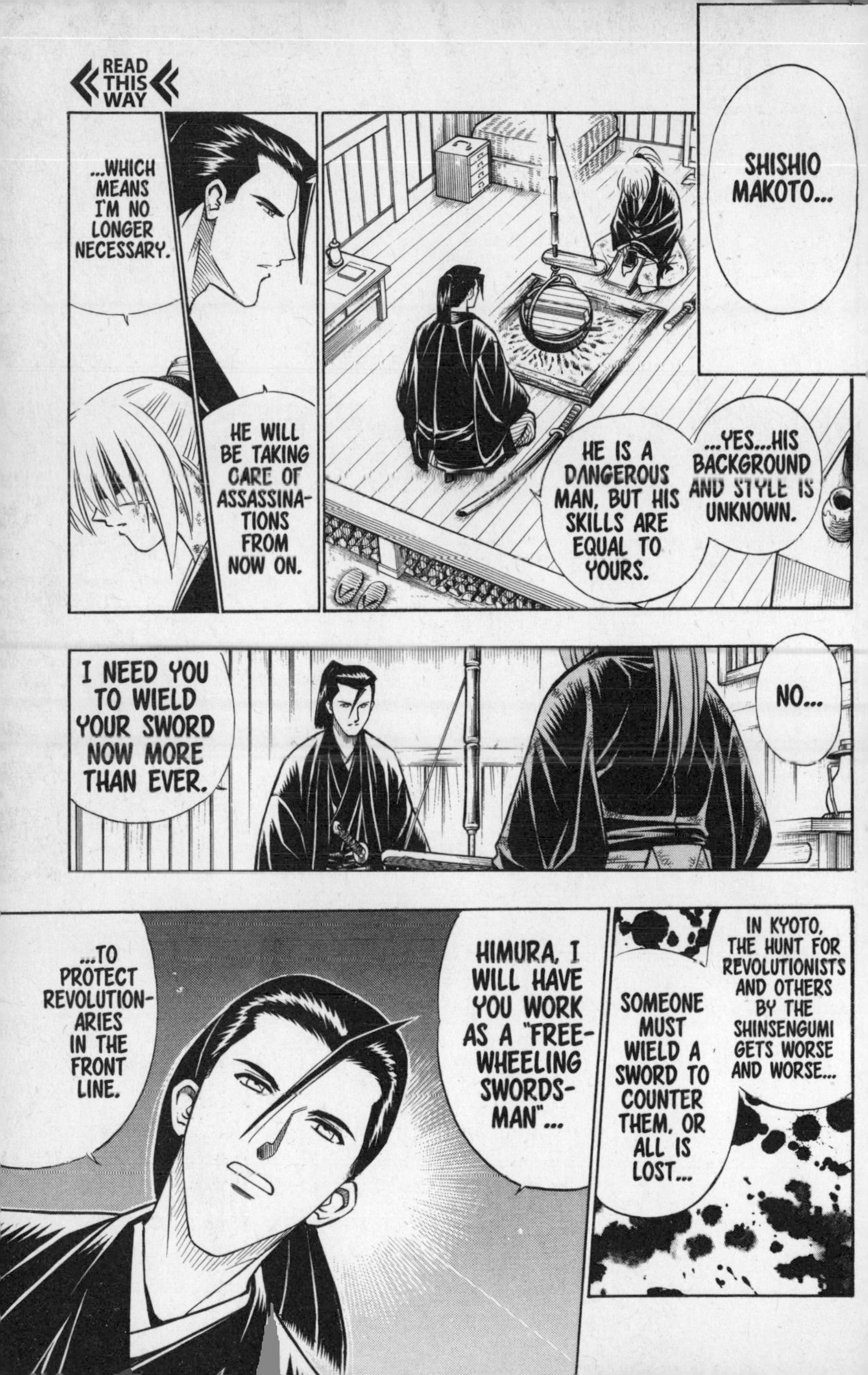
SHISHIO MAKOTO...
...YES...HIS BACKGROUND AND STYLE IS UNKNOWN.
HE IS A DANGEROUS MAN, BUT HIS SKILLS ARE EQUAL TO YOURS.
...WHICH MEANS I'M NO LONGER NECESSARY.
HE WILL BE TAKING CARE OF ASSASSINATIONS FROM NOW ON.
NO...
I NEED YOU TO WIELD YOUR SWORD NOW MORE THAN EVER.
IN KYOTO, THE HUNT FOR REVOLUTIONISTS AND OTHERS BY THE SHINSENGUMI GETS WORSE AND WORSE...
SOMEONE MUST WIELD A SWORD TO COUNTER THEM, OR ALL IS LOST...
HIMURA, I WILL HAVE YOU WORK AS A "FREE-WHEELING SWORDSMAN"...
...TO PROTECT REVOLUTIONARIES IN THE FRONT LINE.

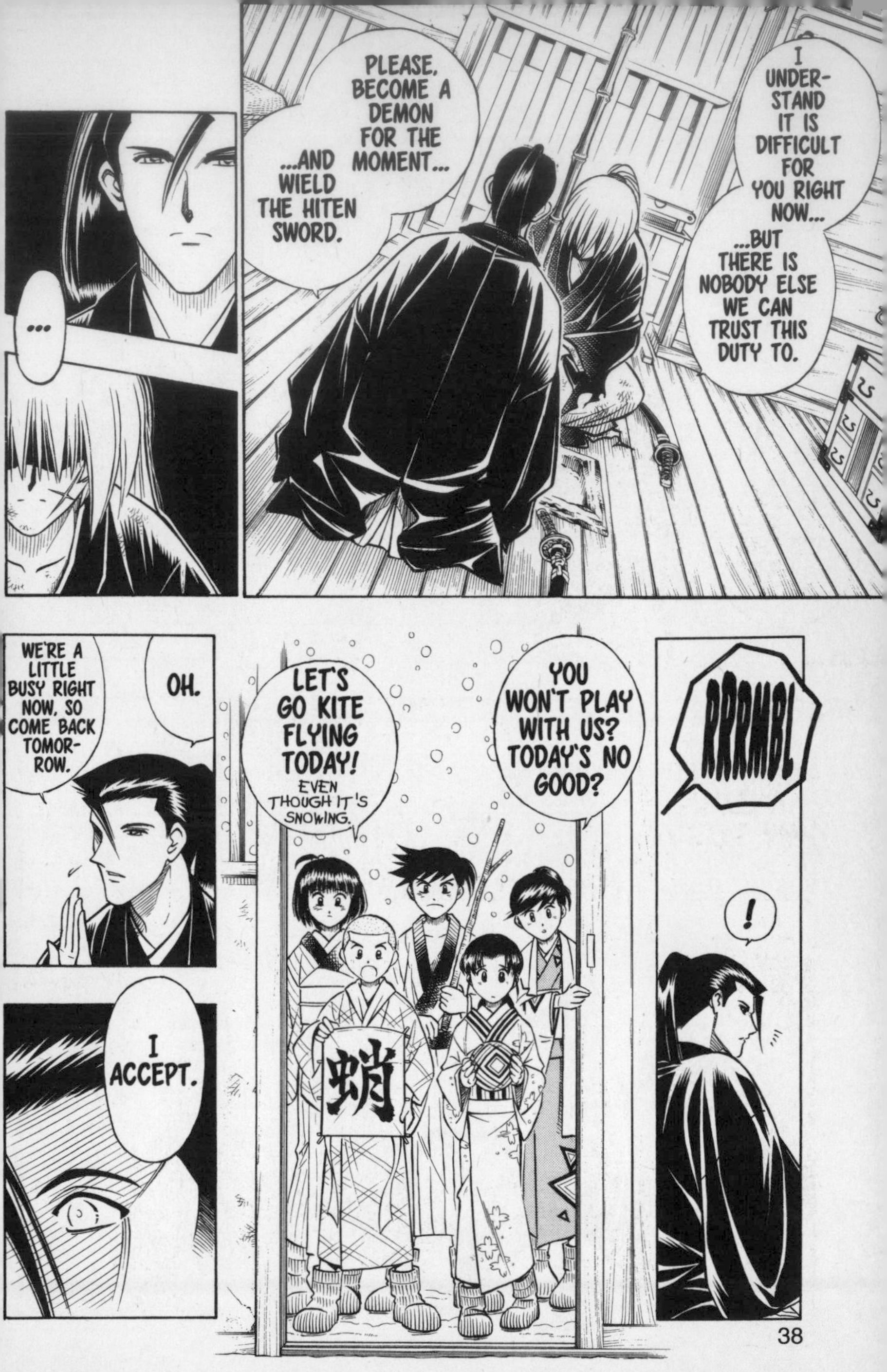
I UNDERSTAND IT IS DIFFICULT FOR YOU RIGHT NOW...
...BUT THERE IS NOBODY ELSE WE CAN TRUST THIS DUTY TO.
PLEASE, BECOME A DEMON FOR THE MOMENT...
...AND WIELD THE HITEN SWORD.
...
RRRMBL
!
YOU WON'T PLAY WITH US? TODAY'S NO GOOD?
LET'S GO KITE FLYING TODAY!
EVEN THOUGH IT'S SNOWING.
蛸
OH.
WE'RE A LITTLE BUSY RIGHT NOW, SO COME BACK TOMORROW.
I ACCEPT.

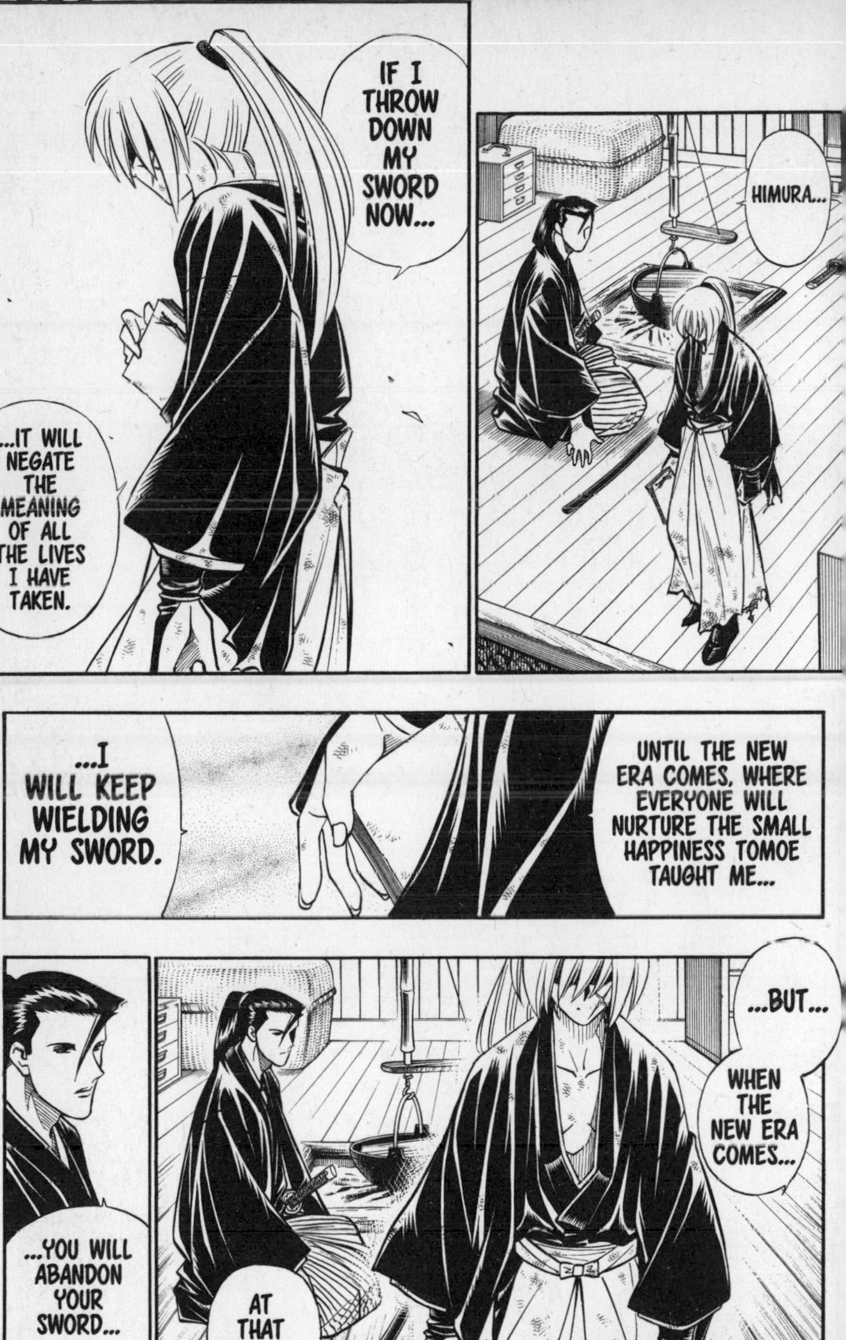
HIMURA...
IF I THROW DOWN MY SWORD NOW...
...IT WILL NEGATE THE MEANING OF ALL THE LIVES I HAVE TAKEN.
UNTIL THE NEW ERA COMES, WHERE EVERYONE WILL NURTURE THE SMALL HAPPINESS TOMOE TAUGHT ME...
...I WILL KEEP WIELDING MY SWORD.
...BUT...
WHEN THE NEW ERA COMES...
AT THAT TIME...
...YOU WILL ABANDON YOUR SWORD...

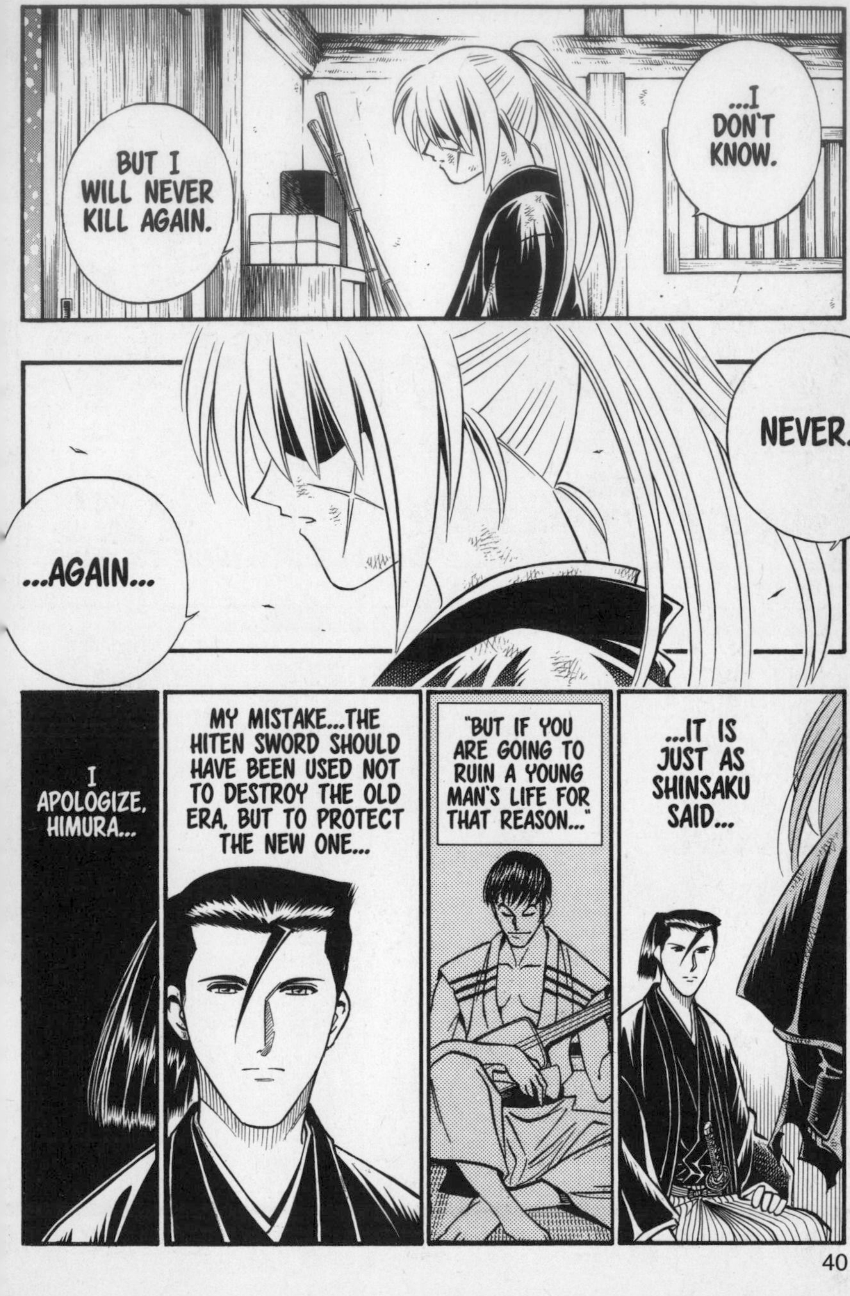
...I DON'T KNOW.
BUT I WILL NEVER KILL AGAIN.
NEVER...
...AGAIN...
...IT IS JUST AS SHINSAKU SAID...
"BUT IF YOU ARE GOING TO RUIN A YOUNG MAN'S LIFE FOR THAT REASON..."
MY MISTAKE...THE HITEN SWORD SHOULD HAVE BEEN USED NOT TO DESTROY THE OLD ERA, BUT TO PROTECT THE NEW ONE...
I APOLOGIZE, HIMURA...

READ THIS WAY

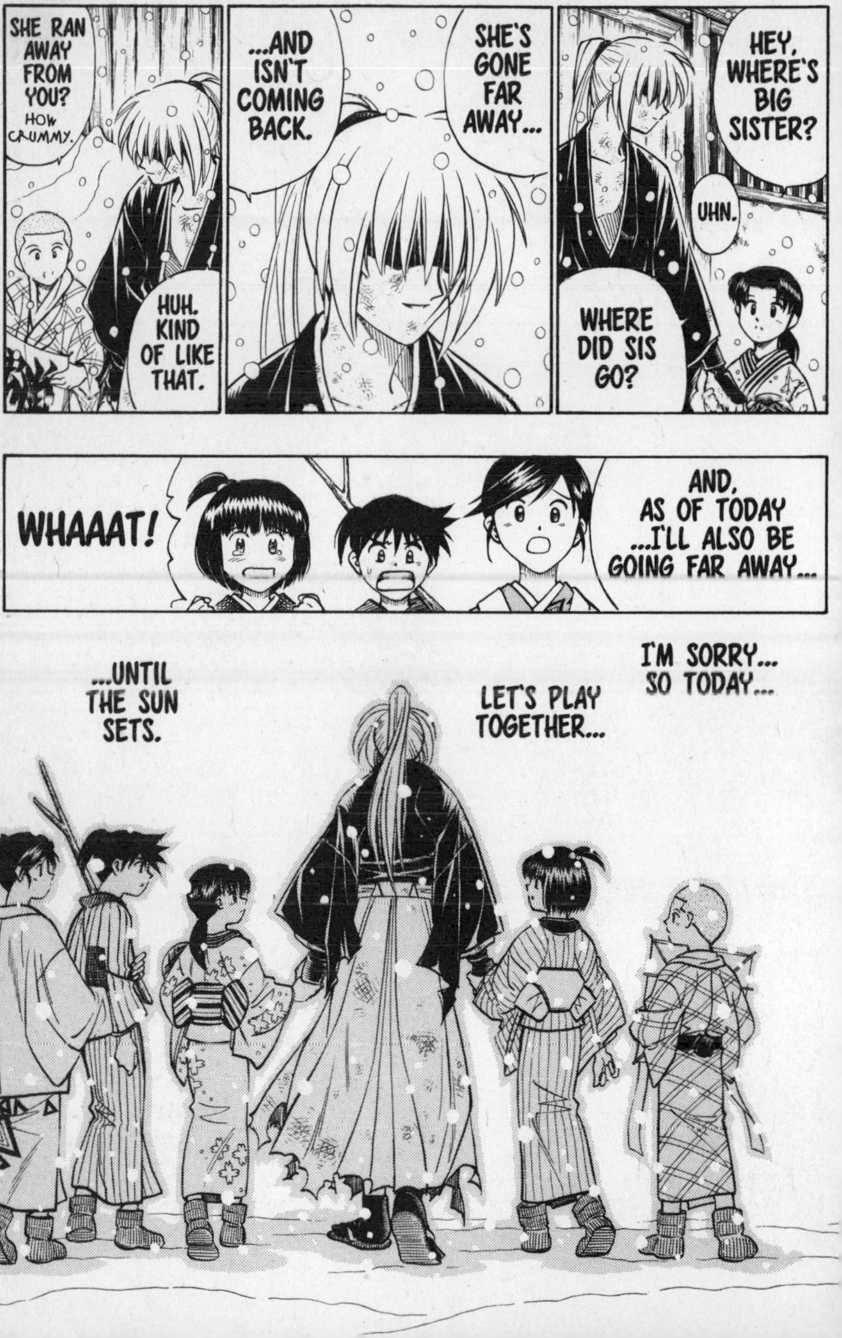
HEY, WHERE'S BIG SISTER?
UHN.
WHERE DID SIS GO?
SHE'S GONE FAR AWAY...
...AND ISN'T COMING BACK.
SHE RAN AWAY FROM YOU? HOW CRUMMY.
HUH. KIND OF LIKE THAT.
AND, AS OF TODAY ...I'LL ALSO BE GOING FAR AWAY...
WHAAAT!
I'M SORRY... SO TODAY...
LET'S PLAY TOGETHER...
...UNTIL THE SUN SETS.

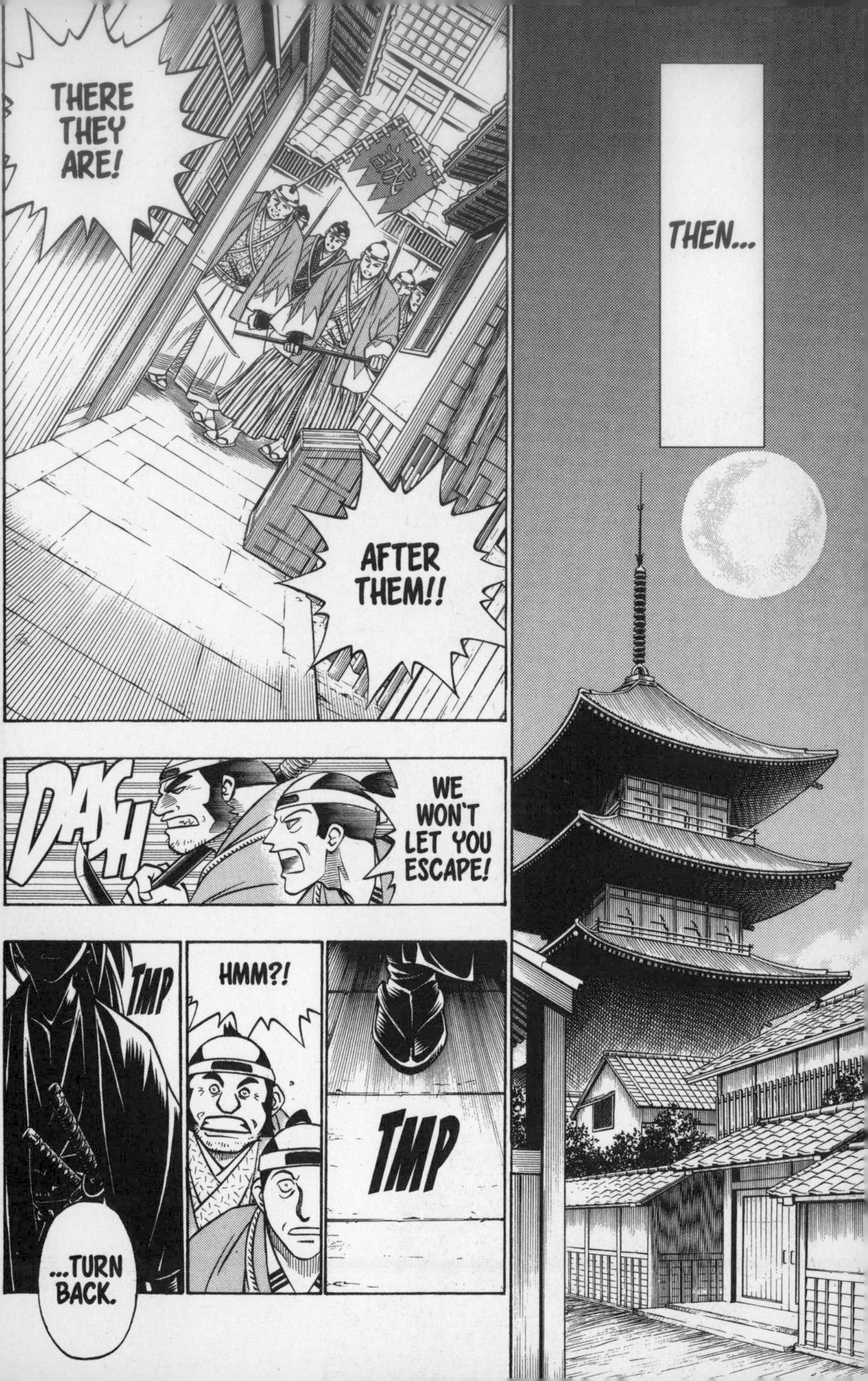
THEN...
THERE THEY ARE!
AFTER THEM!!
WE WON'T LET YOU ESCAPE!
DASH
TMP
HMM?!
TMP
...TURN BACK.

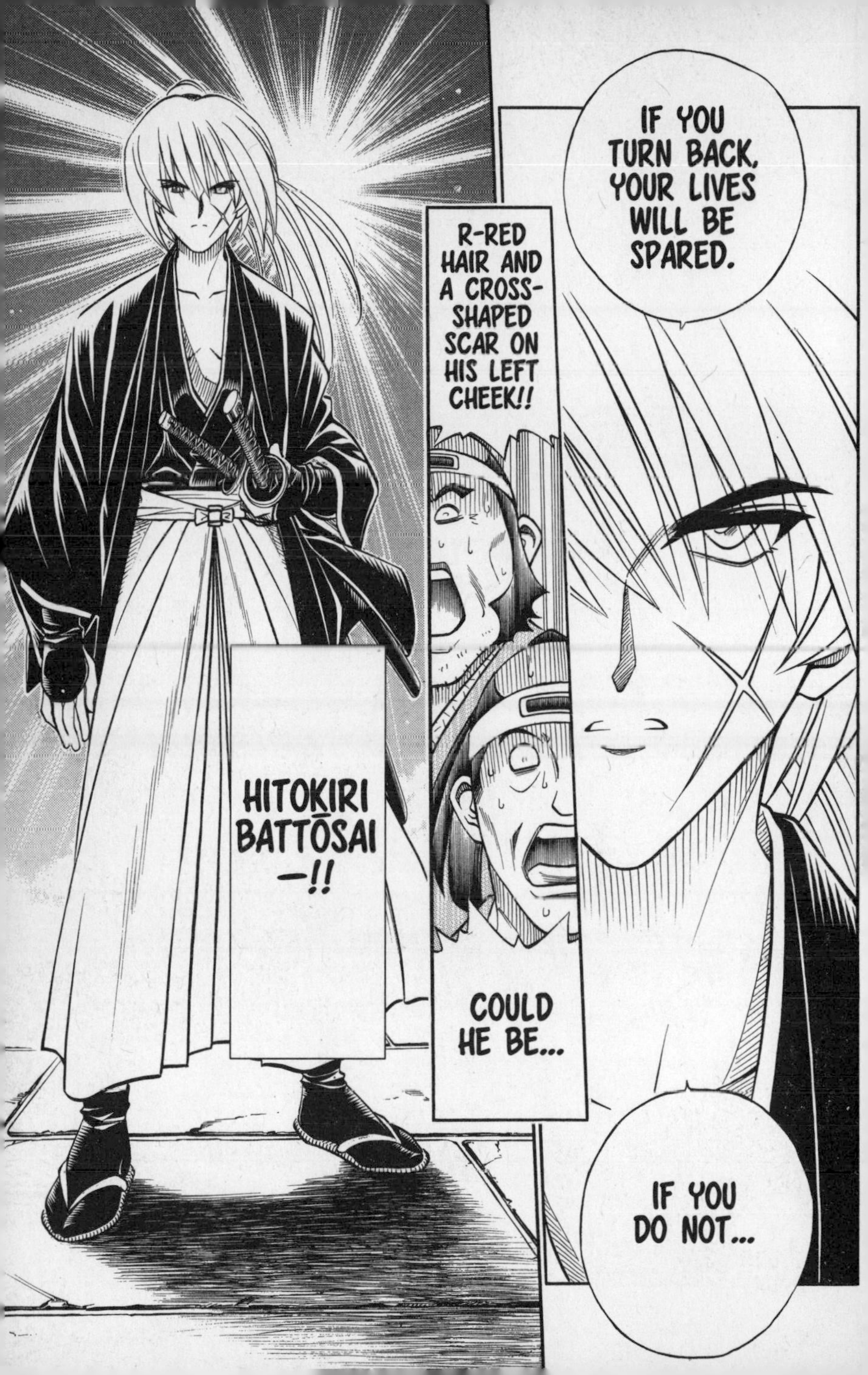
IF YOU TURN BACK, YOUR LIVES WILL BE SPARED.
R-RED HAIR AND A CROSS-SHAPED SCAR ON HIS LEFT CHEEK!!
COULD HE BE...
IF YOU DO NOT...
HITOKIRI BATTŌSAI—!!

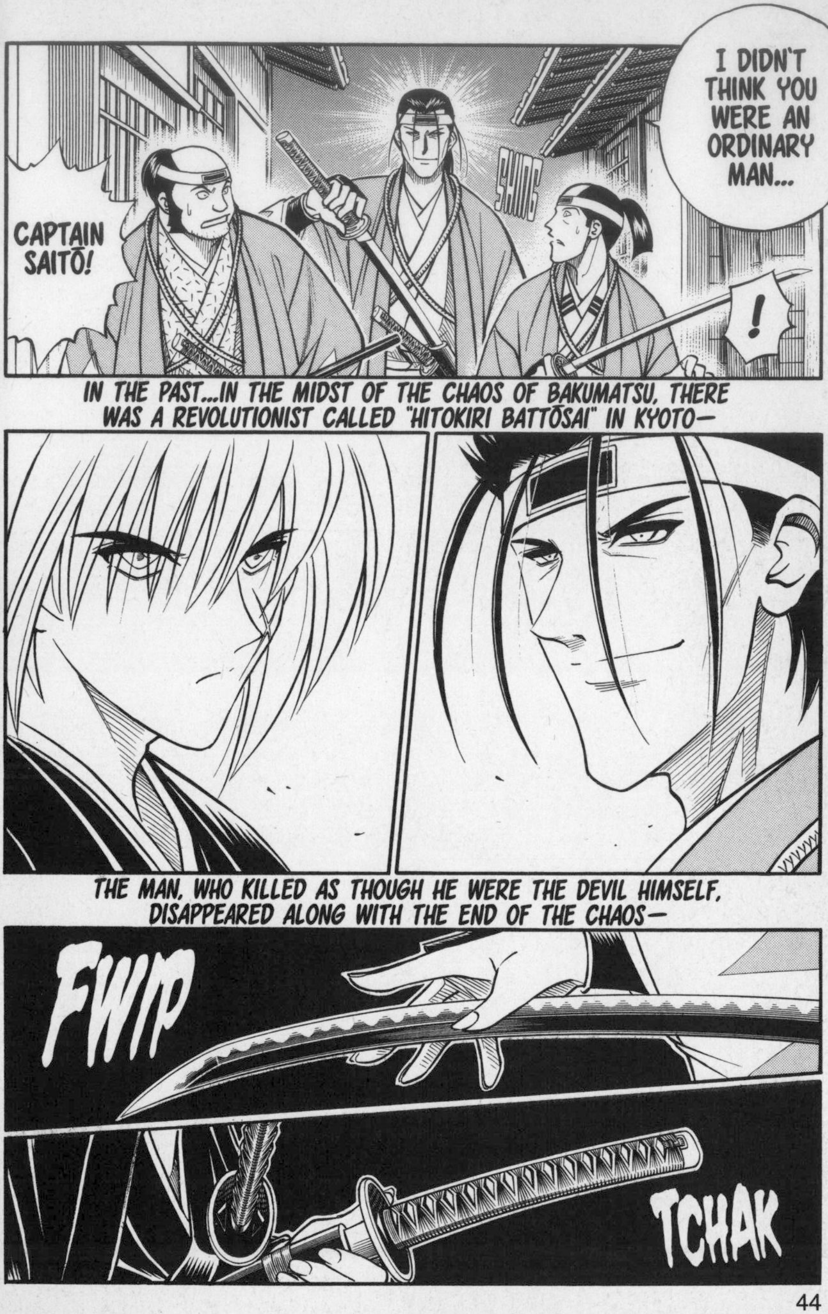
I DIDN'T THINK YOU WERE AN ORDINARY MAN...
!
SHING
CAPTAIN SAITŌ!
IN THE PAST...IN THE MIDST OF THE CHAOS OF BAKUMATSU, THERE WAS A REVOLUTIONIST CALLED "HITOKIRI BATTŌSAI" IN KYOTO—
THE MAN, WHO KILLED AS THOUGH HE WERE THE DEVIL HIMSELF, DISAPPEARED ALONG WITH THE END OF THE CHAOS—
FWIP
TCHAK

READ THIS WAY

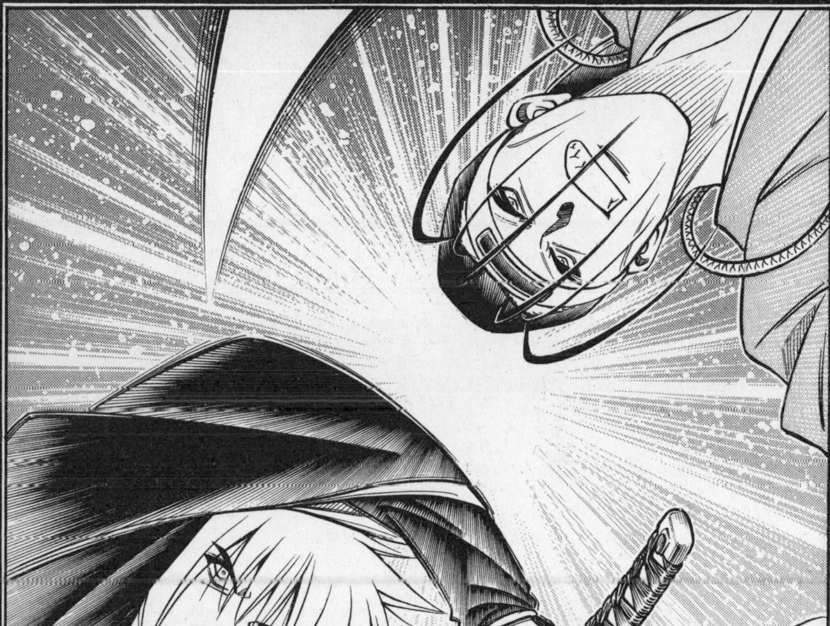

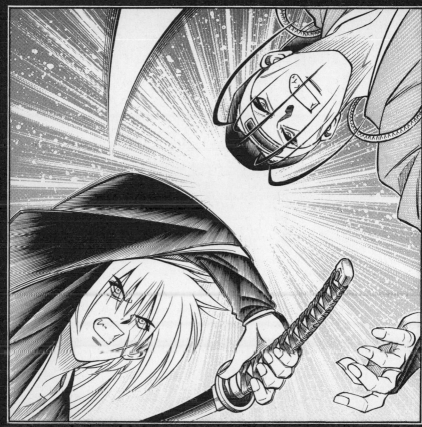

AND SO, TIME PASSED TO THE 11TH YEAR OF MEIJI.

The Secret Life of Characters (41)

—Yukishiro (Himura) Tomoe—

I really don't want to say much about her, but "without lies and deception—no hiding" is the intent of this corner, so I will talk. There was originally no model for Tomoe. The plot for the remembrance episodes was already finished before the series started, and at that point, Tomoe was just going to be a "super beautiful woman whose intent was unclear." To put it simply, "cool beauty." (By the way, when I talked to a friend about this cool beauty concept, he laughed hard. Maybe my idea of a cool beauty is off?) During the three and a half years until she appeared, there was nothing concrete other than what is stated above, and she became an Ayanami look-alike from *Eva*. The basics of drama are the expression of emotions and changes in emotions, but a cool beauty is a cool beauty because she does not reveal her emotions. I didn't realize the important fact that once she revealed her true feelings, it negated all of this, thus turning her into a completely different character towards the end. On top of that, the way she dies is the same way Yumi died. I am not only regretting what I made her into, but also feel disgusted with myself for it. However, it was fun, during the first half, to portray her as a cool beauty. And I do like the character itself, so I would like to bring her back in a different series. At that time, she will be Watsuki's original cool beauty...

Her design, as stated above, turned into an Ayanami look-alike. The only thing original about her is the black pupil, which I put in because I thought, "This way it is easier to create an effect of not knowing her true feelings." But, that's it. To be honest, after doing this series at full tilt for four years, the will, energy, and time to develop my senses rather than just using them—and to nurture a good idea or material, making it my original—are very lacking. Tomoe is a character that reflects my state right now. I am painfully aware that there is a need for me to find a different way to write manga, and am already on the search. For those of you who are angry about Tomoe's character, I would be honored if you would stick with Watsuki's manga a little longer.

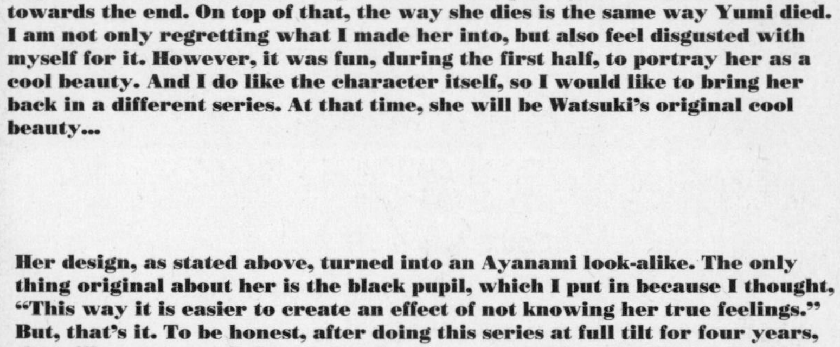

Year	Era	Events
1864		○ IKEDA-YA INCIDENT
	GENJI (1864-1865)	○ KINMON INCIDENT
		○ ENGLAND, FRANCE, USA, HOLLAND ATTACK SHIMONOSEKI WITH CANNON FIRE
1865		○ THE FIRST CHŌSHŪ SUBJUGATION
		○ THE SECOND CHŌSHŪ SUBJUGATION
		○ EDO, OSAKA
1866	**KEIŌ** (1865-1868)	○ SAKAMOTO RYŌMA SATSUMA-CHŌSHŪ
1867		
		○ TOKUGAWA TAKAYOSHI RETURNS POWER TO THE EMPEROR
1868		○ THE OFFICIAL RETURN OF POWER TO THE EMPEROR
	MEIJI (1868-1912)	○ BOSHIN WAR BEGINS
		○ THE MEIJI EMPEROR SUBMITS HIS FIVE LAWS
1869		○ BOSHIN WAR ENDS

AND SO, TIME FLOWED—

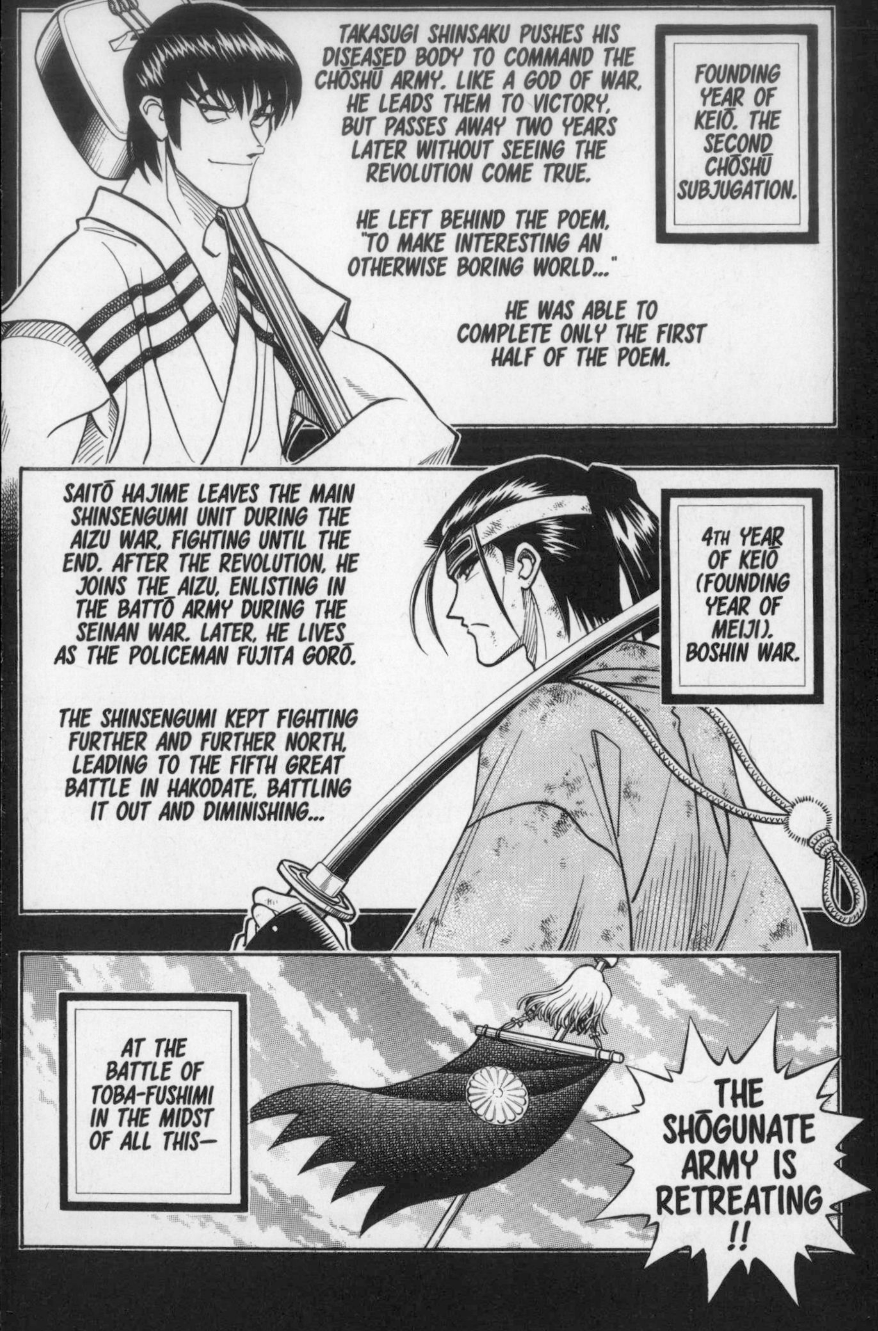
FOUNDING YEAR OF KEIŌ. THE SECOND CHŌSHŪ SUBJUGATION.
TAKASUGI SHINSAKU PUSHES HIS DISEASED BODY TO COMMAND THE CHŌSHŪ ARMY. LIKE A GOD OF WAR, HE LEADS THEM TO VICTORY, BUT PASSES AWAY TWO YEARS LATER WITHOUT SEEING THE REVOLUTION COME TRUE.
HE LEFT BEHIND THE POEM, "TO MAKE INTERESTING AN OTHERWISE BORING WORLD..."
HE WAS ABLE TO COMPLETE ONLY THE FIRST HALF OF THE POEM.
4TH YEAR OF KEIŌ (FOUNDING YEAR OF MEIJI). BOSHIN WAR.
SAITŌ HAJIME LEAVES THE MAIN SHINSENGUMI UNIT DURING THE AIZU WAR, FIGHTING UNTIL THE END. AFTER THE REVOLUTION, HE JOINS THE AIZU, ENLISTING IN THE BATTŌ ARMY DURING THE SEINAN WAR. LATER, HE LIVES AS THE POLICEMAN FUJITA GORŌ.
THE SHINSENGUMI KEPT FIGHTING FURTHER AND FURTHER NORTH, LEADING TO THE FIFTH GREAT BATTLE IN HAKODATE, BATTLING IT OUT AND DIMINISHING...
THE SHŌGUNATE ARMY IS RETREATING!!
AT THE BATTLE OF TOBA-FUSHIMI IN THE MIDST OF ALL THIS—

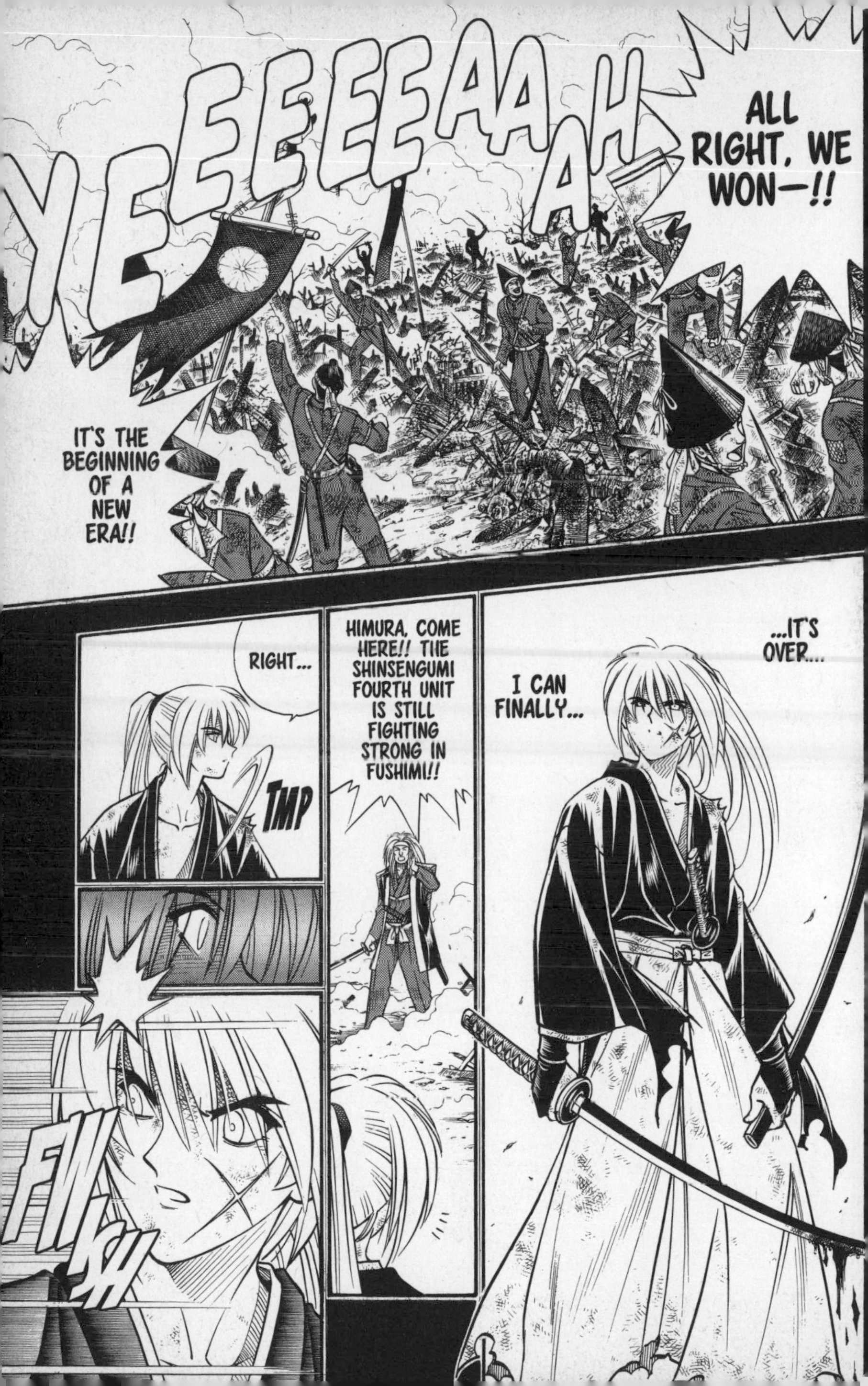
ALL RIGHT, WE WON—!!
YEEEEEAAAH
IT'S THE BEGINNING OF A NEW ERA!!
...IT'S OVER...
I CAN FINALLY...
HIMURA, COME HERE!! THE SHINSENGUMI FOURTH UNIT IS STILL FIGHTING STRONG IN FUSHIMI!!
RIGHT...
TMP
FWSH

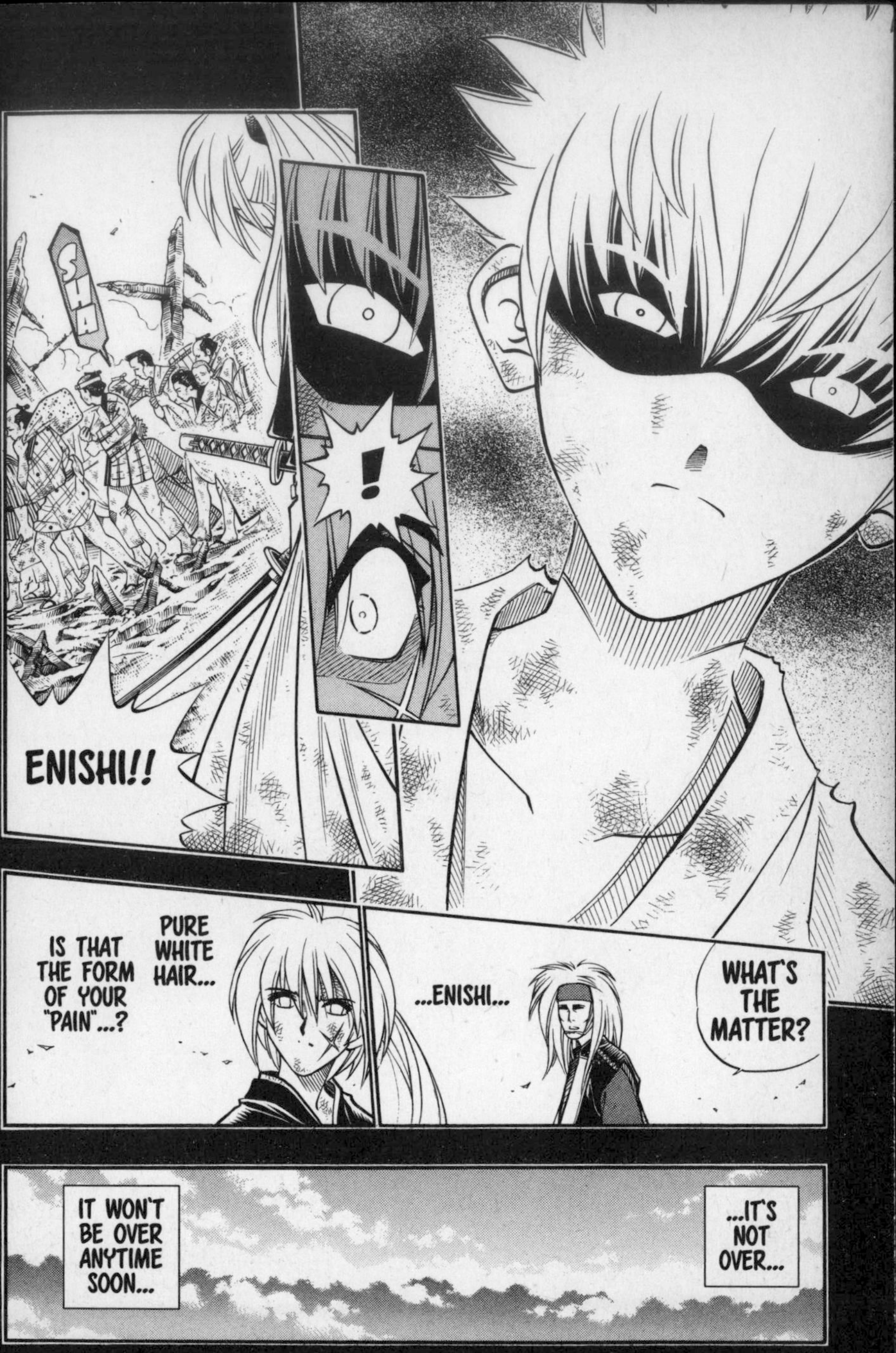
!
SHA
ENISHI!!
WHAT'S THE MATTER?
...ENISHI...
PURE WHITE HAIR...
IS THAT THE FORM OF YOUR "PAIN"...?
...IT'S NOT OVER...
IT WON'T BE OVER ANYTIME SOON...

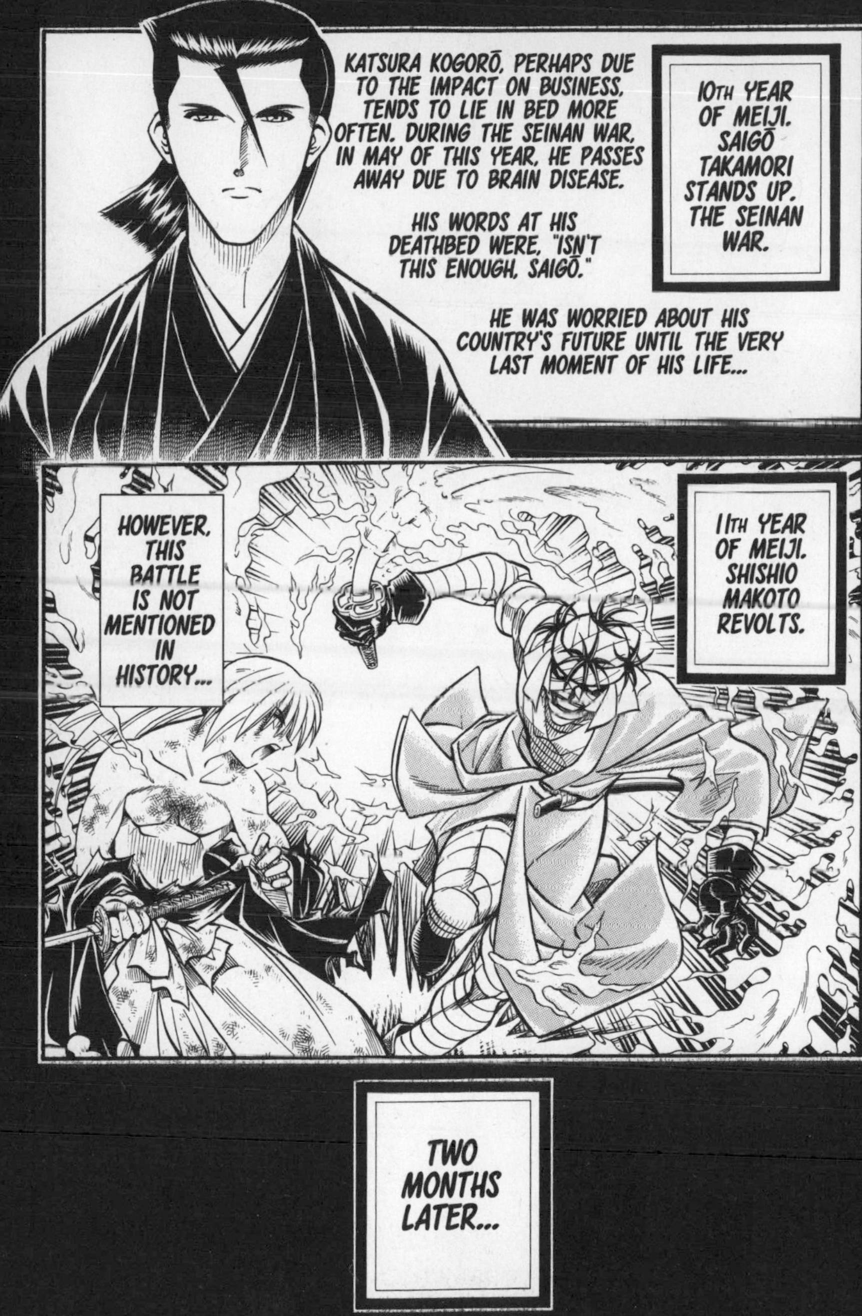
10TH YEAR OF MEIJI. SAIGŌ TAKAMORI STANDS UP. THE SEINAN WAR.
KATSURA KOGORŌ, PERHAPS DUE TO THE IMPACT ON BUSINESS, TENDS TO LIE IN BED MORE OFTEN. DURING THE SEINAN WAR, IN MAY OF THIS YEAR, HE PASSES AWAY DUE TO BRAIN DISEASE.
HIS WORDS AT HIS DEATHBED WERE, "ISN'T THIS ENOUGH, SAIGŌ."
HE WAS WORRIED ABOUT HIS COUNTRY'S FUTURE UNTIL THE VERY LAST MOMENT OF HIS LIFE...
11TH YEAR OF MEIJI. SHISHIO MAKOTO REVOLTS.
HOWEVER, THIS BATTLE IS NOT MENTIONED IN HISTORY...
TWO MONTHS LATER...

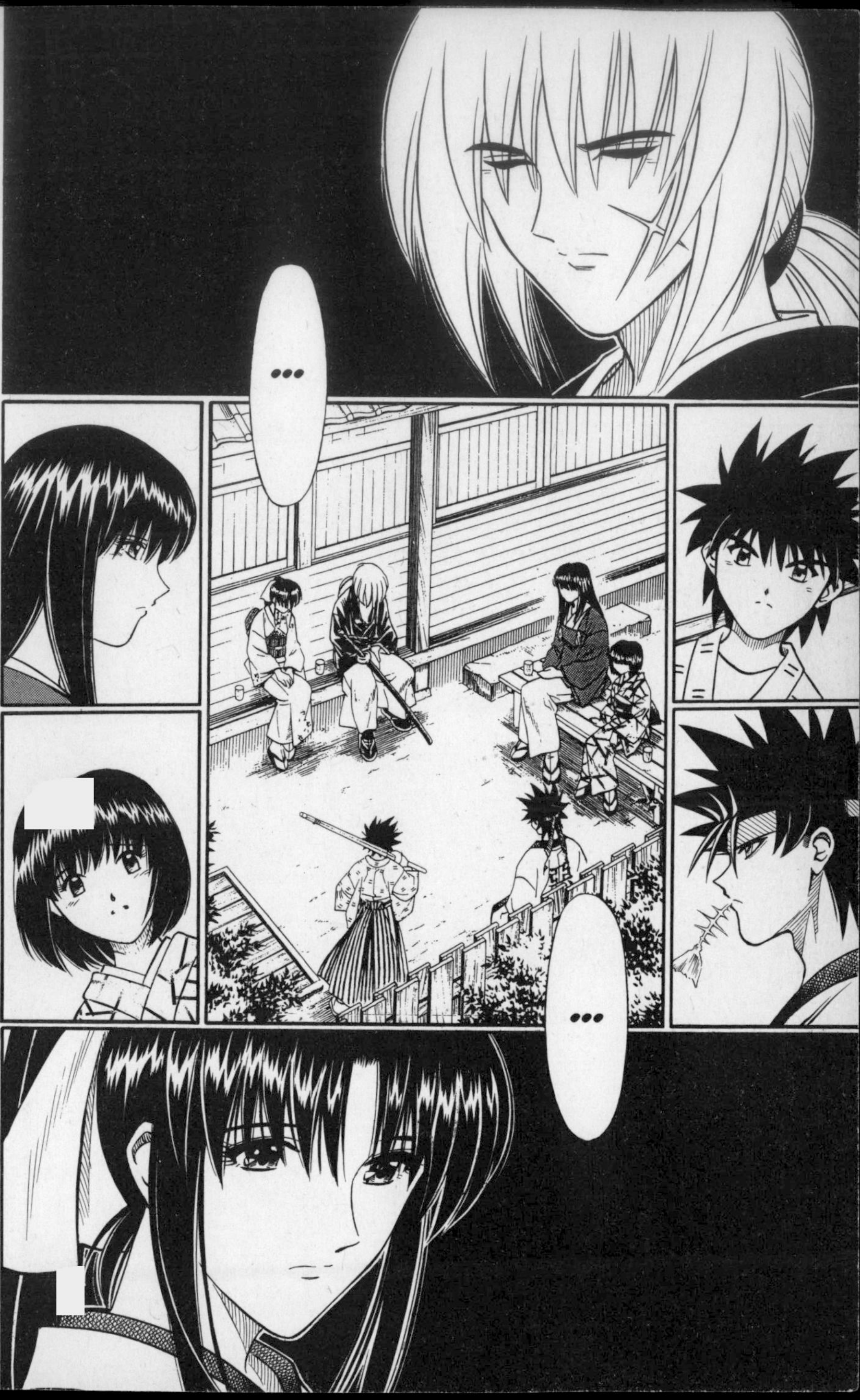
...
...

SILENCE...

NOT ONE OF THEM SAID A WORD...

...AND EVERYONE DISMISSED THEMSELVES ABOUT AN HOUR LATER.

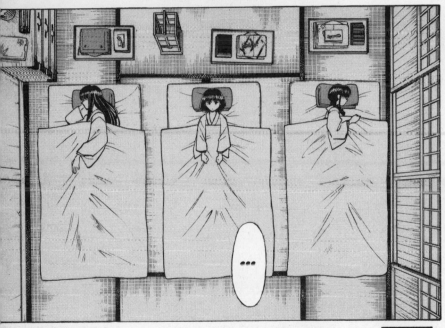

•••

CAN'T SLEEP, TSUBAME-CHAN?

FWIP

SLAM

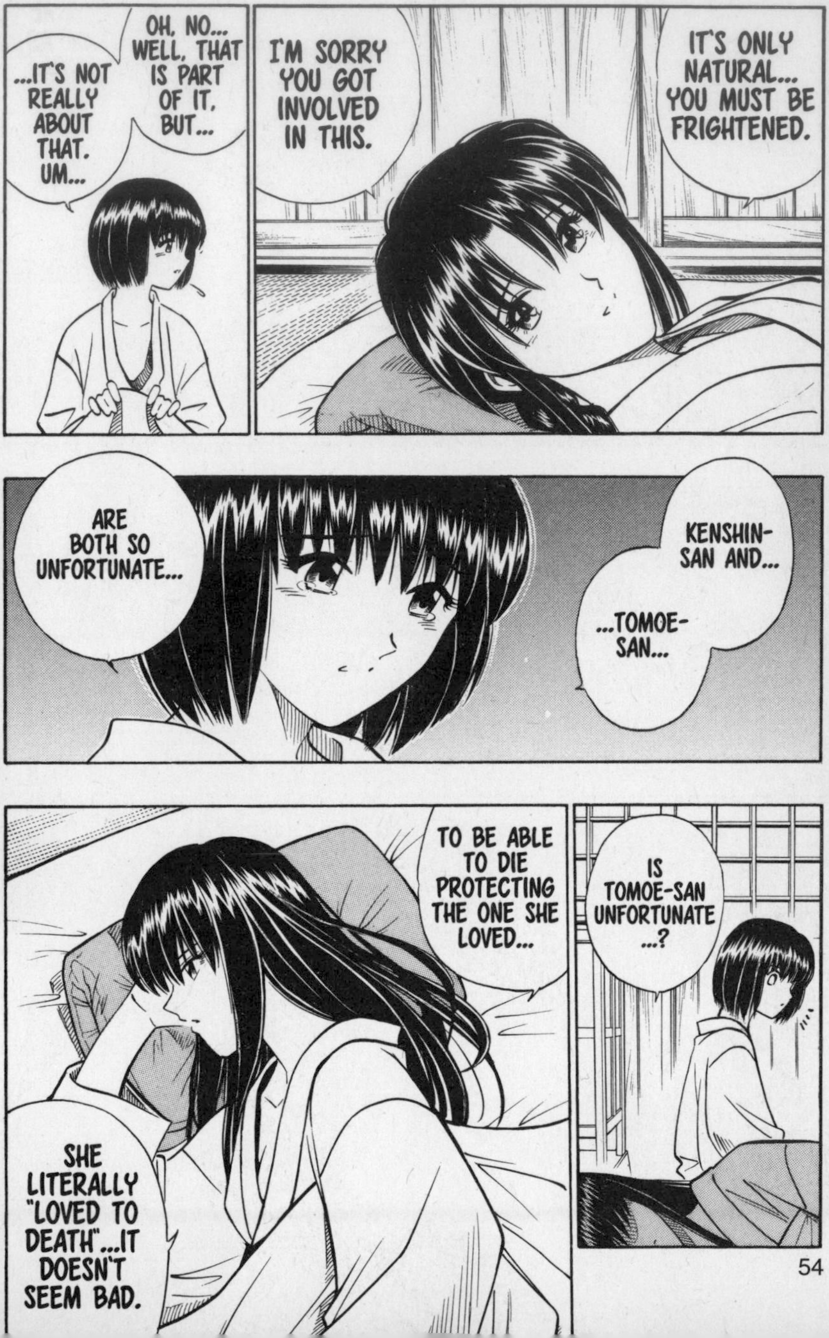
IT'S ONLY NATURAL... YOU MUST BE FRIGHTENED.
I'M SORRY YOU GOT INVOLVED IN THIS.
OH, NO... WELL, THAT IS PART OF IT, BUT...
...IT'S NOT REALLY ABOUT THAT. UM...
KENSHIN-SAN AND...
...TOMOE-SAN...
ARE BOTH SO UNFORTUNATE...
IS TOMOE-SAN UNFORTUNATE ...?
TO BE ABLE TO DIE PROTECTING THE ONE SHE LOVED...
SHE LITERALLY "LOVED TO DEATH"...IT DOESN'T SEEM BAD.

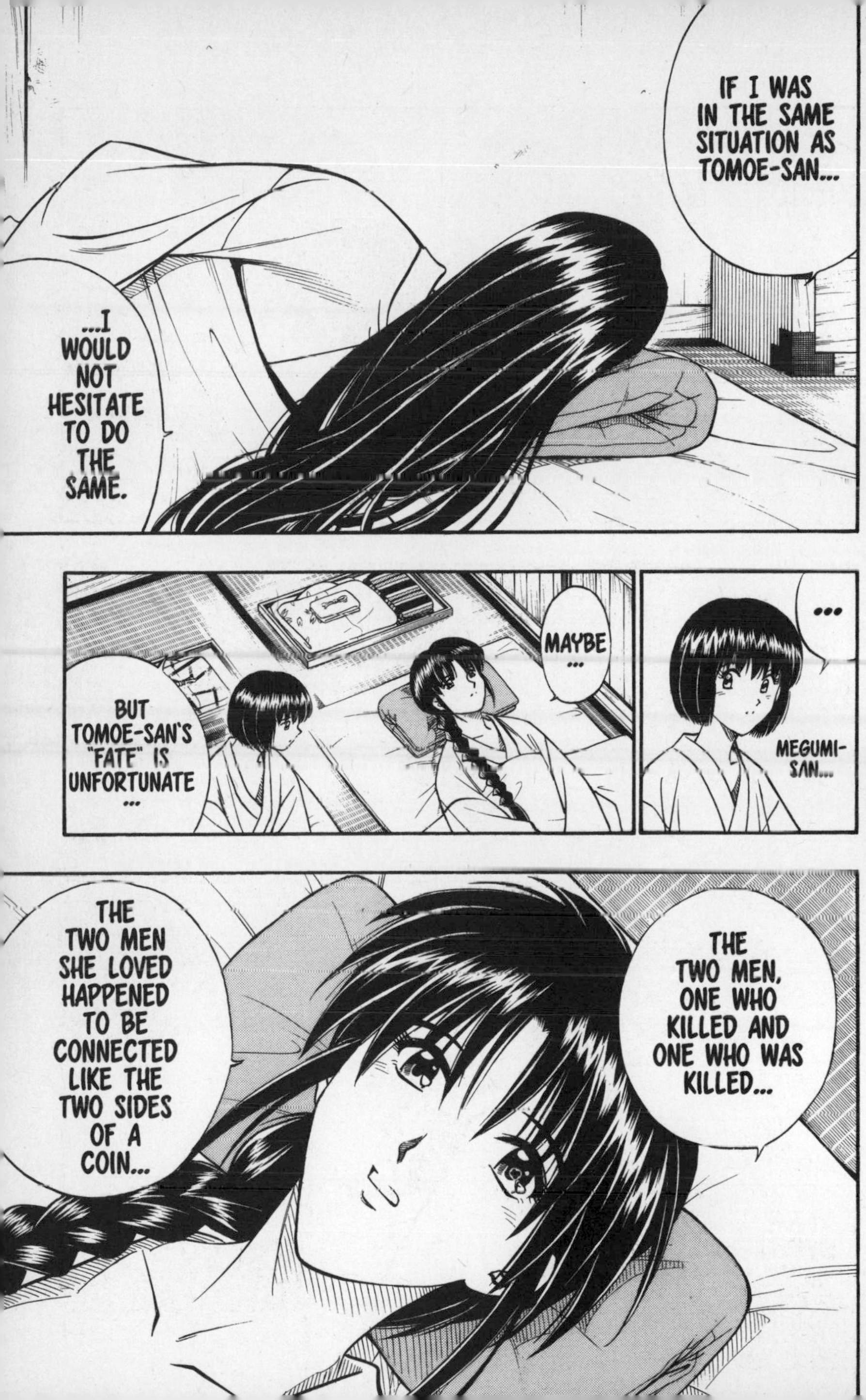
IF I WAS IN THE SAME SITUATION AS TOMOE-SAN...
...I WOULD NOT HESITATE TO DO THE SAME.
...
MEGUMI-SAN...
MAYBE ...
BUT TOMOE-SAN'S "FATE" IS UNFORTUNATE ...
THE TWO MEN, ONE WHO KILLED AND ONE WHO WAS KILLED...
THE TWO MEN SHE LOVED HAPPENED TO BE CONNECTED LIKE THE TWO SIDES OF A COIN...

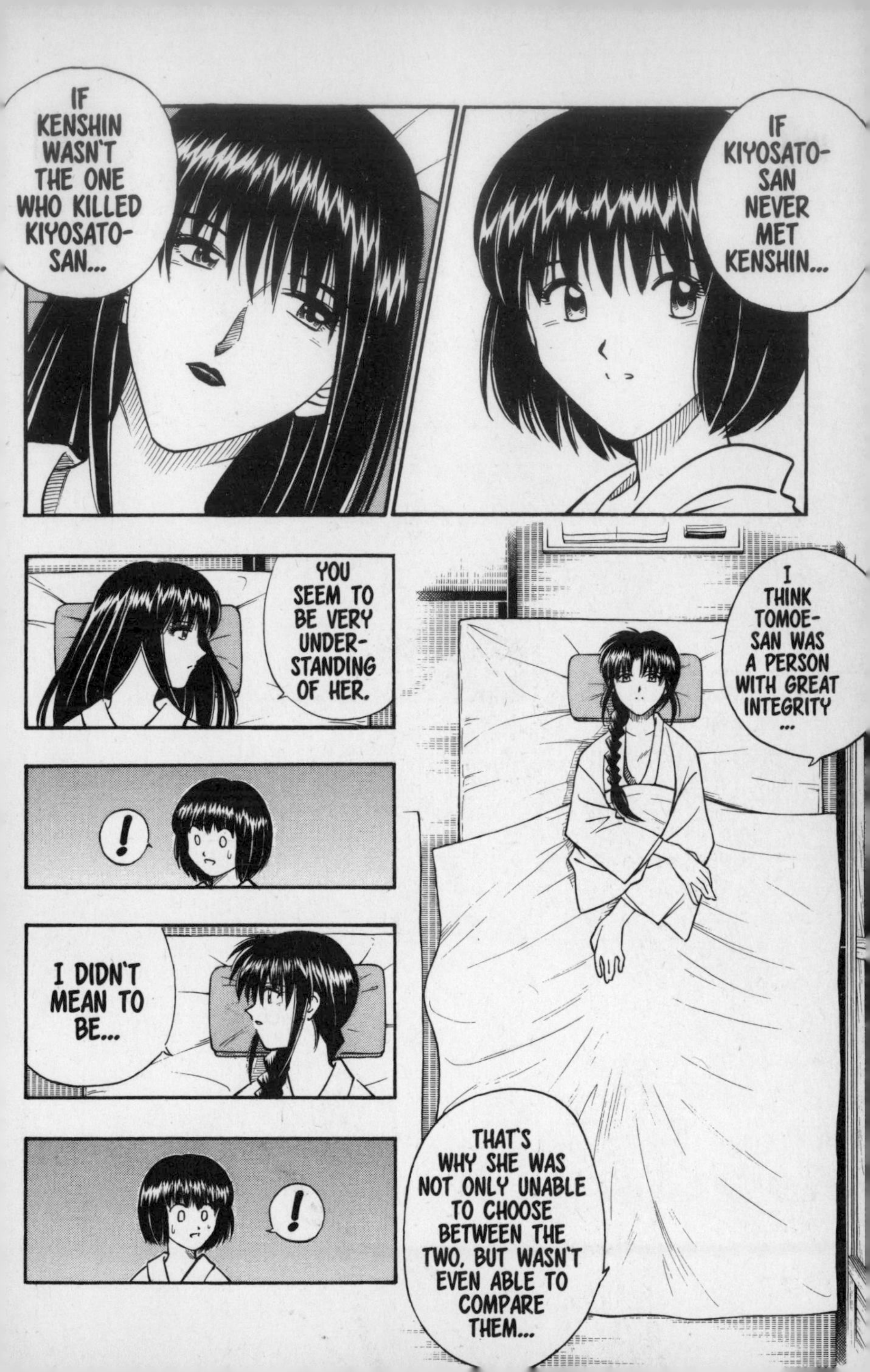
IF KIYOSATO-SAN NEVER MET KENSHIN...
IF KENSHIN WASN'T THE ONE WHO KILLED KIYOSATO-SAN...
I THINK TOMOE-SAN WAS A PERSON WITH GREAT INTEGRITY...
THAT'S WHY SHE WAS NOT ONLY UNABLE TO CHOOSE BETWEEN THE TWO, BUT WASN'T EVEN ABLE TO COMPARE THEM...
YOU SEEM TO BE VERY UNDER-STANDING OF HER.
!
I DIDN'T MEAN TO BE...
!

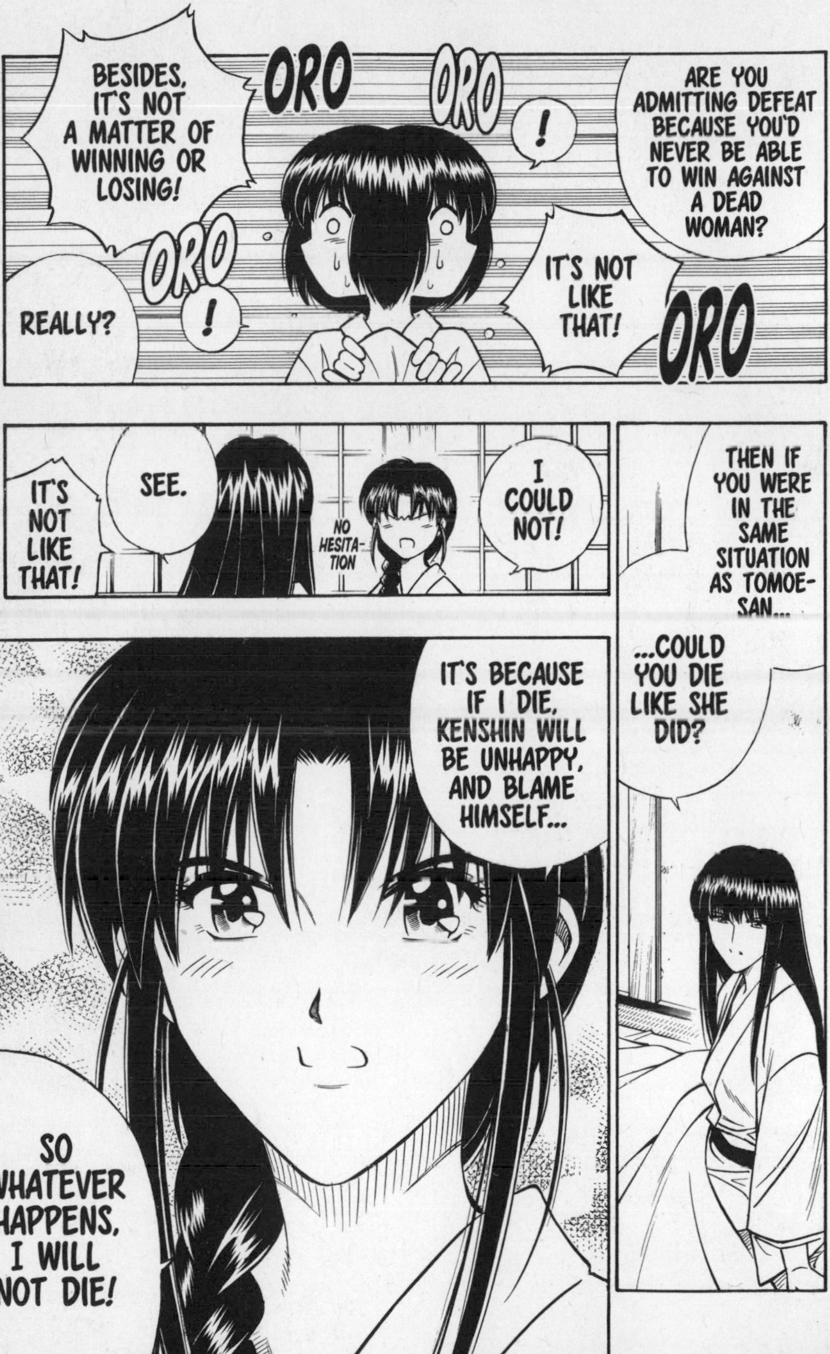
ARE YOU ADMITTING DEFEAT BECAUSE YOU'D NEVER BE ABLE TO WIN AGAINST A DEAD WOMAN?
ORO
IT'S NOT LIKE THAT!
!
ORO
ORO
BESIDES, IT'S NOT A MATTER OF WINNING OR LOSING!
ORO
!
REALLY?
THEN IF YOU WERE IN THE SAME SITUATION AS TOMOE-SAN...
...COULD YOU DIE LIKE SHE DID?
I COULD NOT!
NO HESITATION
SEE.
IT'S NOT LIKE THAT!
IT'S BECAUSE IF I DIE, KENSHIN WILL BE UNHAPPY, AND BLAME HIMSELF...
SO WHATEVER HAPPENS, I WILL NOT DIE!

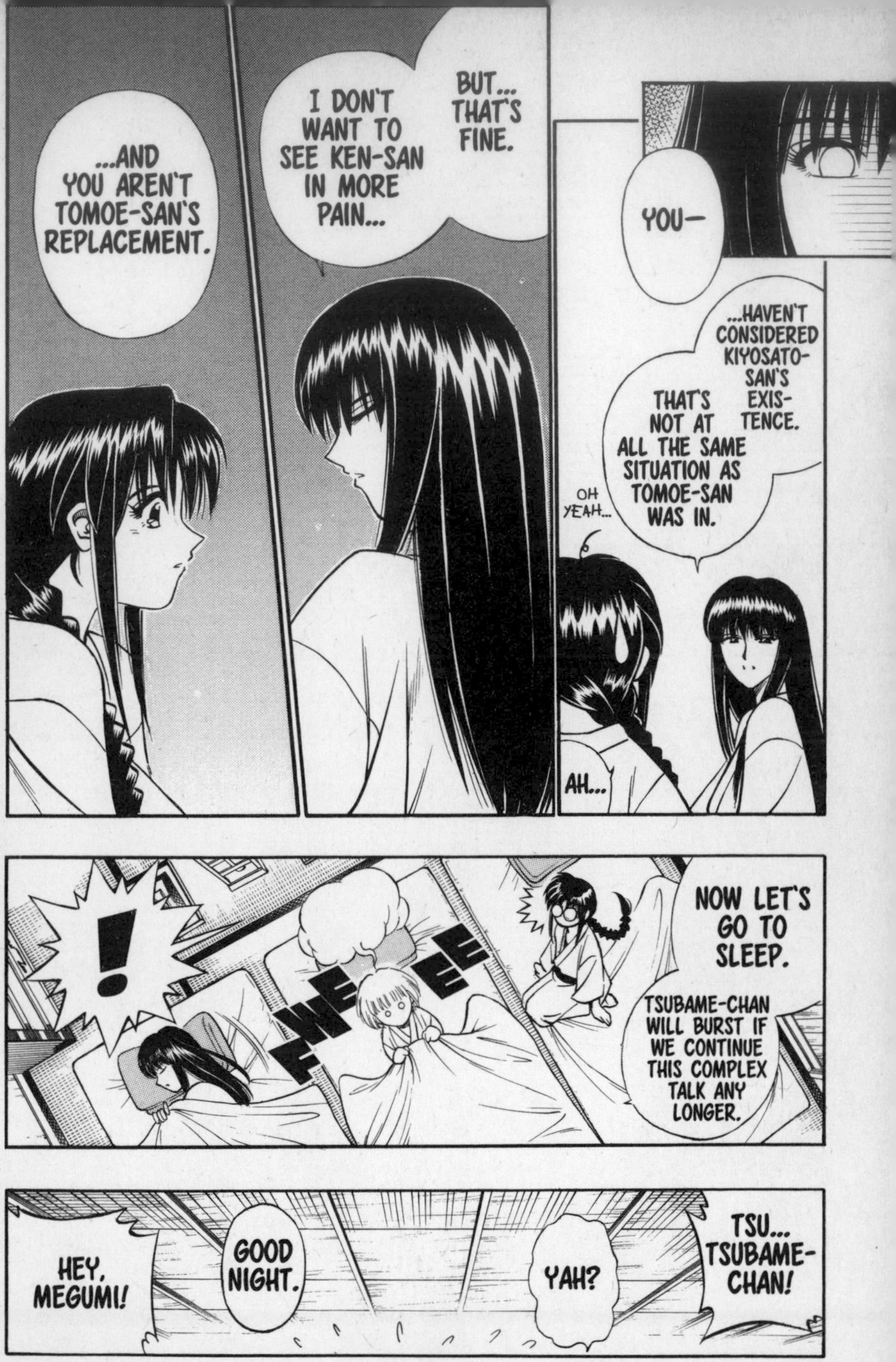
YOU—
...HAVEN'T CONSIDERED KIYOSATO-SAN'S EXISTENCE.
THAT'S NOT AT ALL THE SAME SITUATION AS TOMOE-SAN WAS IN.
OH YEAH...
AH...
BUT... THAT'S FINE.
I DON'T WANT TO SEE KEN-SAN IN MORE PAIN...
...AND YOU AREN'T TOMOE-SAN'S REPLACEMENT.
NOW LET'S GO TO SLEEP.
TSUBAME-CHAN WILL BURST IF WE CONTINUE THIS COMPLEX TALK ANY LONGER.
!
FWEEE
TSU... TSUBAME-CHAN!
YAH?
GOOD NIGHT.
HEY, MEGUMI!

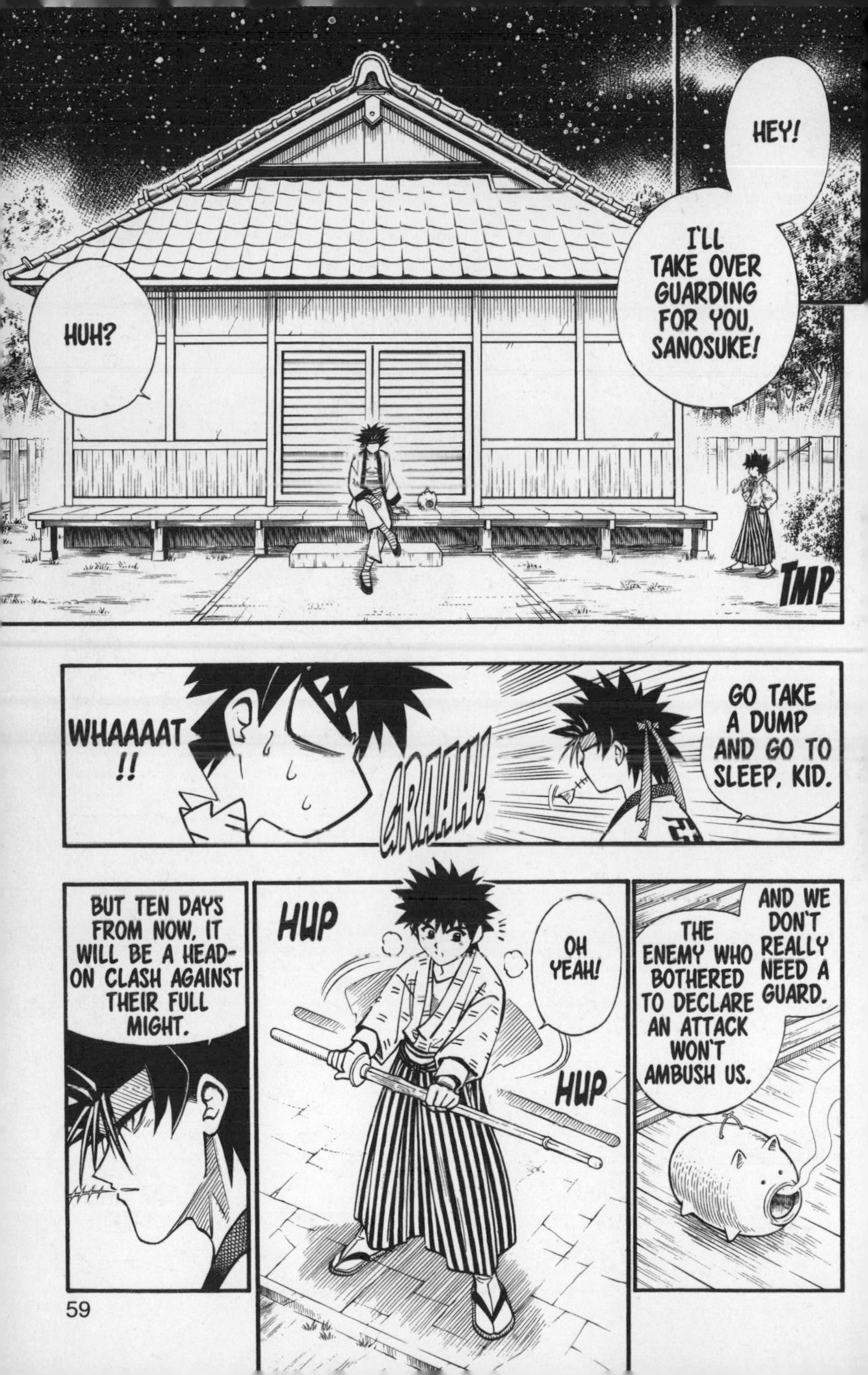
HEY!
I'LL TAKE OVER GUARDING FOR YOU, SANOSUKE!
HUH?
TMP
GO TAKE A DUMP AND GO TO SLEEP, KID.
GRAAAH!
WHAAAAT!!
THE ENEMY WHO BOTHERED TO DECLARE AN ATTACK WON'T AMBUSH US.
AND WE DON'T REALLY NEED A GUARD.
HUP
OH YEAH!
HUP
BUT TEN DAYS FROM NOW, IT WILL BE A HEAD-ON CLASH AGAINST THEIR FULL MIGHT.

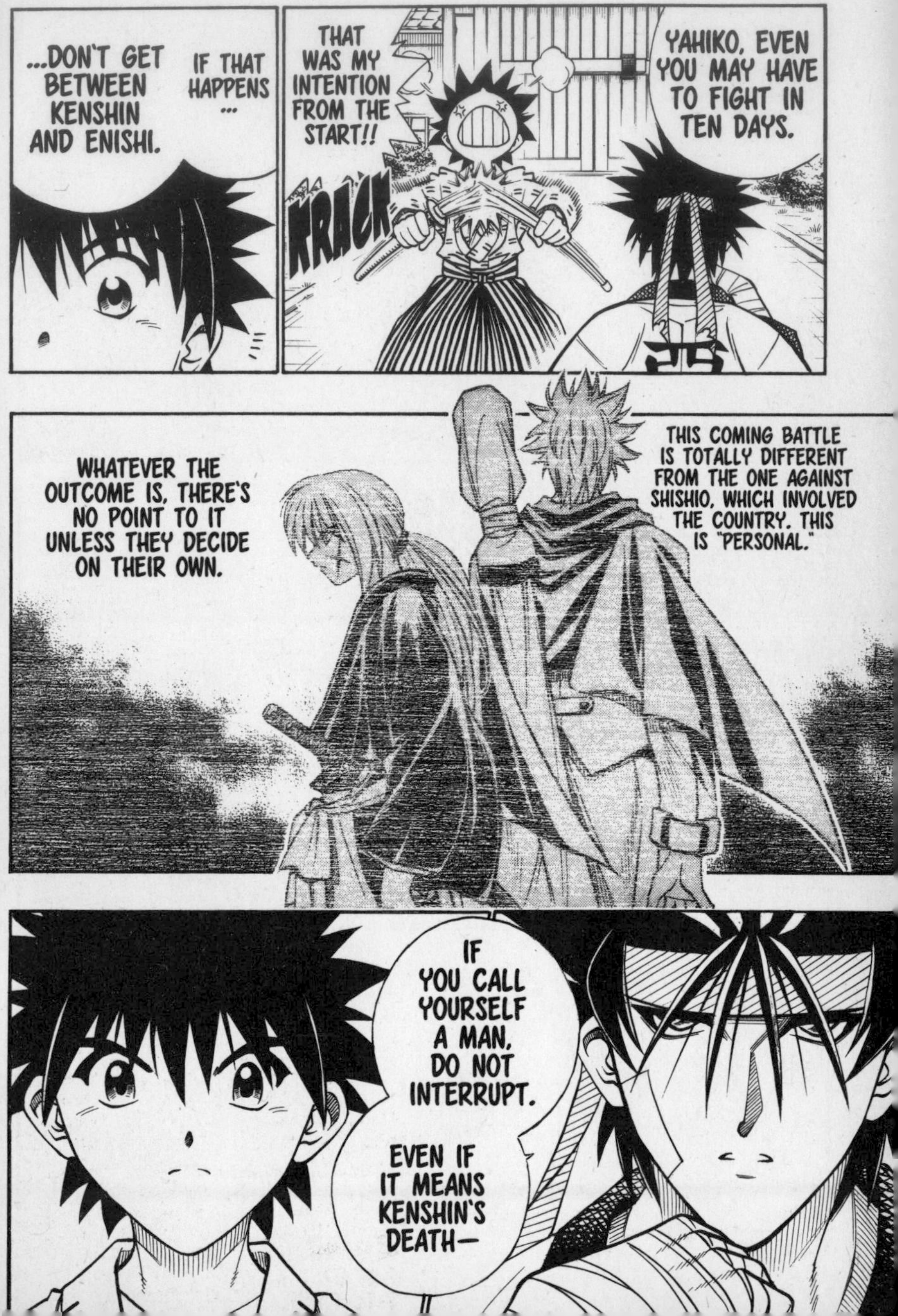
YAHIKO, EVEN YOU MAY HAVE TO FIGHT IN TEN DAYS.
THAT WAS MY INTENTION FROM THE START!!
KRACK
IF THAT HAPPENS...
...DON'T GET BETWEEN KENSHIN AND ENISHI.
THIS COMING BATTLE IS TOTALLY DIFFERENT FROM THE ONE AGAINST SHISHIO, WHICH INVOLVED THE COUNTRY. THIS IS "PERSONAL."
WHATEVER THE OUTCOME IS, THERE'S NO POINT TO IT UNLESS THEY DECIDE ON THEIR OWN.
IF YOU CALL YOURSELF A MAN, DO NOT INTERRUPT.
EVEN IF IT MEANS KENSHIN'S DEATH—

READ THIS WAY

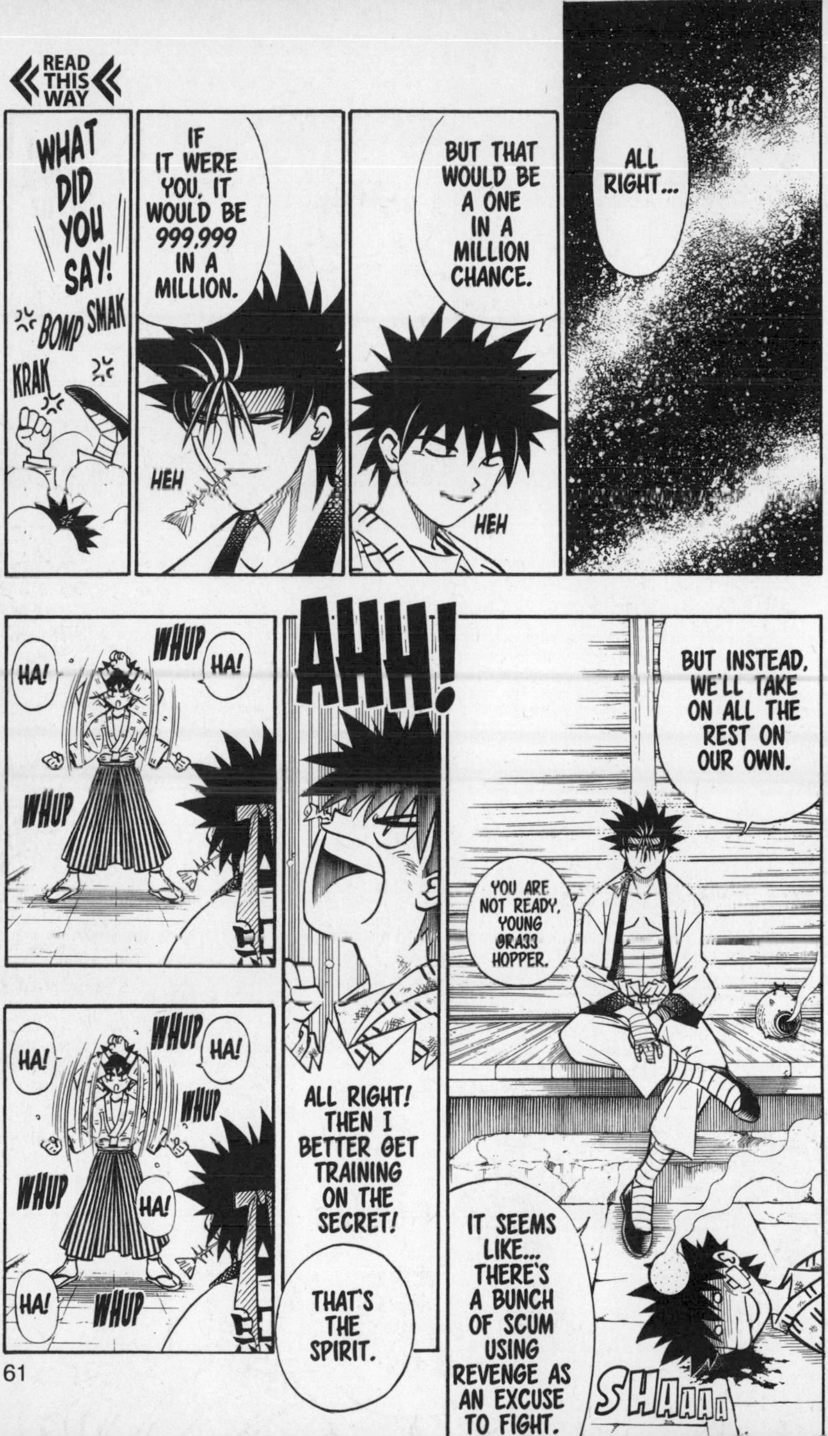
ALL RIGHT...
BUT THAT WOULD BE A ONE IN A MILLION CHANCE.
HEH
IF IT WERE YOU, IT WOULD BE 999,999 IN A MILLION.
HEH
WHAT DID YOU SAY!
BOMP
SMAK
KRAK
BUT INSTEAD, WE'LL TAKE ON ALL THE REST ON OUR OWN.
YOU ARE NOT READY, YOUNG GRASS HOPPER.
IT SEEMS LIKE... THERE'S A BUNCH OF SCUM USING REVENGE AS AN EXCUSE TO FIGHT.
SHAAAA
AHH!
ALL RIGHT! THEN I BETTER GET TRAINING ON THE SECRET!
THAT'S THE SPIRIT.
HA!
WHUP
HA!
WHUP
HA!
WHUP
HA!
WHUP
HA!
HA!
WHUP

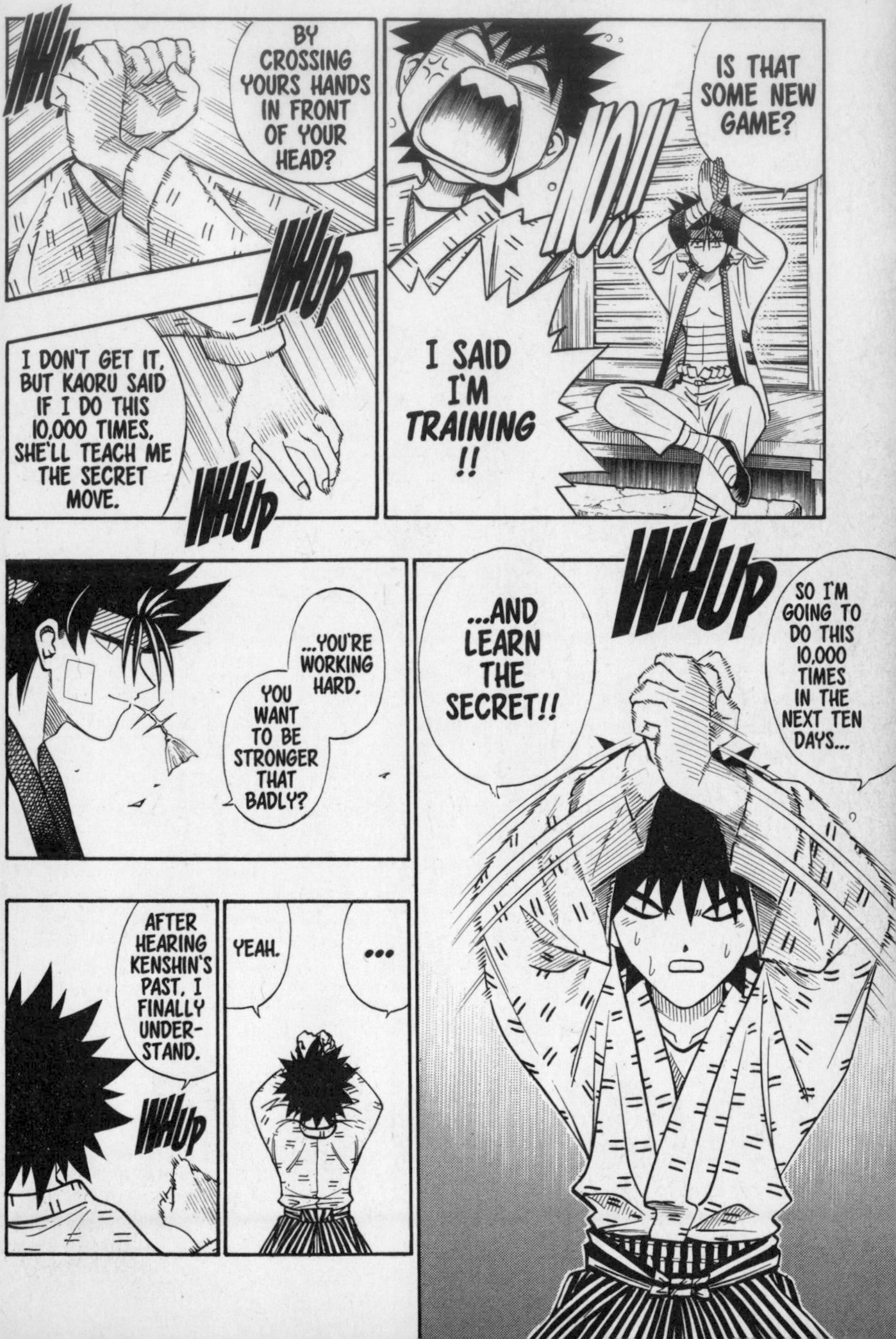
IS THAT SOME NEW GAME?
NO!!
I SAID I'M TRAINING!!
BY CROSSING YOURS HANDS IN FRONT OF YOUR HEAD?
WHUP
I DON'T GET IT, BUT KAORU SAID IF I DO THIS 10,000 TIMES, SHE'LL TEACH ME THE SECRET MOVE.
WHUP
WHUP
SO I'M GOING TO DO THIS 10,000 TIMES IN THE NEXT TEN DAYS...
...AND LEARN THE SECRET!!
...YOU'RE WORKING HARD.
YOU WANT TO BE STRONGER THAT BADLY?
...
YEAH.
AFTER HEARING KENSHIN'S PAST, I FINALLY UNDER-STAND.
WHUP

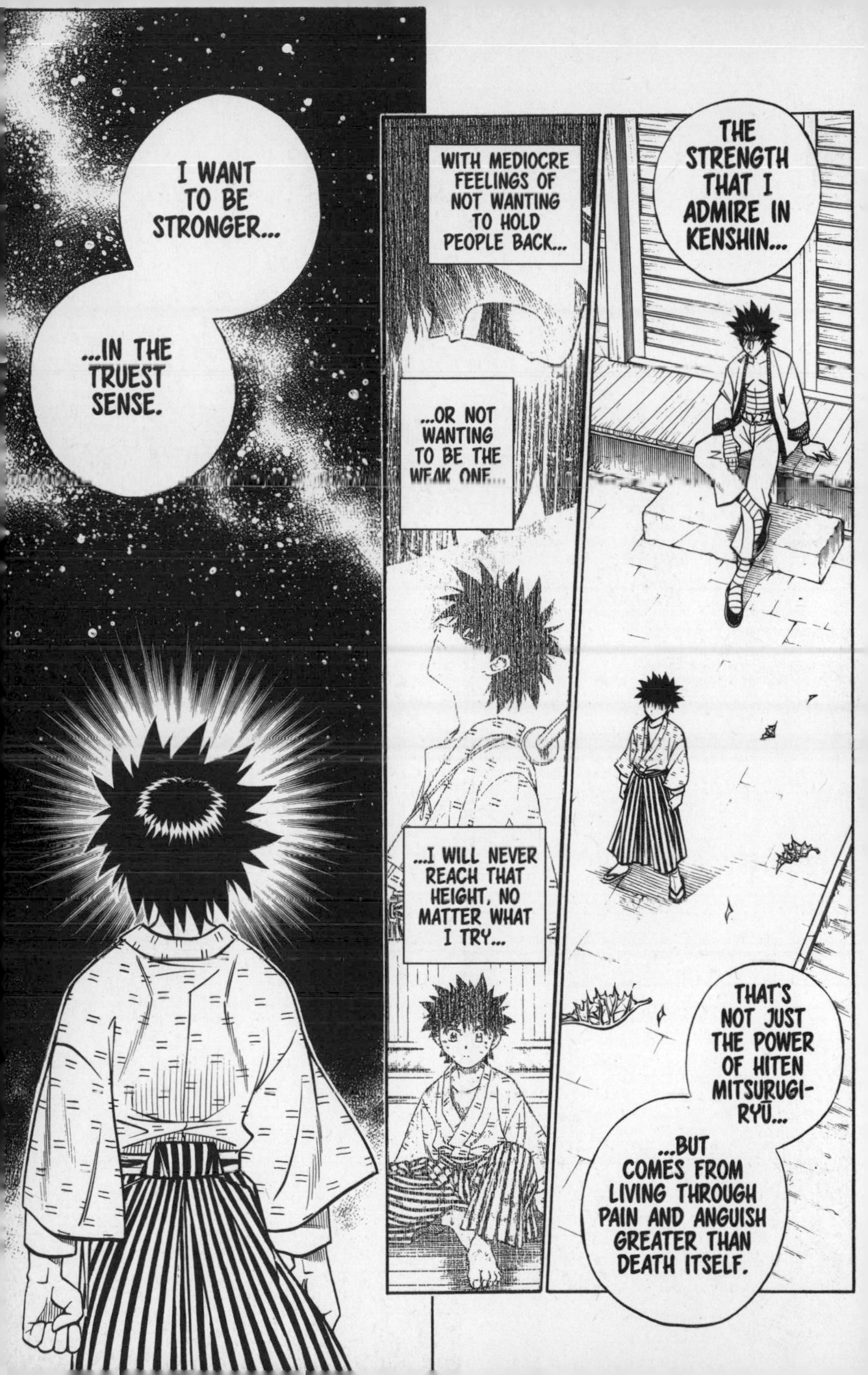
THE STRENGTH THAT I ADMIRE IN KENSHIN...
THAT'S NOT JUST THE POWER OF HITEN MITSURUGI-RYŪ...
...BUT COMES FROM LIVING THROUGH PAIN AND ANGUISH GREATER THAN DEATH ITSELF.
WITH MEDIOCRE FEELINGS OF NOT WANTING TO HOLD PEOPLE BACK...
...OR NOT WANTING TO BE THE WEAK ONE...
...I WILL NEVER REACH THAT HEIGHT, NO MATTER WHAT I TRY...
I WANT TO BE STRONGER...
...IN THE TRUEST SENSE.

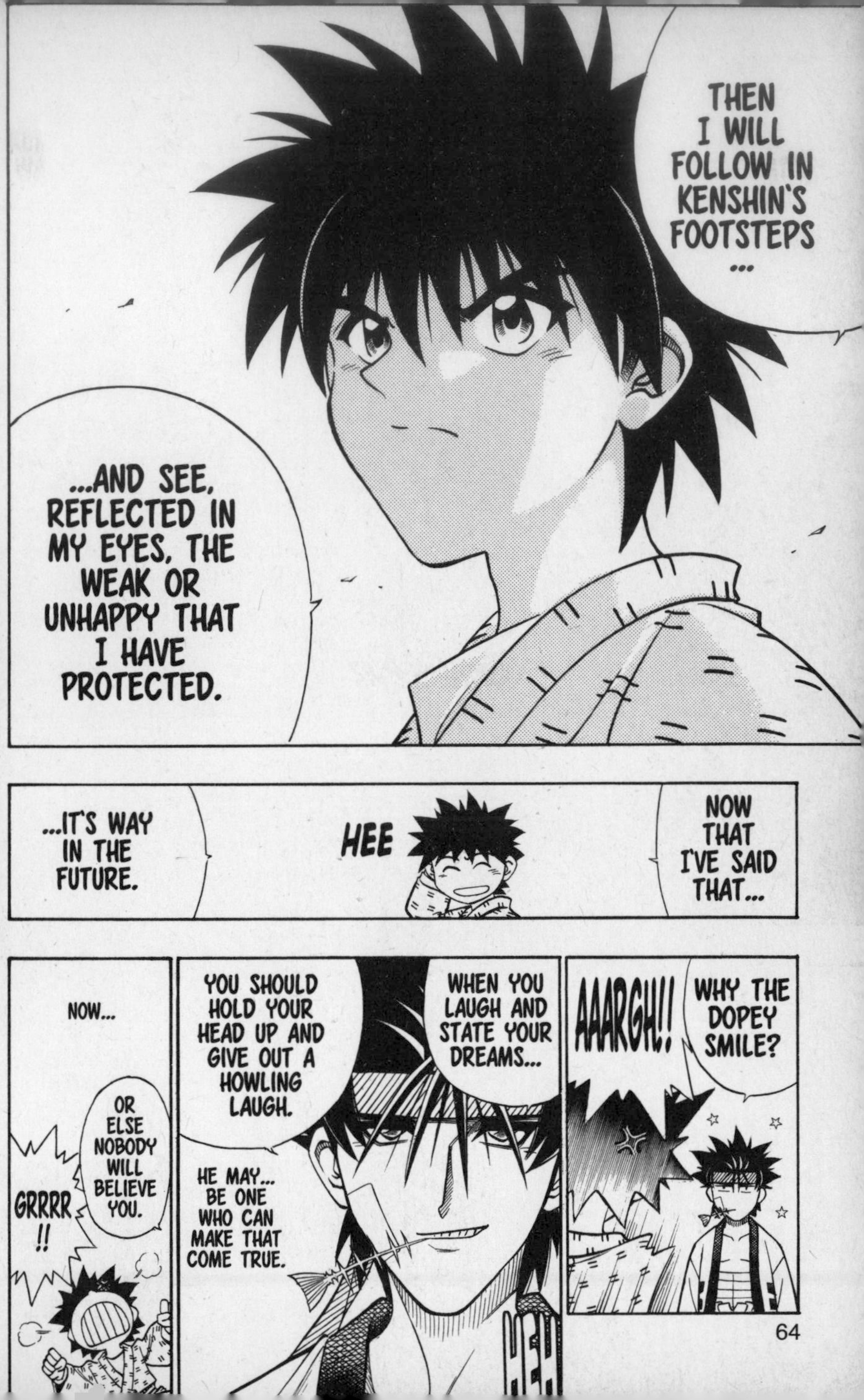
THEN I WILL FOLLOW IN KENSHIN'S FOOTSTEPS ...
...AND SEE, REFLECTED IN MY EYES, THE WEAK OR UNHAPPY THAT I HAVE PROTECTED.
NOW THAT I'VE SAID THAT...
HEE
...IT'S WAY IN THE FUTURE.
WHY THE DOPEY SMILE?
AAARGH!!
WHEN YOU LAUGH AND STATE YOUR DREAMS...
YOU SHOULD HOLD YOUR HEAD UP AND GIVE OUT A HOWLING LAUGH.
HE MAY... BE ONE WHO CAN MAKE THAT COME TRUE.
HEH
NOW...
OR ELSE NOBODY WILL BELIEVE YOU.
GRRRR !!

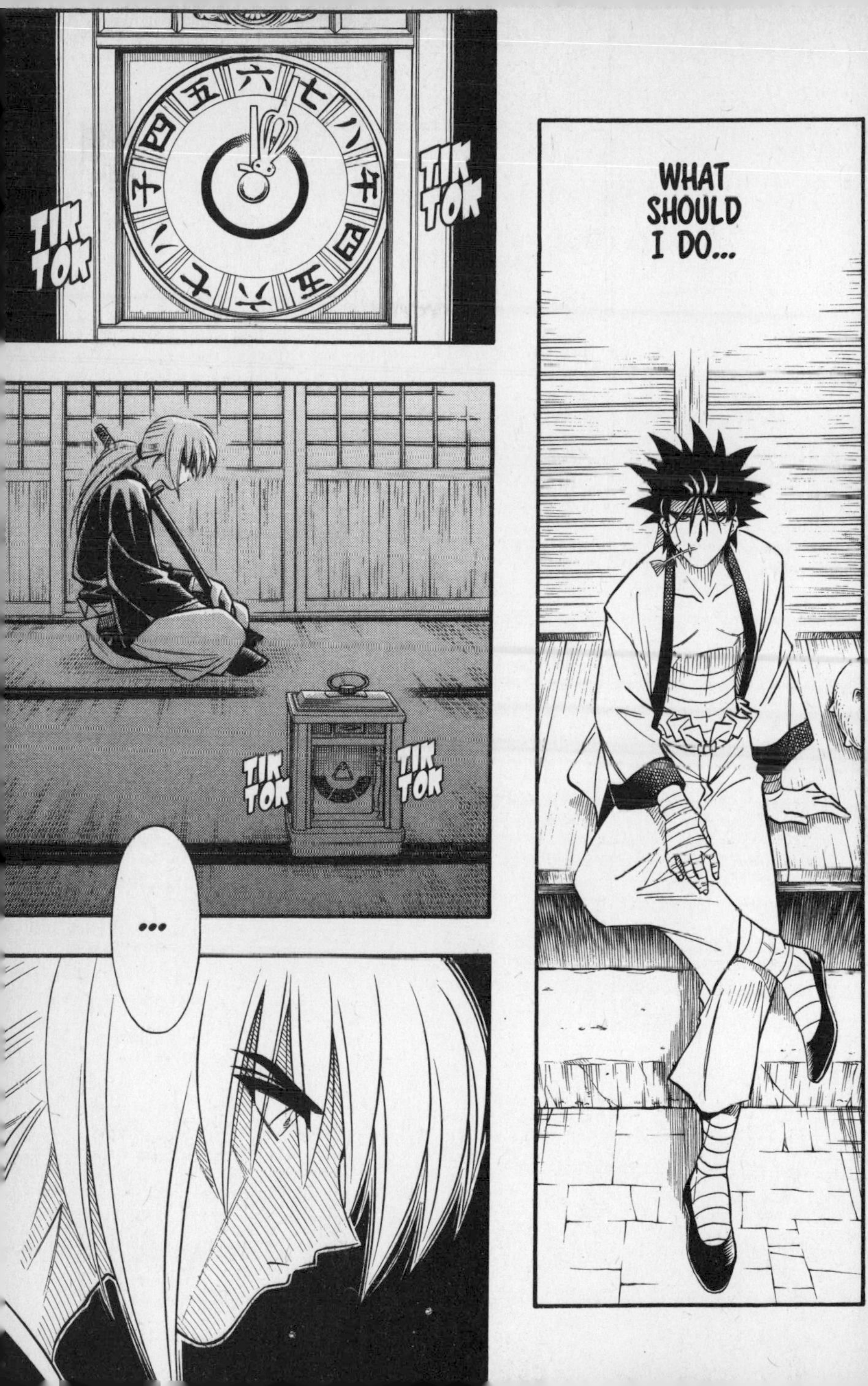
WHAT SHOULD I DO...
TIK TOK
TIK TOK
TIK TOK
TIK TOK
...

The Secret Life of Characters (42)
—Katsura Kogorō and Takasugi Shinsaku—

The two huge Chōshū stars of the Bakumatsu that everyone knows. They have already appeared in many works in different forms, both taking off on their own directions. So, what are their forms in *Ruro-Ken*? They are "the intellectual Katsura, and the free Takasugi," the most orthodox forms they take. Watsuki has the image of Katsura as a strategist, who has more deep thoughts and calculations, and of Takasugi as a snapped madman. But since the remembrance episodes are centered on the story of Kenshin and Tomoe, those were all cut out. Reading back, I regret that they seem too bland and lacking in flavor.

If I ever have a chance to write something really set in the Bakumatsu, I would like to bring out the Katsura and Takasugi I have imagined. A violent and picaresque pair that will bring in many letters of objections, like the time Saitō first appeared.

In terms of design, I quickly drafted Katsura from photos remaining of him, but adjusting to make him a gentle, good-looking man with an accent added by the forelock. Like I have stated above, I just meant to make him the most orthodox image, but Takei-sensei of *Shaman King* complimented it, saying, "A great design with the simple forelock adding to the character expression," which made me happy, but at the same time a little embarrassed. The senses of each individual person are not to be taken lightly.

Takasugi is made of a rejected design for Nagaoka Mikio in volume five. When I created this design for Nagaoka, I felt, "He's too wild and cool! Too good to use for a villain," and switched it out. When looked at closely, they look very much alike. I had actually wanted to use it for a brotherly figure in my next work, but I thought "Why not?" and went free falling with it. Recently, I tend to like these wild outlaw types more than the gentle good-looking types.

I am a bit tired of drawing the good-looking types for now.

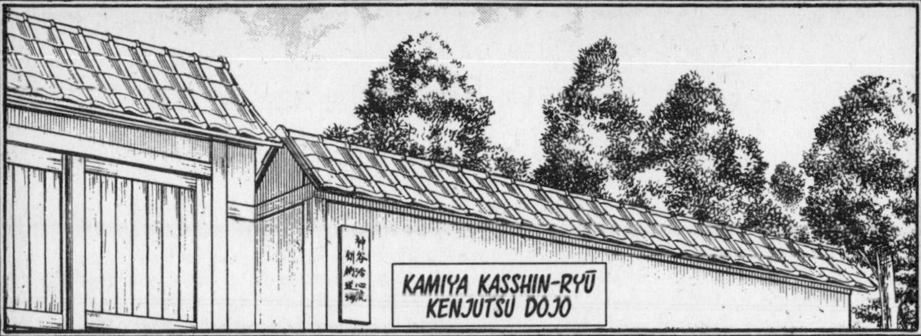
KAMIYA KASSHIN-RYŪ
KENJUTSU DOJO

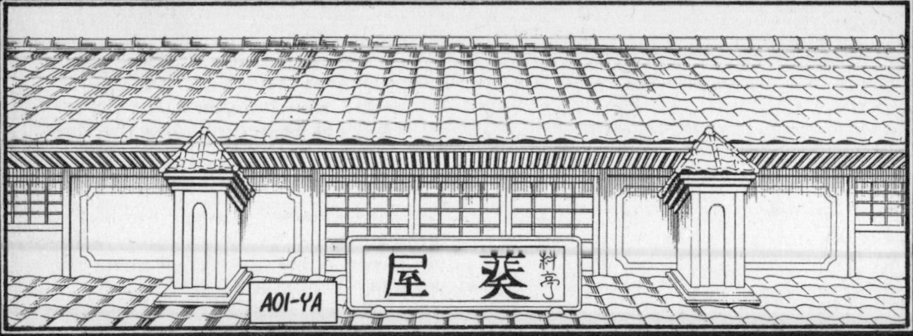
料亭
葵屋
AOI-YA

Act 181
A Strand of Hope

和月伸宏

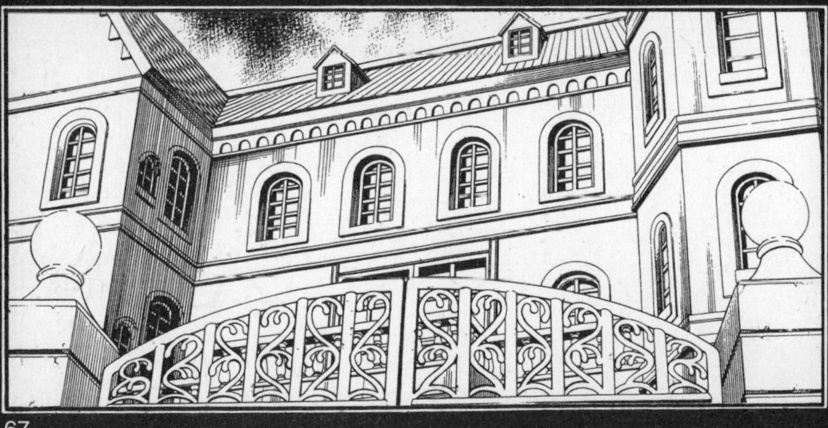

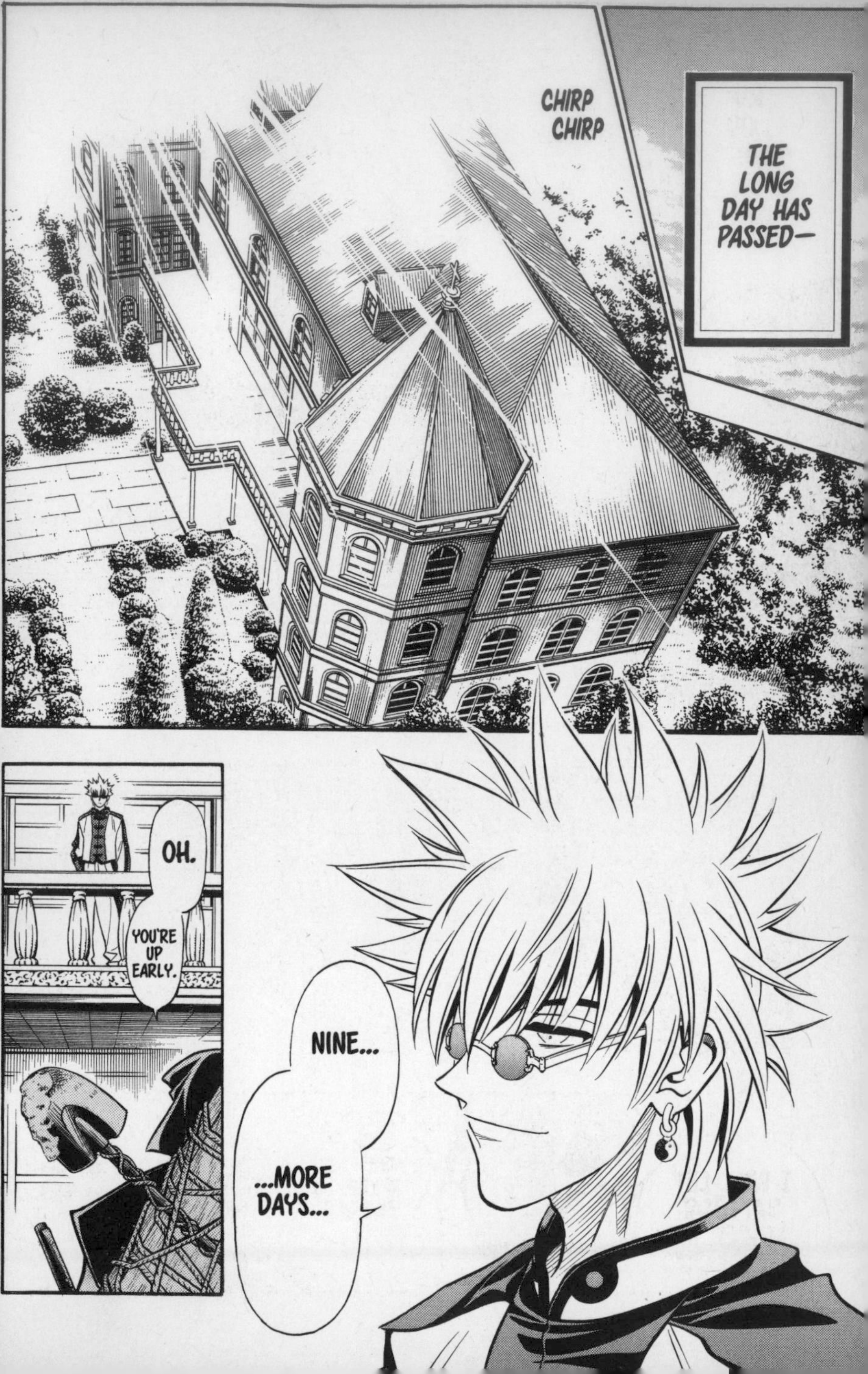
THE LONG DAY HAS PASSED—
CHIRP CHIRP
NINE...
...MORE DAYS...
OH.
YOU'RE UP EARLY.

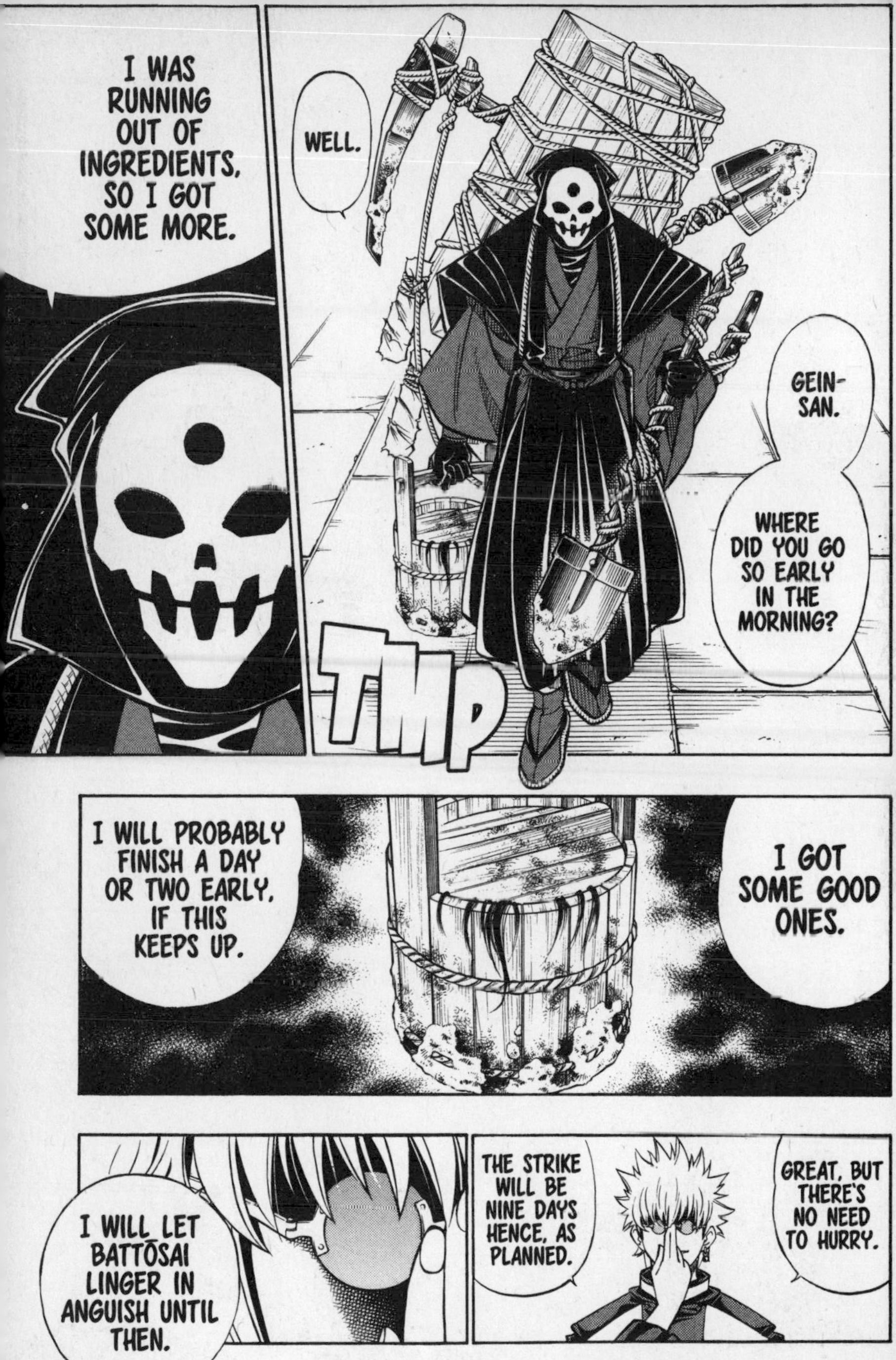
GEIN-SAN.
WHERE DID YOU GO SO EARLY IN THE MORNING?
WELL.
TMP
I WAS RUNNING OUT OF INGREDIENTS, SO I GOT SOME MORE.
I GOT SOME GOOD ONES.
I WILL PROBABLY FINISH A DAY OR TWO EARLY, IF THIS KEEPS UP.
GREAT, BUT THERE'S NO NEED TO HURRY.
THE STRIKE WILL BE NINE DAYS HENCE, AS PLANNED.
I WILL LET BATTŌSAI LINGER IN ANGUISH UNTIL THEN.

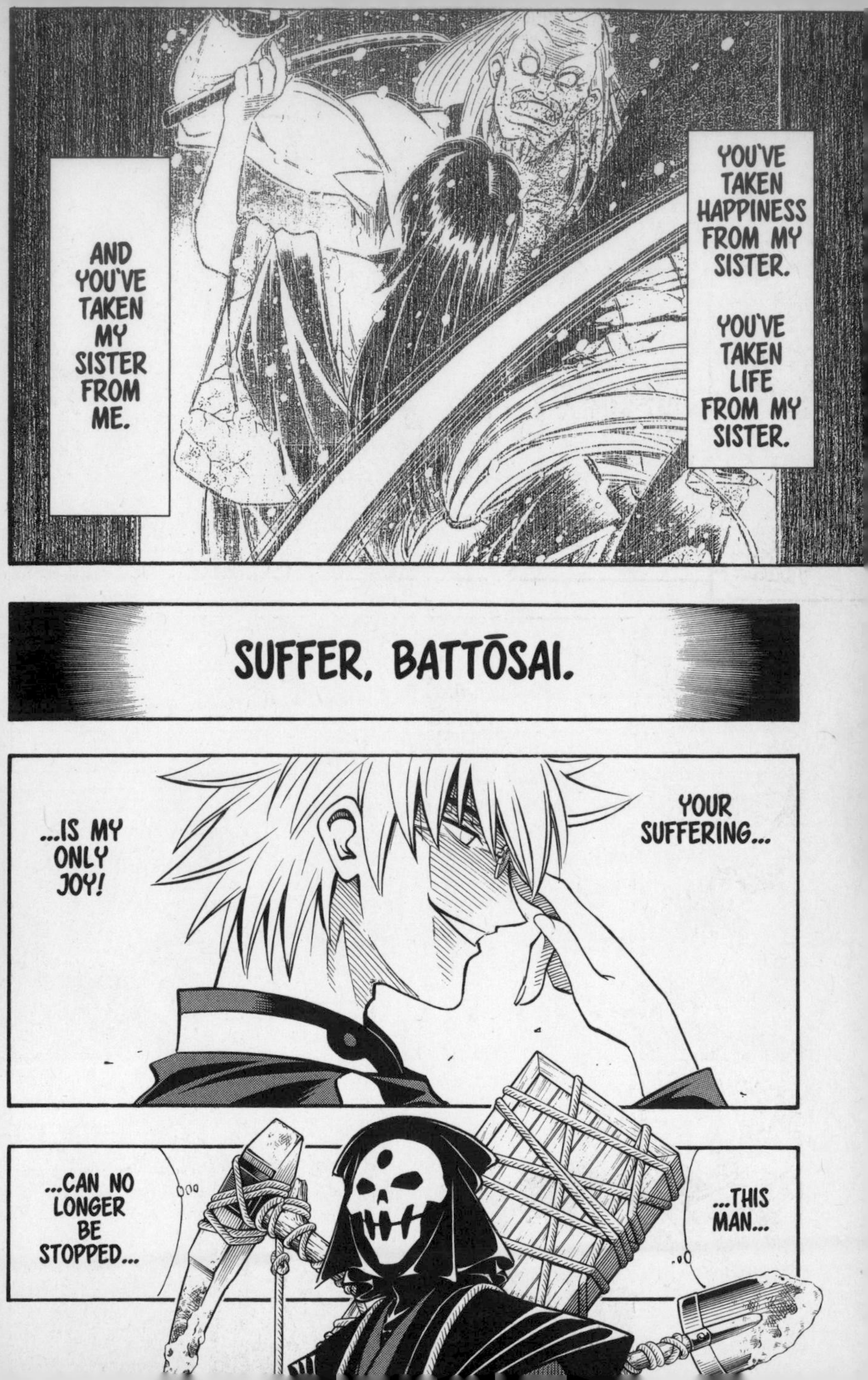
YOU'VE TAKEN HAPPINESS FROM MY SISTER.
YOU'VE TAKEN LIFE FROM MY SISTER.
AND YOU'VE TAKEN MY SISTER FROM ME.
SUFFER, BATTŌSAI.
YOUR SUFFERING...
...IS MY ONLY JOY!
...THIS MAN...
...CAN NO LONGER BE STOPPED...

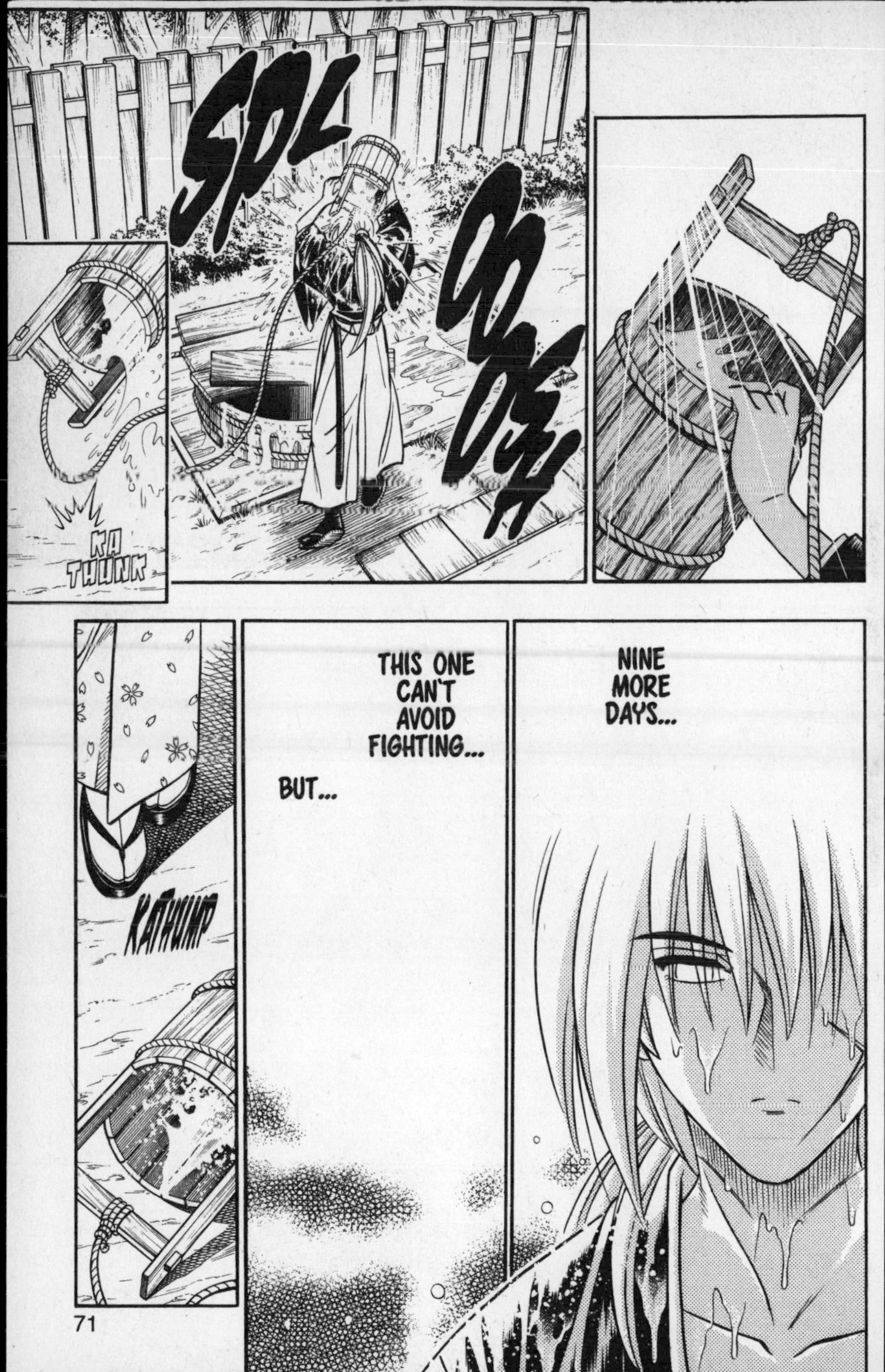
SPLOOSH
KA THUNK
NINE MORE DAYS...
THIS ONE CAN'T AVOID FIGHTING...
BUT...
KATHUMP

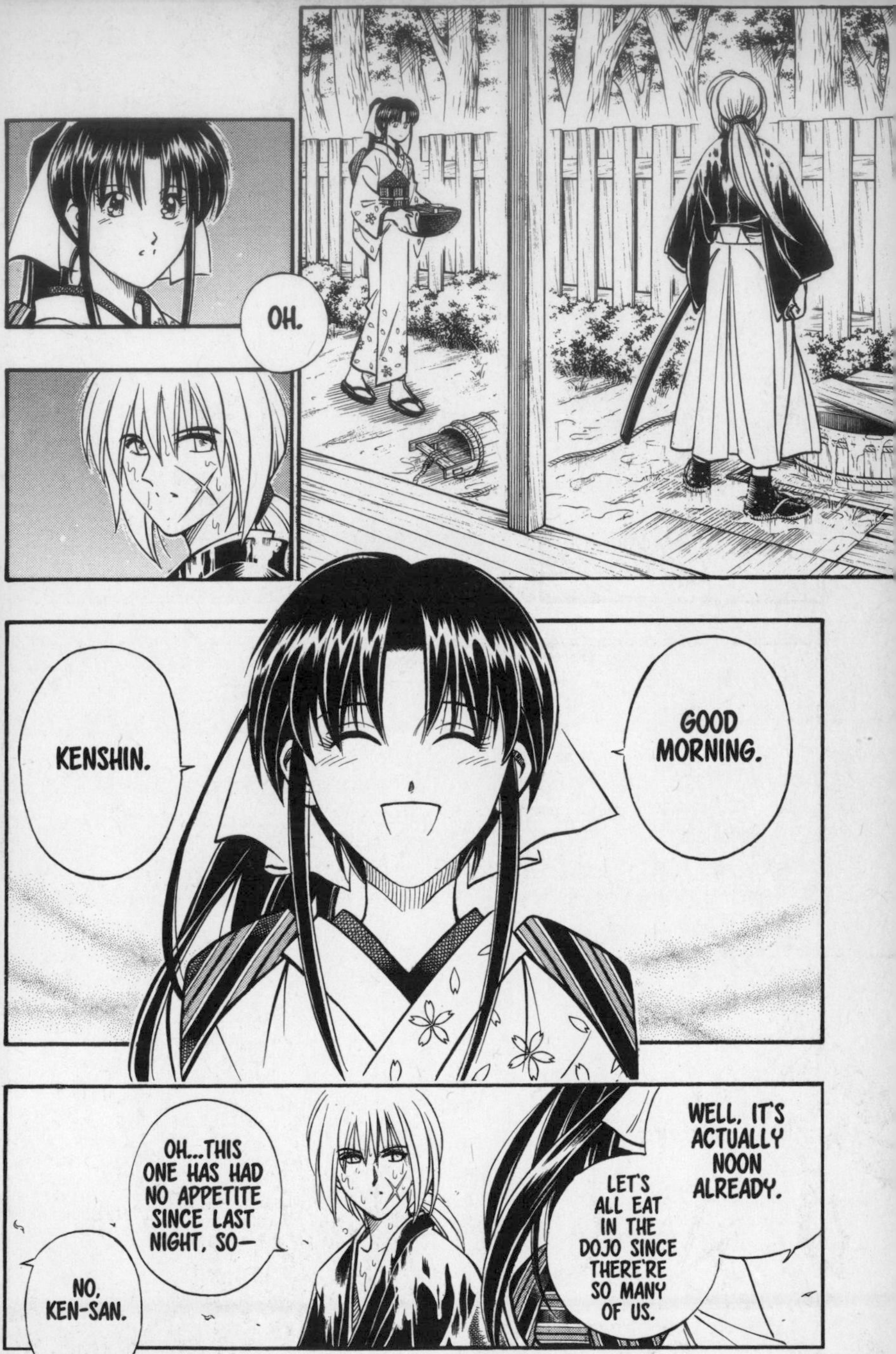
OH.
GOOD MORNING.
KENSHIN.
WELL, IT'S ACTUALLY NOON ALREADY.
LET'S ALL EAT IN THE DOJO SINCE THERE'RE SO MANY OF US.
OH...THIS ONE HAS HAD NO APPETITE SINCE LAST NIGHT, SO—
NO, KEN-SAN.

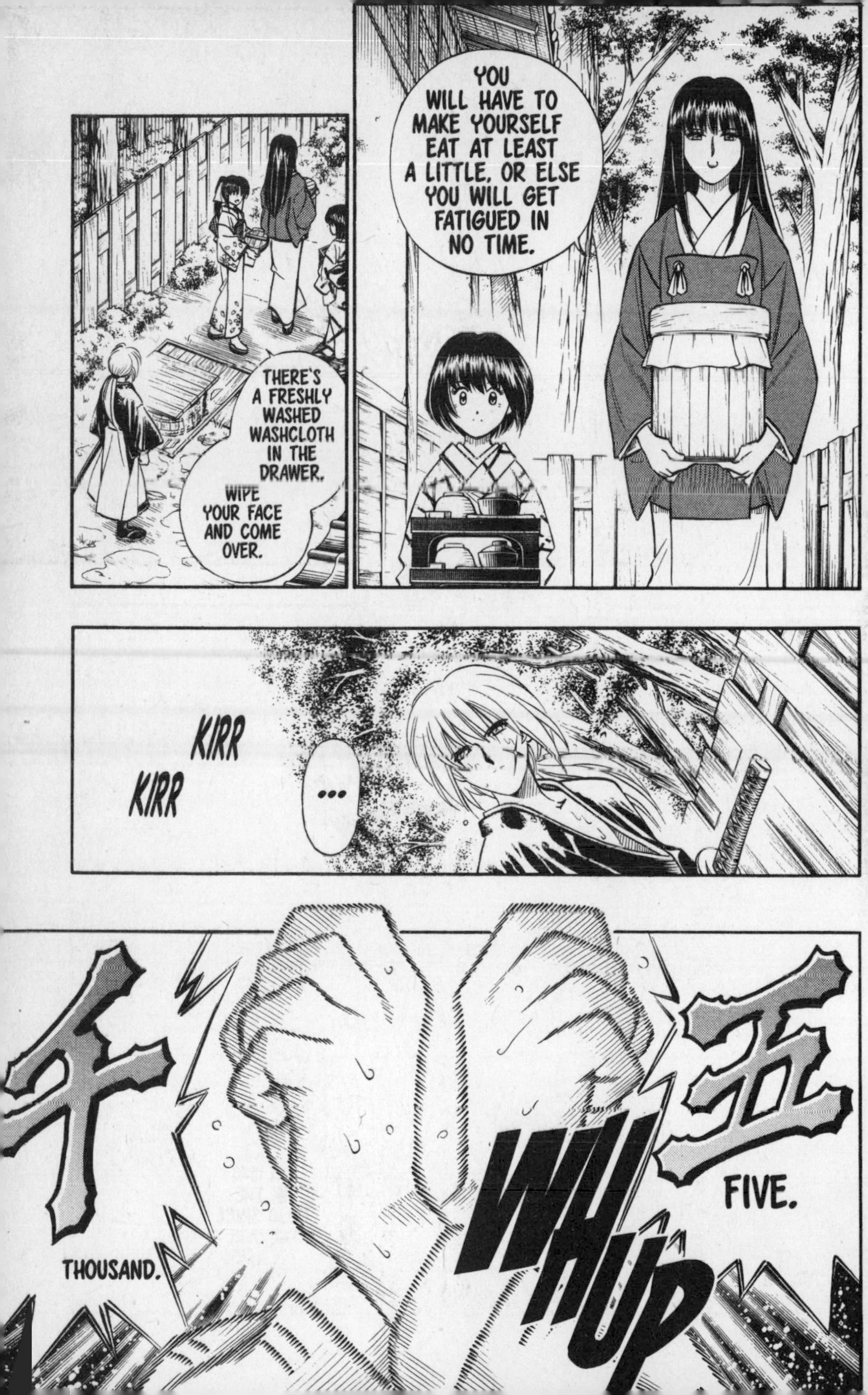
YOU WILL HAVE TO MAKE YOURSELF EAT AT LEAST A LITTLE, OR ELSE YOU WILL GET FATIGUED IN NO TIME.
THERE'S A FRESHLY WASHED WASHCLOTH IN THE DRAWER.
WIPE YOUR FACE AND COME OVER.
KIRR
KIRR
...
五
FIVE.
WHUP
千
THOUSAND.

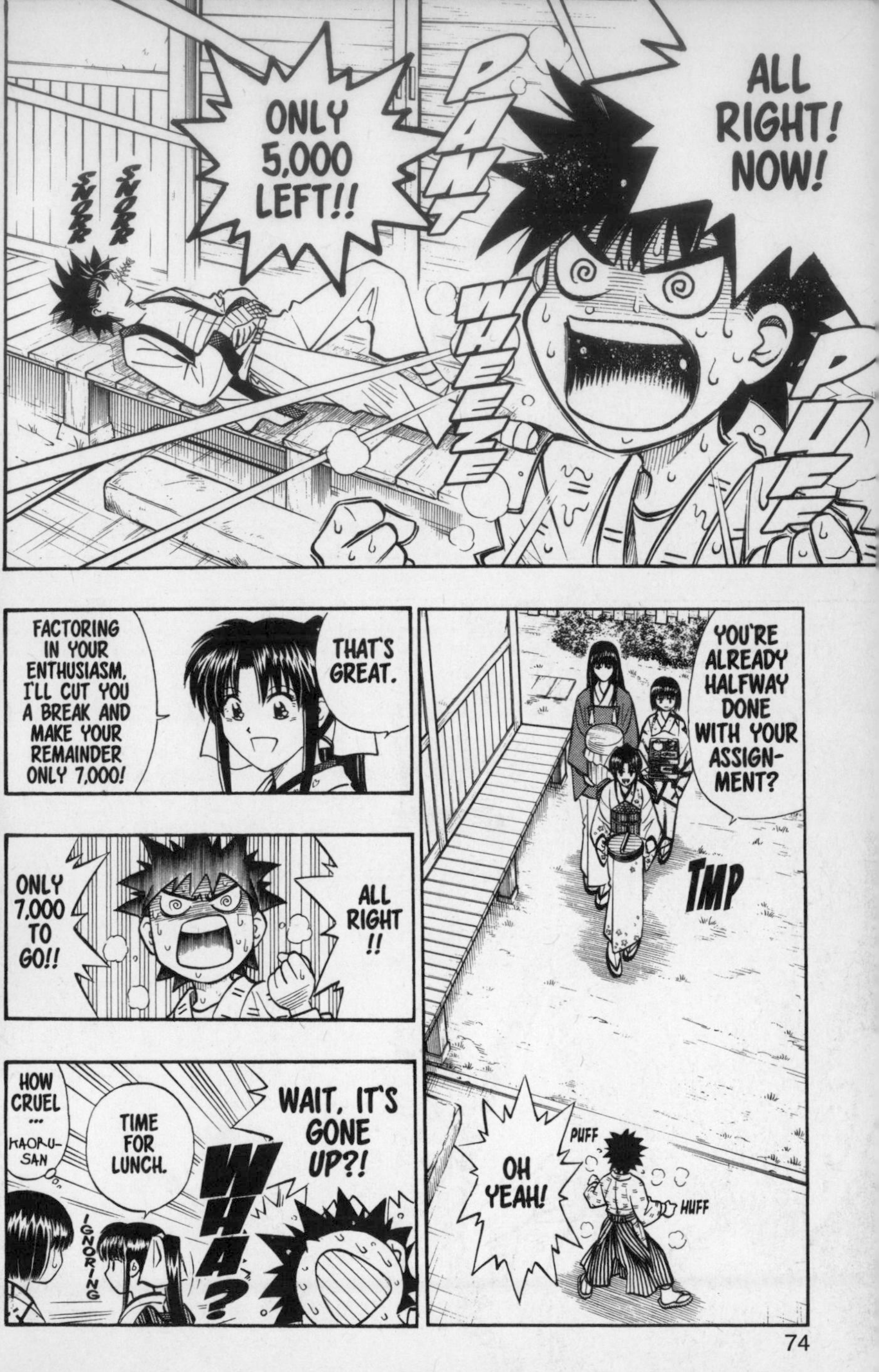
ALL RIGHT! NOW!
PANT
ONLY 5,000 LEFT!!
PUFF
WHEEZE
SNORR
SNORR
YOU'RE ALREADY HALFWAY DONE WITH YOUR ASSIGNMENT?
TMP
PUFF
OH YEAH!
HUFF
THAT'S GREAT.
FACTORING IN YOUR ENTHUSIASM, I'LL CUT YOU A BREAK AND MAKE YOUR REMAINDER ONLY 7,000!
ALL RIGHT!!
ONLY 7,000 TO GO!!
WAIT, IT'S GONE UP?!
WHA?
TIME FOR LUNCH.
IGNORING
HOW CRUEL... KAORU-SAN

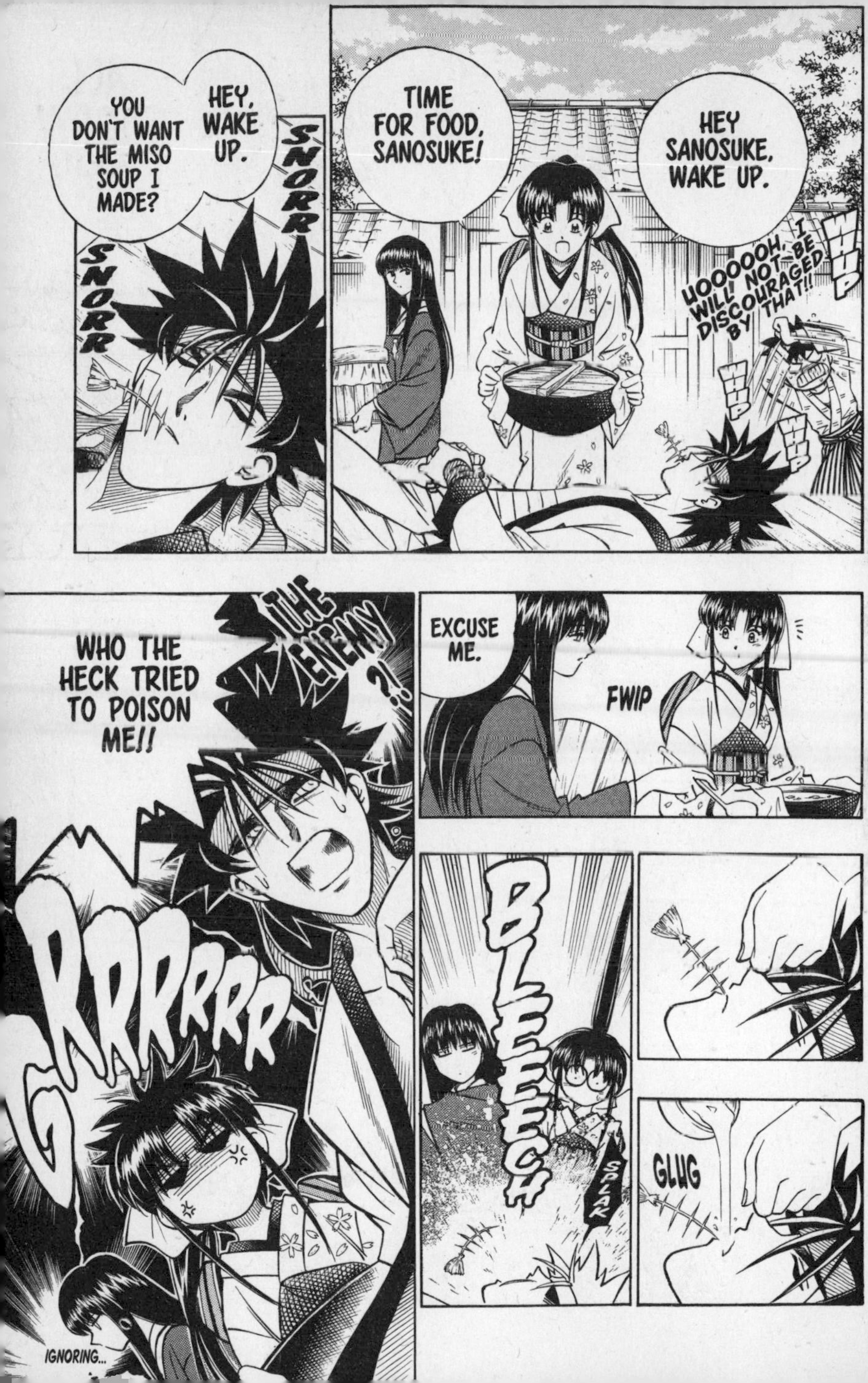
HEY SANOSUKE, WAKE UP.
TIME FOR FOOD, SANOSUKE!
UOOOOOH, I WILL NOT BE DISCOURAGED BY THAT!!
WHUP
WHUP
WHUP
SNORR
SNORR
HEY, WAKE UP.
YOU DON'T WANT THE MISO SOUP I MADE?
EXCUSE ME.
FWIP
GLUG
BLEECH
SPLAK
THE ENEMY?!
WHO THE HECK TRIED TO POISON ME!!
GRRRRRR
IGNORING...

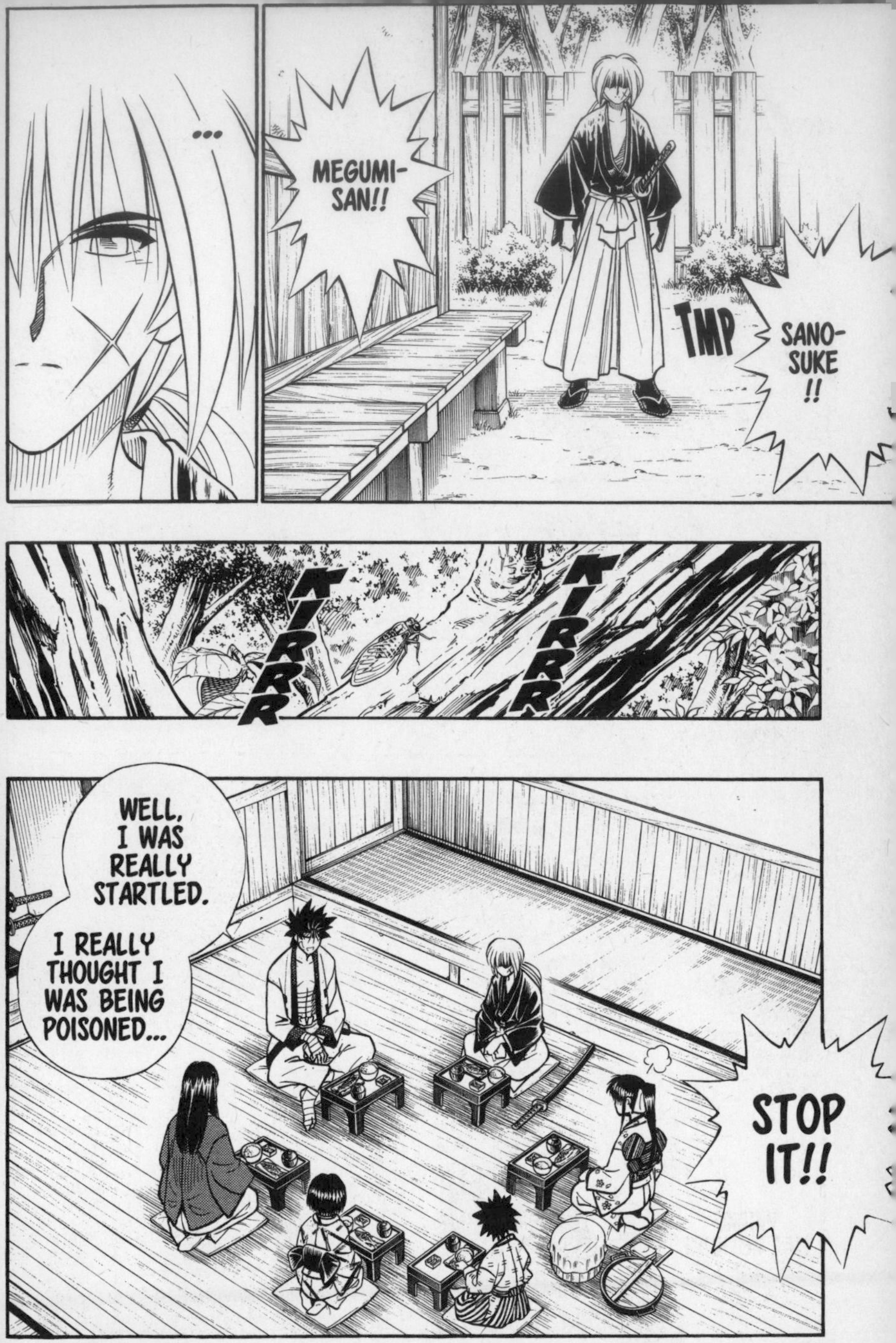
SANO-SUKE!!
TMP
MEGUMI-SAN!!
...
KIRRR
KIRRR
STOP IT!!
WELL, I WAS REALLY STARTLED.
I REALLY THOUGHT I WAS BEING POISONED...

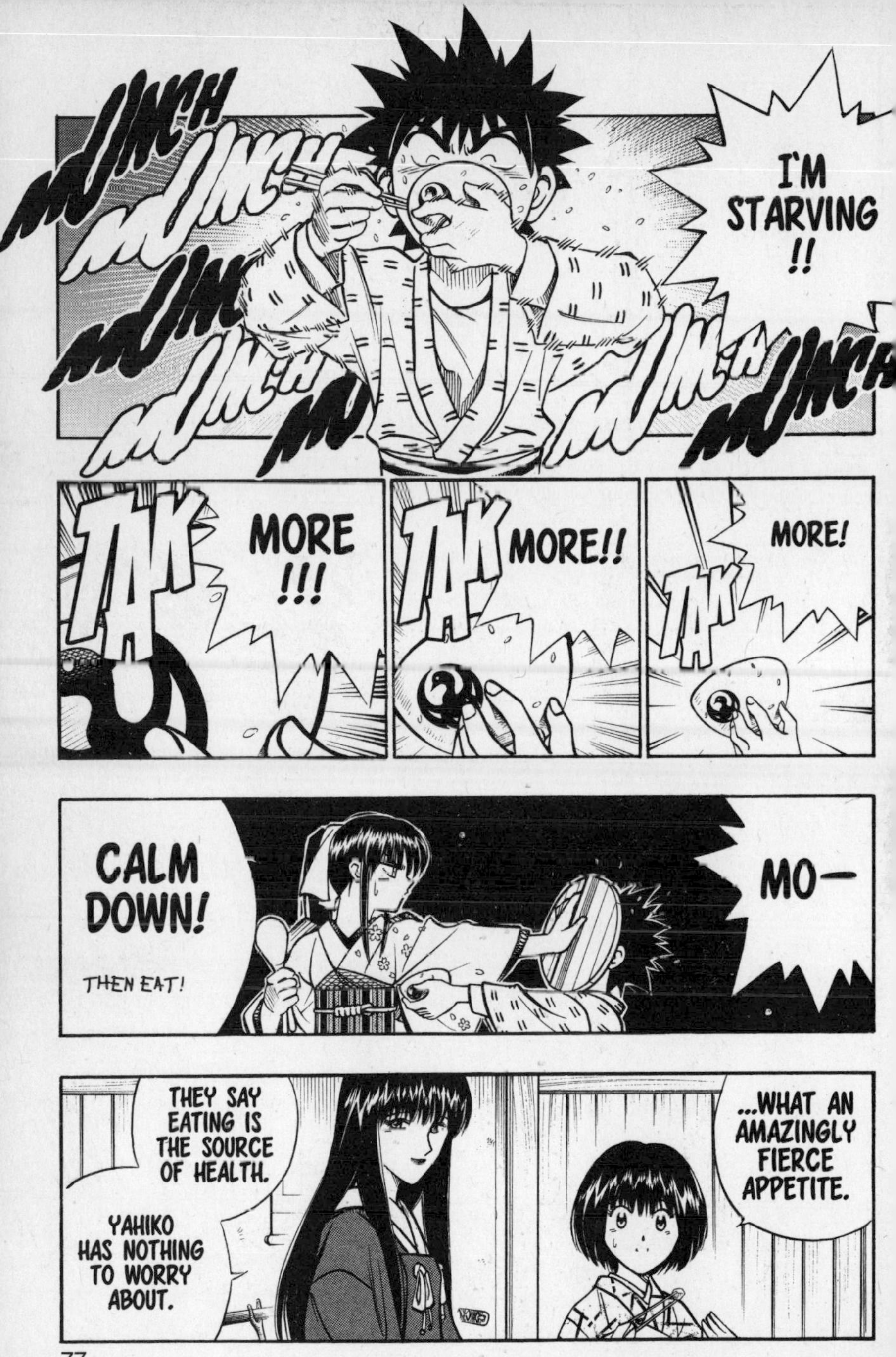
I'M STARVING!!
MUNCH
MUNCH
MUNCH
MUNCH
MUNCH
MUNCH
MUNCH
TAK
MORE!
TAK
MORE!!
TAK
MORE!!!
MO—
CALM DOWN!
THEN EAT!
...WHAT AN AMAZINGLY FIERCE APPETITE.
THEY SAY EATING IS THE SOURCE OF HEALTH.
YAHIKO HAS NOTHING TO WORRY ABOUT.

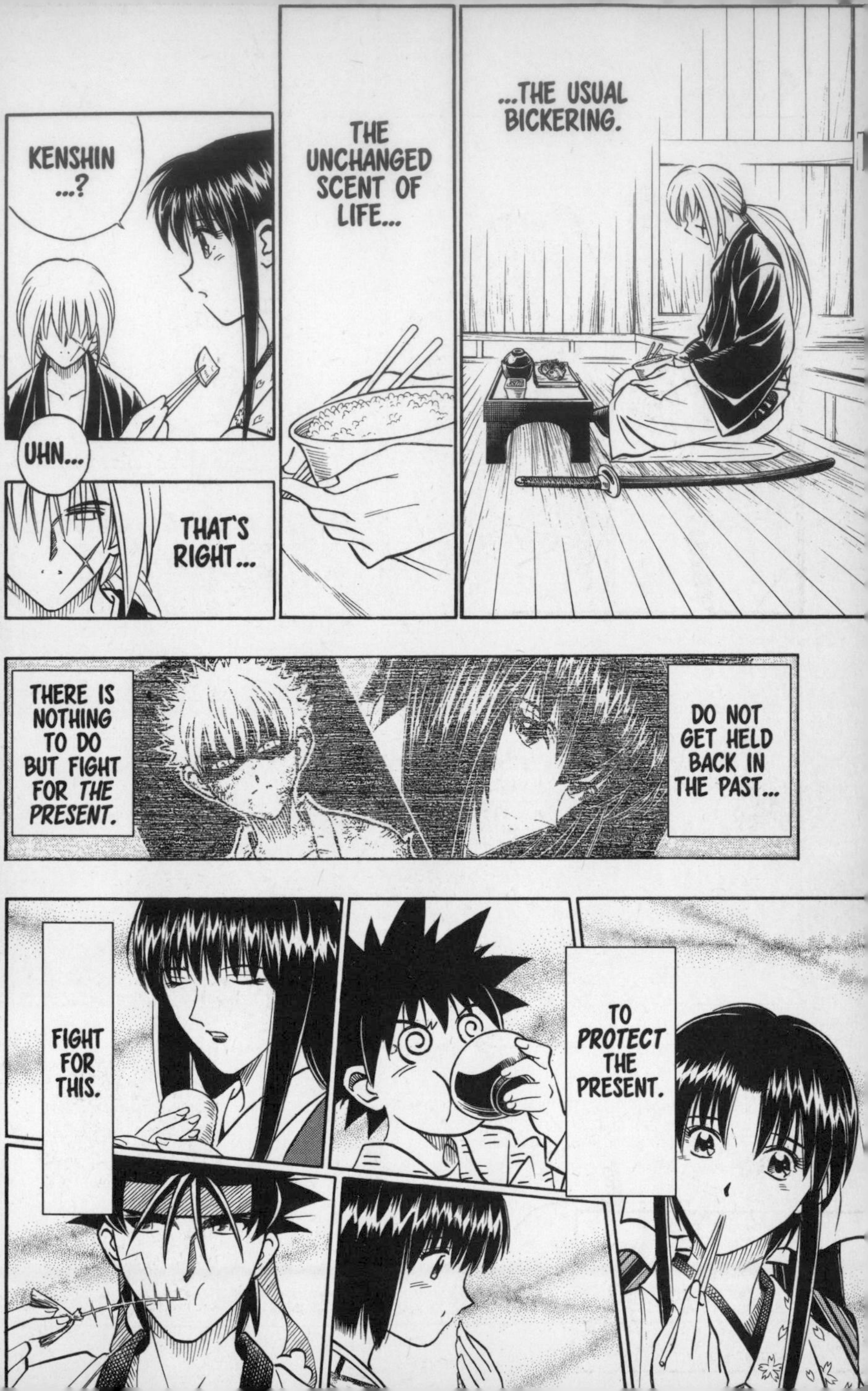
...THE USUAL BICKERING.
THE UNCHANGED SCENT OF LIFE...
KENSHIN ...?
UHN...
THAT'S RIGHT...
DO NOT GET HELD BACK IN THE PAST...
THERE IS NOTHING TO DO BUT FIGHT FOR *THE PRESENT.*
TO *PROTECT* THE PRESENT.
FIGHT FOR THIS.

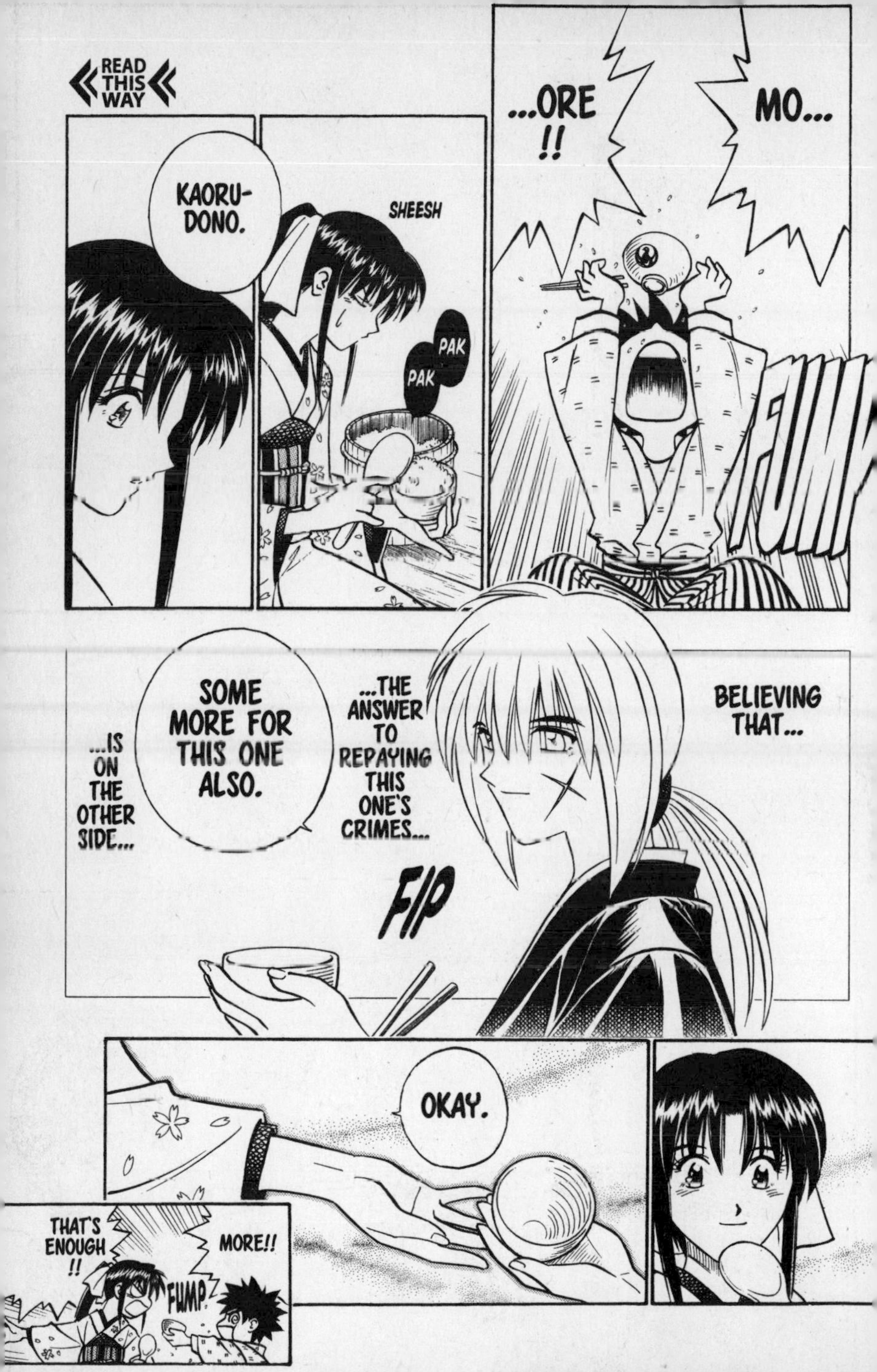
READ THIS WAY
MO...
...ORE !!
SHEESH
PAK
PAK
KAORU-DONO.
BELIEVING THAT...
...THE ANSWER TO REPAYING THIS ONE'S CRIMES...
SOME MORE FOR THIS ONE ALSO.
...IS ON THE OTHER SIDE...
FIP
OKAY.
MORE!!
FUMP
THAT'S ENOUGH !!

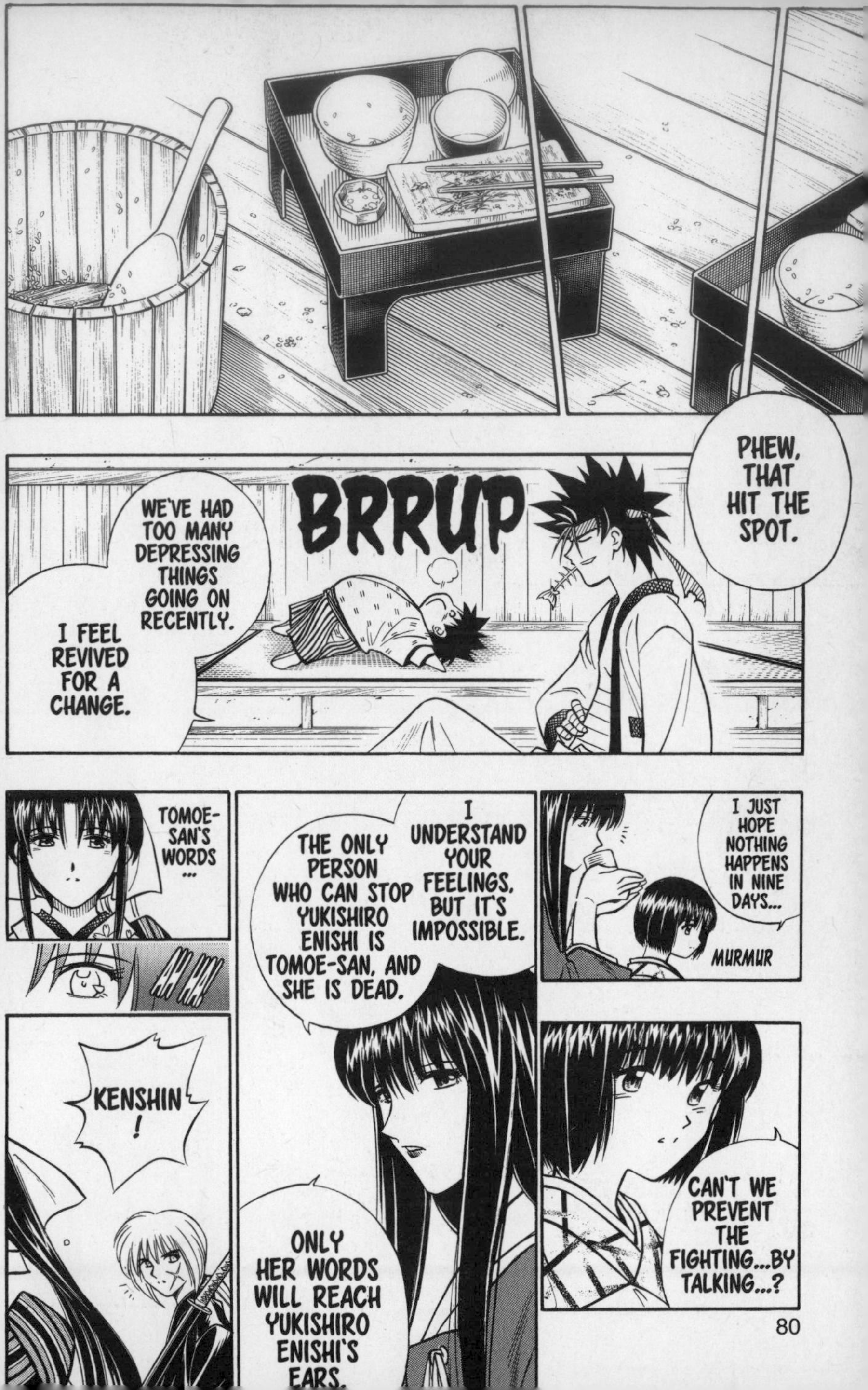
PHEW, THAT HIT THE SPOT.
BRRUP
WE'VE HAD TOO MANY DEPRESSING THINGS GOING ON RECENTLY.
I FEEL REVIVED FOR A CHANGE.
I JUST HOPE NOTHING HAPPENS IN NINE DAYS...
MURMUR
CAN'T WE PREVENT THE FIGHTING...BY TALKING...?
I UNDERSTAND YOUR FEELINGS, BUT IT'S IMPOSSIBLE.
THE ONLY PERSON WHO CAN STOP YUKISHIRO ENISHI IS TOMOE-SAN, AND SHE IS DEAD.
ONLY HER WORDS WILL REACH YUKISHIRO ENISHI'S EARS.
TOMOE-SAN'S WORDS ...
KENSHIN !

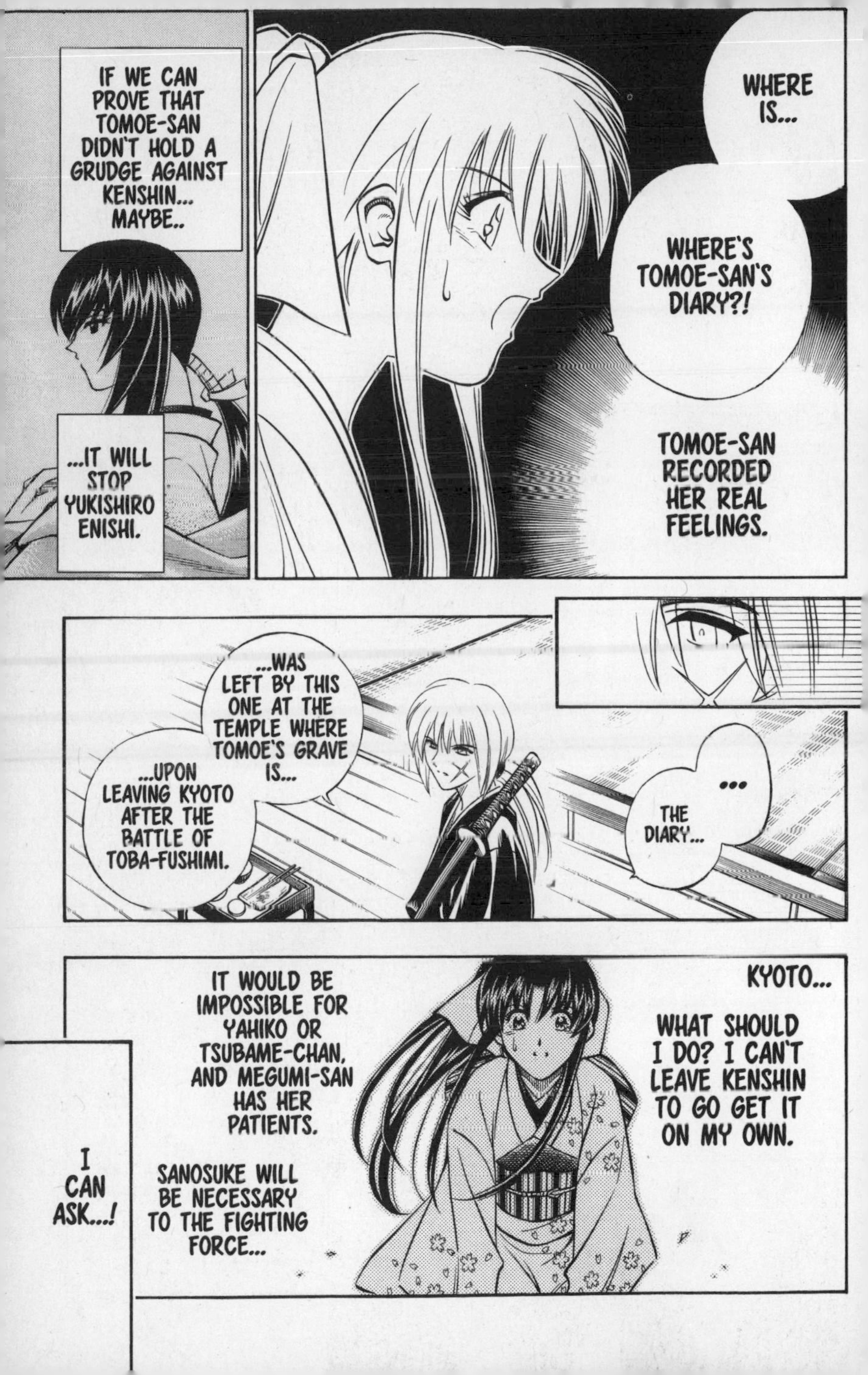
WHERE IS...
WHERE'S TOMOE-SAN'S DIARY?!
TOMOE-SAN RECORDED HER REAL FEELINGS.
IF WE CAN PROVE THAT TOMOE-SAN DIDN'T HOLD A GRUDGE AGAINST KENSHIN... MAYBE..
...IT WILL STOP YUKISHIRO ENISHI.
...
THE DIARY...
...WAS LEFT BY THIS ONE AT THE TEMPLE WHERE TOMOE'S GRAVE IS...
...UPON LEAVING KYOTO AFTER THE BATTLE OF TOBA-FUSHIMI.
KYOTO...
WHAT SHOULD I DO? I CAN'T LEAVE KENSHIN TO GO GET IT ON MY OWN.
IT WOULD BE IMPOSSIBLE FOR YAHIKO OR TSUBAME-CHAN, AND MEGUMI-SAN HAS HER PATIENTS.
SANOSUKE WILL BE NECESSARY TO THE FIGHTING FORCE...
I CAN ASK...!

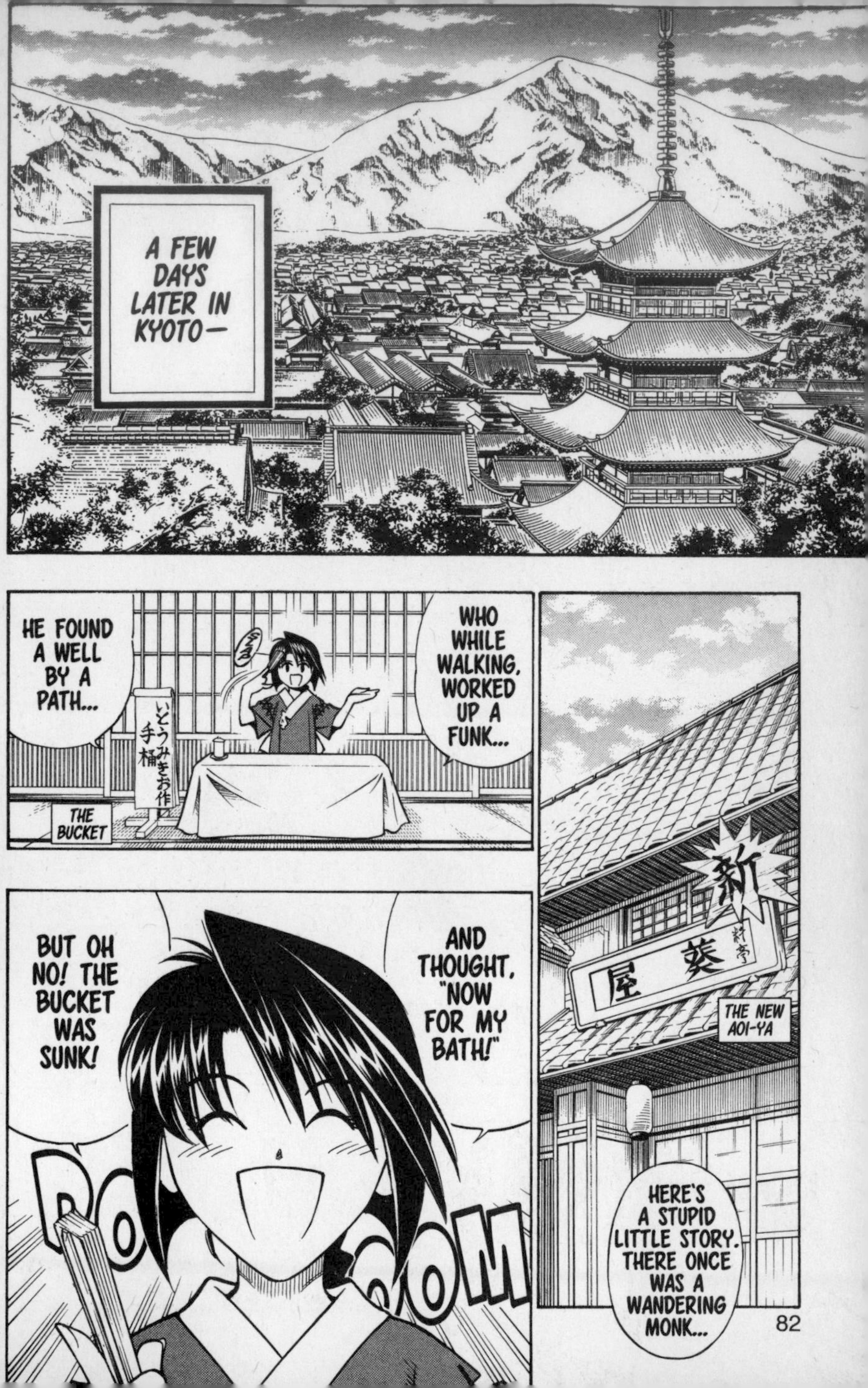
A FEW DAYS LATER IN KYOTO—
新
料亭
葵屋
THE NEW AOI-YA
HERE'S A STUPID LITTLE STORY. THERE ONCE WAS A WANDERING MONK...
WHO WHILE WALKING, WORKED UP A FUNK...
HE FOUND A WELL BY A PATH...
いとうみきお作
手桶
THE BUCKET
AND THOUGHT, "NOW FOR MY BATH!"
BUT OH NO! THE BUCKET WAS SUNK!
DOOOOM

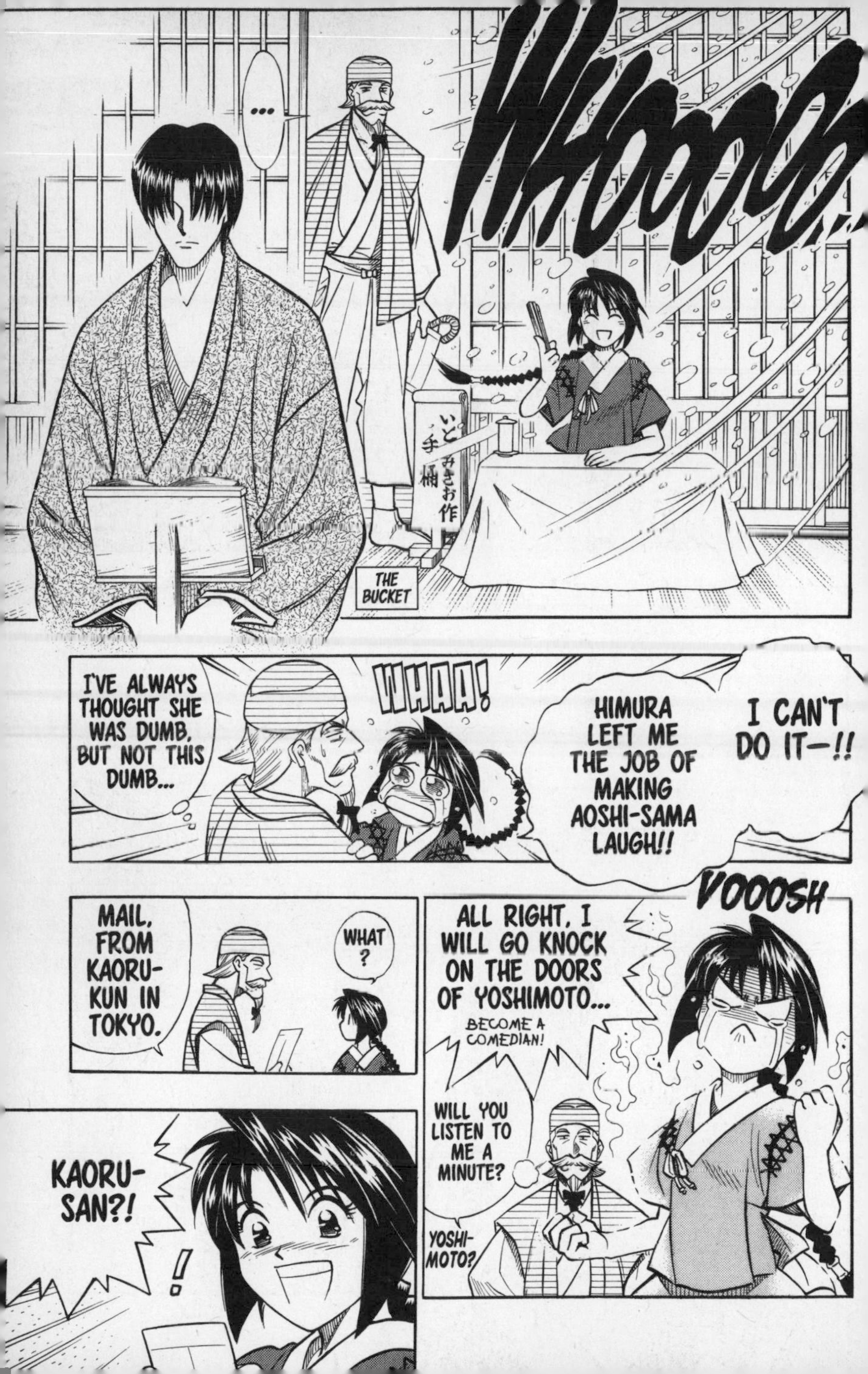
Whooa...
...
いど
手桶
みきお作
THE BUCKET
I CAN'T DO IT—!!
HIMURA LEFT ME THE JOB OF MAKING AOSHI-SAMA LAUGH!!
WHAA!
I'VE ALWAYS THOUGHT SHE WAS DUMB, BUT NOT THIS DUMB...
VOOOSH
ALL RIGHT, I WILL GO KNOCK ON THE DOORS OF YOSHIMOTO...
BECOME A COMEDIAN!
WILL YOU LISTEN TO ME A MINUTE?
YOSHI-MOTO?
MAIL, FROM KAORU-KUN IN TOKYO.
WHAT?
KAORU-SAN?!
!

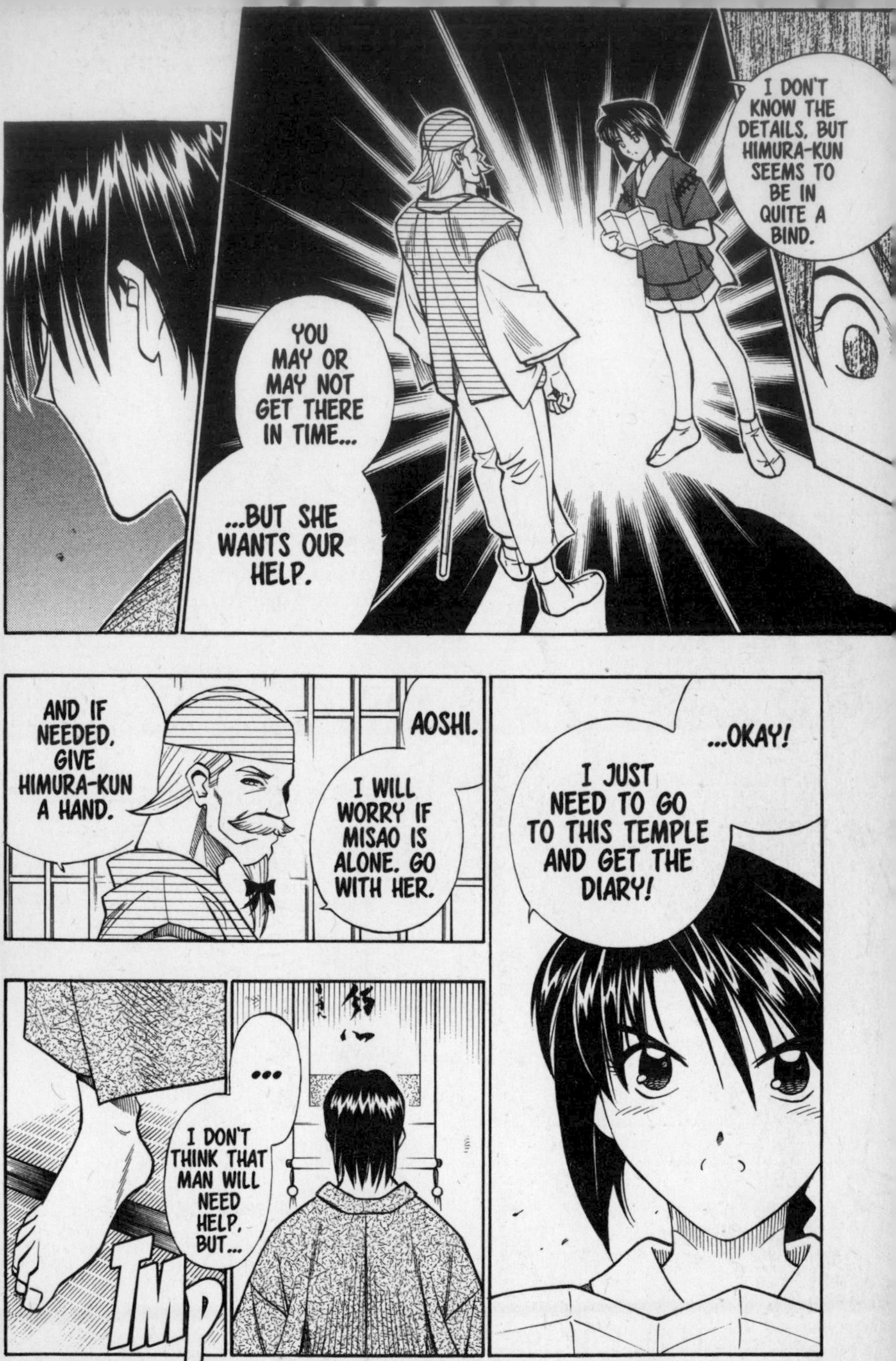
I DON'T KNOW THE DETAILS, BUT HIMURA-KUN SEEMS TO BE IN QUITE A BIND.
YOU MAY OR MAY NOT GET THERE IN TIME...
...BUT SHE WANTS OUR HELP.
...OKAY!
I JUST NEED TO GO TO THIS TEMPLE AND GET THE DIARY!
AOSHI.
I WILL WORRY IF MISAO IS ALONE. GO WITH HER.
AND IF NEEDED, GIVE HIMURA-KUN A HAND.
...
I DON'T THINK THAT MAN WILL NEED HELP, BUT...
TMP

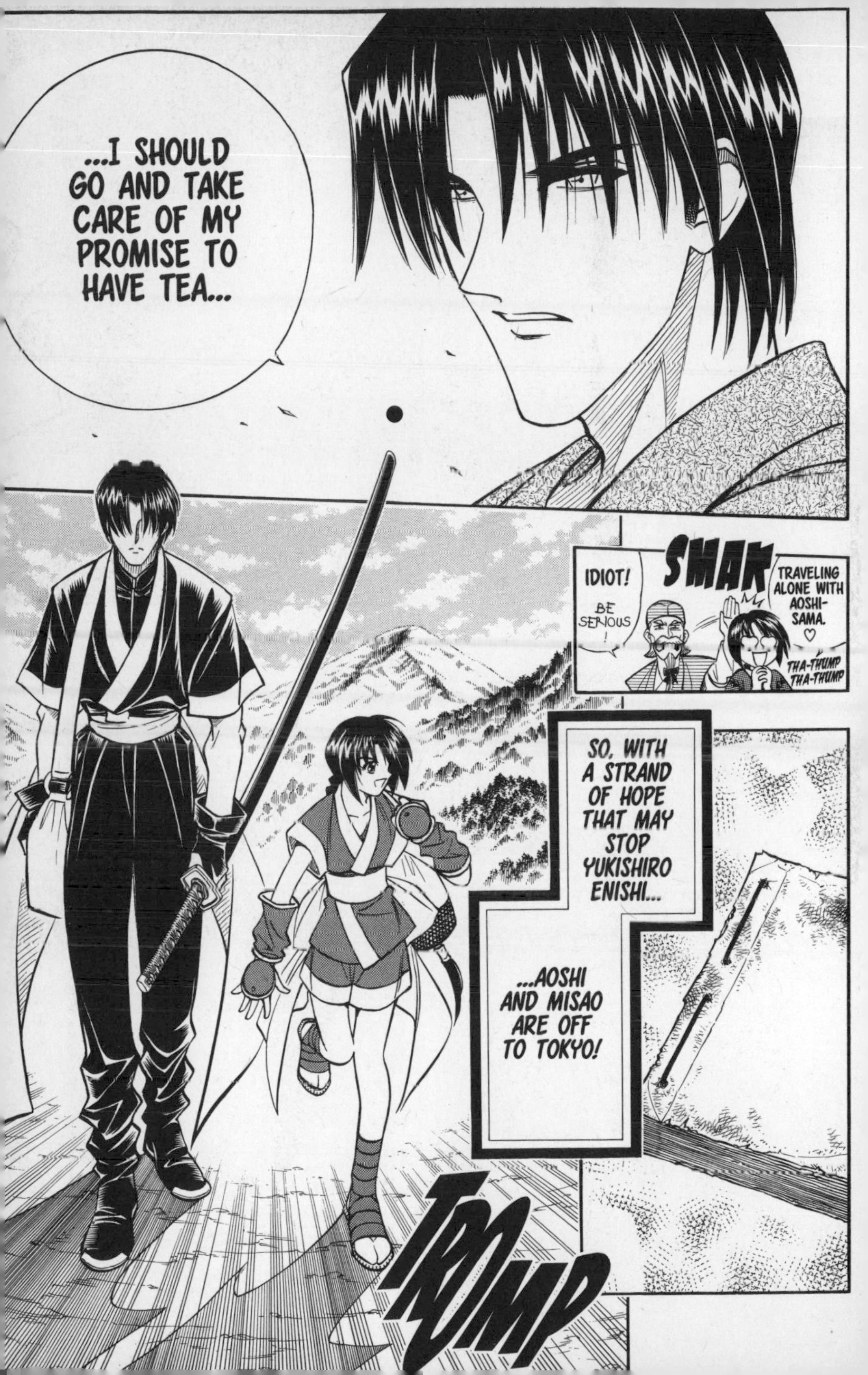
...I SHOULD GO AND TAKE CARE OF MY PROMISE TO HAVE TEA...
TRAVELING ALONE WITH AOSHI-SAMA. ♡
THA-THUMP THA-THUMP
SMAK
IDIOT!
BE SERIOUS!
SO, WITH A STRAND OF HOPE THAT MAY STOP YUKISHIRO ENISHI...
...AOSHI AND MISAO ARE OFF TO TOKYO!
TROMP

Rurouni Kenshin

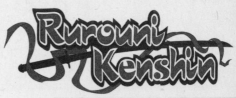

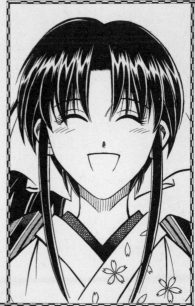

Act 182
Confession (Part 1)

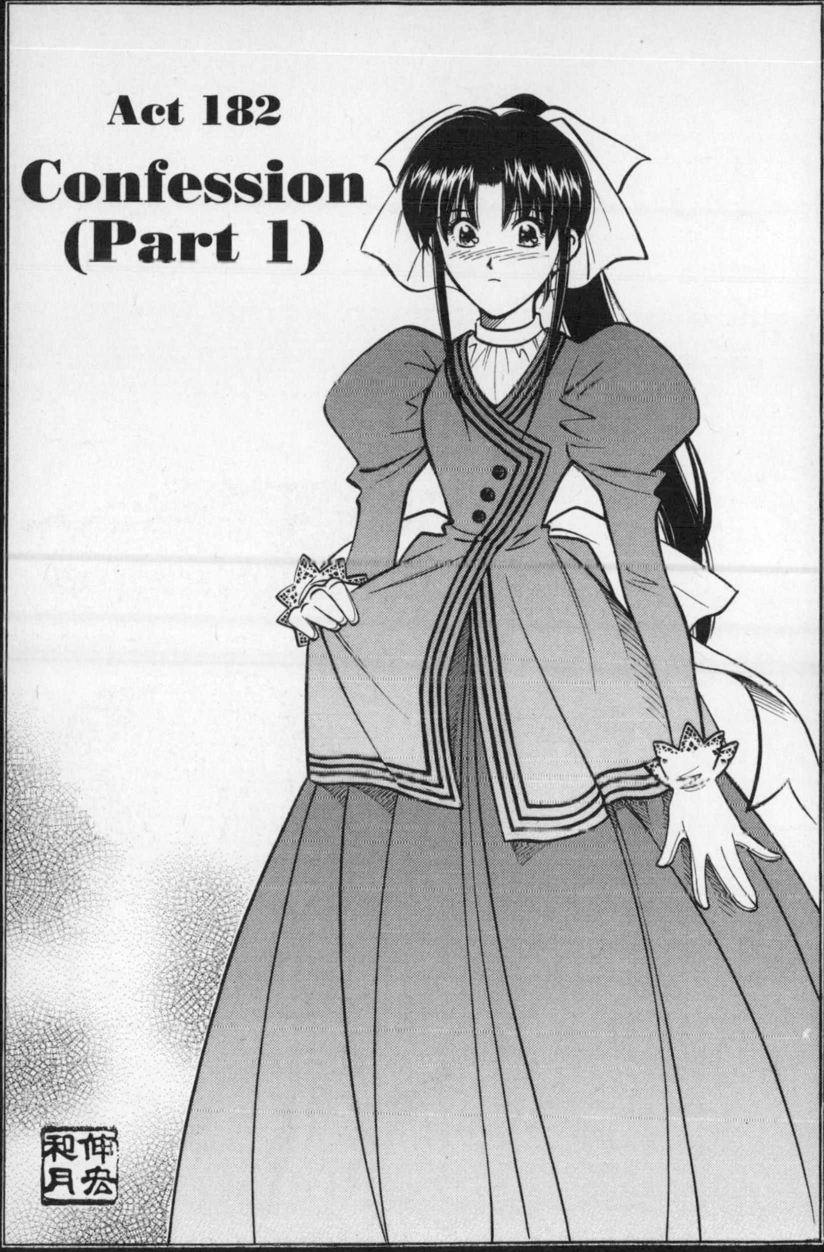
伸宏和月

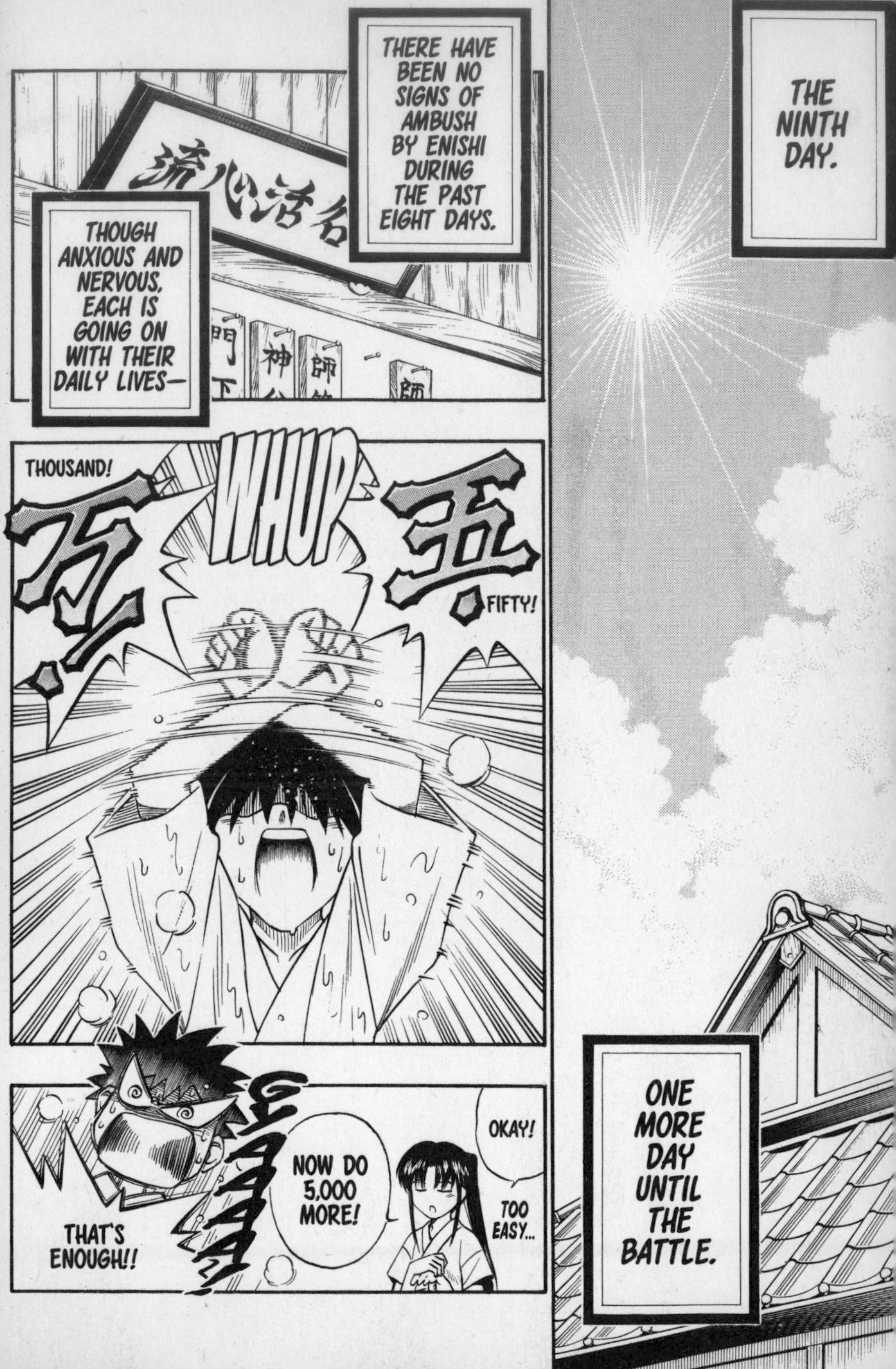
THE NINTH DAY.
ONE MORE DAY UNTIL THE BATTLE.
THERE HAVE BEEN NO SIGNS OF AMBUSH BY ENISHI DURING THE PAST EIGHT DAYS.
THOUGH ANXIOUS AND NERVOUS, EACH IS GOING ON WITH THEIR DAILY LIVES—
五
FIFTY!
WHUP
万
THOUSAND!
OKAY!
TOO EASY...
NOW DO 5,000 MORE!
THAT'S ENOUGH!!

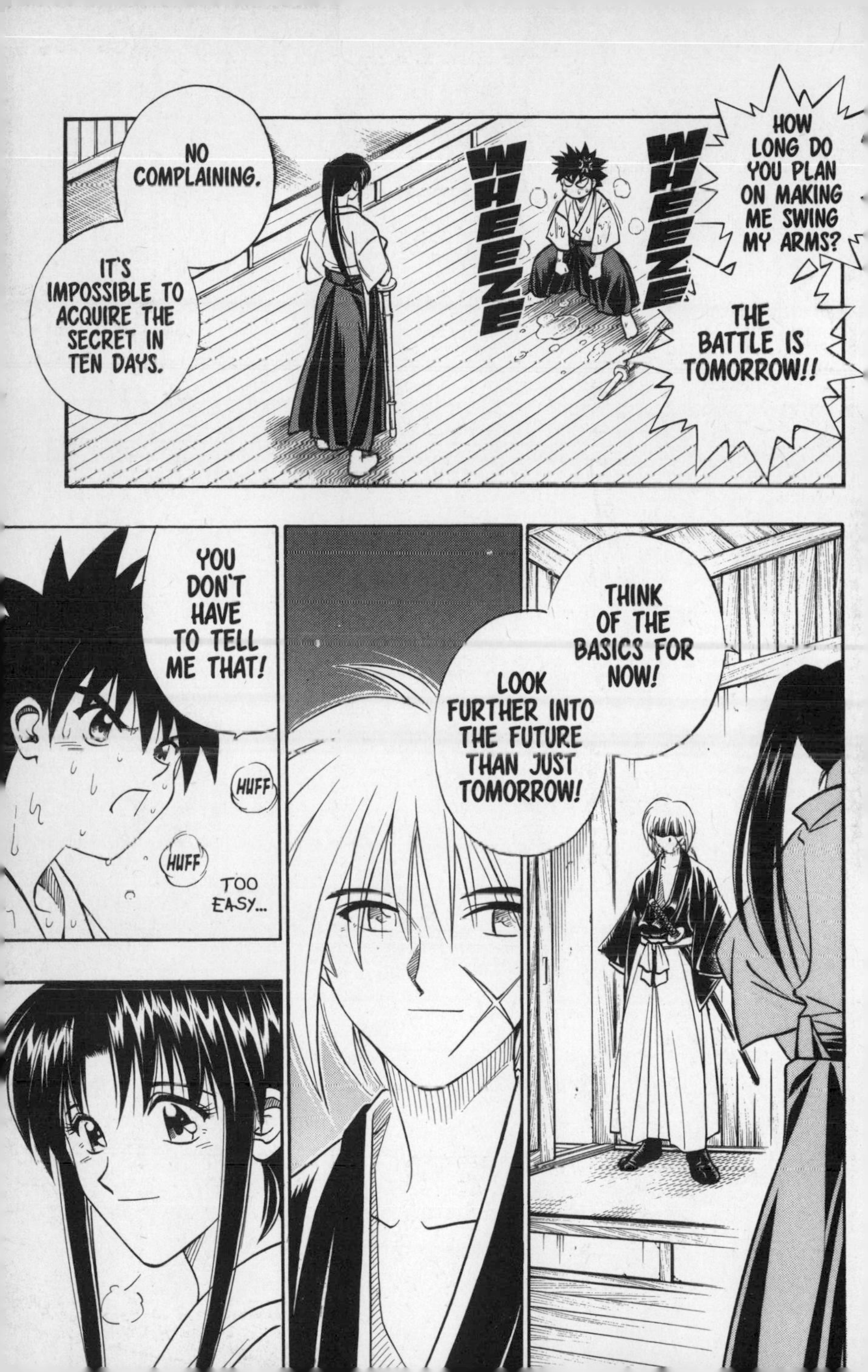
HOW LONG DO YOU PLAN ON MAKING ME SWING MY ARMS?
THE BATTLE IS TOMORROW!!
WHEEZE
WHEEZE
NO COMPLAINING.
IT'S IMPOSSIBLE TO ACQUIRE THE SECRET IN TEN DAYS.
THINK OF THE BASICS FOR NOW!
LOOK FURTHER INTO THE FUTURE THAN JUST TOMORROW!
YOU DON'T HAVE TO TELL ME THAT!
HUFF
HUFF
TOO EASY...

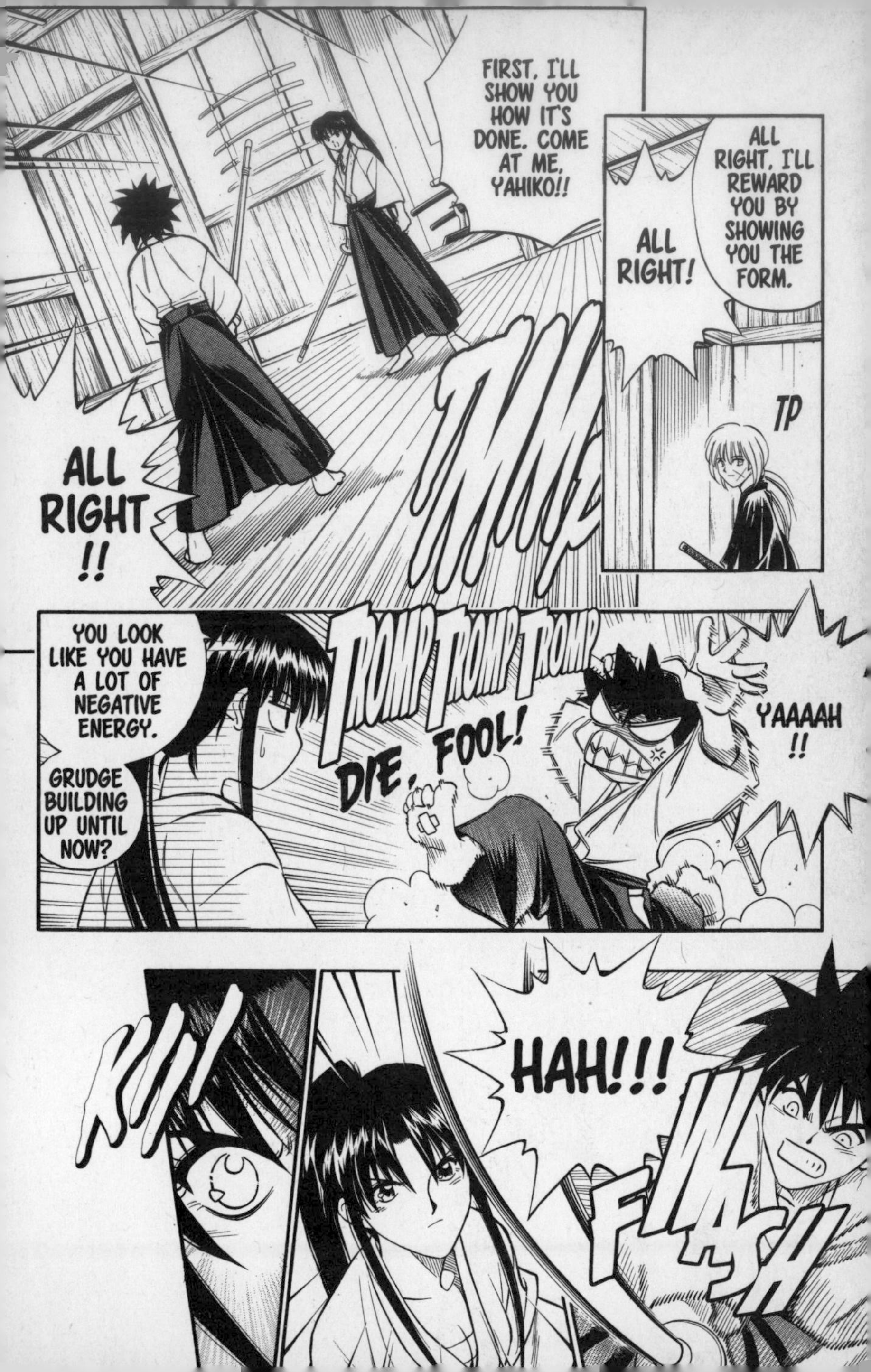
ALL RIGHT. I'LL REWARD YOU BY SHOWING YOU THE FORM.
ALL RIGHT!
TP
FIRST, I'LL SHOW YOU HOW IT'S DONE. COME AT ME, YAHIKO!!
ALL RIGHT !!
YAAAAH !!
TROMP TROMP TROMP
DIE, FOOL!
YOU LOOK LIKE YOU HAVE A LOT OF NEGATIVE ENERGY.
GRUDGE BUILDING UP UNTIL NOW?
FLASH
HAH!!!

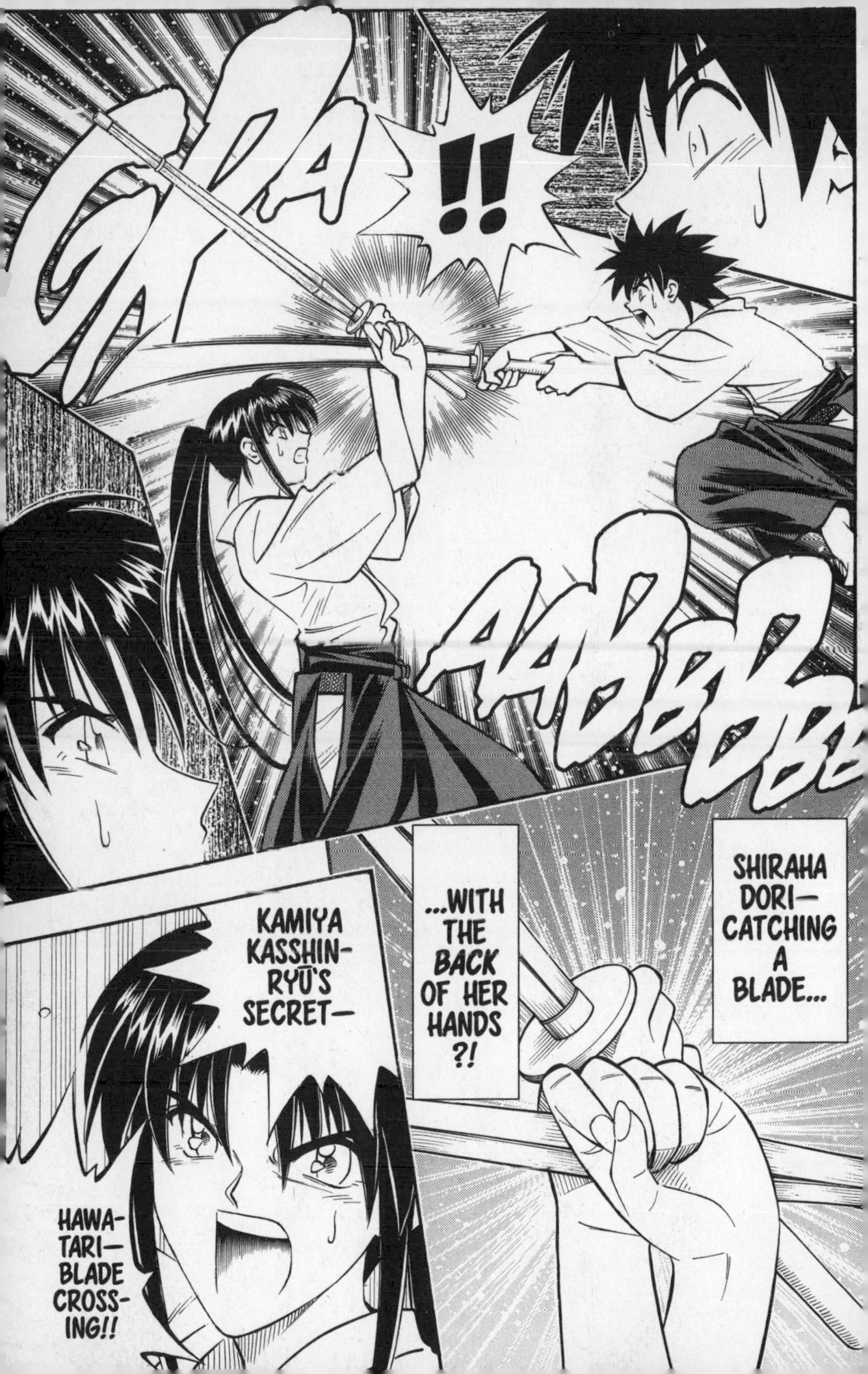
SHIRAHA DORI—CATCHING A BLADE...
...WITH THE BACK OF HER HANDS?!
KAMIYA KASSHIN-RYŪ'S SECRET—
HAWATARI—BLADE CROSSING!!

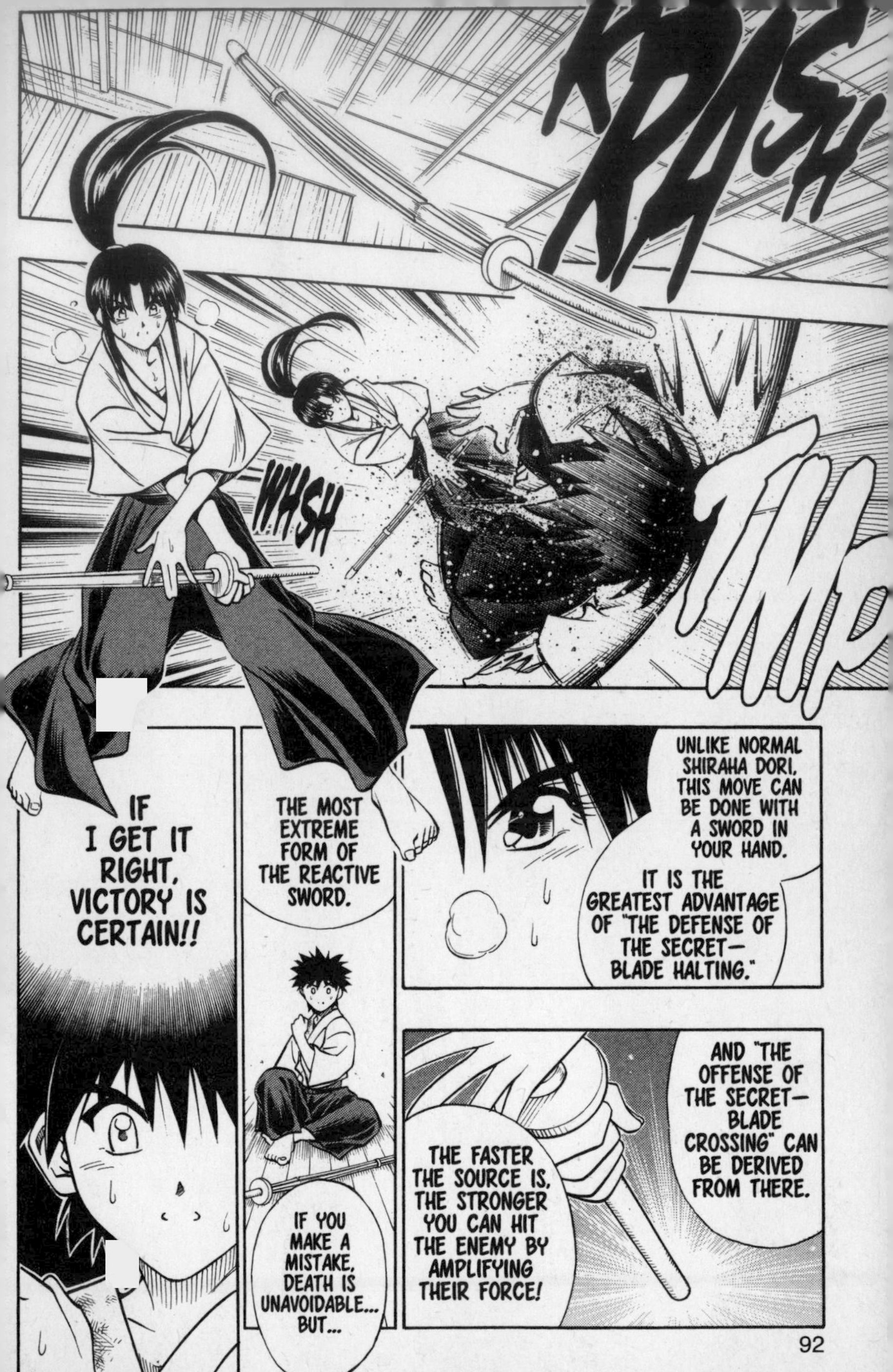
KRASH
TMP
WHSH
UNLIKE NORMAL SHIRAHA DORI, THIS MOVE CAN BE DONE WITH A SWORD IN YOUR HAND.
IT IS THE GREATEST ADVANTAGE OF "THE DEFENSE OF THE SECRET-BLADE HALTING."
AND "THE OFFENSE OF THE SECRET-BLADE CROSSING" CAN BE DERIVED FROM THERE.
THE FASTER THE SOURCE IS, THE STRONGER YOU CAN HIT THE ENEMY BY AMPLIFYING THEIR FORCE!
THE MOST EXTREME FORM OF THE REACTIVE SWORD.
IF YOU MAKE A MISTAKE, DEATH IS UNAVOIDABLE... BUT...
IF I GET IT RIGHT, VICTORY IS CERTAIN!!

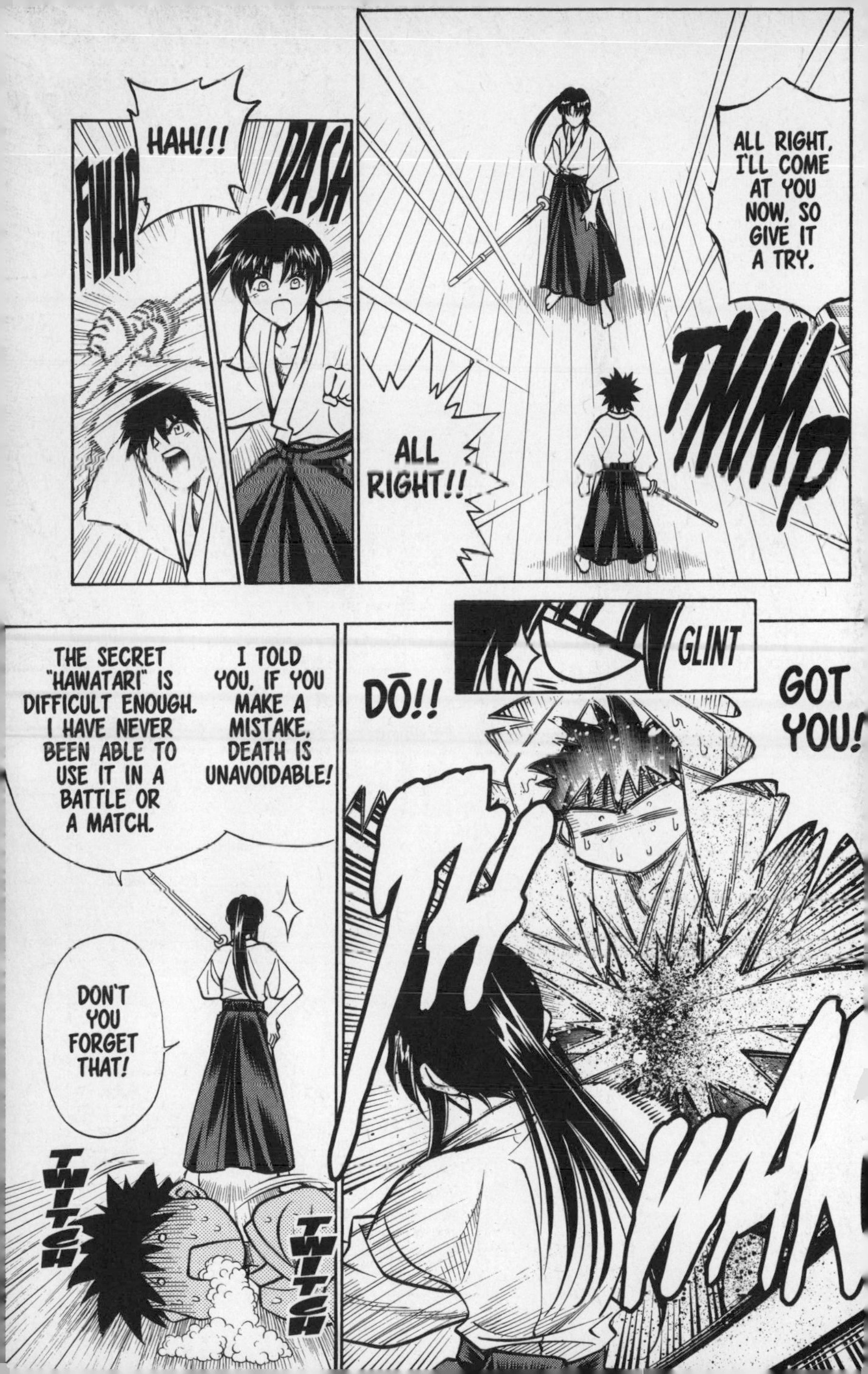
ALL RIGHT, I'LL COME AT YOU NOW, SO GIVE IT A TRY.
TMMP
ALL RIGHT!!
DASH
HAH!!!
FWAP
GLINT
GOT YOU!
DŌ!!
I TOLD YOU, IF YOU MAKE A MISTAKE, DEATH IS UNAVOIDABLE!
THE SECRET "HAWATARI" IS DIFFICULT ENOUGH. I HAVE NEVER BEEN ABLE TO USE IT IN A BATTLE OR A MATCH.
DON'T YOU FORGET THAT!
TWITCH
TWITCH

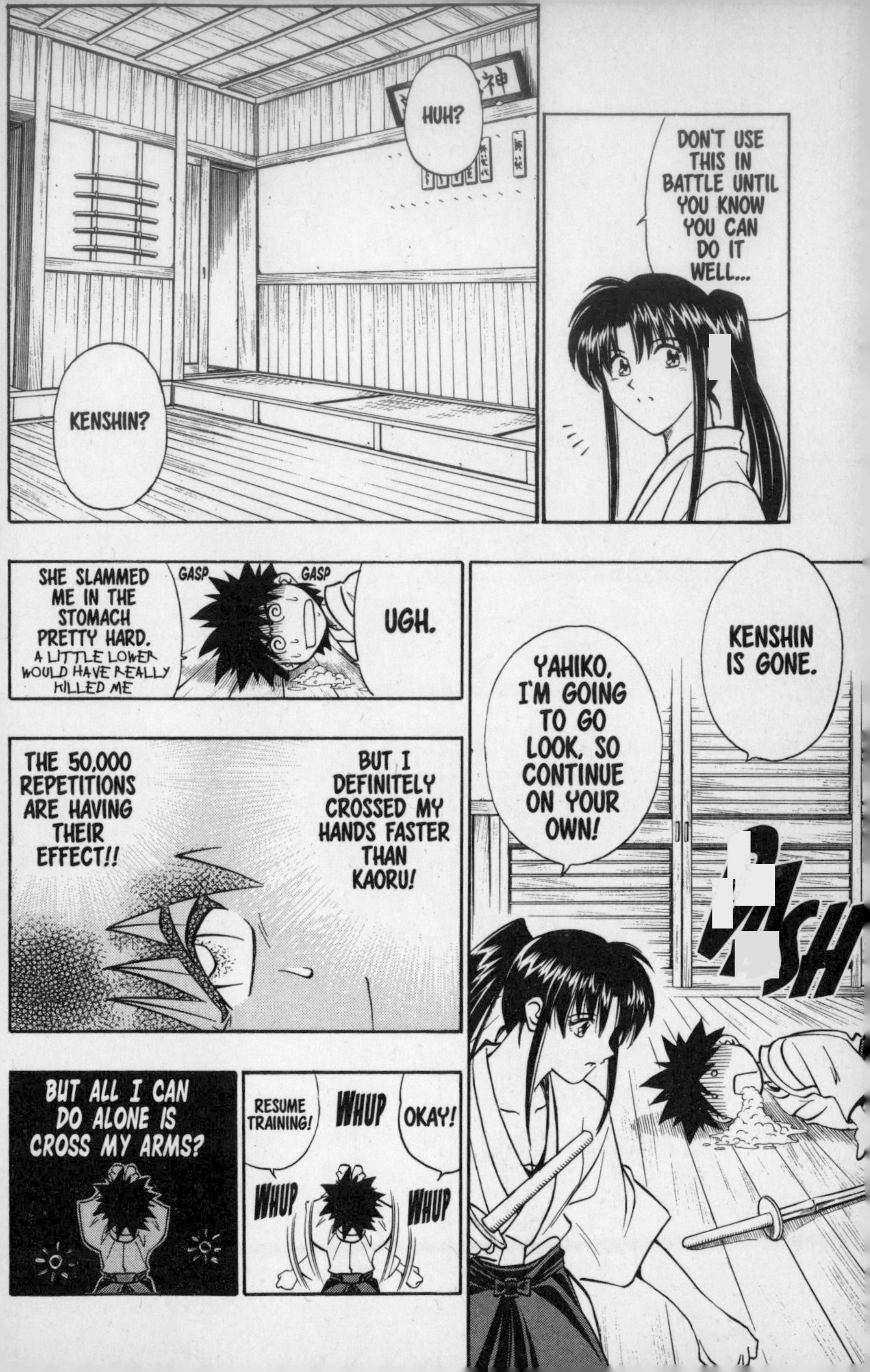
DON'T USE THIS IN BATTLE UNTIL YOU KNOW YOU CAN DO IT WELL...
HUH?
KENSHIN?
KENSHIN IS GONE.
YAHIKO, I'M GOING TO GO LOOK, SO CONTINUE ON YOUR OWN!
UGH.
GASP
GASP
SHE SLAMMED ME IN THE STOMACH PRETTY HARD.
A LITTLE LOWER WOULD HAVE REALLY KILLED ME
BUT I DEFINITELY CROSSED MY HANDS FASTER THAN KAORU!
THE 50,000 REPETITIONS ARE HAVING THEIR EFFECT!!
OKAY!
WHUP
RESUME TRAINING!
WHUP
WHUP
BUT ALL I CAN DO ALONE IS CROSS MY ARMS?

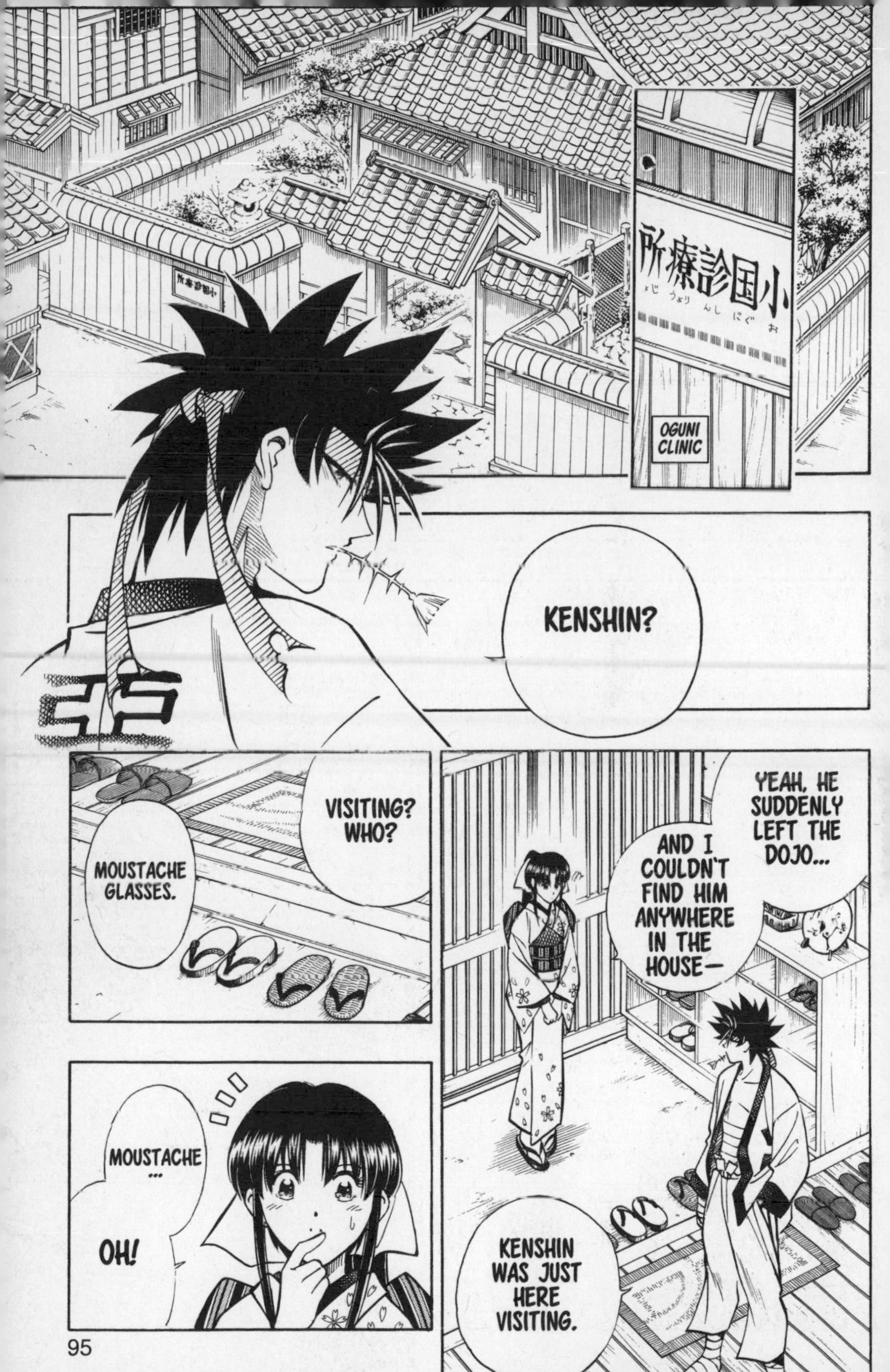
小国診療所
OGUNI CLINIC
KENSHIN?
YEAH, HE SUDDENLY LEFT THE DOJO...
AND I COULDN'T FIND HIM ANYWHERE IN THE HOUSE—
KENSHIN WAS JUST HERE VISITING.
VISITING? WHO?
MOUSTACHE GLASSES.
MOUSTACHE ...
OH!

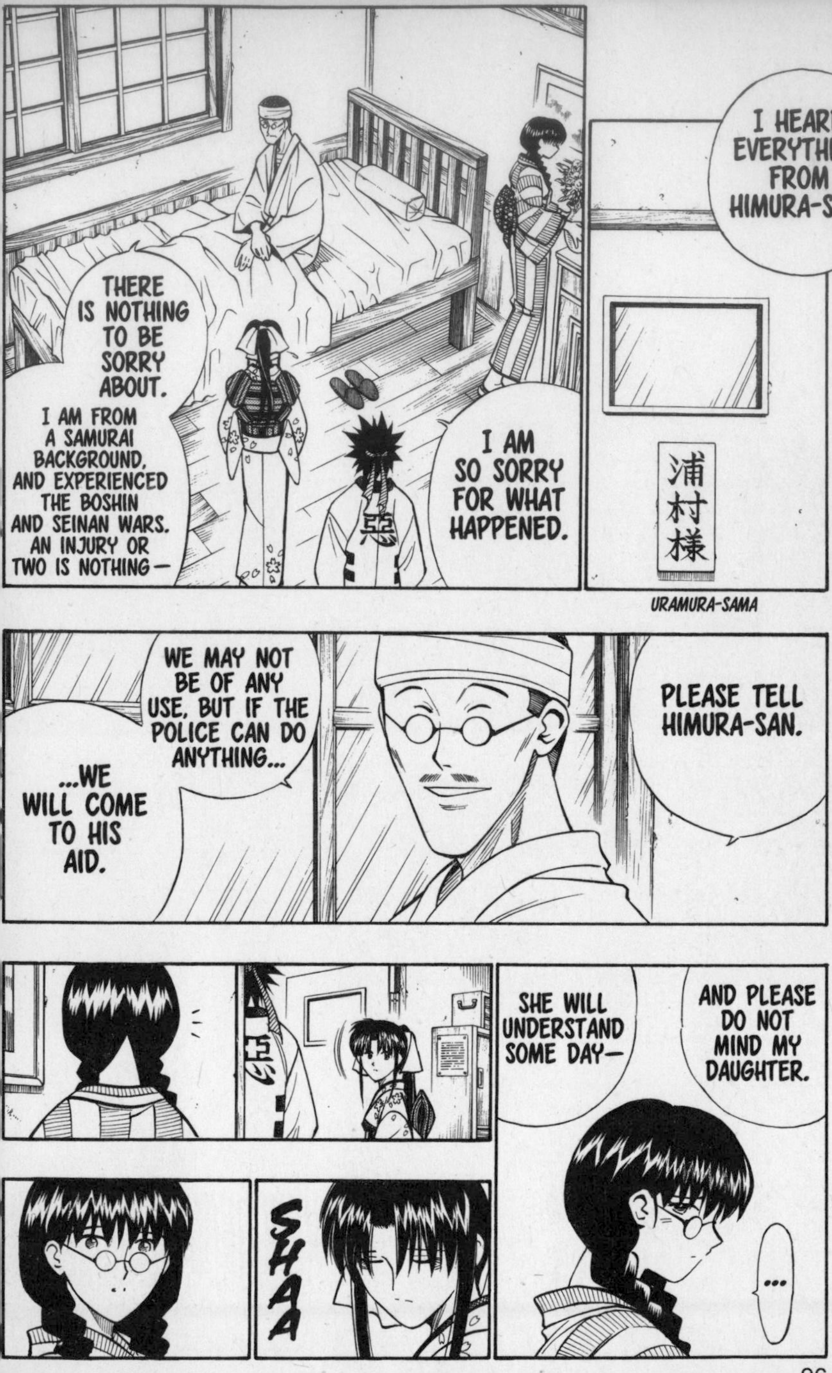
I HEARD EVERYTHING FROM HIMURA-SAN.
浦村様
URAMURA-SAMA
I AM SO SORRY FOR WHAT HAPPENED.
THERE IS NOTHING TO BE SORRY ABOUT.
I AM FROM A SAMURAI BACKGROUND, AND EXPERIENCED THE BOSHIN AND SEINAN WARS. AN INJURY OR TWO IS NOTHING—
PLEASE TELL HIMURA-SAN.
WE MAY NOT BE OF ANY USE, BUT IF THE POLICE CAN DO ANYTHING...
...WE WILL COME TO HIS AID.
AND PLEASE DO NOT MIND MY DAUGHTER.
SHE WILL UNDERSTAND SOME DAY—
...
SHAA

READ THIS WAY

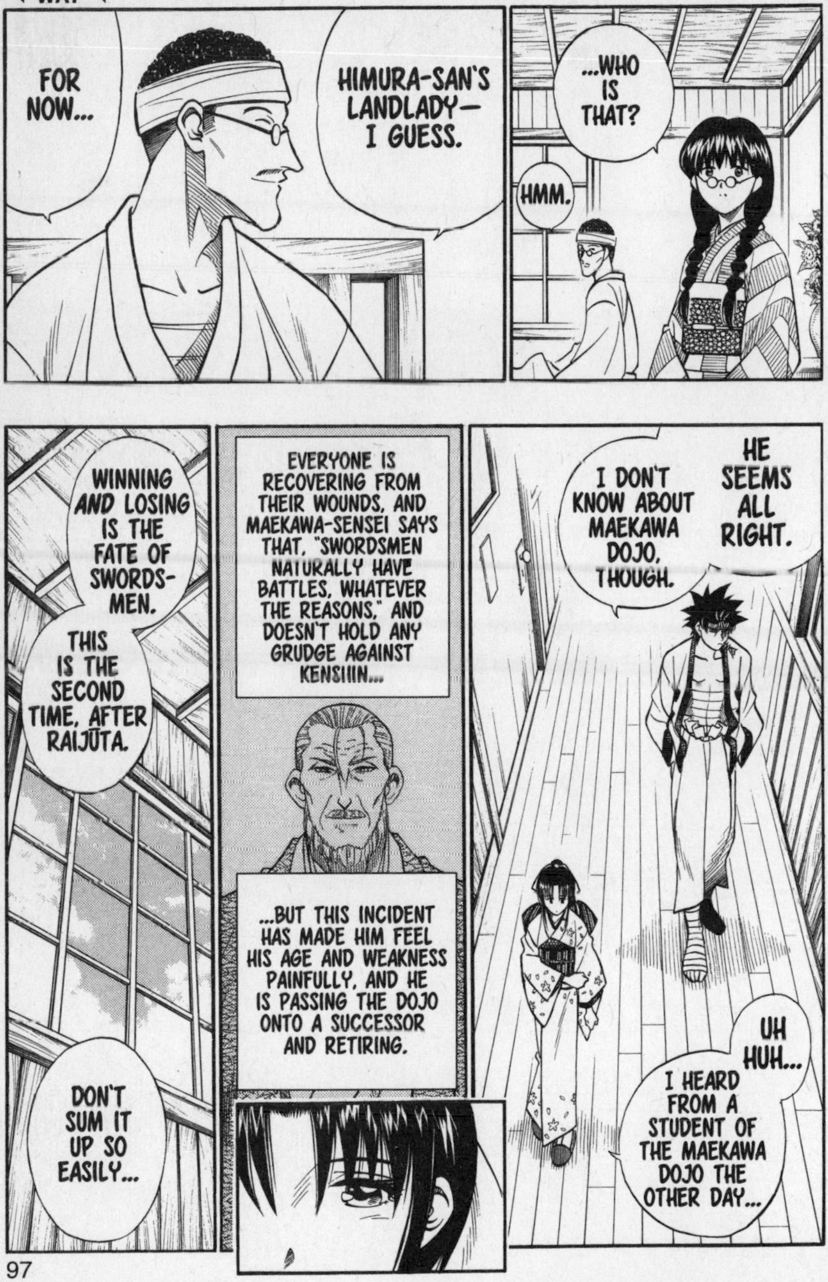
...WHO IS THAT?
HMM.
HIMURA-SAN'S LANDLADY— I GUESS.
FOR NOW...
HE SEEMS ALL RIGHT.
I DON'T KNOW ABOUT MAEKAWA DOJO, THOUGH.
UH HUH...
I HEARD FROM A STUDENT OF THE MAEKAWA DOJO THE OTHER DAY...
EVERYONE IS RECOVERING FROM THEIR WOUNDS, AND MAEKAWA-SENSEI SAYS THAT, "SWORDSMEN NATURALLY HAVE BATTLES, WHATEVER THE REASONS," AND DOESN'T HOLD ANY GRUDGE AGAINST KENSHIN...
...BUT THIS INCIDENT HAS MADE HIM FEEL HIS AGE AND WEAKNESS PAINFULLY, AND HE IS PASSING THE DOJO ONTO A SUCCESSOR AND RETIRING.
WINNING *AND* LOSING IS THE FATE OF SWORDSMEN.
THIS IS THE SECOND TIME, AFTER RAIJŪTA.
DON'T SUM IT UP SO EASILY...

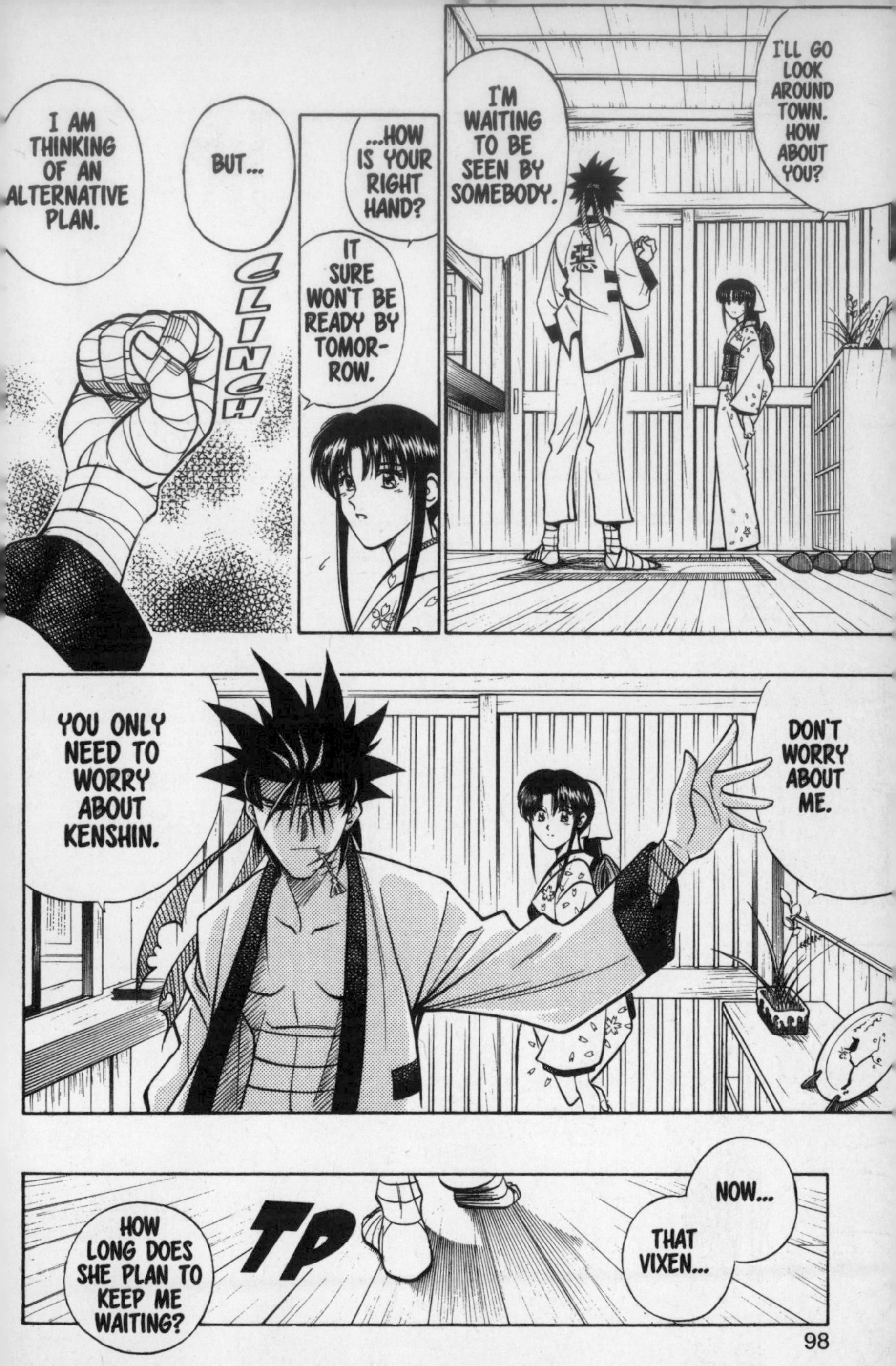
I'LL GO LOOK AROUND TOWN. HOW ABOUT YOU?
I'M WAITING TO BE SEEN BY SOMEBODY.
...HOW IS YOUR RIGHT HAND?
IT SURE WON'T BE READY BY TOMORROW.
BUT...
I AM THINKING OF AN ALTERNATIVE PLAN.
CLINCH
DON'T WORRY ABOUT ME.
YOU ONLY NEED TO WORRY ABOUT KENSHIN.
NOW...
THAT VIXEN...
TP
HOW LONG DOES SHE PLAN TO KEEP ME WAITING?

READ THIS WAY

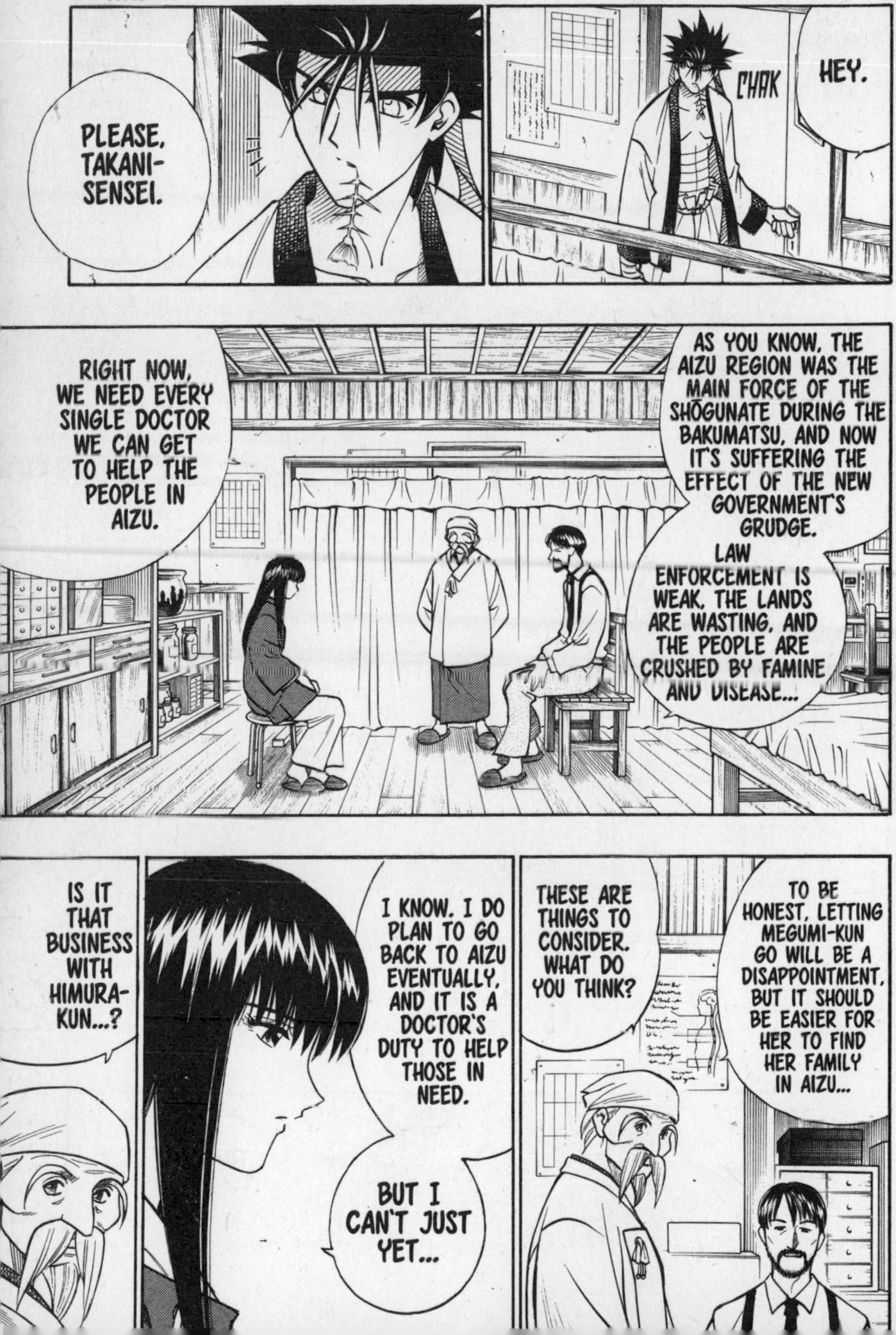
CHAK
HEY.
PLEASE, TAKANI-SENSEI.
AS YOU KNOW, THE AIZU REGION WAS THE MAIN FORCE OF THE SHŌGUNATE DURING THE BAKUMATSU, AND NOW IT'S SUFFERING THE EFFECT OF THE NEW GOVERNMENT'S GRUDGE.
LAW ENFORCEMENT IS WEAK, THE LANDS ARE WASTING, AND THE PEOPLE ARE CRUSHED BY FAMINE AND DISEASE...
RIGHT NOW, WE NEED EVERY SINGLE DOCTOR WE CAN GET TO HELP THE PEOPLE IN AIZU.
TO BE HONEST, LETTING MEGUMI-KUN GO WILL BE A DISAPPOINTMENT, BUT IT SHOULD BE EASIER FOR HER TO FIND HER FAMILY IN AIZU...
THESE ARE THINGS TO CONSIDER. WHAT DO YOU THINK?
I KNOW. I DO PLAN TO GO BACK TO AIZU EVENTUALLY, AND IT IS A DOCTOR'S DUTY TO HELP THOSE IN NEED.
BUT I CAN'T JUST YET...
IS IT THAT BUSINESS WITH HIMURA-KUN...?

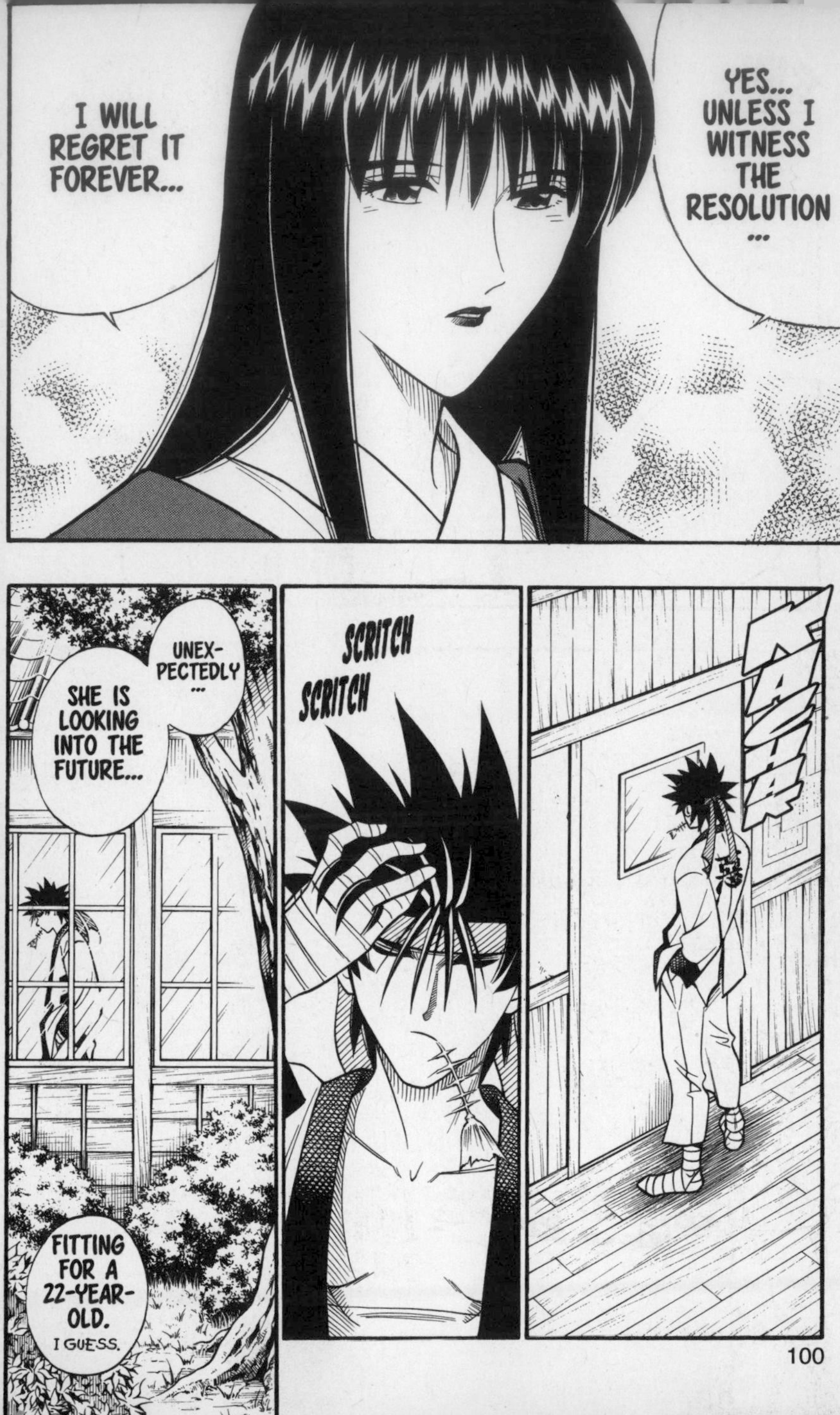

YES... UNLESS I WITNESS THE RESOLUTION ...
I WILL REGRET IT FOREVER...
SCRITCH
SCRITCH
UNEX-PECTEDLY ...
SHE IS LOOKING INTO THE FUTURE...
FITTING FOR A 22-YEAR-OLD.
I GUESS.

READ THIS WAY

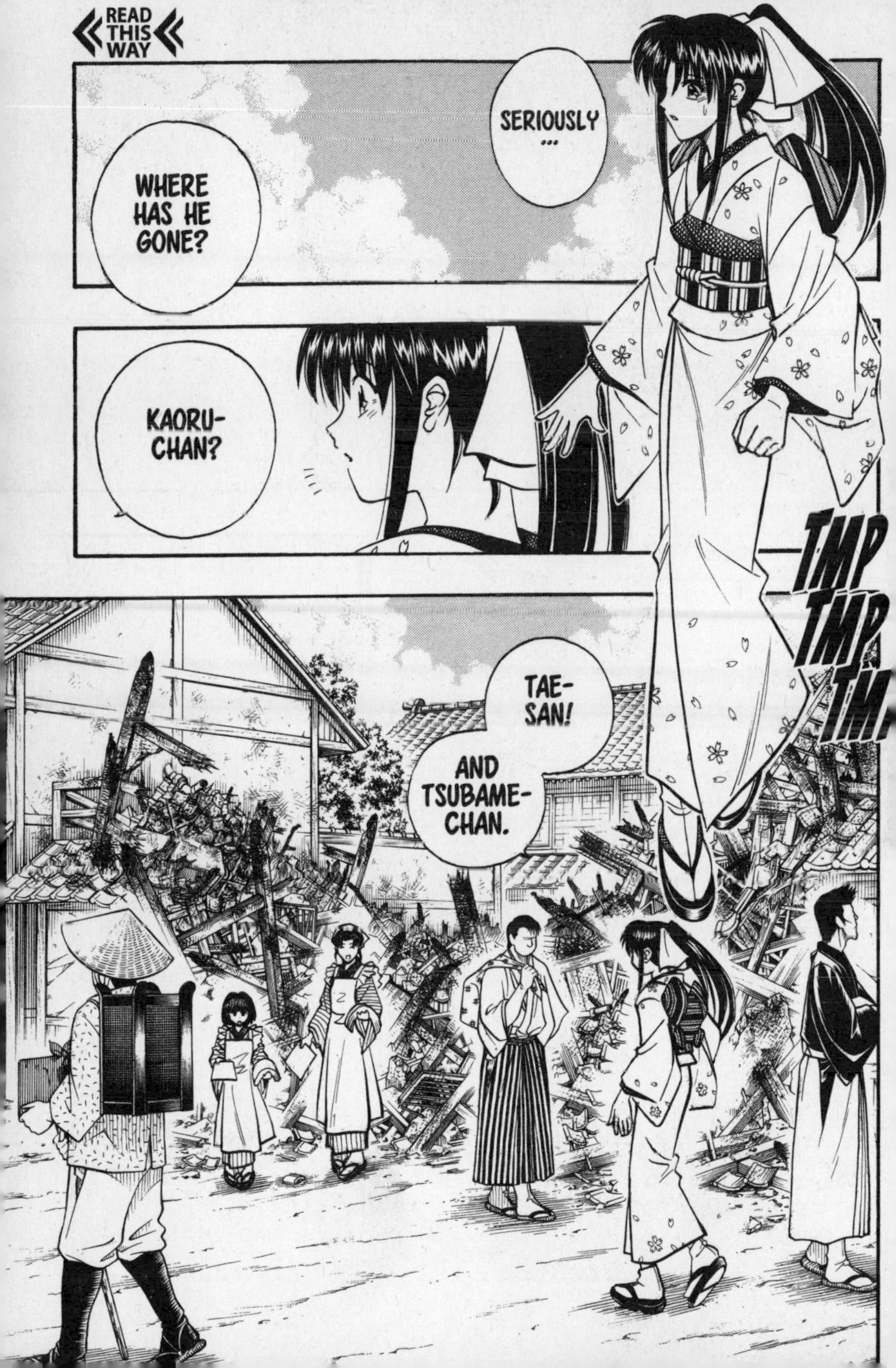
SERIOUSLY ...
WHERE HAS HE GONE?
KAORU-CHAN?
TMP TMP TMP
TAE-SAN!
AND TSUBAME-CHAN.

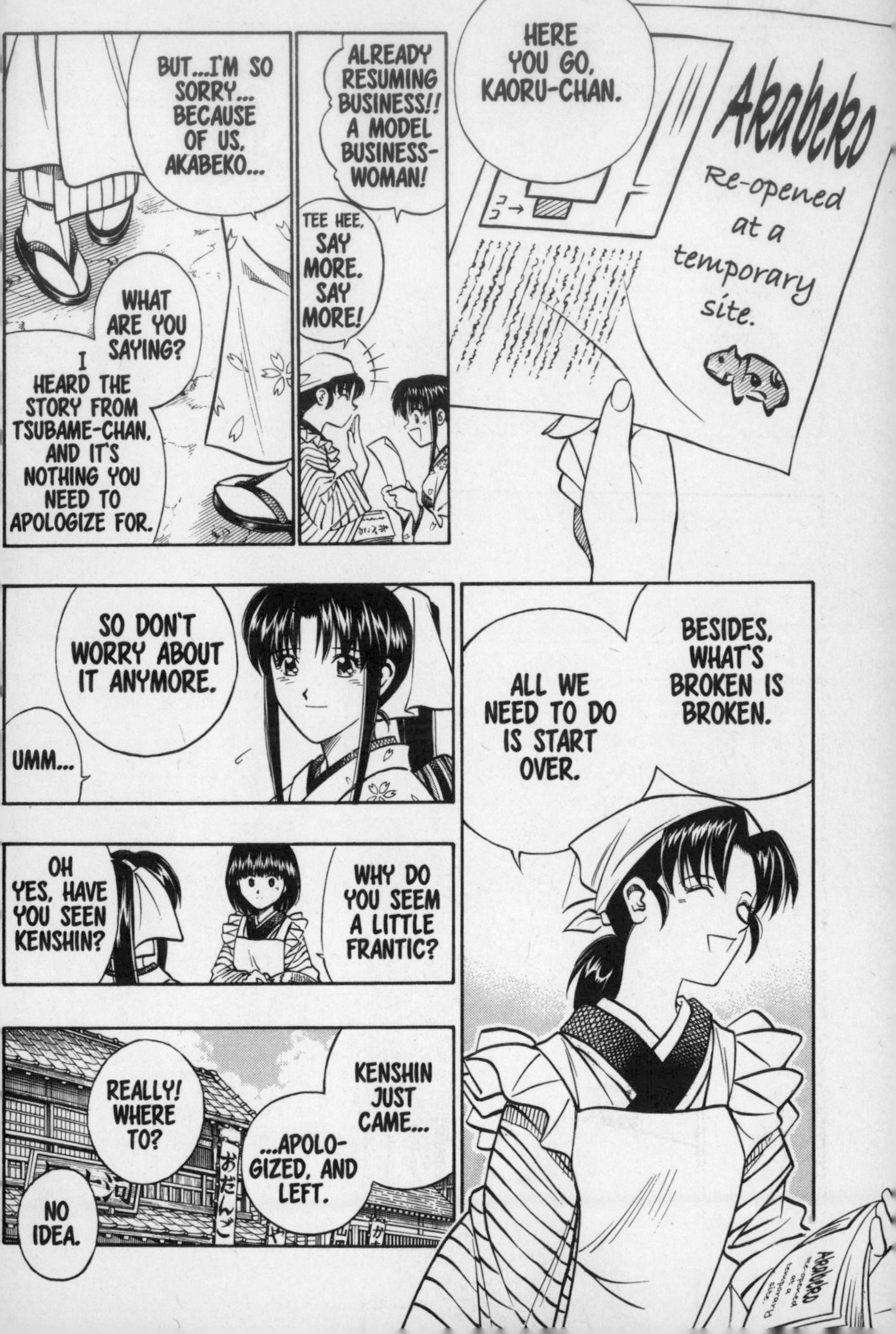
HERE YOU GO, KAORU-CHAN.
Akabeko
Re-opened at a temporary site.
ALREADY RESUMING BUSINESS!! A MODEL BUSINESS-WOMAN!
TEE HEE, SAY MORE. SAY MORE!
BUT...I'M SO SORRY... BECAUSE OF US, AKABEKO...
WHAT ARE YOU SAYING?
I HEARD THE STORY FROM TSUBAME-CHAN, AND IT'S NOTHING YOU NEED TO APOLOGIZE FOR.
BESIDES, WHAT'S BROKEN IS BROKEN.
ALL WE NEED TO DO IS START OVER.
Akabeko Re-opened at a temporary site.
SO DON'T WORRY ABOUT IT ANYMORE.
UMM...
WHY DO YOU SEEM A LITTLE FRANTIC?
OH YES, HAVE YOU SEEN KENSHIN?
KENSHIN JUST CAME...
...APOLO-GIZED, AND LEFT.
REALLY! WHERE TO?
NO IDEA.
おだんご

READ THIS WAY

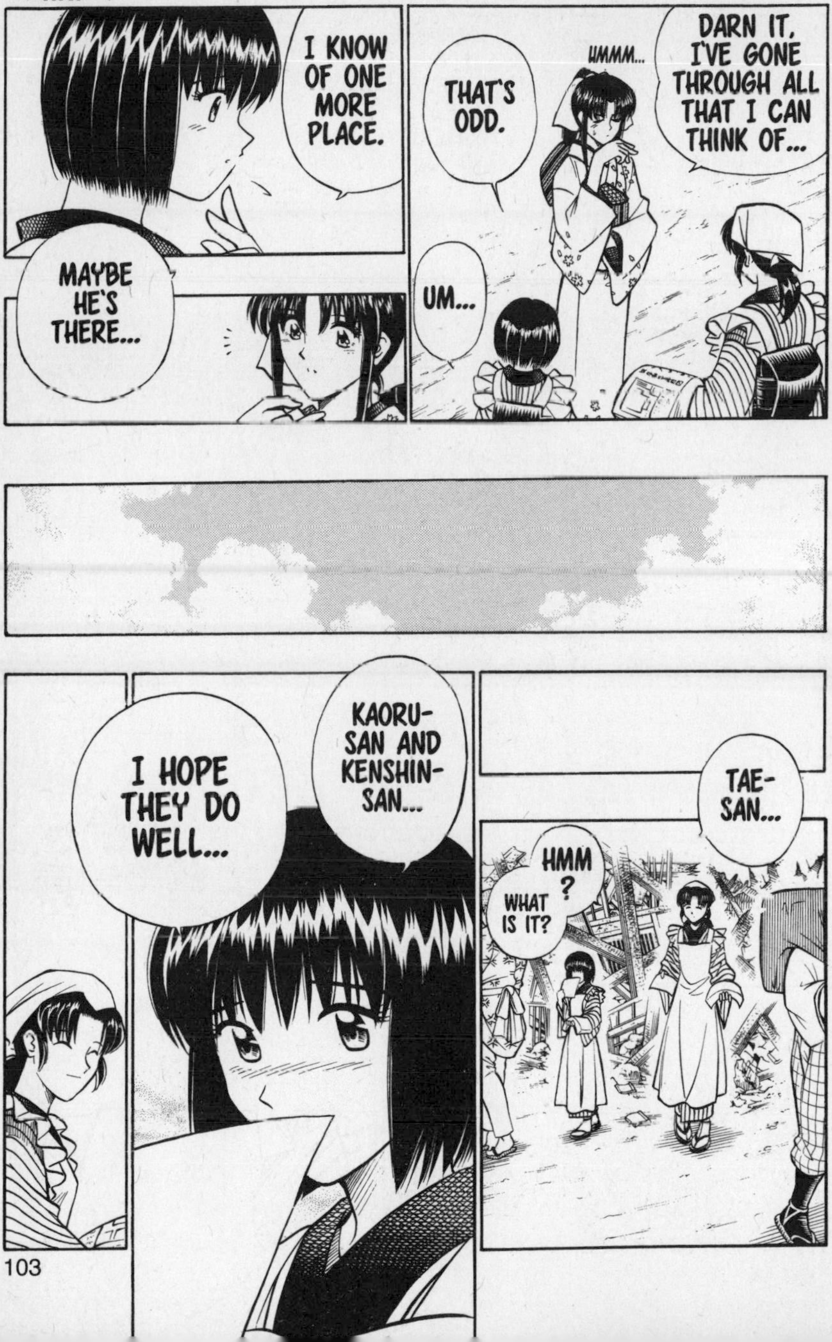
DARN IT, I'VE GONE THROUGH ALL THAT I CAN THINK OF...
UMMM...
THAT'S ODD.
UM...
I KNOW OF ONE MORE PLACE.
MAYBE HE'S THERE...
TAE-SAN...
HMM?
WHAT IS IT?
KAORU-SAN AND KENSHIN-SAN...
I HOPE THEY DO WELL...

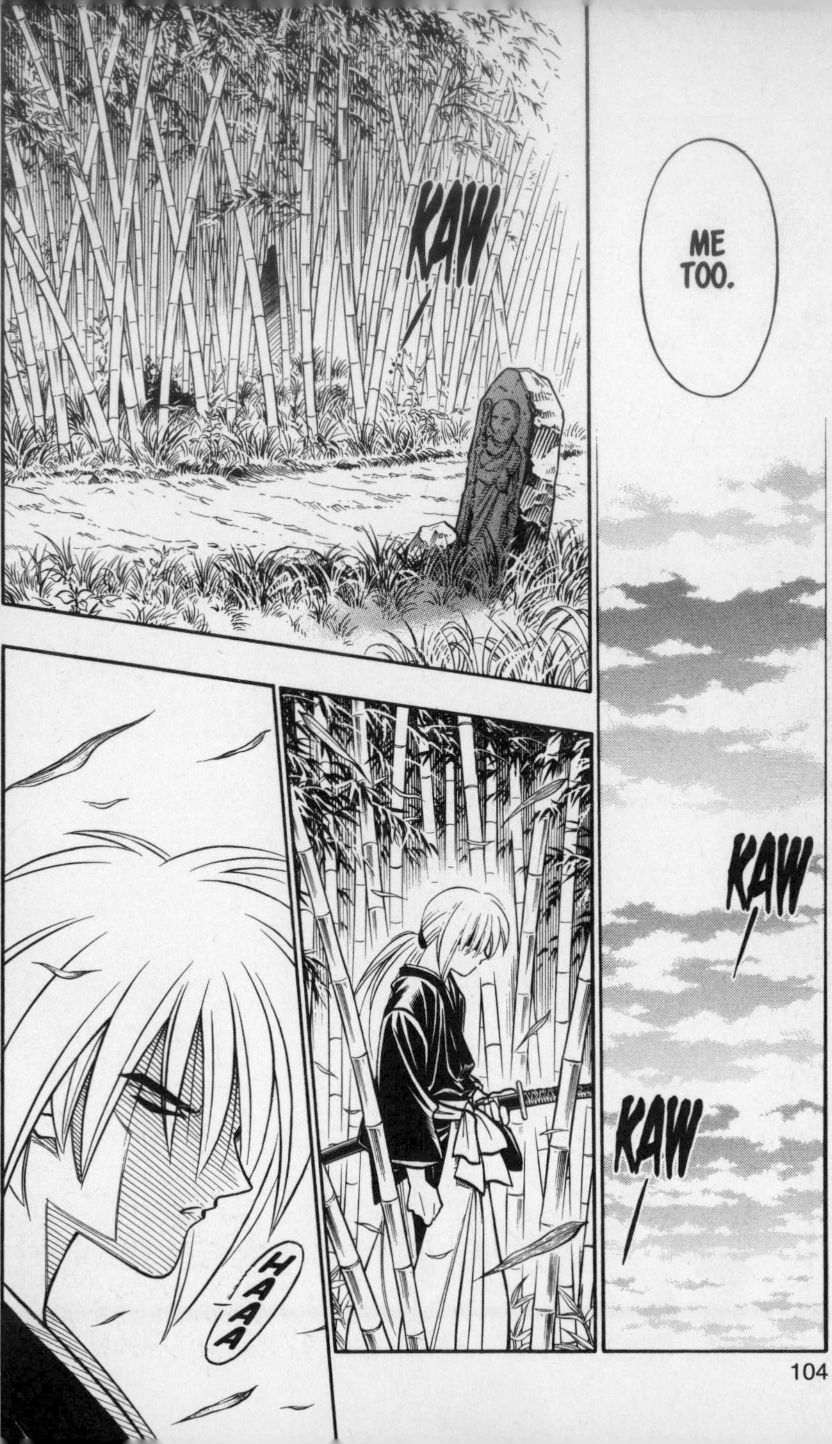
ME TOO.
KAW
KAW
KAW
HAAAA

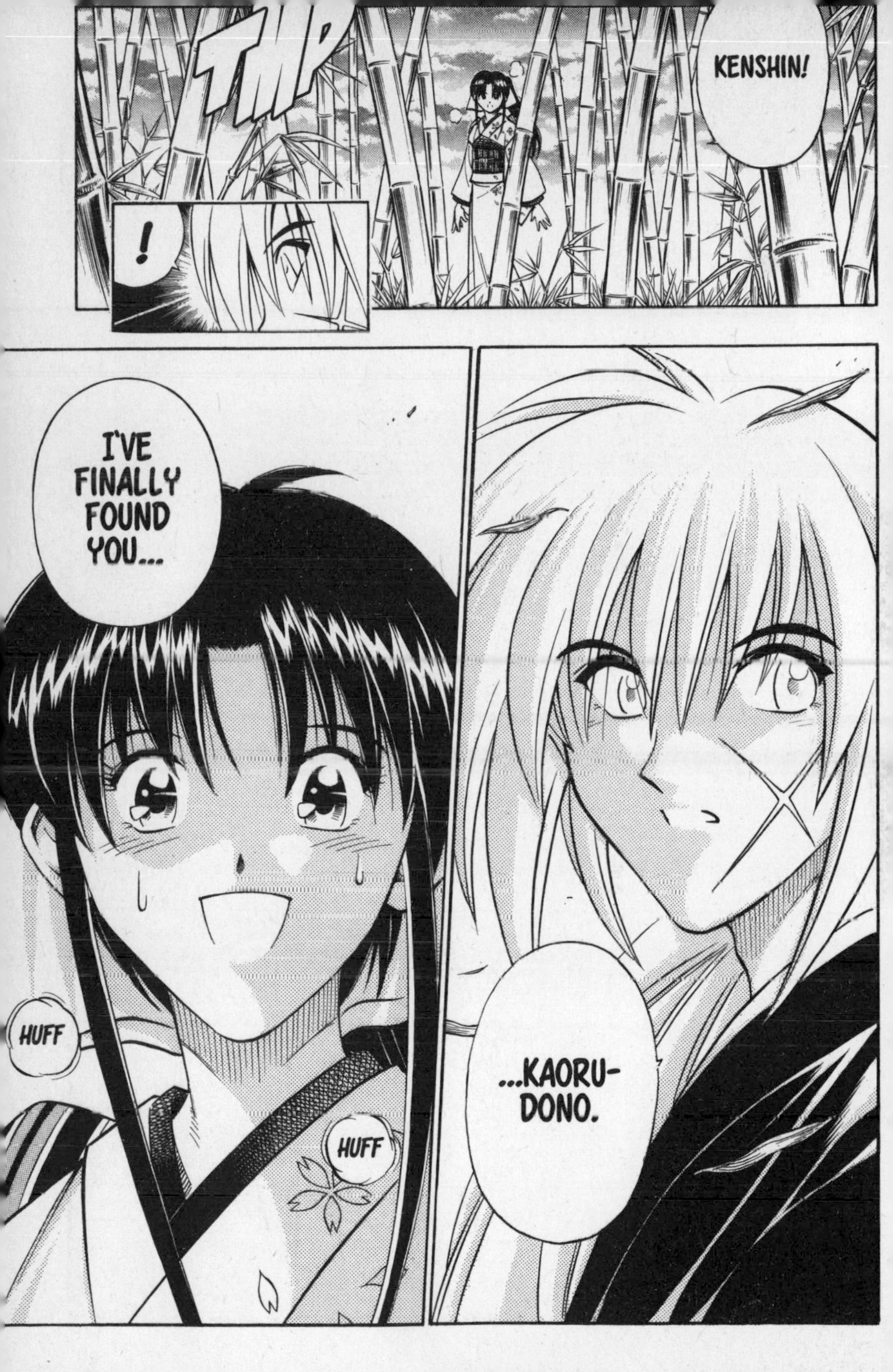
KENSHIN!
THP
!
...KAORU-DONO.
I'VE FINALLY FOUND YOU...
HUFF
HUFF

Rurouni Kenshin

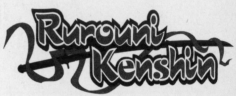

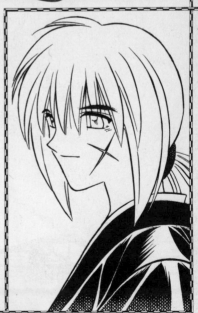

Act 183
Confession (Part 2)

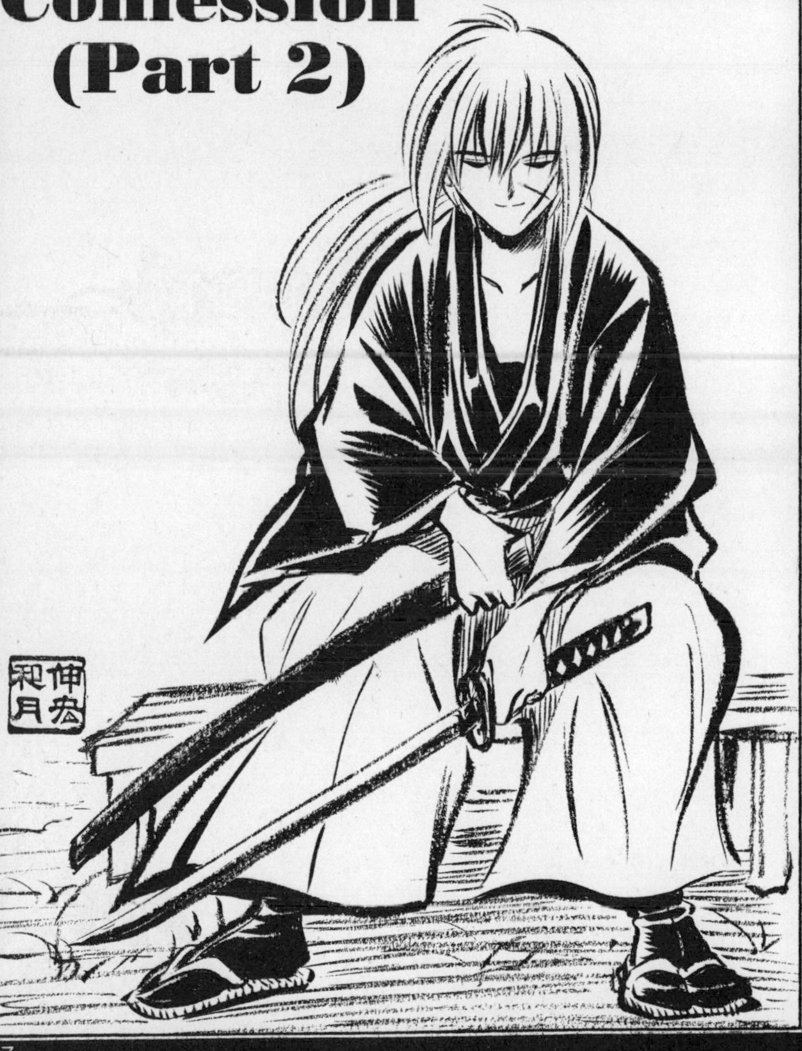
伸宏和月

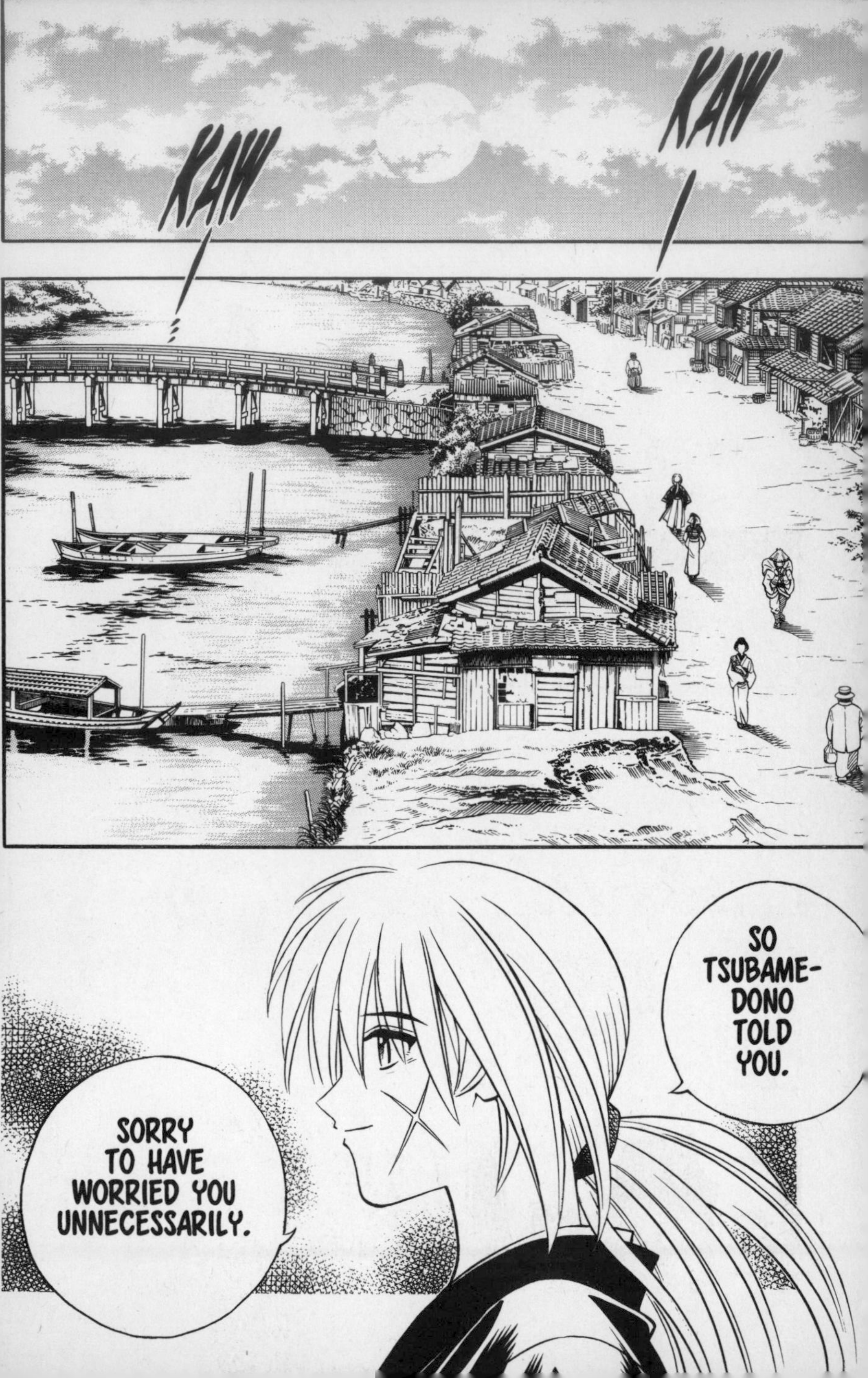
KAW
KAW
SO TSUBAME-DONO TOLD YOU.
SORRY TO HAVE WORRIED YOU UNNECESSARILY.

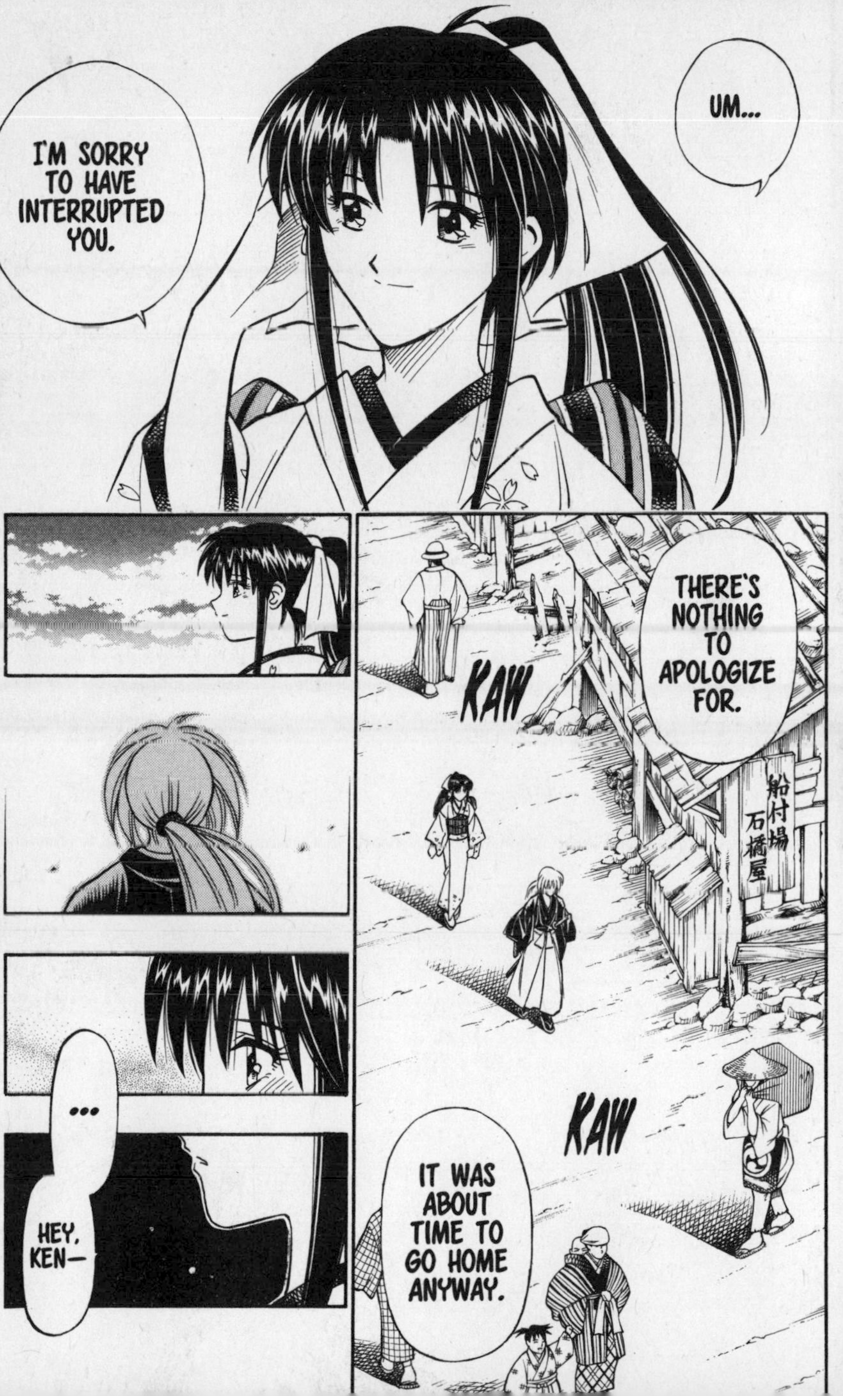
UM...
I'M SORRY TO HAVE INTERRUPTED YOU.
THERE'S NOTHING TO APOLOGIZE FOR.
KAW
船付場
石橋屋
KAW
IT WAS ABOUT TIME TO GO HOME ANYWAY.
...
HEY, KEN—

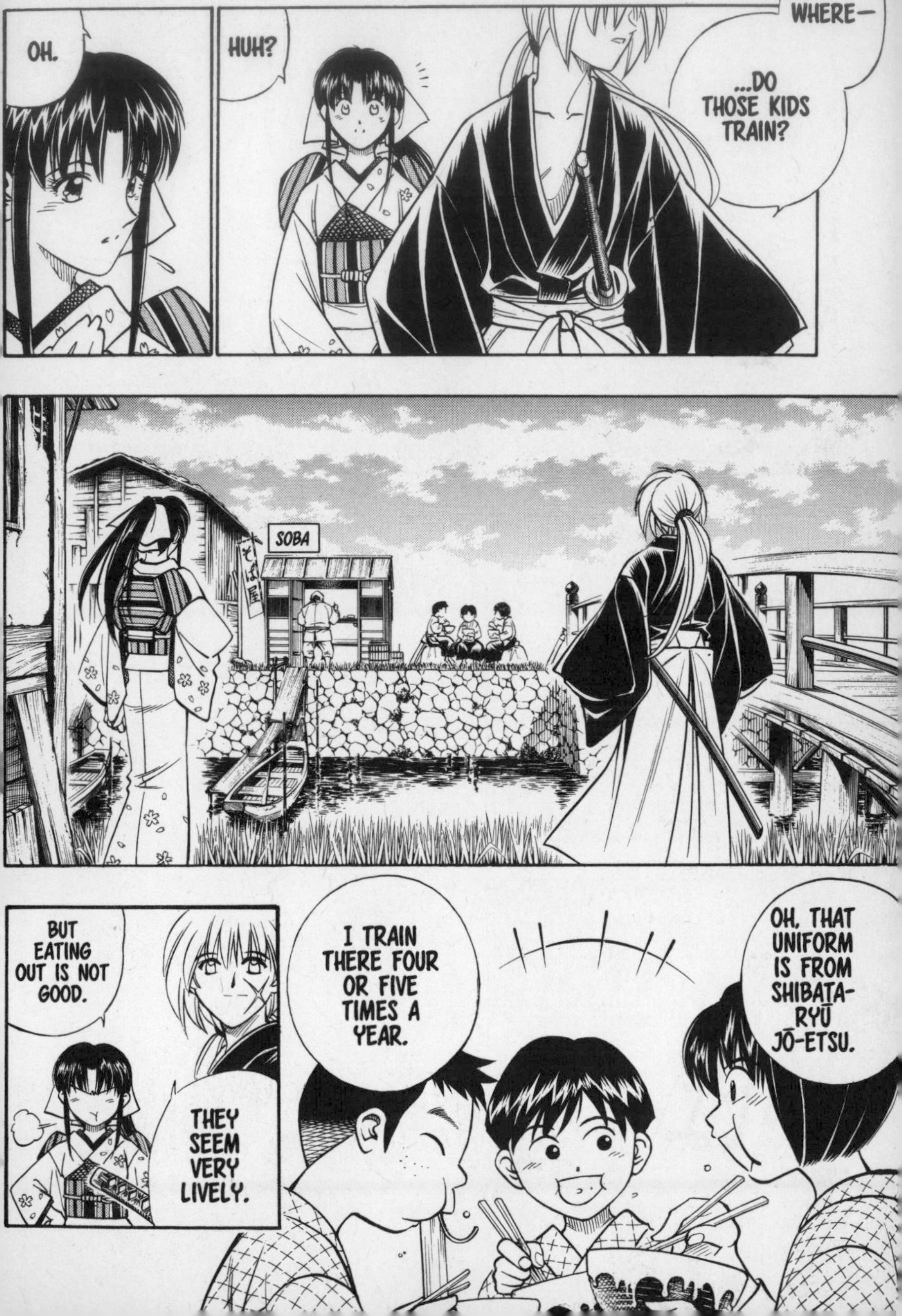
WHERE—
...DO THOSE KIDS TRAIN?
HUH?
OH.
SOBA
そば屋
OH, THAT UNIFORM IS FROM SHIBATA-RYŪ JŌ-ETSU.
I TRAIN THERE FOUR OR FIVE TIMES A YEAR.
BUT EATING OUT IS NOT GOOD.
THEY SEEM VERY LIVELY.

READ THIS WAY

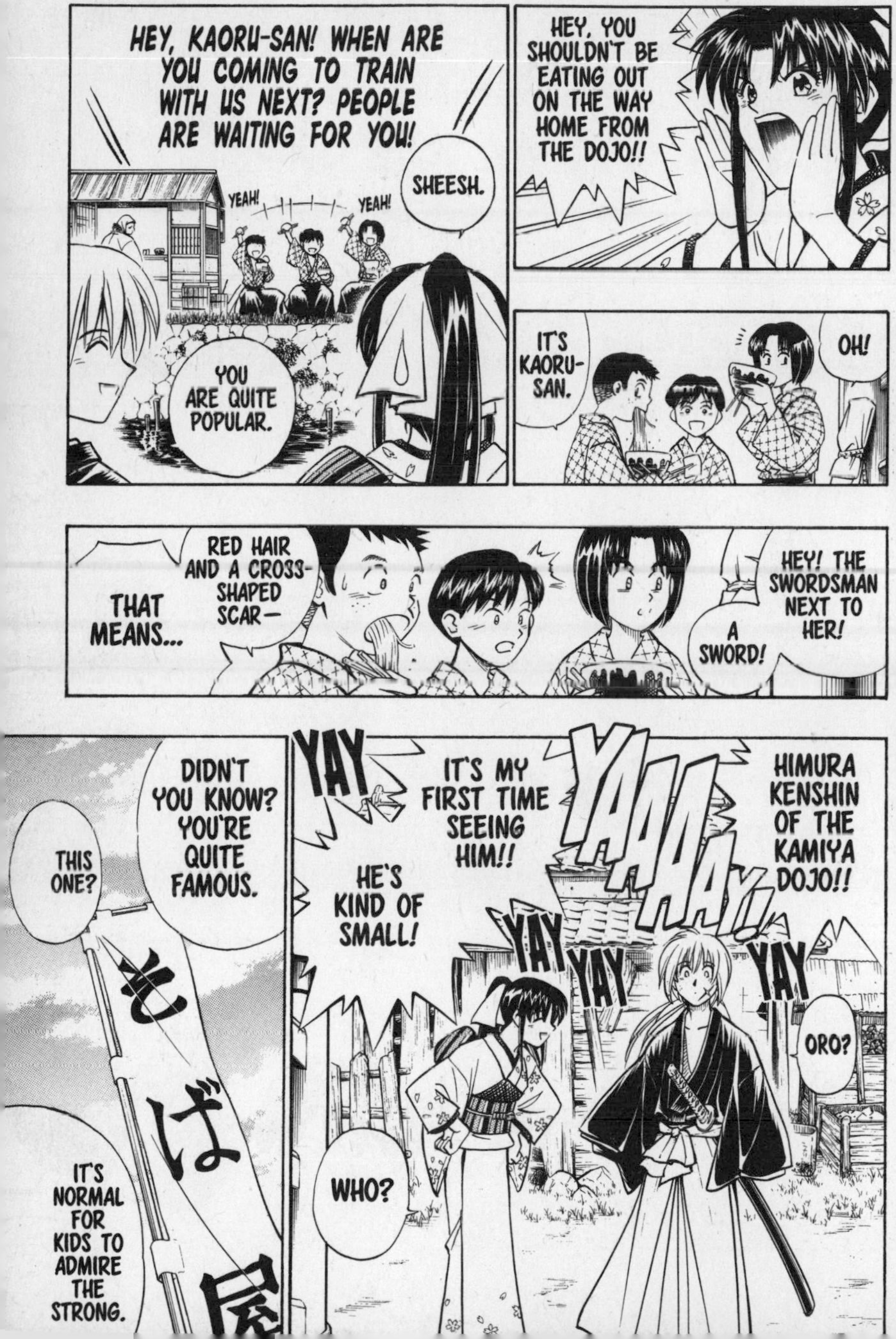
HEY, YOU SHOULDN'T BE EATING OUT ON THE WAY HOME FROM THE DOJO!!
OH!
IT'S KAORU-SAN.
HEY, KAORU-SAN! WHEN ARE YOU COMING TO TRAIN WITH US NEXT? PEOPLE ARE WAITING FOR YOU!
YEAH!
YEAH!
SHEESH.
YOU ARE QUITE POPULAR.
HEY! THE SWORDSMAN NEXT TO HER!
A SWORD!
RED HAIR AND A CROSS-SHAPED SCAR—
THAT MEANS...
HIMURA KENSHIN OF THE KAMIYA DOJO!!
YAAAAY!!
IT'S MY FIRST TIME SEEING HIM!!
YAY
HE'S KIND OF SMALL!
YAY
YAY
YAY
ORO?
WHO?
DIDN'T YOU KNOW? YOU'RE QUITE FAMOUS.
THIS ONE?
そば
IT'S NORMAL FOR KIDS TO ADMIRE THE STRONG.

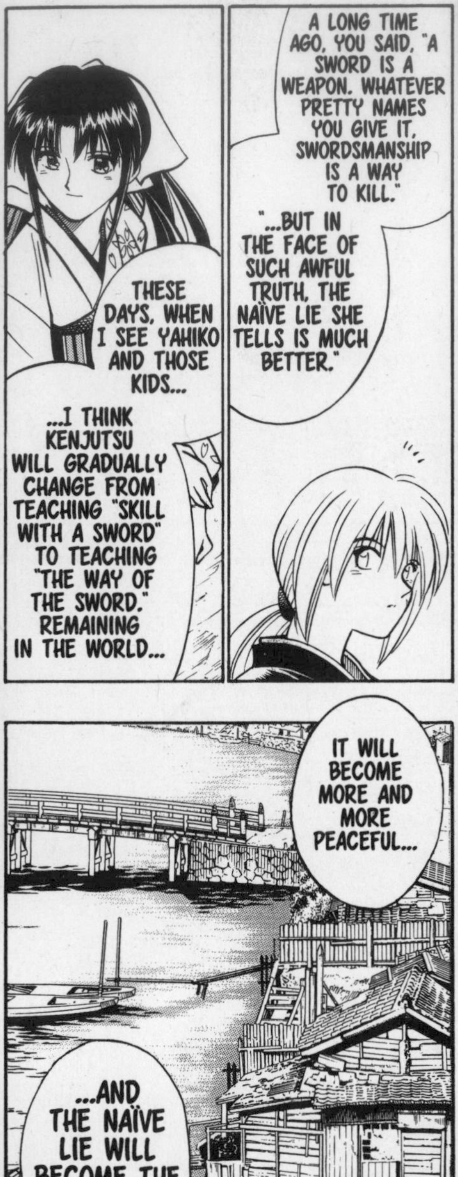
A LONG TIME AGO, YOU SAID, "A SWORD IS A WEAPON. WHATEVER PRETTY NAMES YOU GIVE IT, SWORDSMANSHIP IS A WAY TO KILL."
"...BUT IN THE FACE OF SUCH AWFUL TRUTH, THE NAÏVE LIE SHE TELLS IS MUCH BETTER."
THESE DAYS, WHEN I SEE YAHIKO AND THOSE KIDS...
...I THINK KENJUTSU WILL GRADUALLY CHANGE FROM TEACHING "SKILL WITH A SWORD" TO TEACHING "THE WAY OF THE SWORD." REMAINING IN THE WORLD...
IT WILL BECOME MORE AND MORE PEACEFUL...
...AND THE NAÏVE LIE WILL BECOME THE TRUTH...
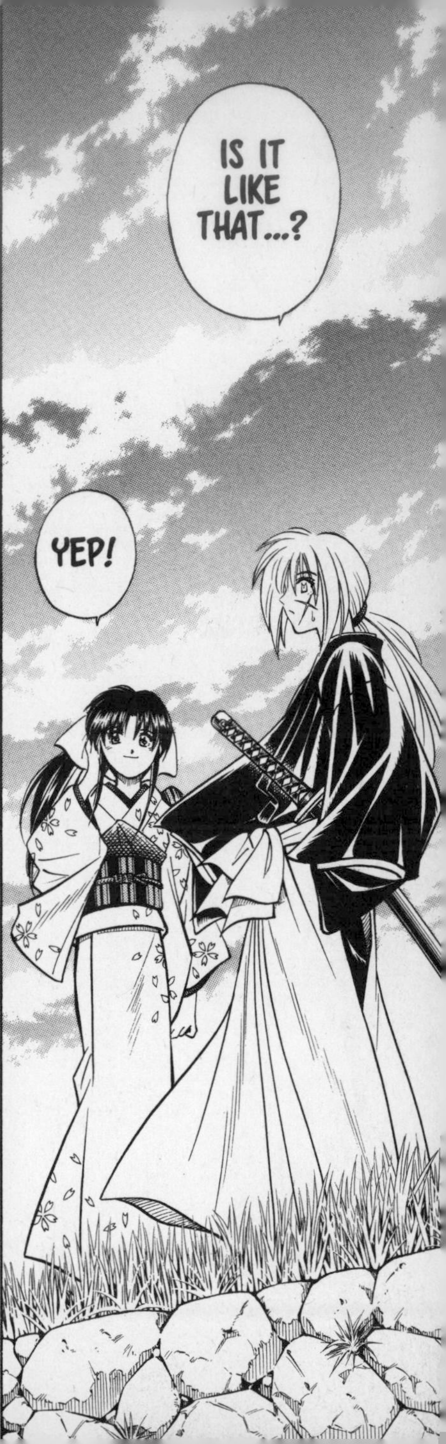
IS IT LIKE THAT...?
YEP!

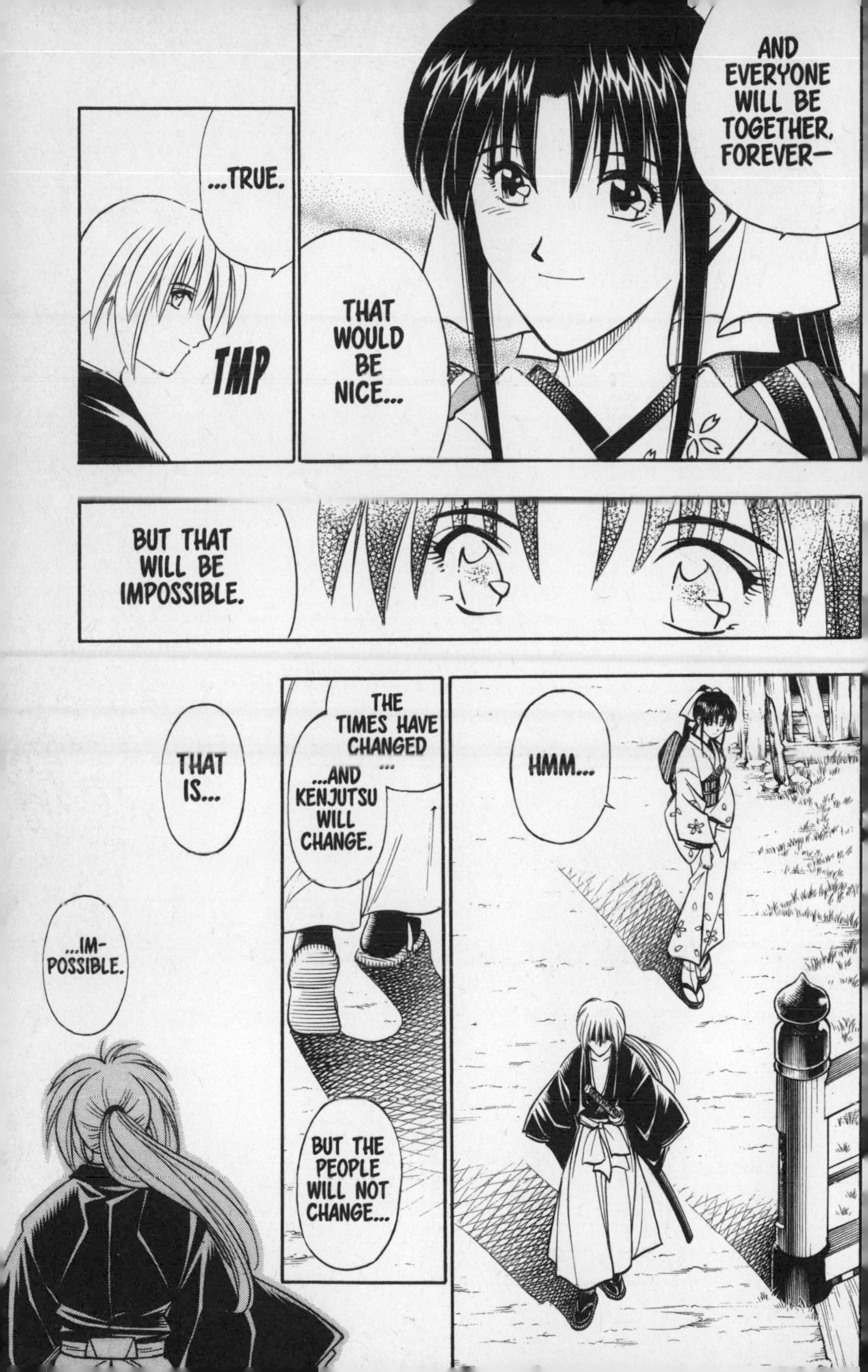
AND EVERYONE WILL BE TOGETHER, FOREVER—
THAT WOULD BE NICE...
...TRUE.
TMP
BUT THAT WILL BE IMPOSSIBLE.
HMM...
THE TIMES HAVE CHANGED ...
...AND KENJUTSU WILL CHANGE.
BUT THE PEOPLE WILL NOT CHANGE...
THAT IS...
...IM-POSSIBLE.

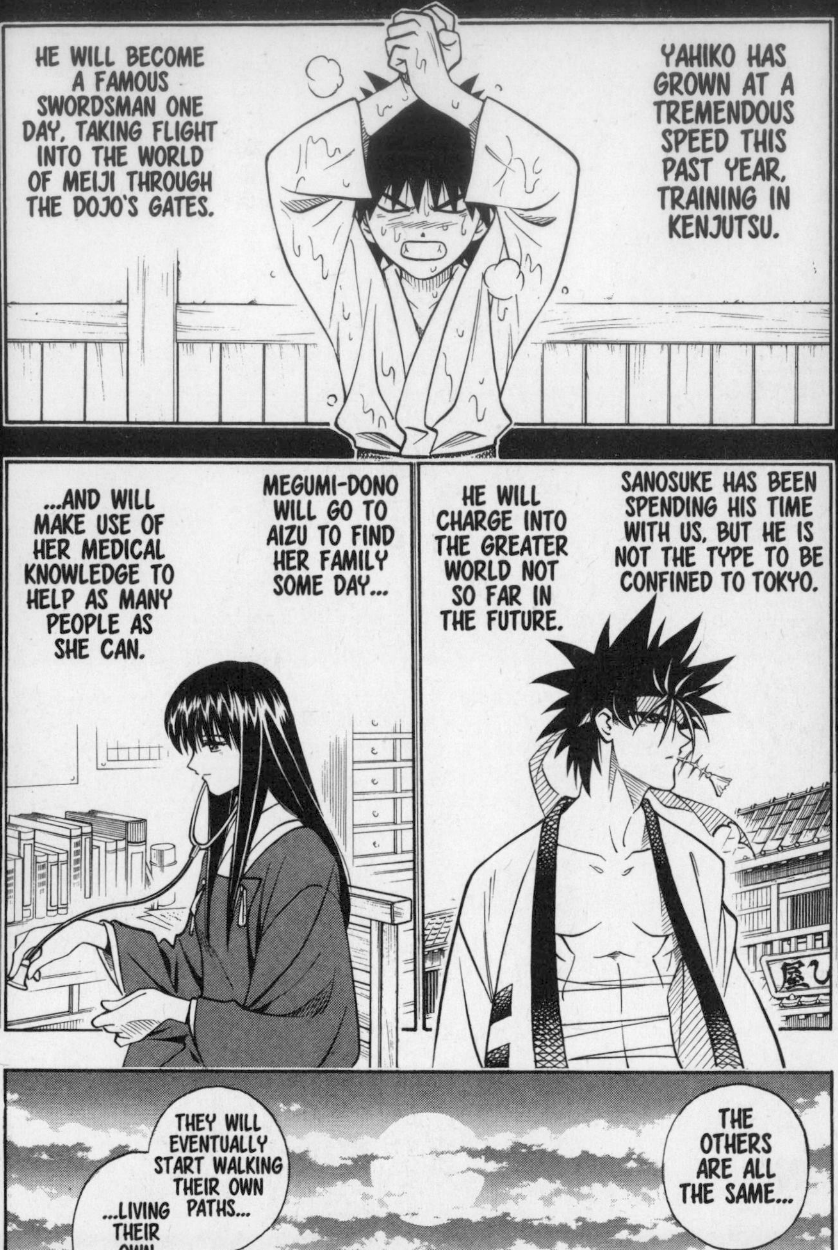
YAHIKO HAS GROWN AT A TREMENDOUS SPEED THIS PAST YEAR, TRAINING IN KENJUTSU.
HE WILL BECOME A FAMOUS SWORDSMAN ONE DAY, TAKING FLIGHT INTO THE WORLD OF MEIJI THROUGH THE DOJO'S GATES.
SANOSUKE HAS BEEN SPENDING HIS TIME WITH US, BUT HE IS NOT THE TYPE TO BE CONFINED TO TOKYO.
HE WILL CHARGE INTO THE GREATER WORLD NOT SO FAR IN THE FUTURE.
MEGUMI-DONO WILL GO TO AIZU TO FIND HER FAMILY SOME DAY...
...AND WILL MAKE USE OF HER MEDICAL KNOWLEDGE TO HELP AS MANY PEOPLE AS SHE CAN.
THE OTHERS ARE ALL THE SAME...
THEY WILL EVENTUALLY START WALKING THEIR OWN PATHS...
...LIVING THEIR OWN LIVES.

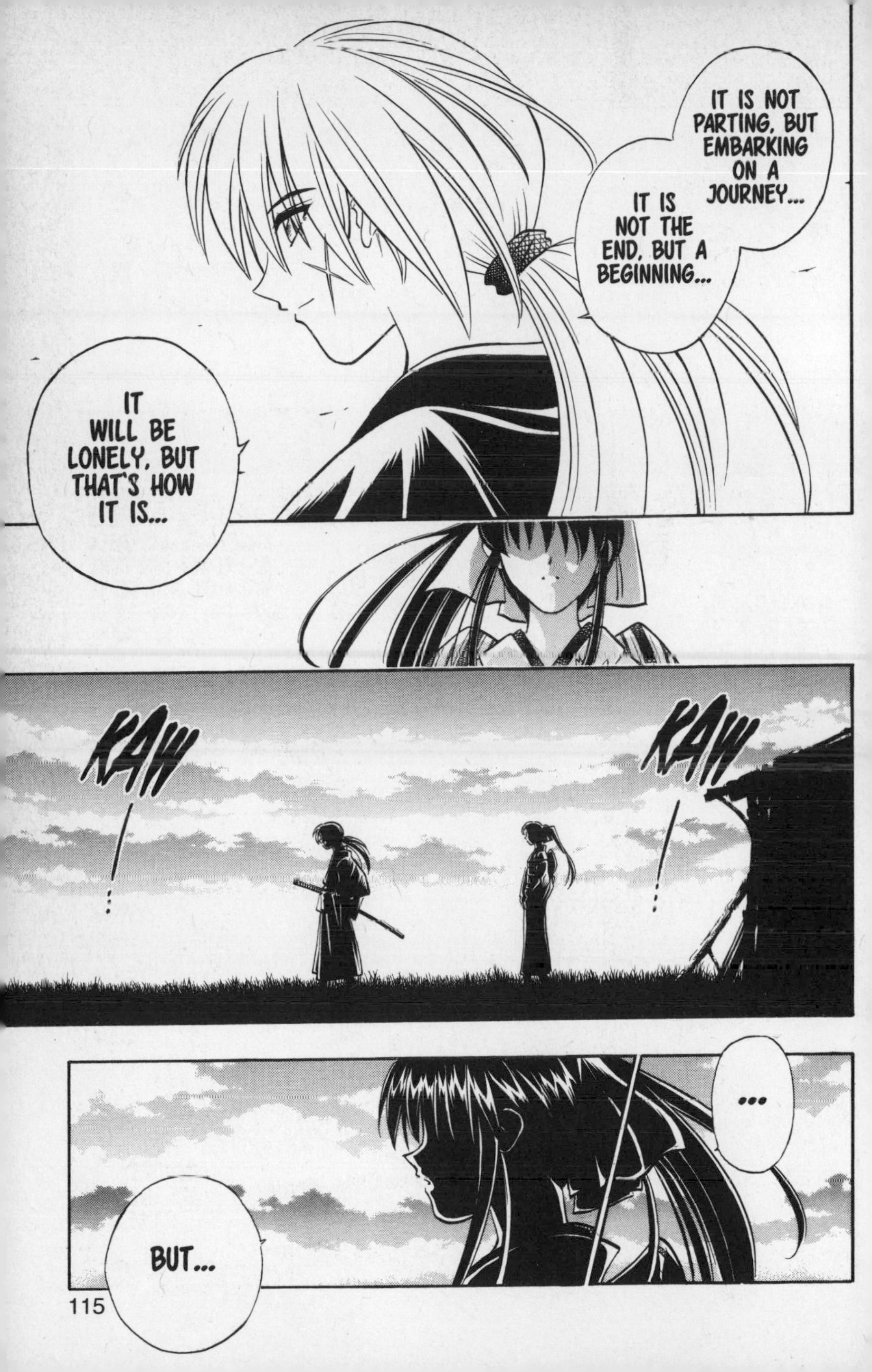
IT IS NOT PARTING, BUT EMBARKING ON A JOURNEY...
IT IS NOT THE END, BUT A BEGINNING...
IT WILL BE LONELY, BUT THAT'S HOW IT IS...
KAW
KAW
...
BUT...

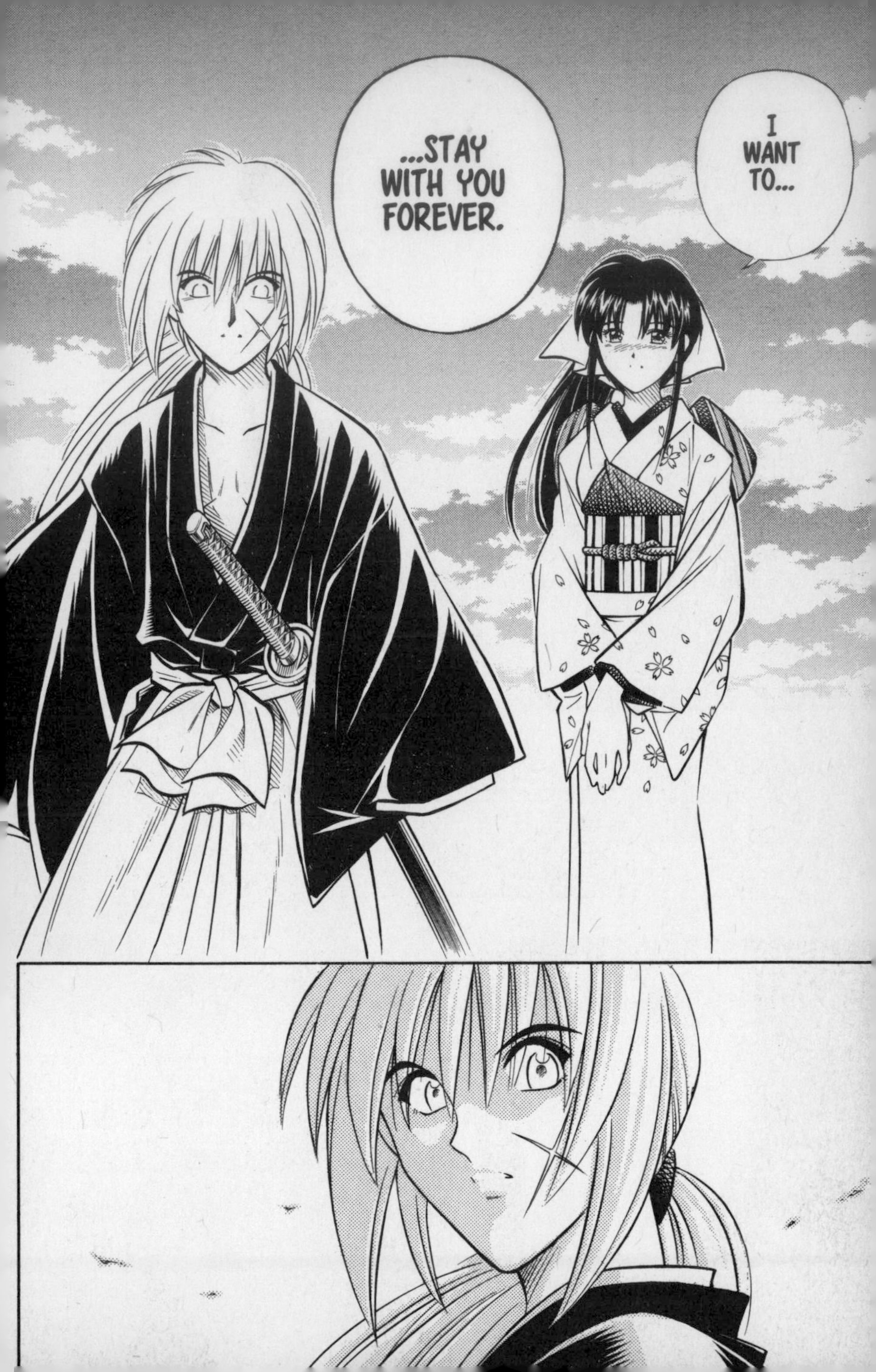
I WANT TO...
...STAY WITH YOU FOREVER.

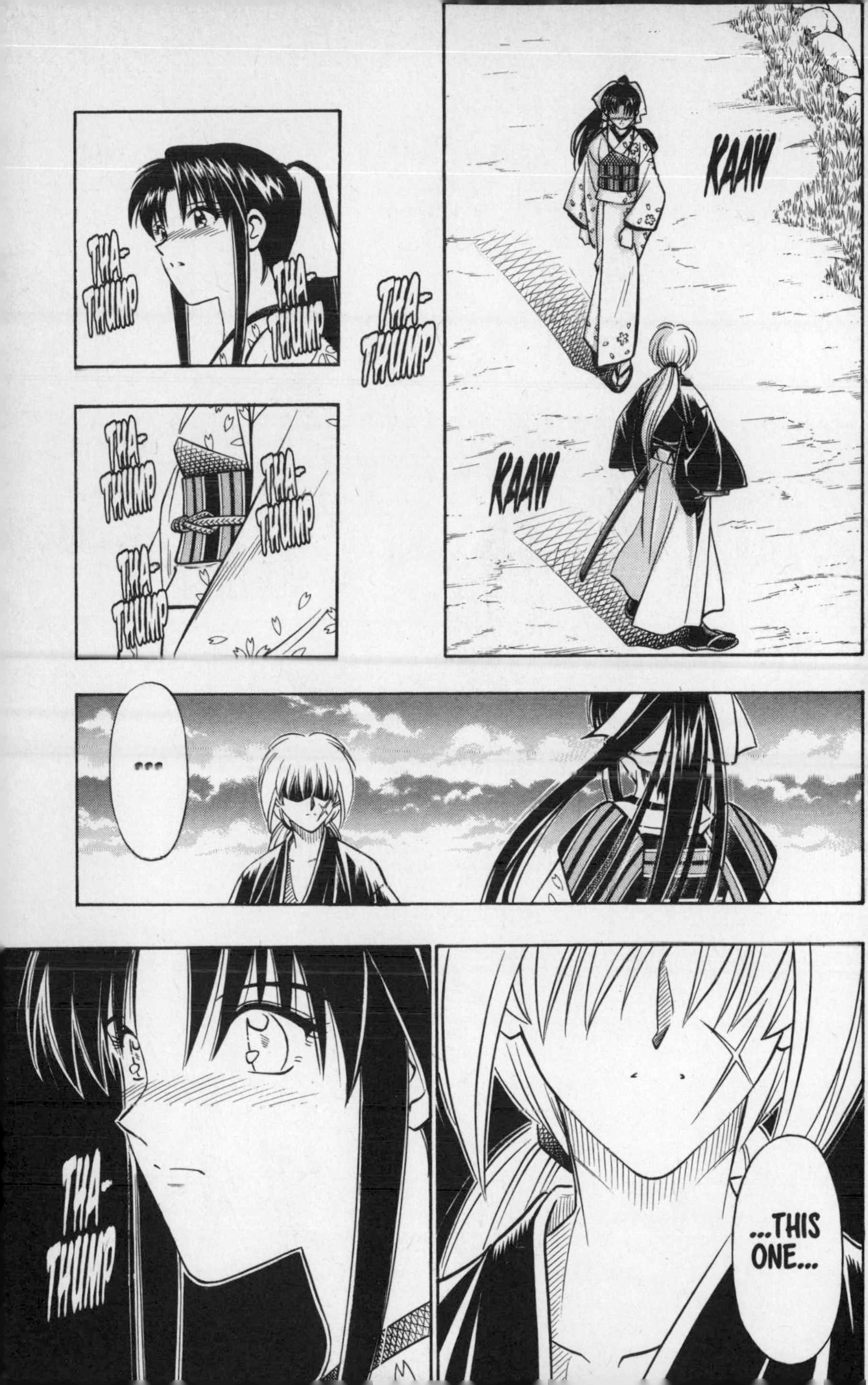
KAAW
KAAW
THA-THUMP
THA-THUMP
THA-THUMP
THA-THUMP
THA-THUMP
THA-THUMP
...
...THIS ONE...
THA-THUMP

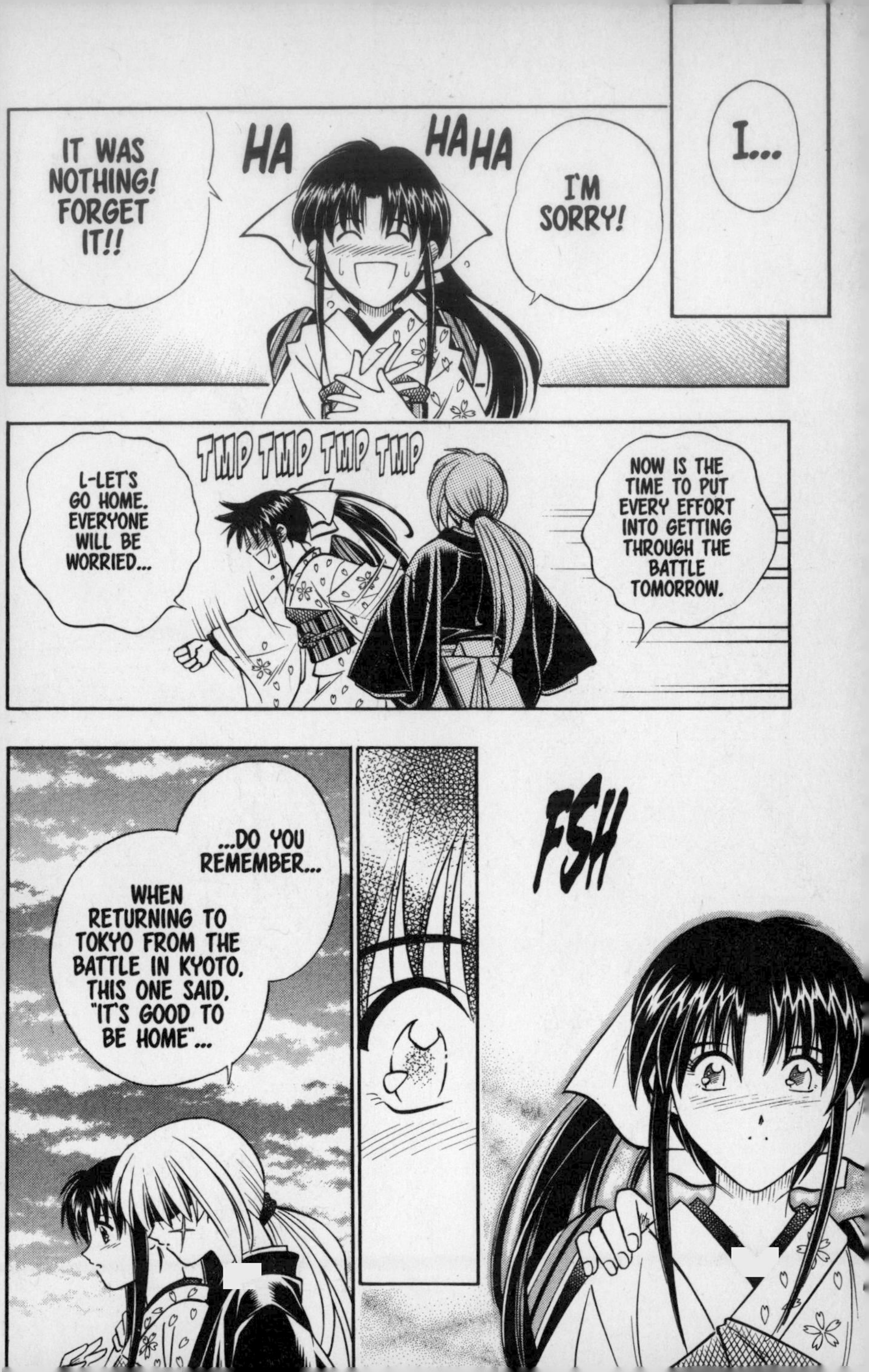
I...
I'M SORRY!
HA HA
HA
IT WAS NOTHING! FORGET IT!!
NOW IS THE TIME TO PUT EVERY EFFORT INTO GETTING THROUGH THE BATTLE TOMORROW.
TMP TMP TMP TMP
L-LET'S GO HOME. EVERYONE WILL BE WORRIED...
FSH
...DO YOU REMEMBER...
WHEN RETURNING TO TOKYO FROM THE BATTLE IN KYOTO, THIS ONE SAID, "IT'S GOOD TO BE HOME"...

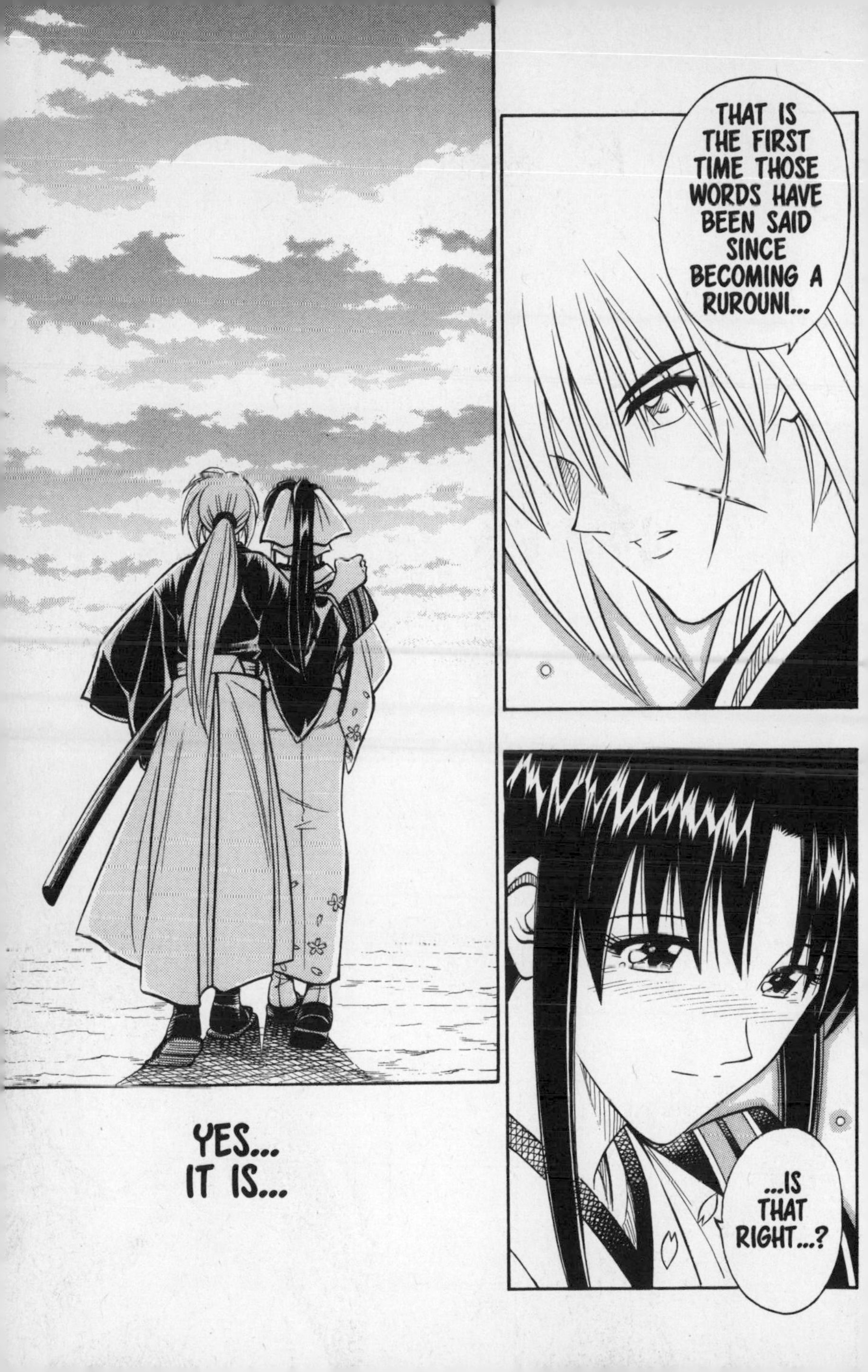
THAT IS THE FIRST TIME THOSE WORDS HAVE BEEN SAID SINCE BECOMING A RUROUNI...
...IS THAT RIGHT...?
YES... IT IS...

SOBA

BLAH

BLAH

BLAH

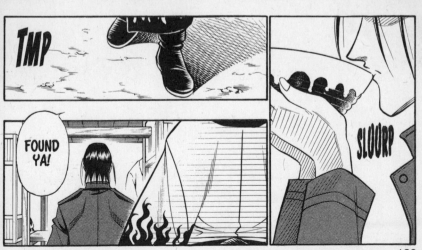

TMP

FOUND YA!

SLUURP

120

READ THIS WAY

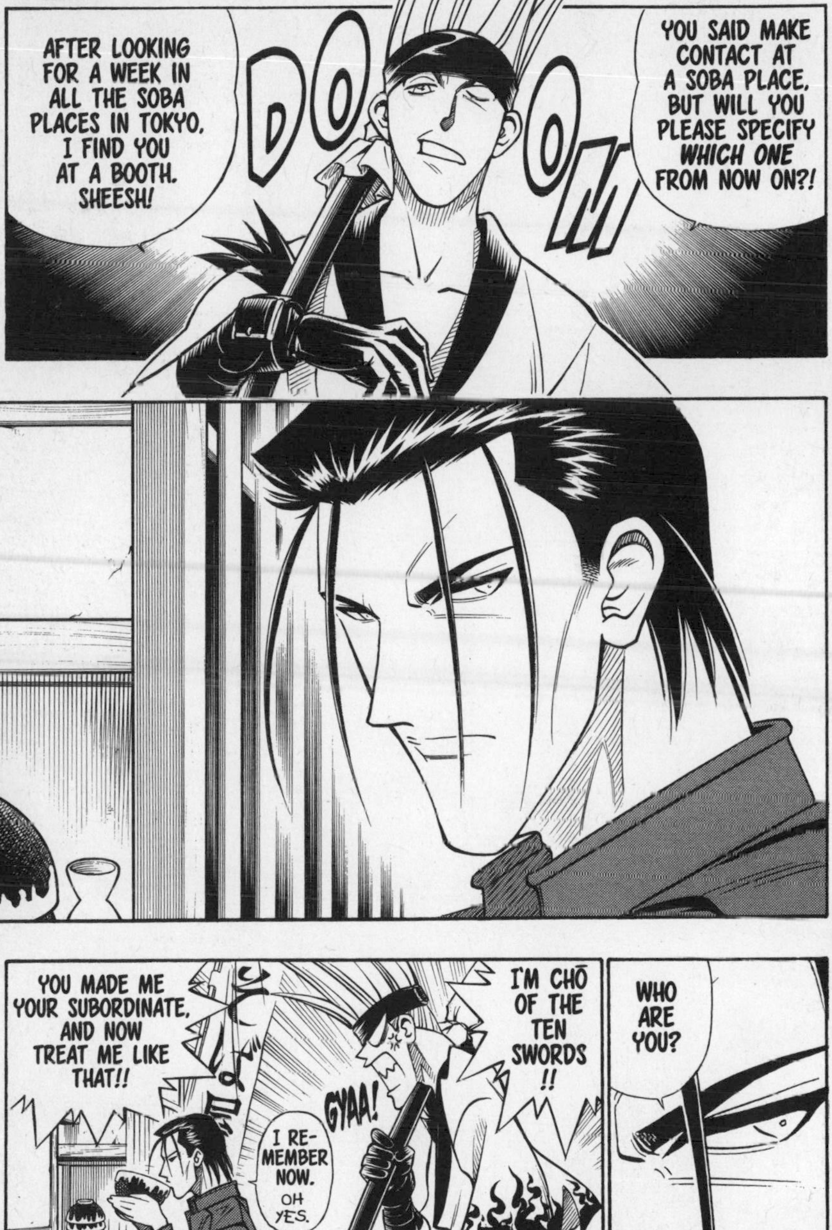

YOU SAID MAKE CONTACT AT A SOBA PLACE, BUT WILL YOU PLEASE SPECIFY *WHICH ONE* FROM NOW ON?!
DOOOM
AFTER LOOKING FOR A WEEK IN ALL THE SOBA PLACES IN TOKYO, I FIND YOU AT A BOOTH. SHEESH!
WHO ARE YOU?
I'M CHŌ OF THE TEN SWORDS!!
YOU MADE ME YOUR SUBORDINATE, AND NOW TREAT ME LIKE THAT!!
GYAA!
I RE-MEMBER NOW.
OH YES.

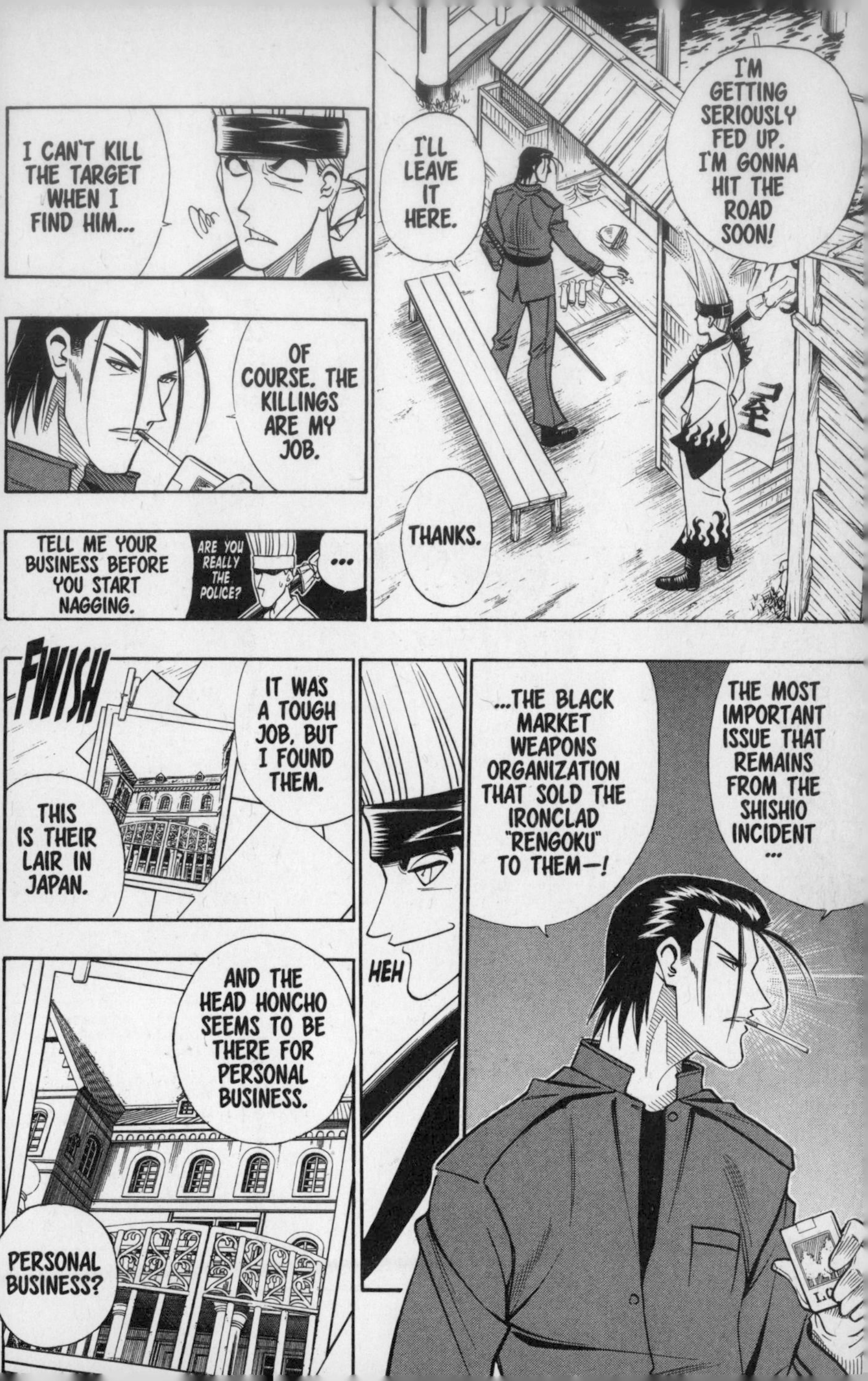
I'M GETTING SERIOUSLY FED UP. I'M GONNA HIT THE ROAD SOON!
I'LL LEAVE IT HERE.
THANKS.
I CAN'T KILL THE TARGET WHEN I FIND HIM...
OF COURSE. THE KILLINGS ARE MY JOB.
...
ARE YOU REALLY THE POLICE?
TELL ME YOUR BUSINESS BEFORE YOU START NAGGING.
THE MOST IMPORTANT ISSUE THAT REMAINS FROM THE SHISHIO INCIDENT ...
...THE BLACK MARKET WEAPONS ORGANIZATION THAT SOLD THE IRONCLAD "RENGOKU" TO THEM—!
HEH
FWISH
IT WAS A TOUGH JOB, BUT I FOUND THEM.
THIS IS THEIR LAIR IN JAPAN.
AND THE HEAD HONCHO SEEMS TO BE THERE FOR PERSONAL BUSINESS.
PERSONAL BUSINESS?

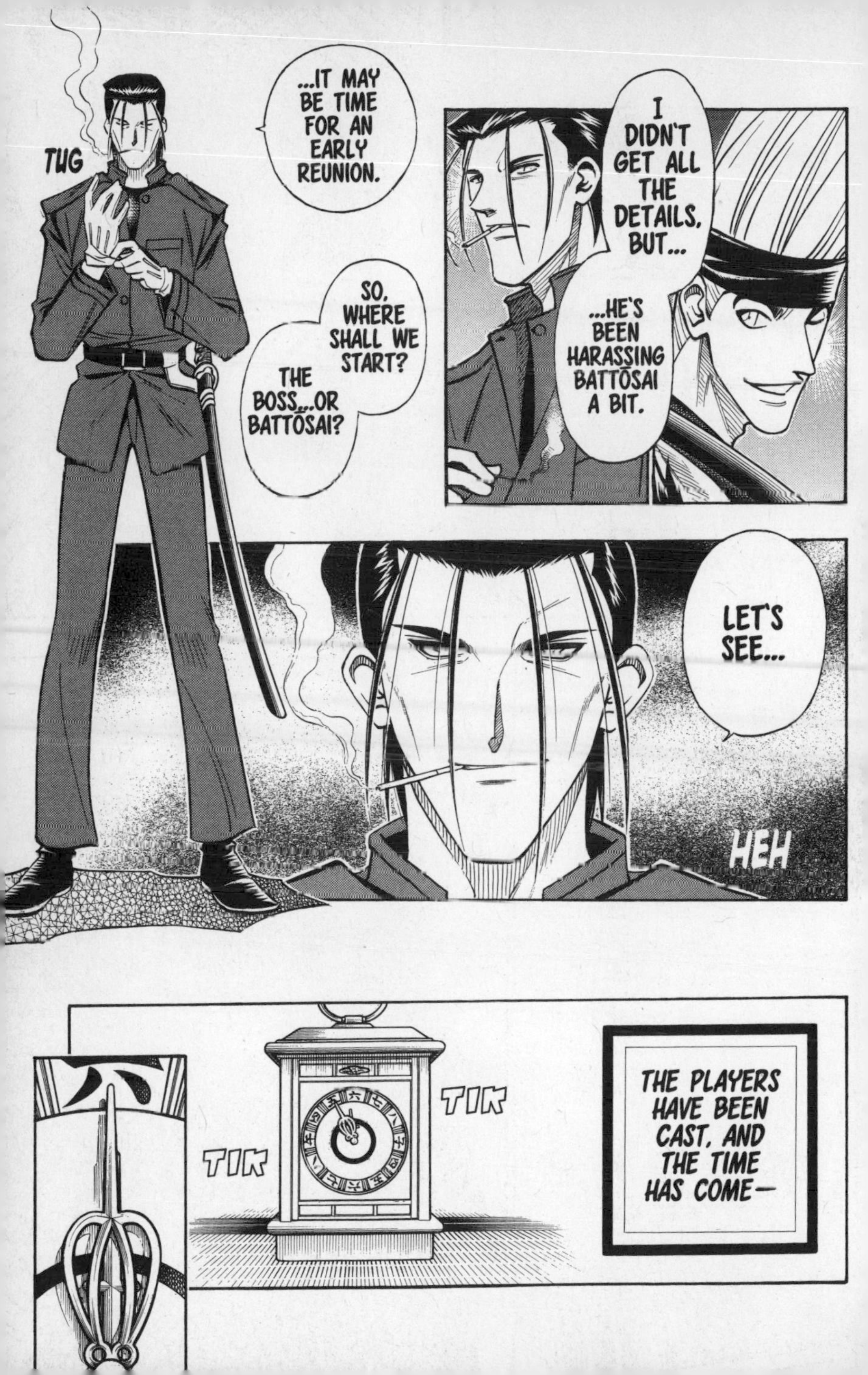
I DIDN'T GET ALL THE DETAILS, BUT...
...HE'S BEEN HARASSING BATTŌSAI A BIT.
LET'S SEE...
HEH
...IT MAY BE TIME FOR AN EARLY REUNION.
TUG
SO, WHERE SHALL WE START?
THE BOSS,...OR BATTŌSAI?
THE PLAYERS HAVE BEEN CAST, AND THE TIME HAS COME—
TIK
TIK

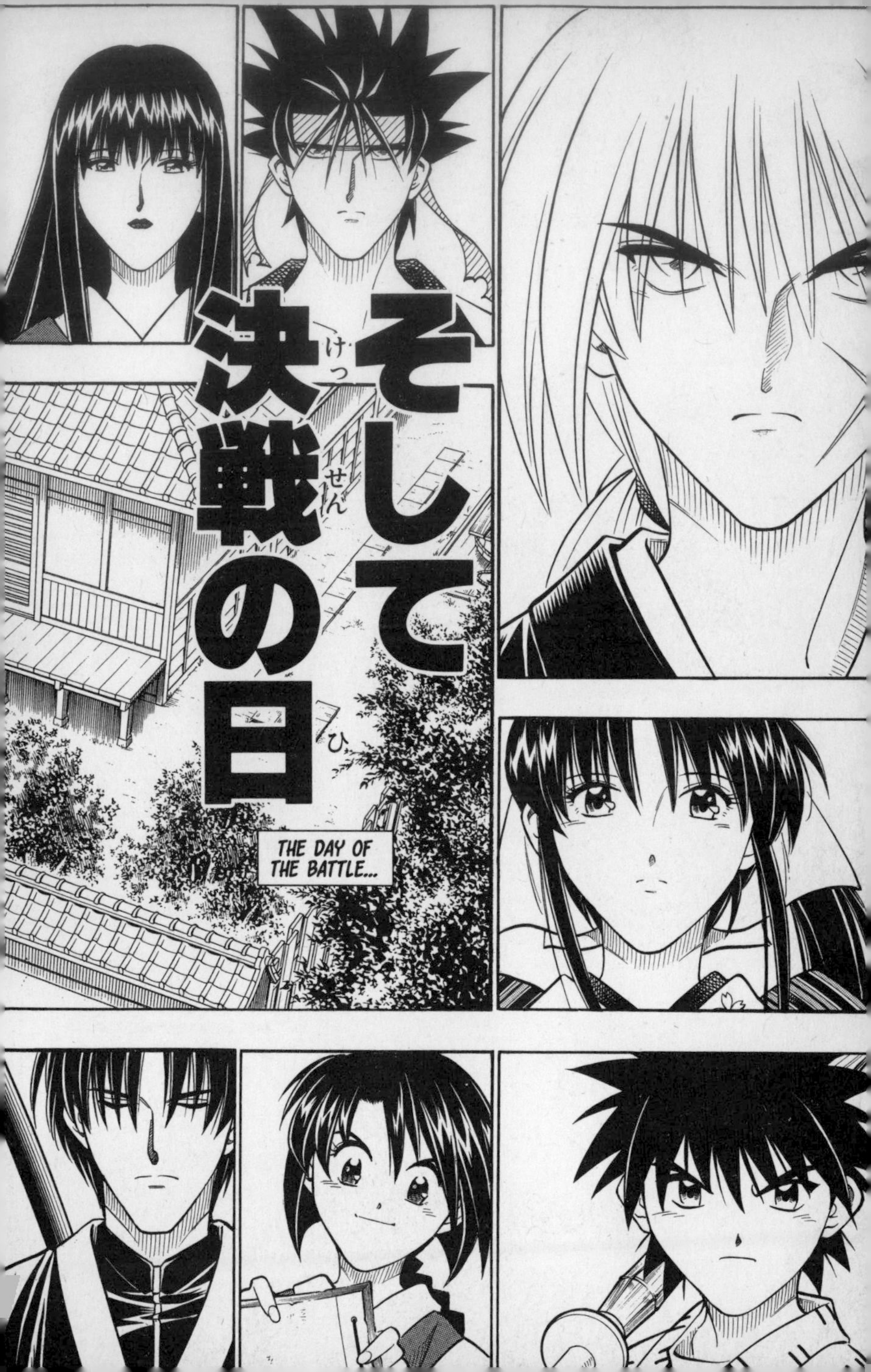

そして決戦の日
THE DAY OF THE BATTLE...

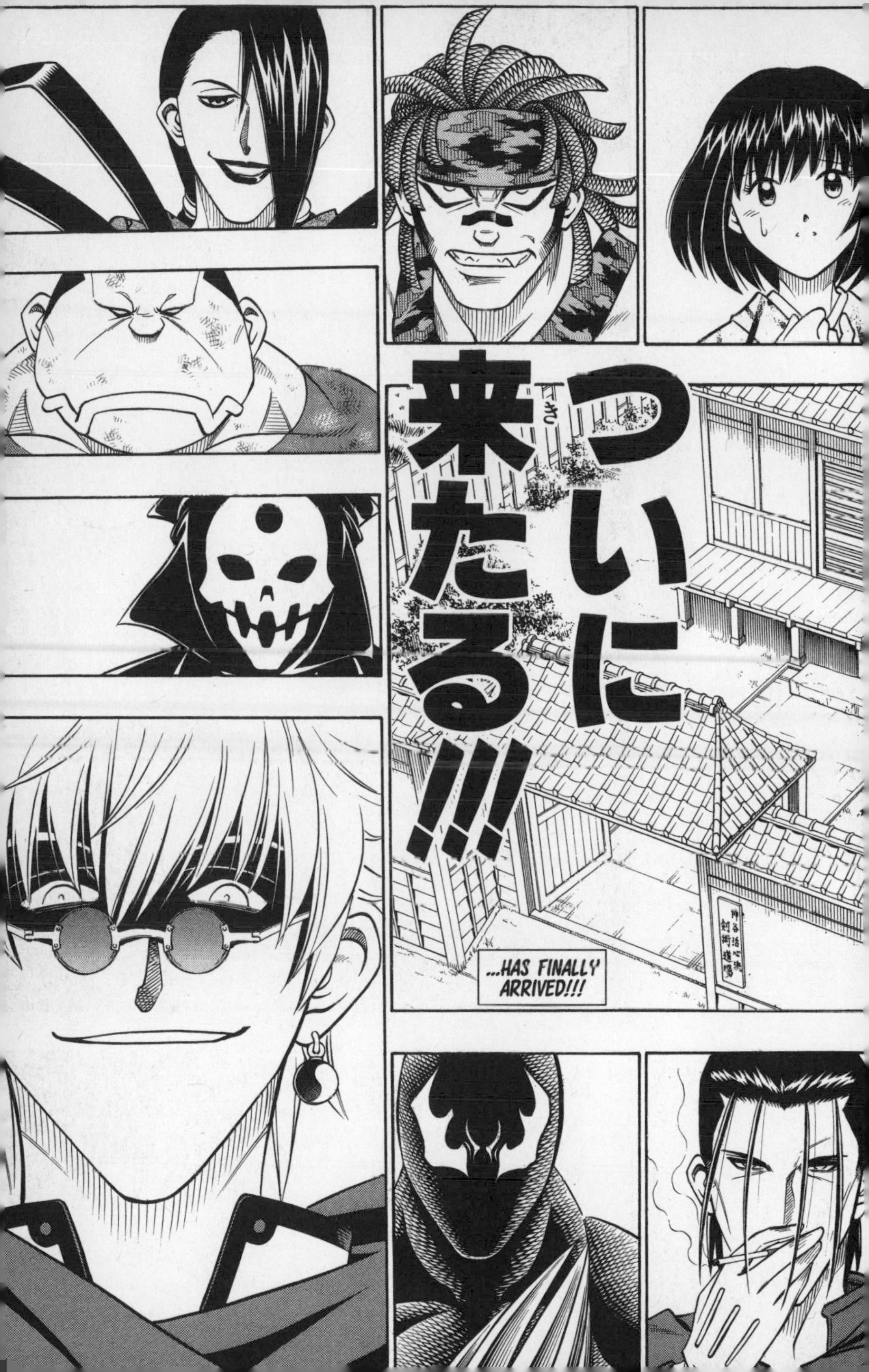
ついに来たる!!!
...HAS FINALLY ARRIVED!!!
神谷活心流
剣術道場

Rurouni Kenshin

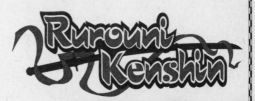

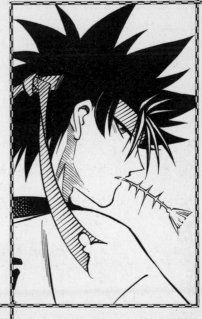

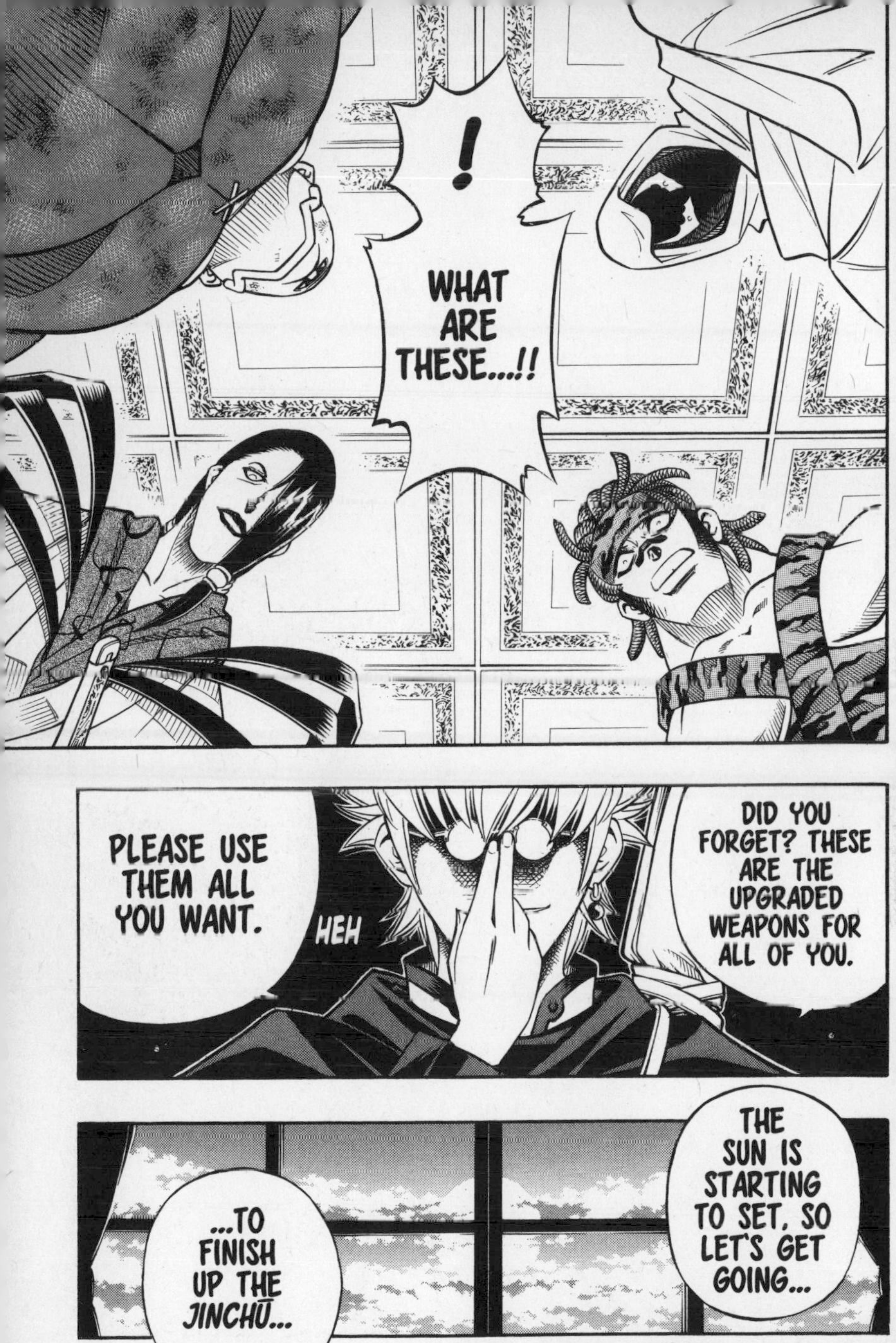
!
WHAT ARE THESE...!!
DID YOU FORGET? THESE ARE THE UPGRADED WEAPONS FOR ALL OF YOU.
HEH
PLEASE USE THEM ALL YOU WANT.
THE SUN IS STARTING TO SET, SO LET'S GET GOING...
...TO FINISH UP THE JINCHŪ...

Act 184—Fireworks

Fireworks

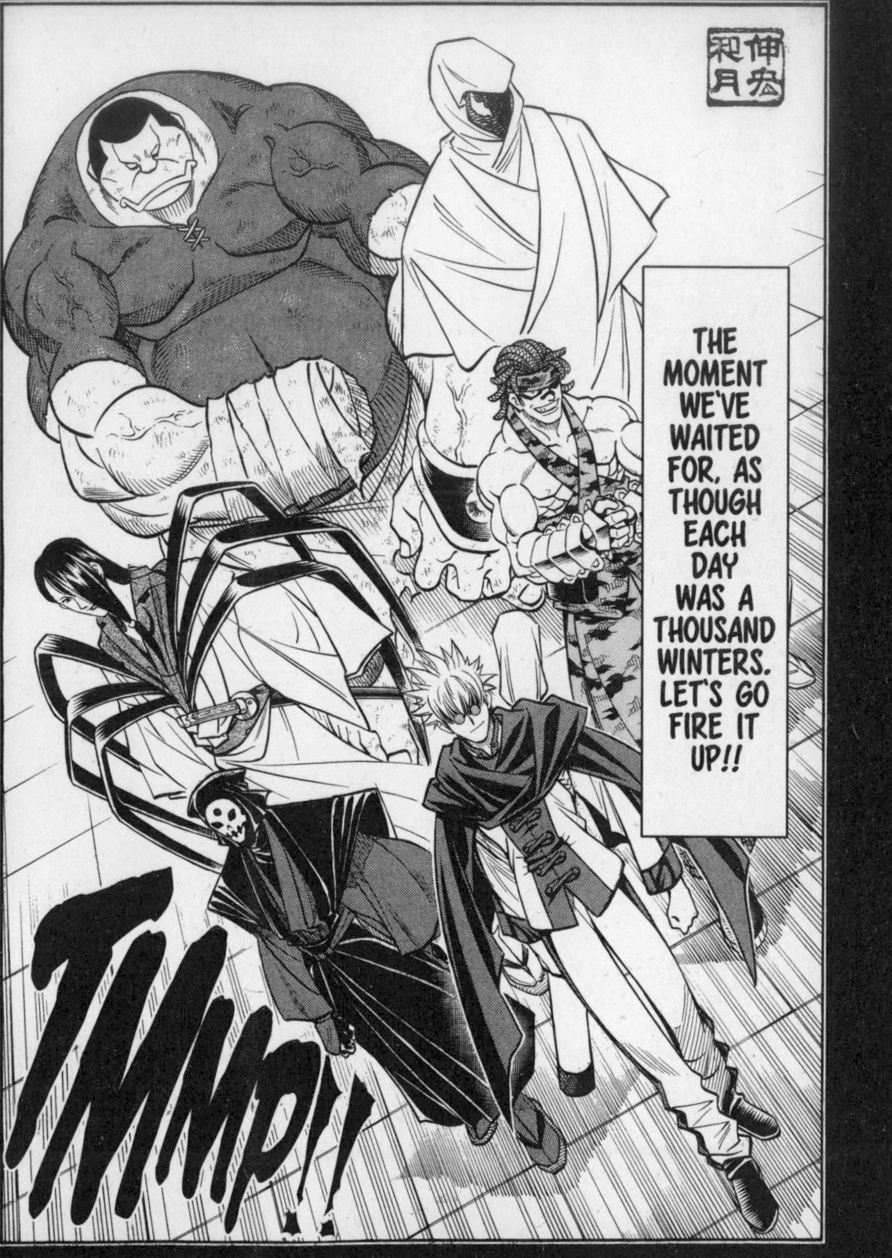
伸宏和月
THE MOMENT WE'VE WAITED FOR, AS THOUGH EACH DAY WAS A THOUSAND WINTERS. LET'S GO FIRE IT UP!!
THMP!!

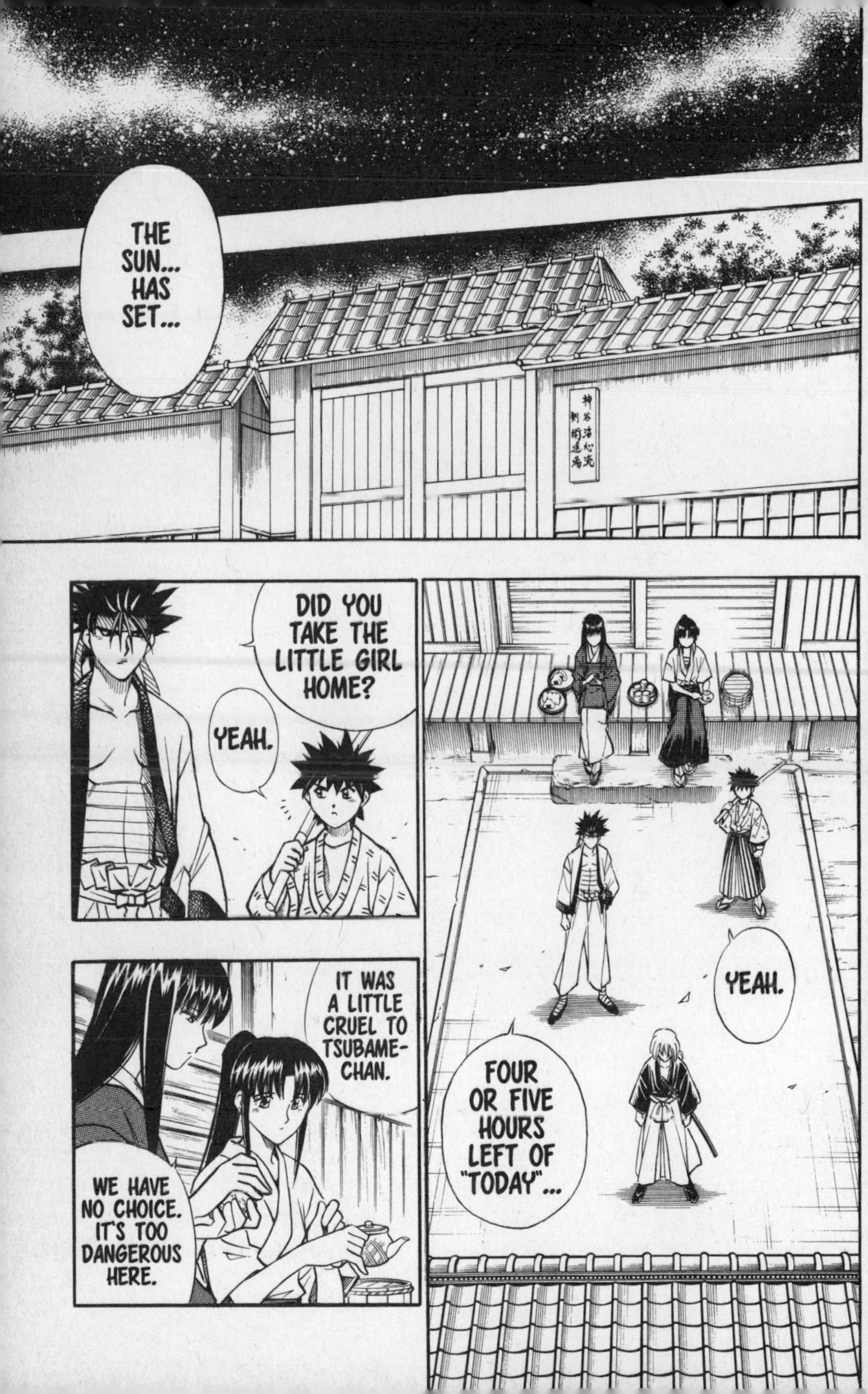
THE SUN... HAS SET...
神谷活心流
剣術道場
YEAH.
FOUR OR FIVE HOURS LEFT OF "TODAY"...
DID YOU TAKE THE LITTLE GIRL HOME?
YEAH.
IT WAS A LITTLE CRUEL TO TSUBAME-CHAN.
WE HAVE NO CHOICE. IT'S TOO DANGEROUS HERE.

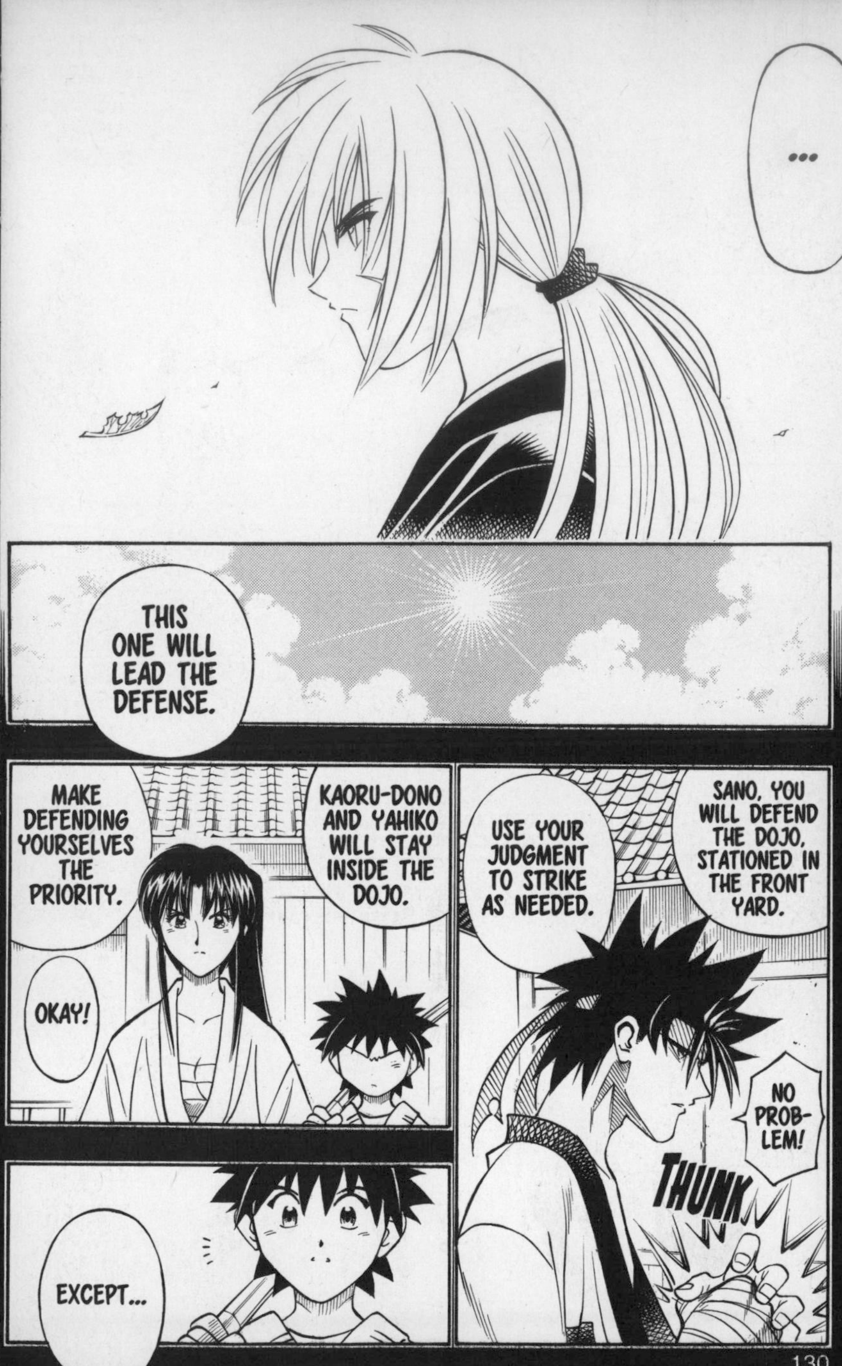
...
THIS ONE WILL LEAD THE DEFENSE.
SANO, YOU WILL DEFEND THE DOJO, STATIONED IN THE FRONT YARD.
USE YOUR JUDGMENT TO STRIKE AS NEEDED.
NO PROB-LEM!
THUNK
KAORU-DONO AND YAHIKO WILL STAY INSIDE THE DOJO.
MAKE DEFENDING YOURSELVES THE PRIORITY.
OKAY!
EXCEPT...

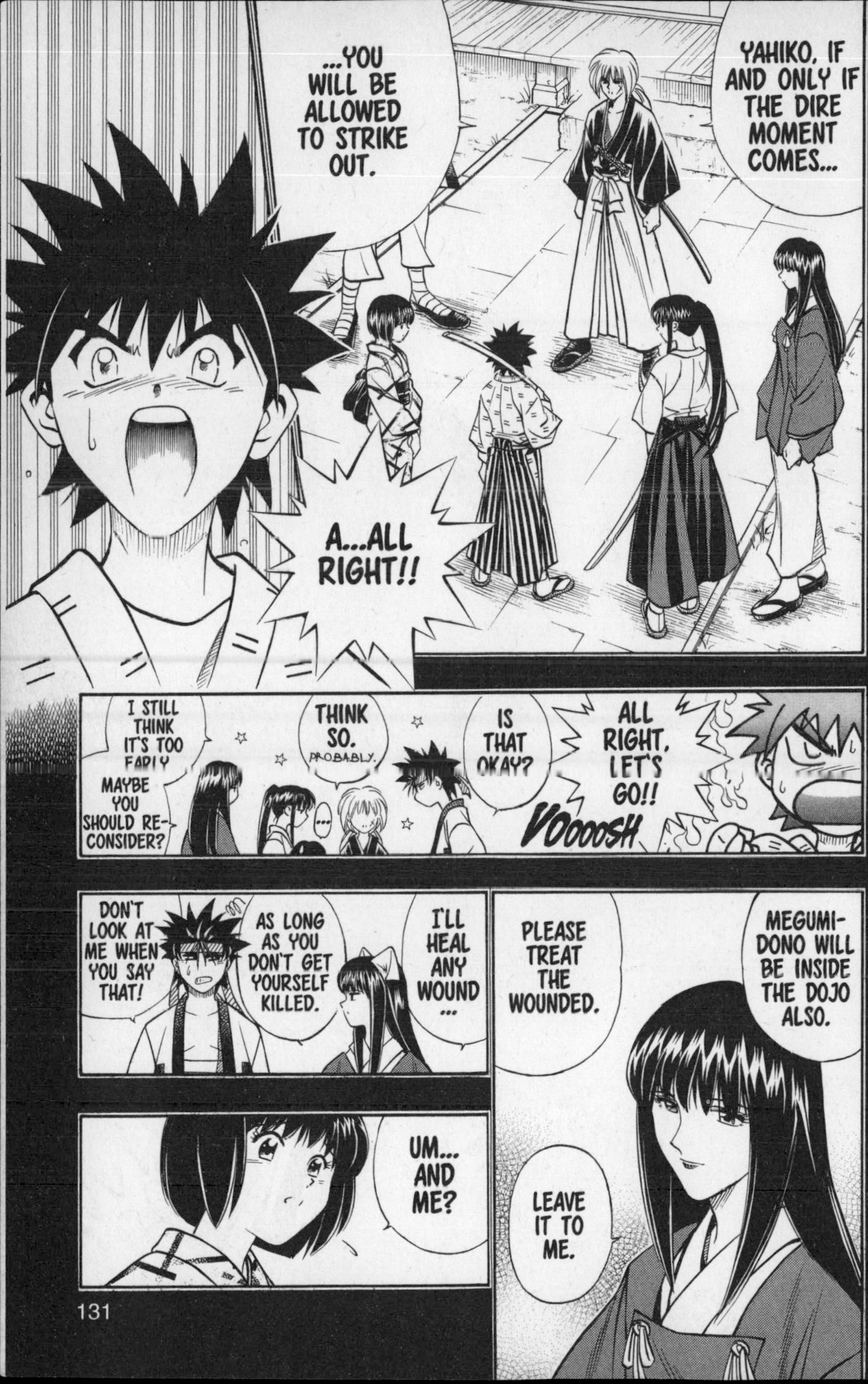
YAHIKO, IF AND ONLY IF THE DIRE MOMENT COMES...
...YOU WILL BE ALLOWED TO STRIKE OUT.
A...ALL RIGHT!!
ALL RIGHT, LET'S GO!!
VOOOOSH
IS THAT OKAY?
THINK SO.
PROBABLY.
I STILL THINK IT'S TOO EARLY
MAYBE YOU SHOULD RE-CONSIDER?
...
MEGUMI-DONO WILL BE INSIDE THE DOJO ALSO.
PLEASE TREAT THE WOUNDED.
LEAVE IT TO ME.
I'LL HEAL ANY WOUND...
AS LONG AS YOU DON'T GET YOURSELF KILLED.
DON'T LOOK AT ME WHEN YOU SAY THAT!
UM... AND ME?

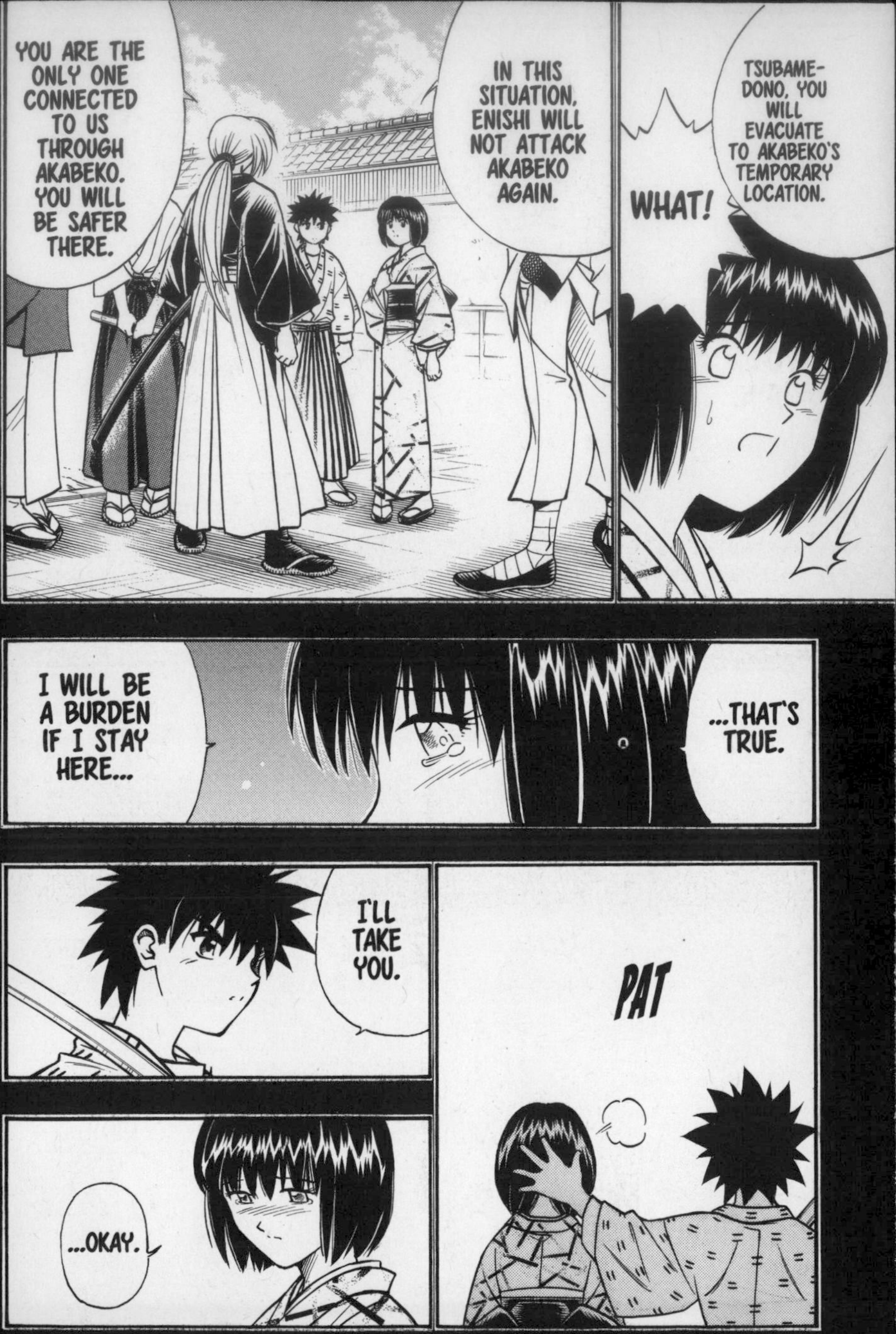
TSUBAME-DONO, YOU WILL EVACUATE TO AKABEKO'S TEMPORARY LOCATION.
WHAT!
IN THIS SITUATION, ENISHI WILL NOT ATTACK AKABEKO AGAIN.
YOU ARE THE ONLY ONE CONNECTED TO US THROUGH AKABEKO. YOU WILL BE SAFER THERE.
...THAT'S TRUE.
I WILL BE A BURDEN IF I STAY HERE...
PAT
I'LL TAKE YOU.
...OKAY.

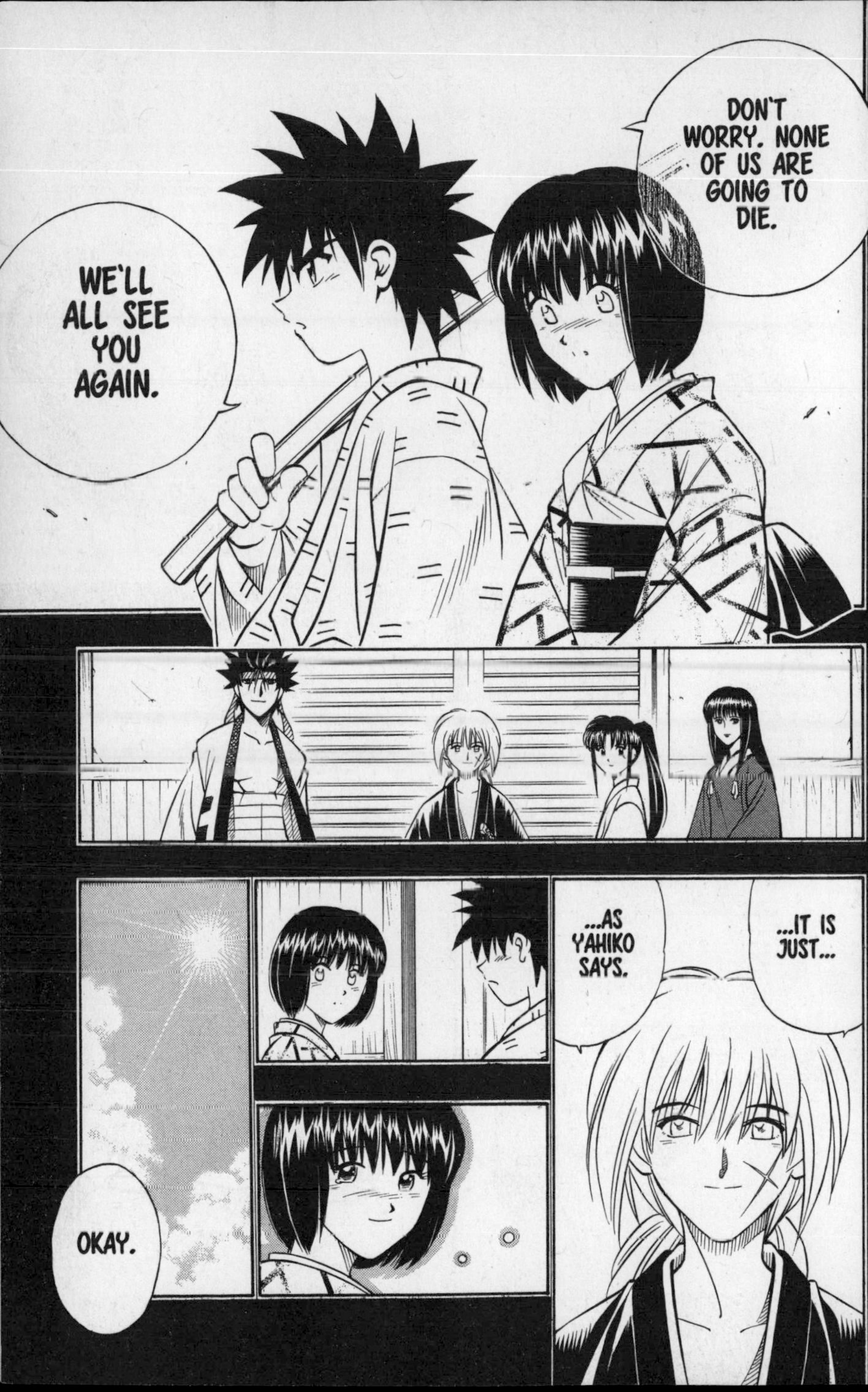
DON'T WORRY. NONE OF US ARE GOING TO DIE.
WE'LL ALL SEE YOU AGAIN.
...IT IS JUST...
...AS YAHIKO SAYS.
OKAY.

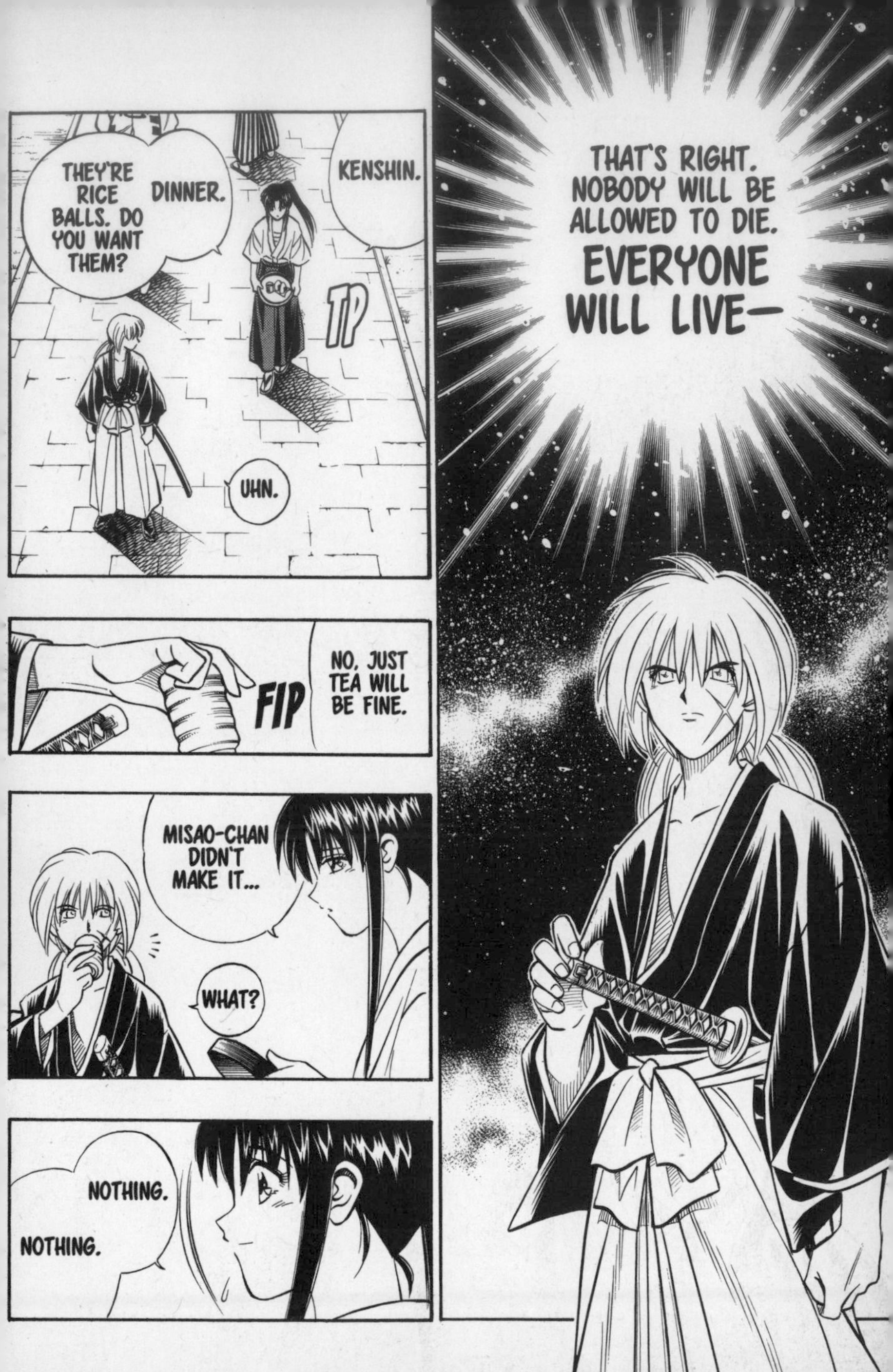
THAT'S RIGHT. NOBODY WILL BE ALLOWED TO DIE.
EVERYONE WILL LIVE—
KENSHIN.
TP
DINNER.
THEY'RE RICE BALLS. DO YOU WANT THEM?
UHN.
NO, JUST TEA WILL BE FINE.
FIP
MISAO-CHAN DIDN'T MAKE IT...
WHAT?
NOTHING.
NOTHING.

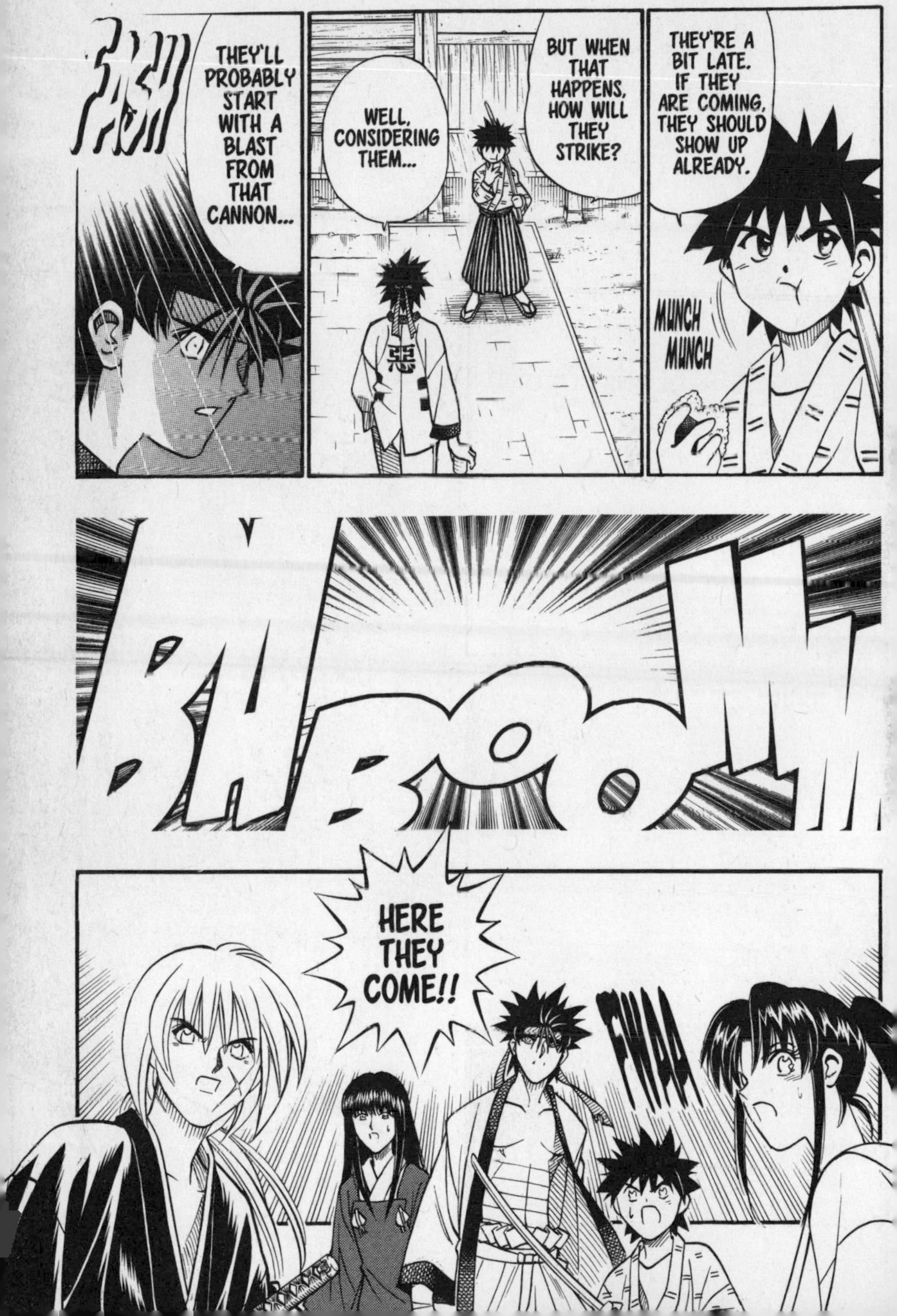
THEY'RE A BIT LATE. IF THEY ARE COMING, THEY SHOULD SHOW UP ALREADY.
MUNCH MUNCH
BUT WHEN THAT HAPPENS, HOW WILL THEY STRIKE?
WELL, CONSIDERING THEM...
THEY'LL PROBABLY START WITH A BLAST FROM THAT CANNON...
KA-BOOM
HERE THEY COME!!

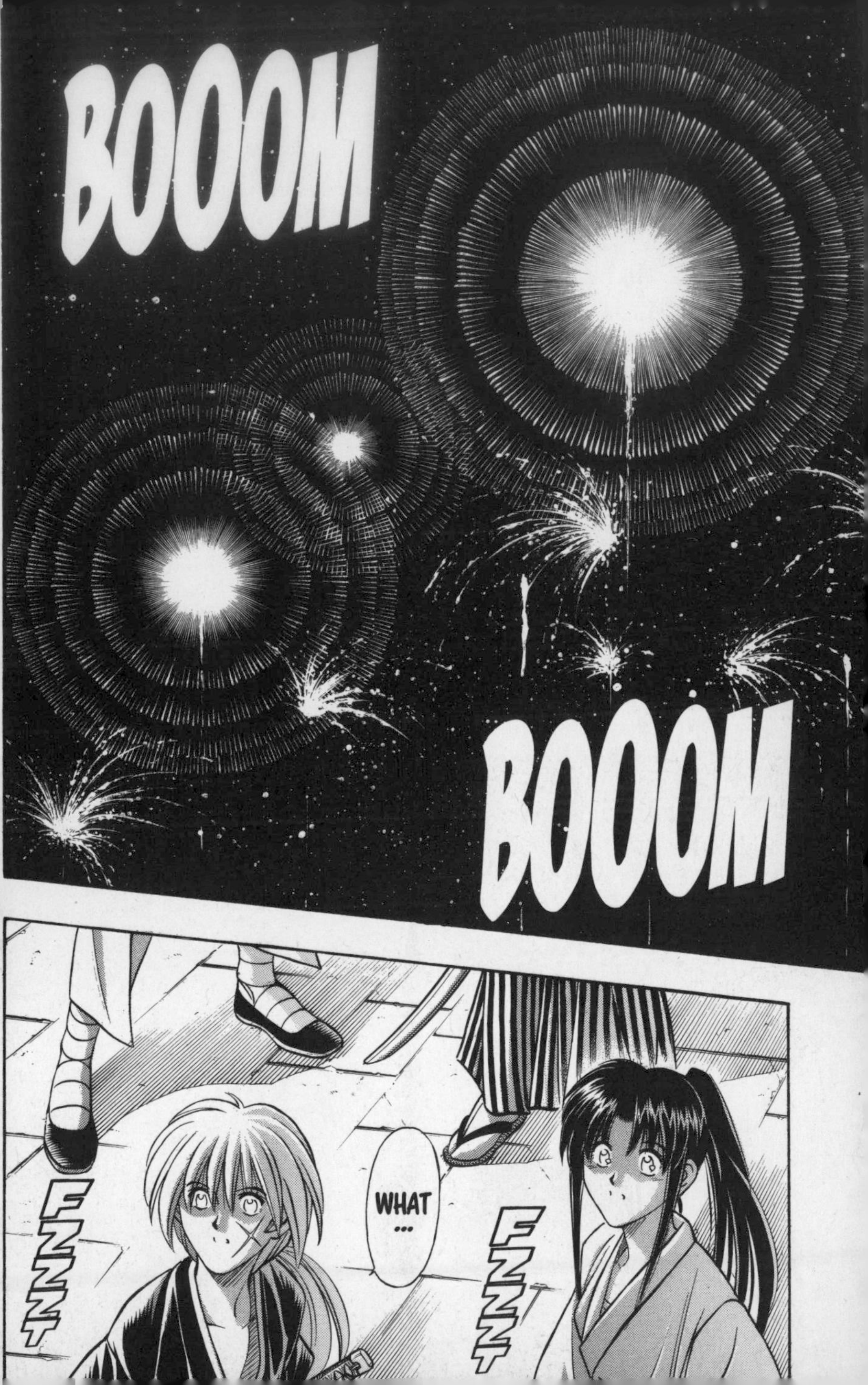
BOOOM
BOOOM
FZZZT
WHAT ...
FZZZT

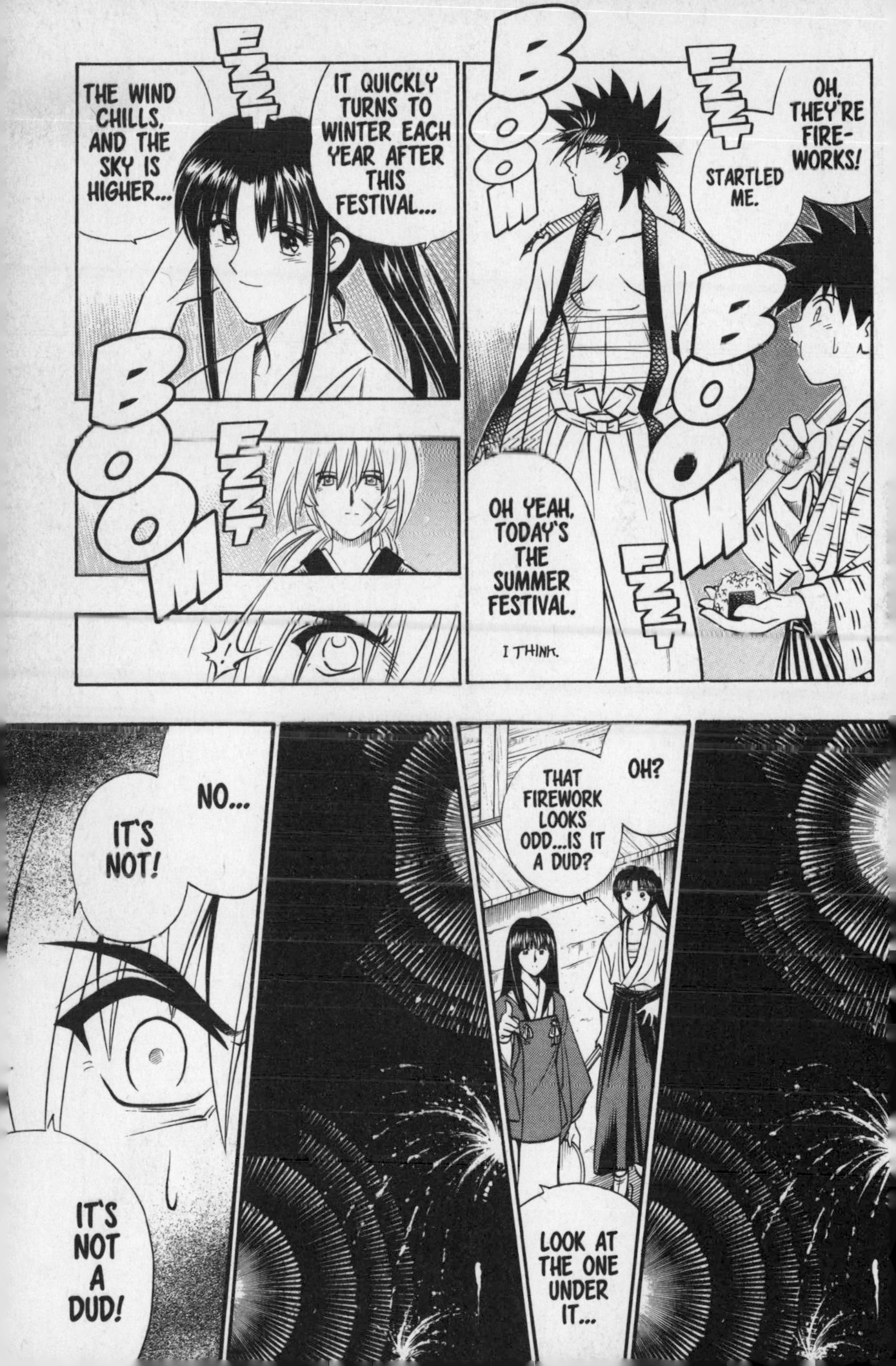
BOOM
FZZT
OH, THEY'RE FIRE-WORKS!
STARTLED ME.
BOOM
FZZT
OH YEAH, TODAY'S THE SUMMER FESTIVAL.
I THINK.
FZZT
IT QUICKLY TURNS TO WINTER EACH YEAR AFTER THIS FESTIVAL...
THE WIND CHILLS, AND THE SKY IS HIGHER...
BOOM
FZZT
OH?
THAT FIREWORK LOOKS ODD...IS IT A DUD?
LOOK AT THE ONE UNDER IT...
NO...
IT'S NOT!
IT'S NOT A DUD!

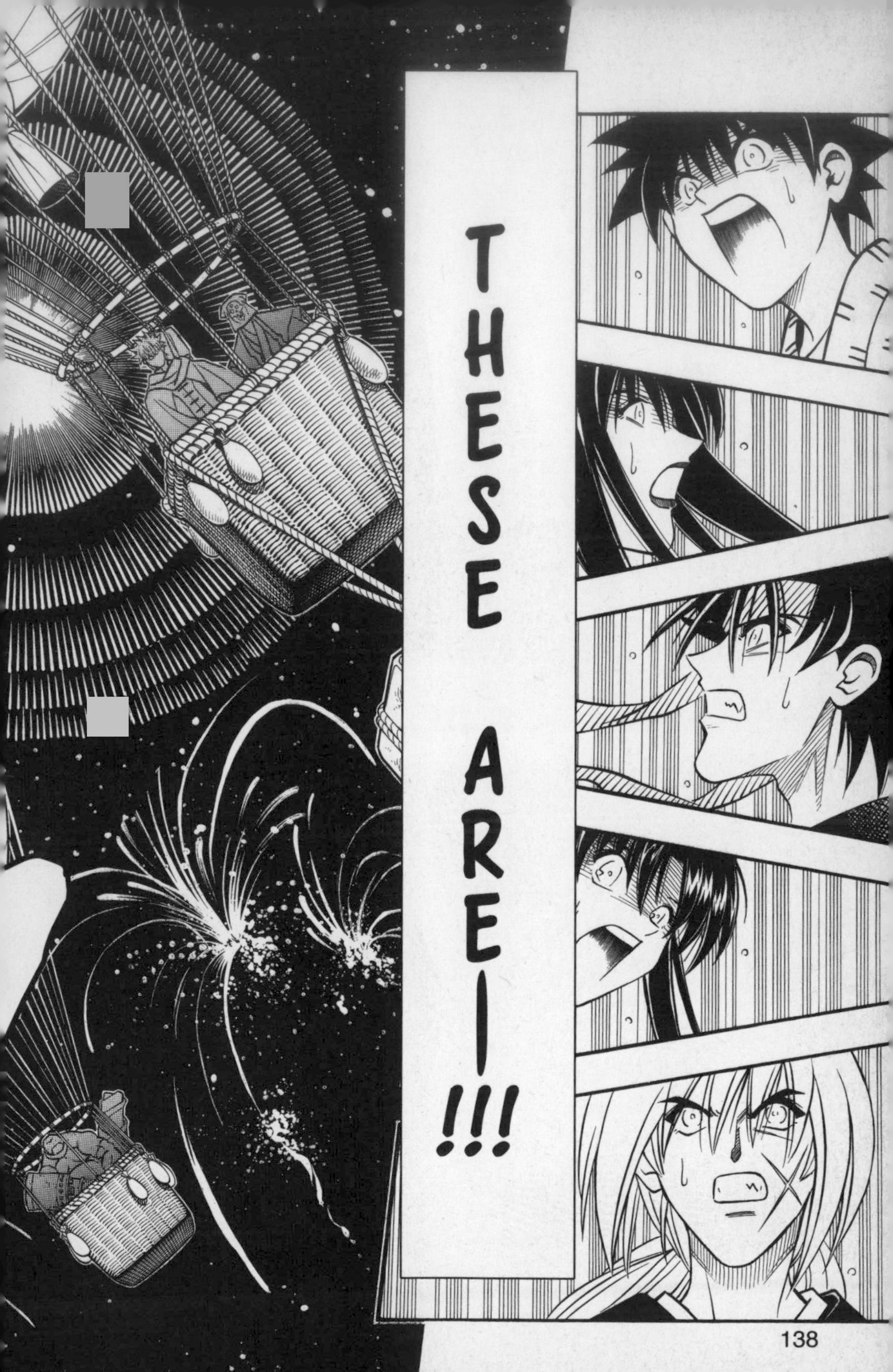
THESE ARE!!!

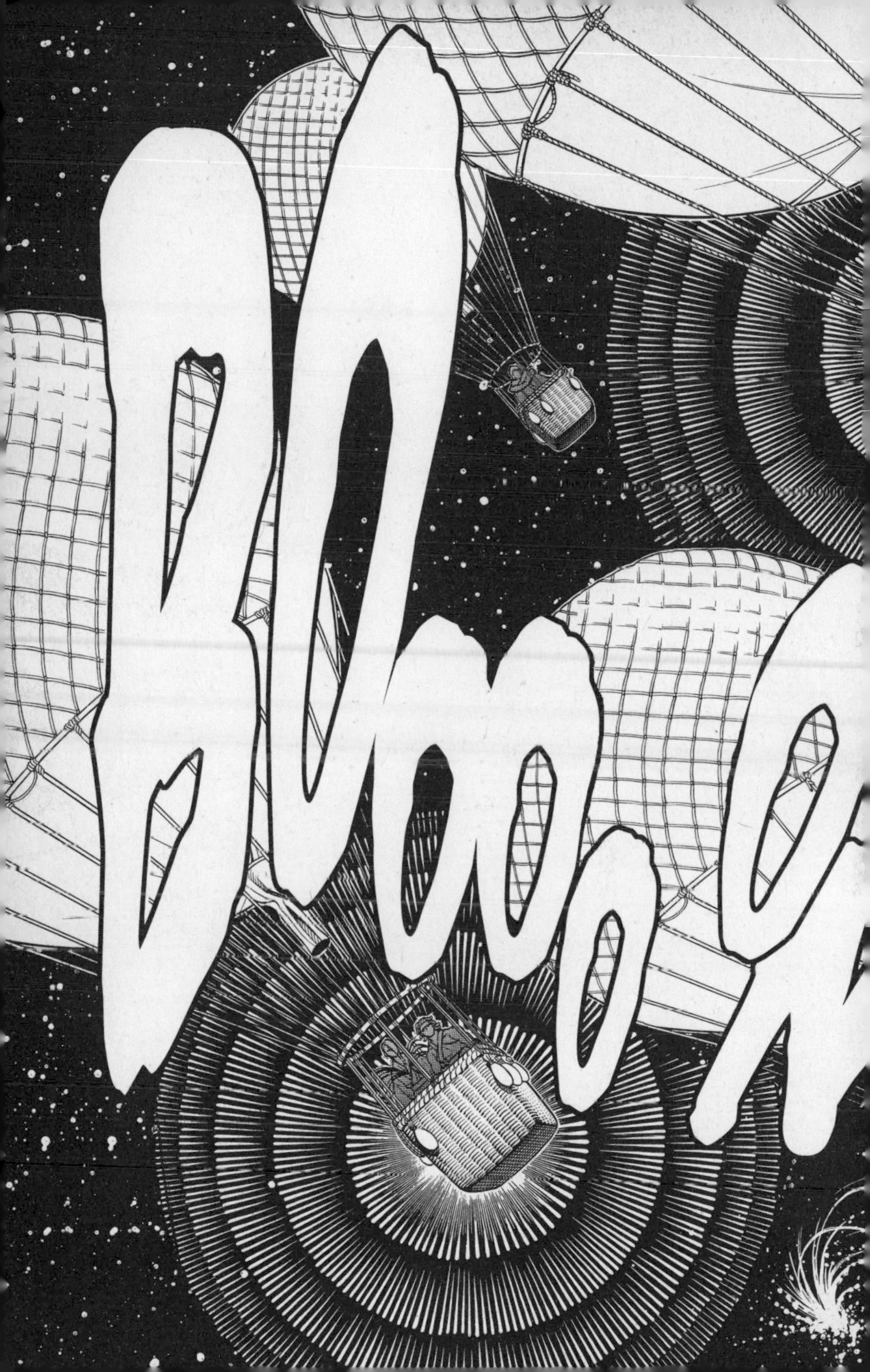

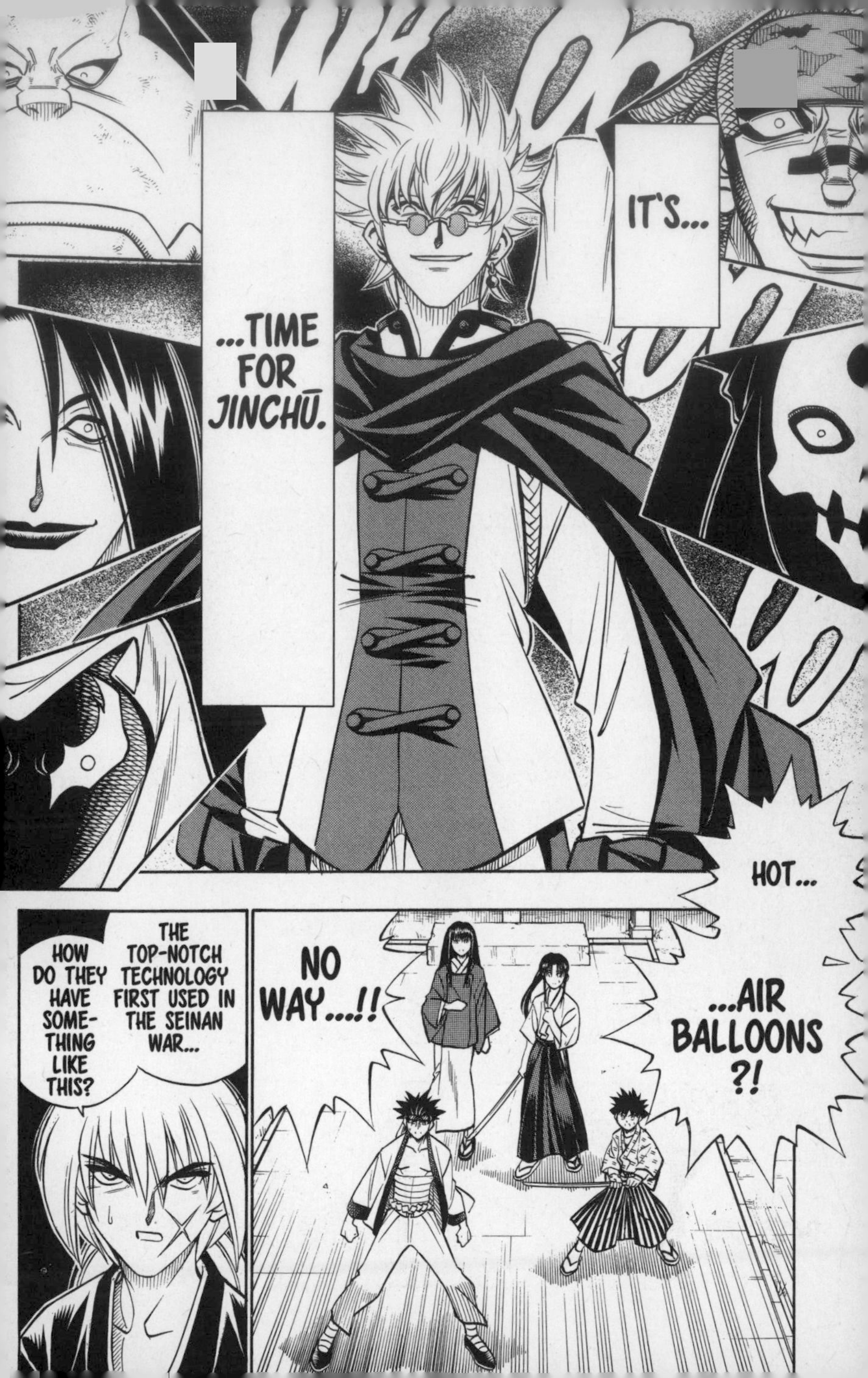
IT'S...
...TIME FOR JINCHŪ.
HOT...
...AIR BALLOONS?!
NO WAY...!!
THE TOP-NOTCH TECHNOLOGY FIRST USED IN THE SEINAN WAR...
HOW DO THEY HAVE SOME-THING LIKE THIS?

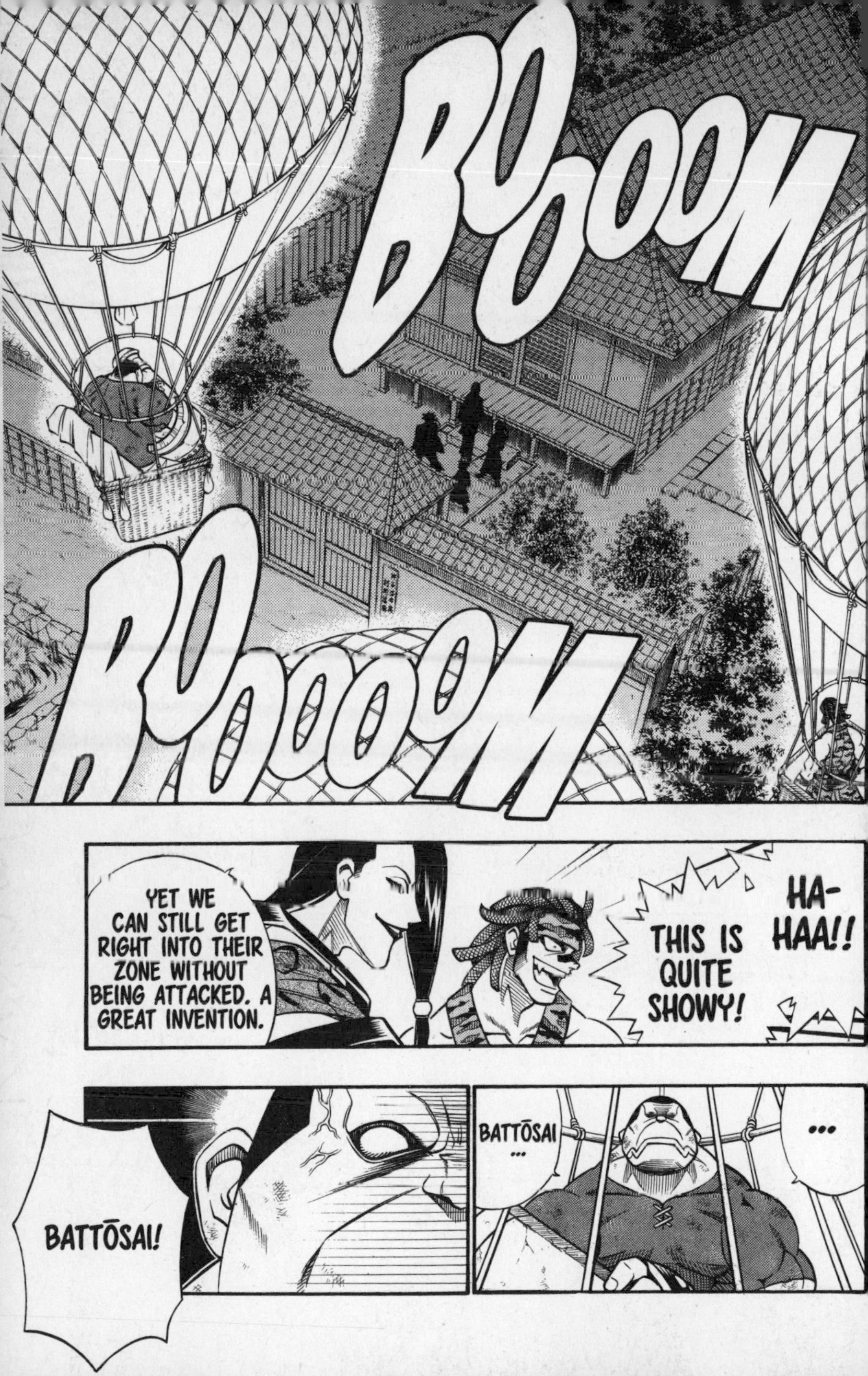
BOOOM
BOOOOM
HA-HAA!!
THIS IS QUITE SHOWY!
YET WE CAN STILL GET RIGHT INTO THEIR ZONE WITHOUT BEING ATTACKED. A GREAT INVENTION.
...
BATTŌSAI ...
BATTŌSAI!

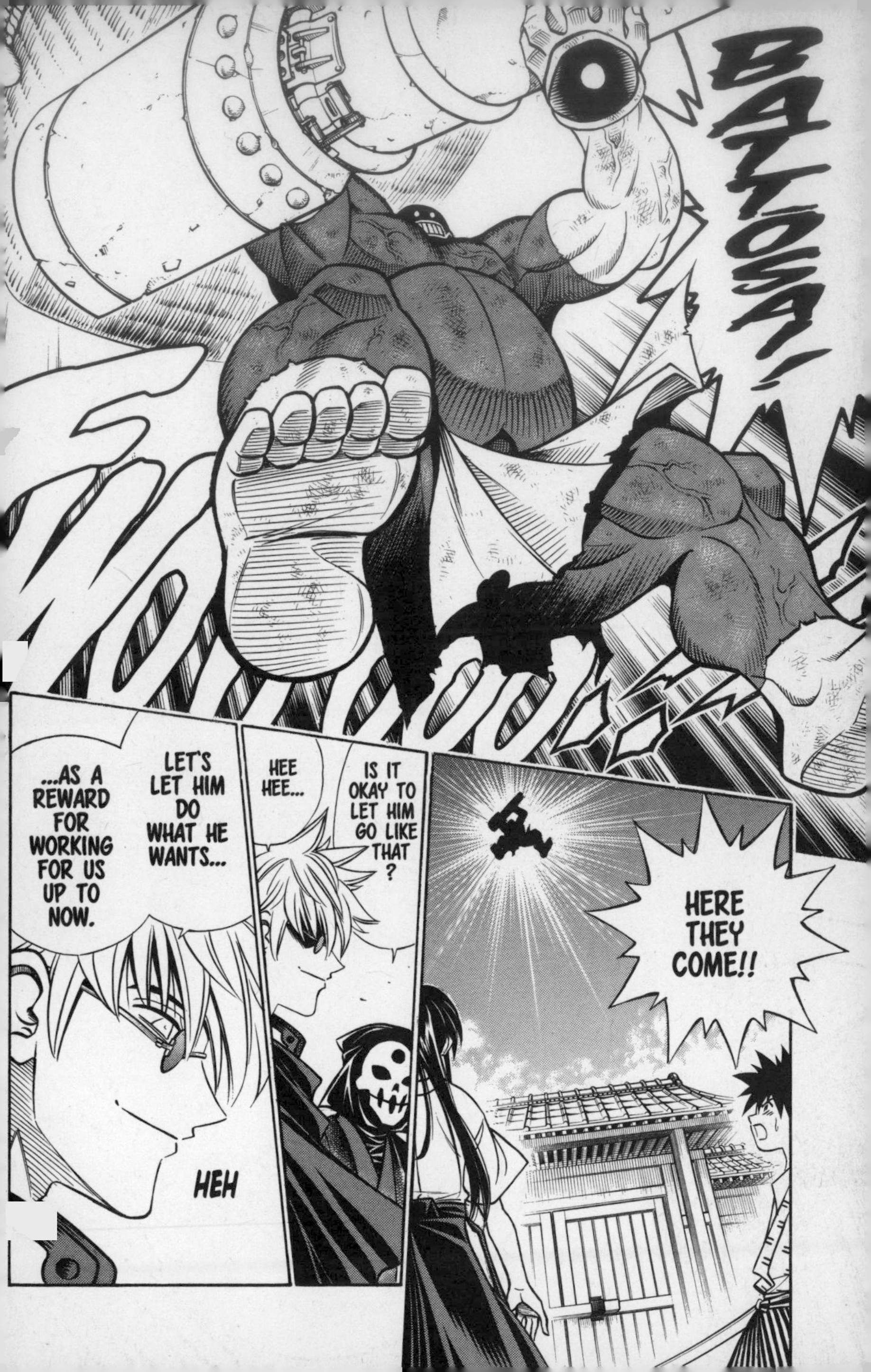
BATTOSAI!!
HERE THEY COME!!
IS IT OKAY TO LET HIM GO LIKE THAT?
HEE HEE...
LET'S LET HIM DO WHAT HE WANTS...
...AS A REWARD FOR WORKING FOR US UP TO NOW.
HEH

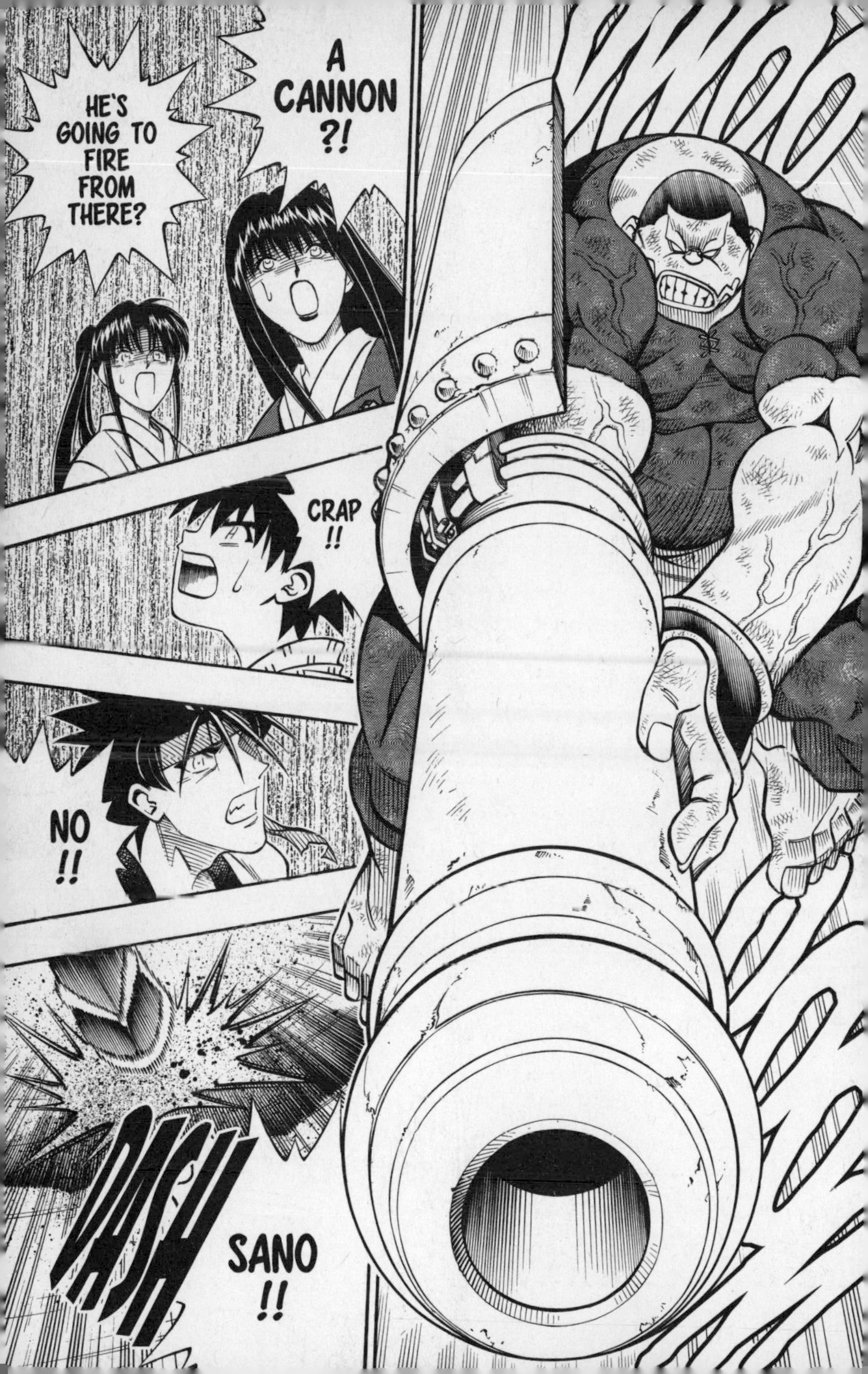
A CANNON ?!
HE'S GOING TO FIRE FROM THERE?
CRAP !!
NO !!
SANO !!

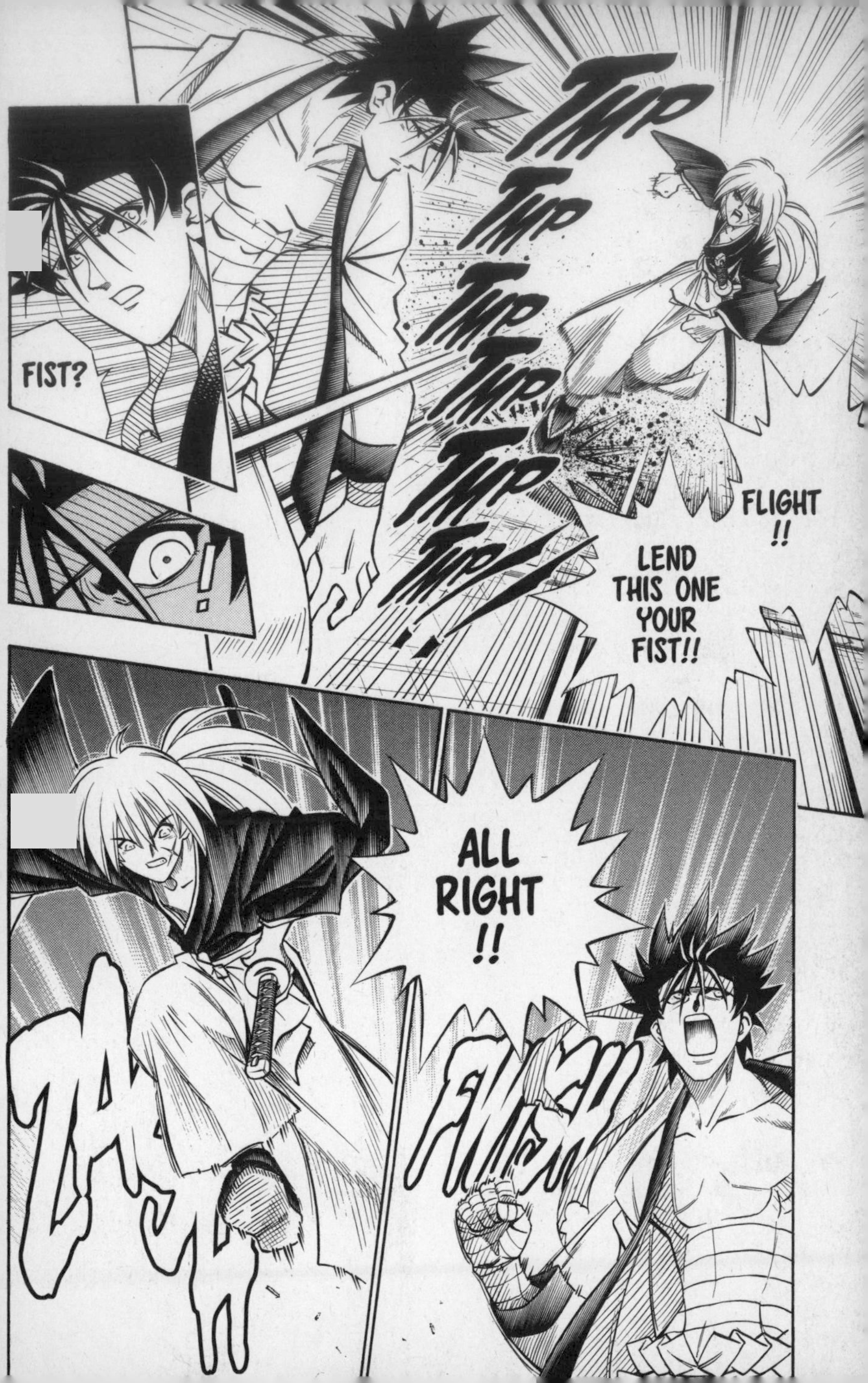
FLIGHT
!!
LEND THIS ONE YOUR FIST!!
FIST?
!
ALL RIGHT !!

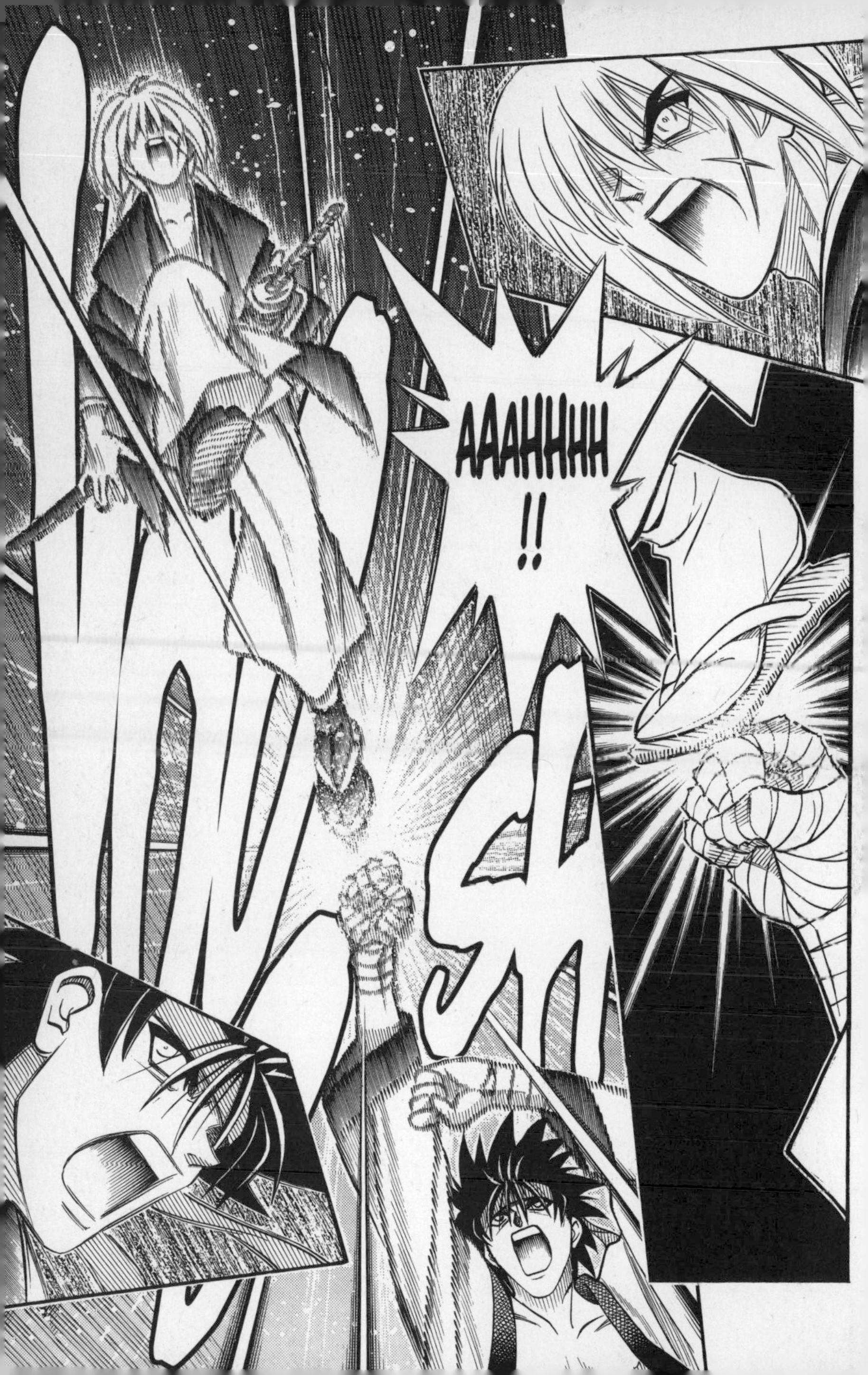
AAAHHHH
!!

Rurouni Kenshin

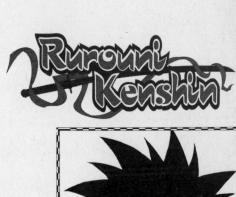

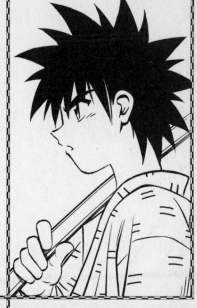

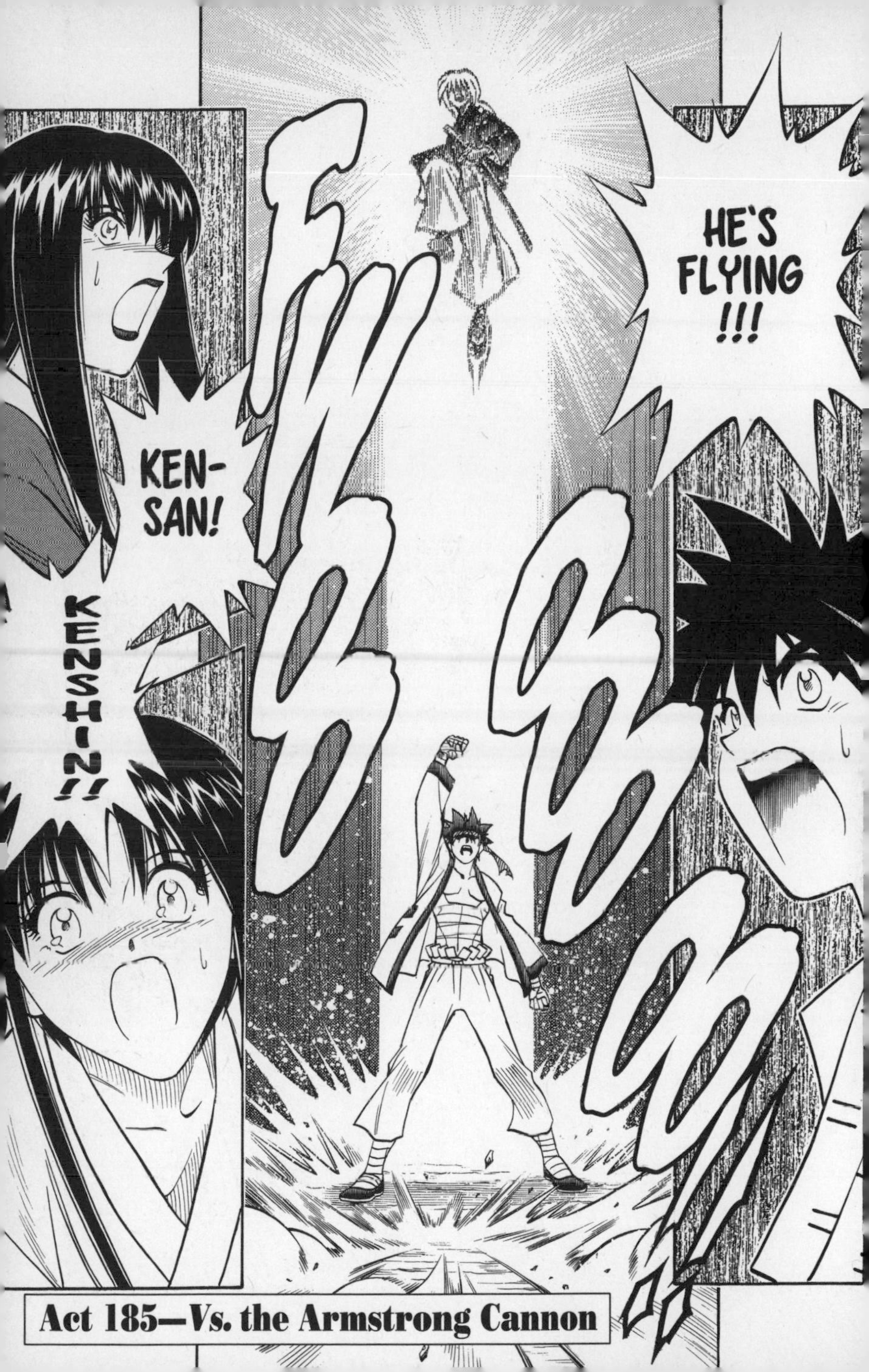
HE'S FLYING !!!
KEN-SAN!
KENSHIN!!

Act 185—Vs. the Armstrong Cannon

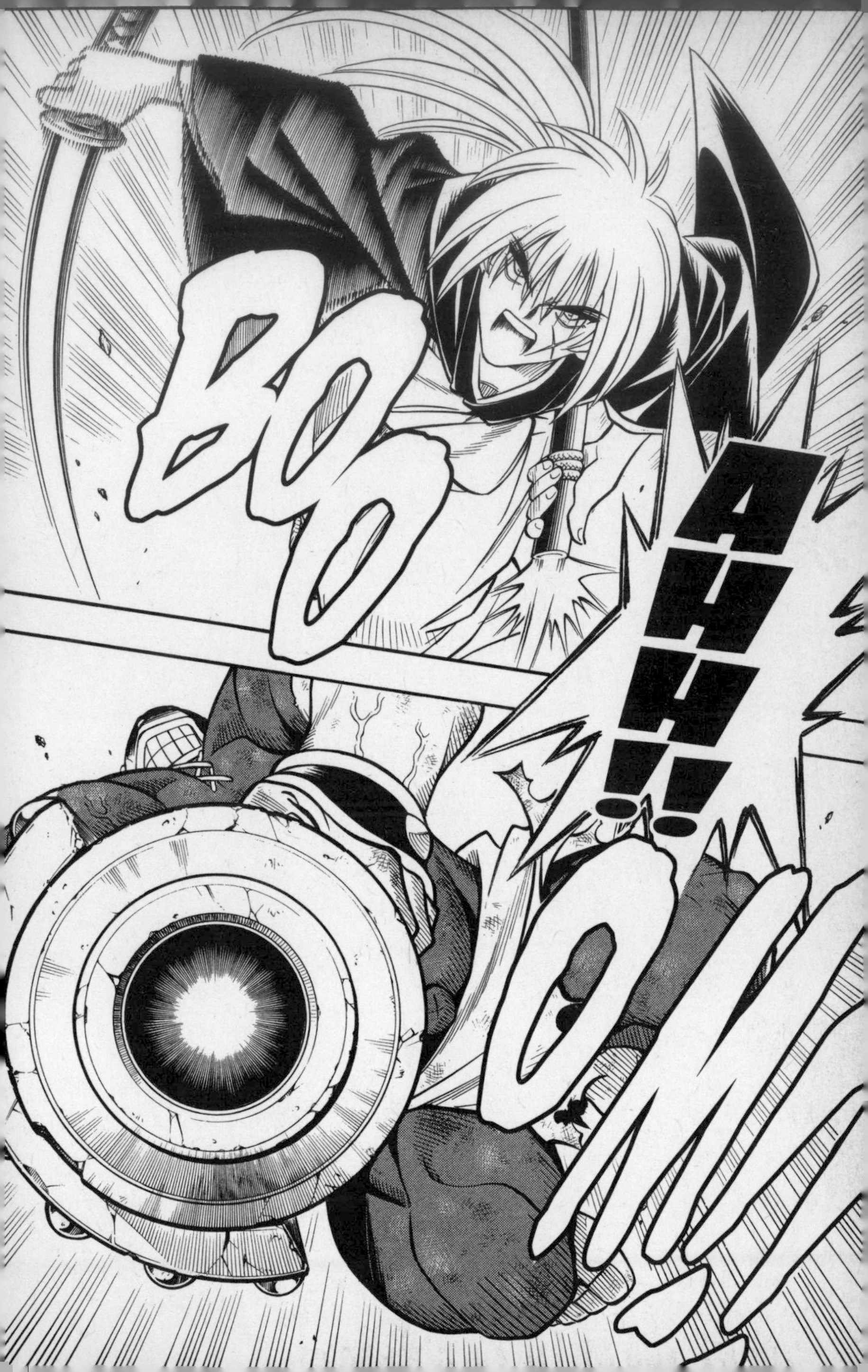
AHH!!
BOOOM

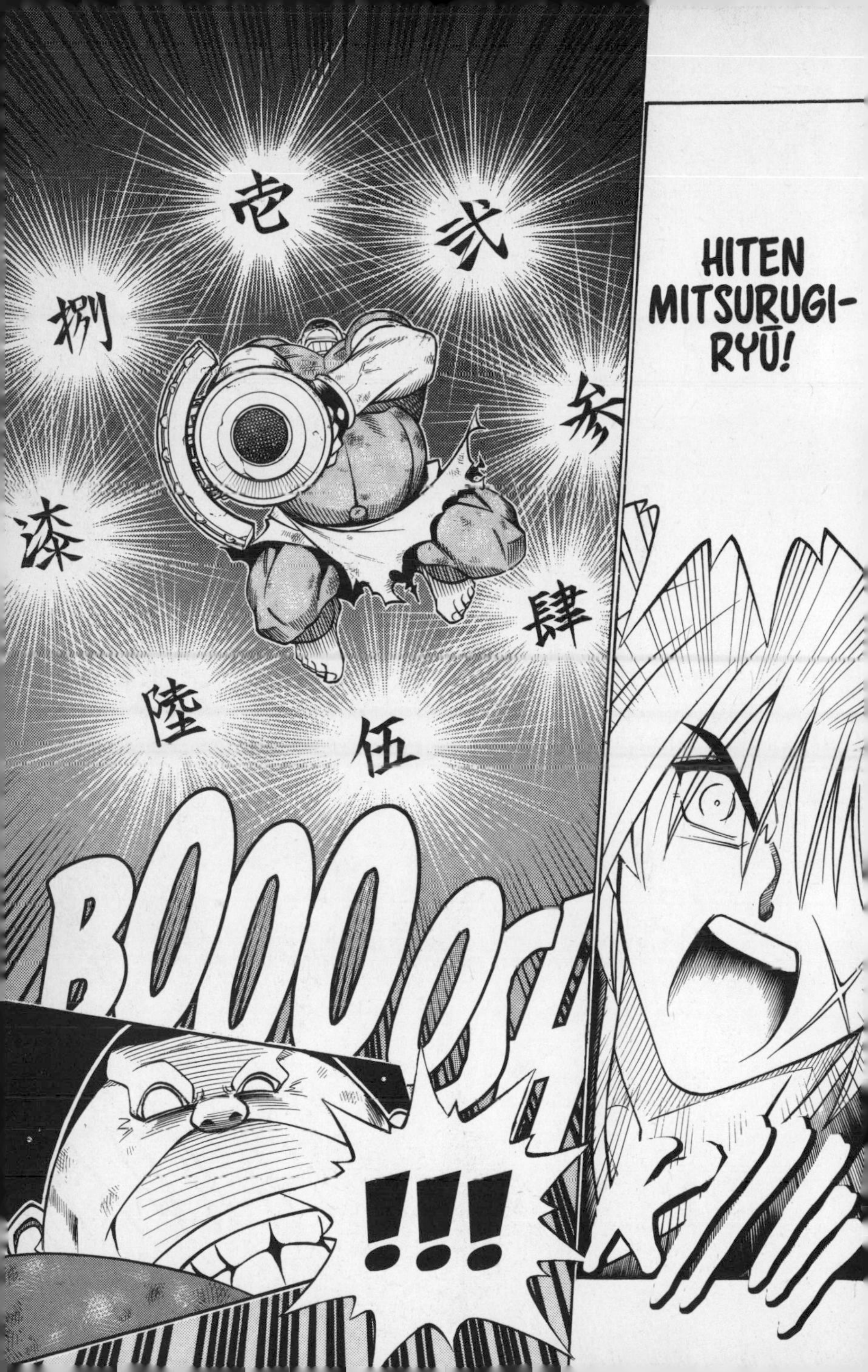
HITEN MITSURUGI-RYŪ!
壱
弐
参
肆
伍
陸
漆
捌
!!!

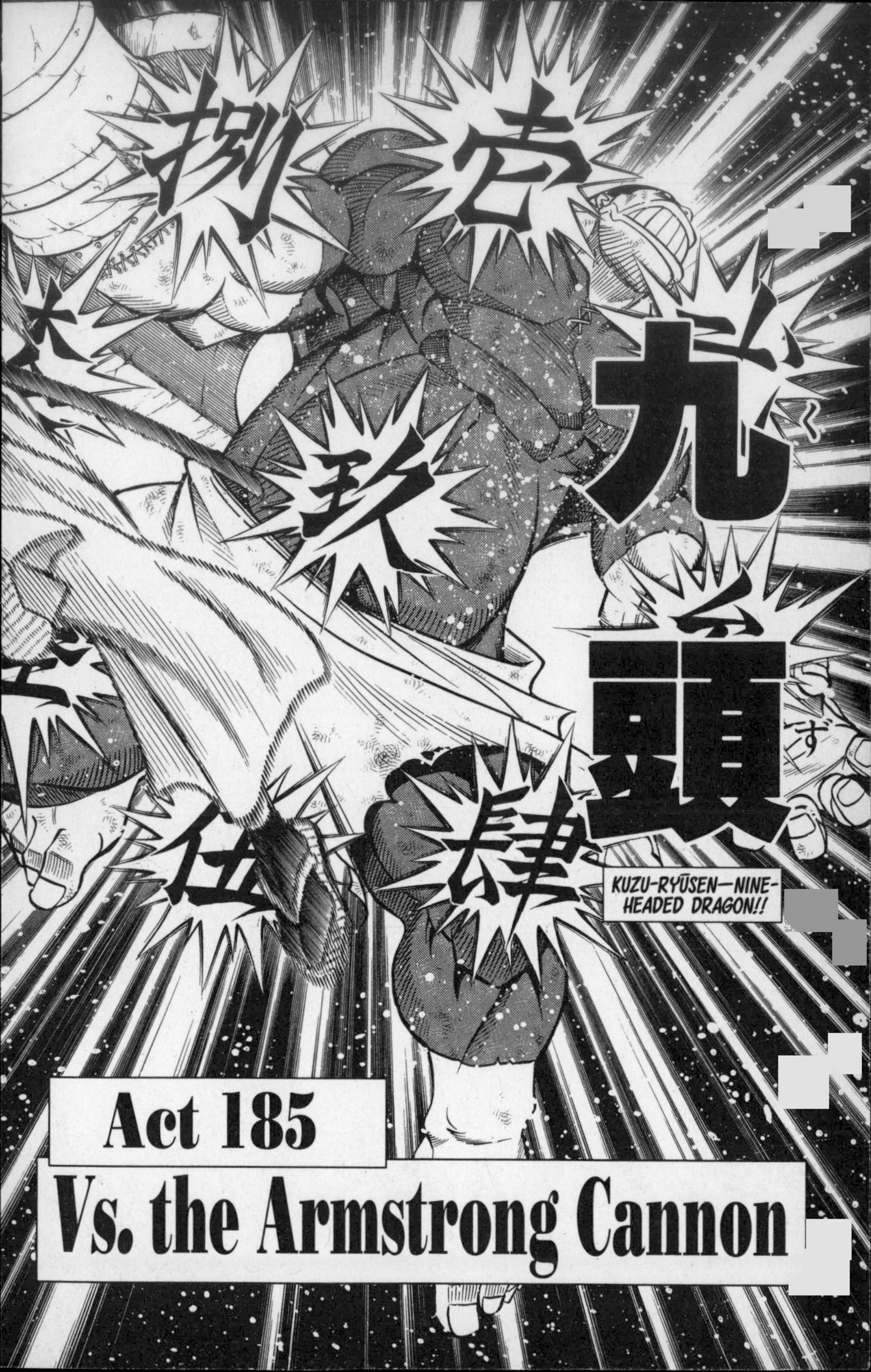
捌
壱
玖
九頭
肆
伍
KUZU-RYŪSEN—NINE-HEADED DRAGON!!
Act 185
Vs. the Armstrong Cannon

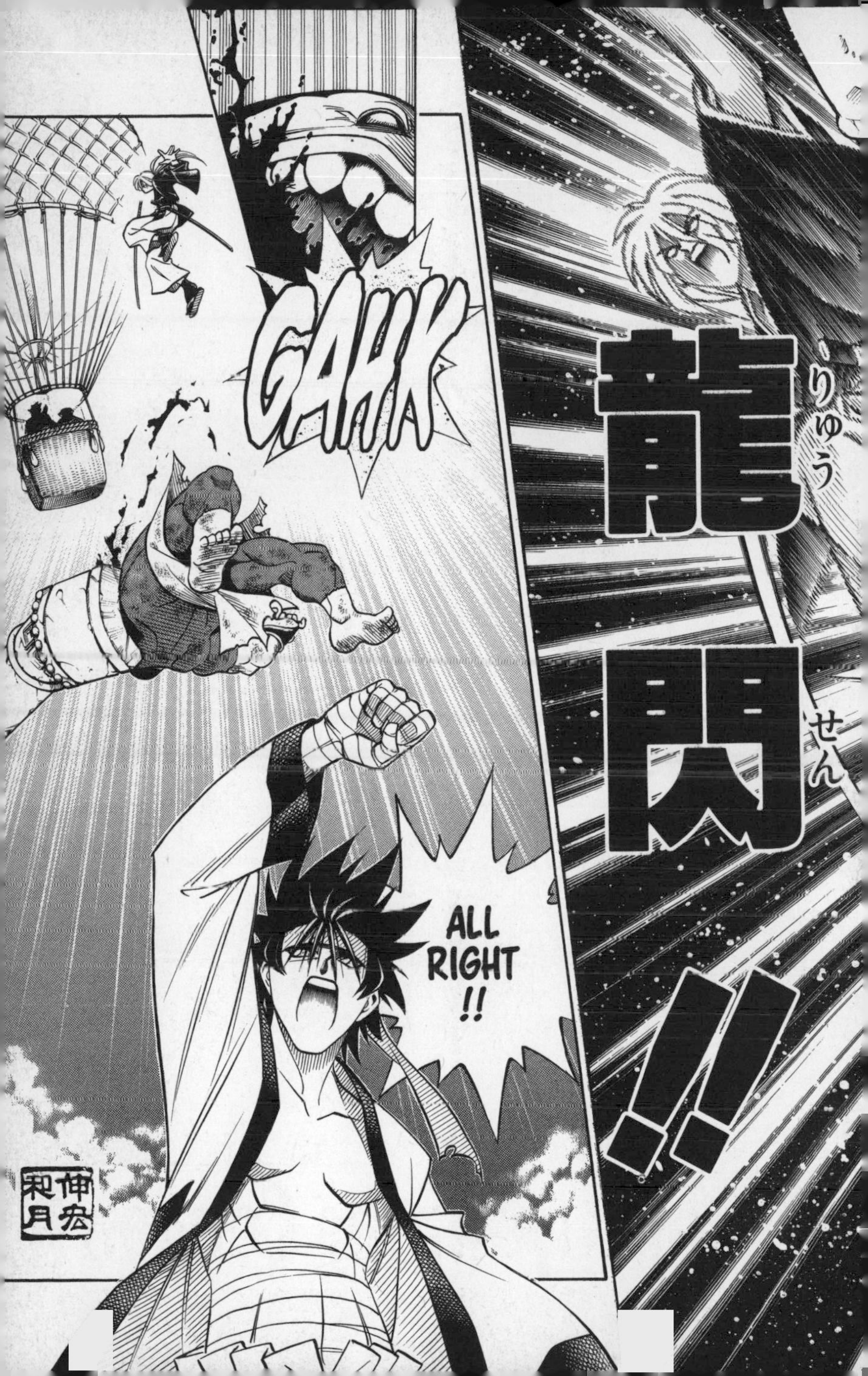
龍閃!!
りゅう せん
GAHK
ALL RIGHT !!

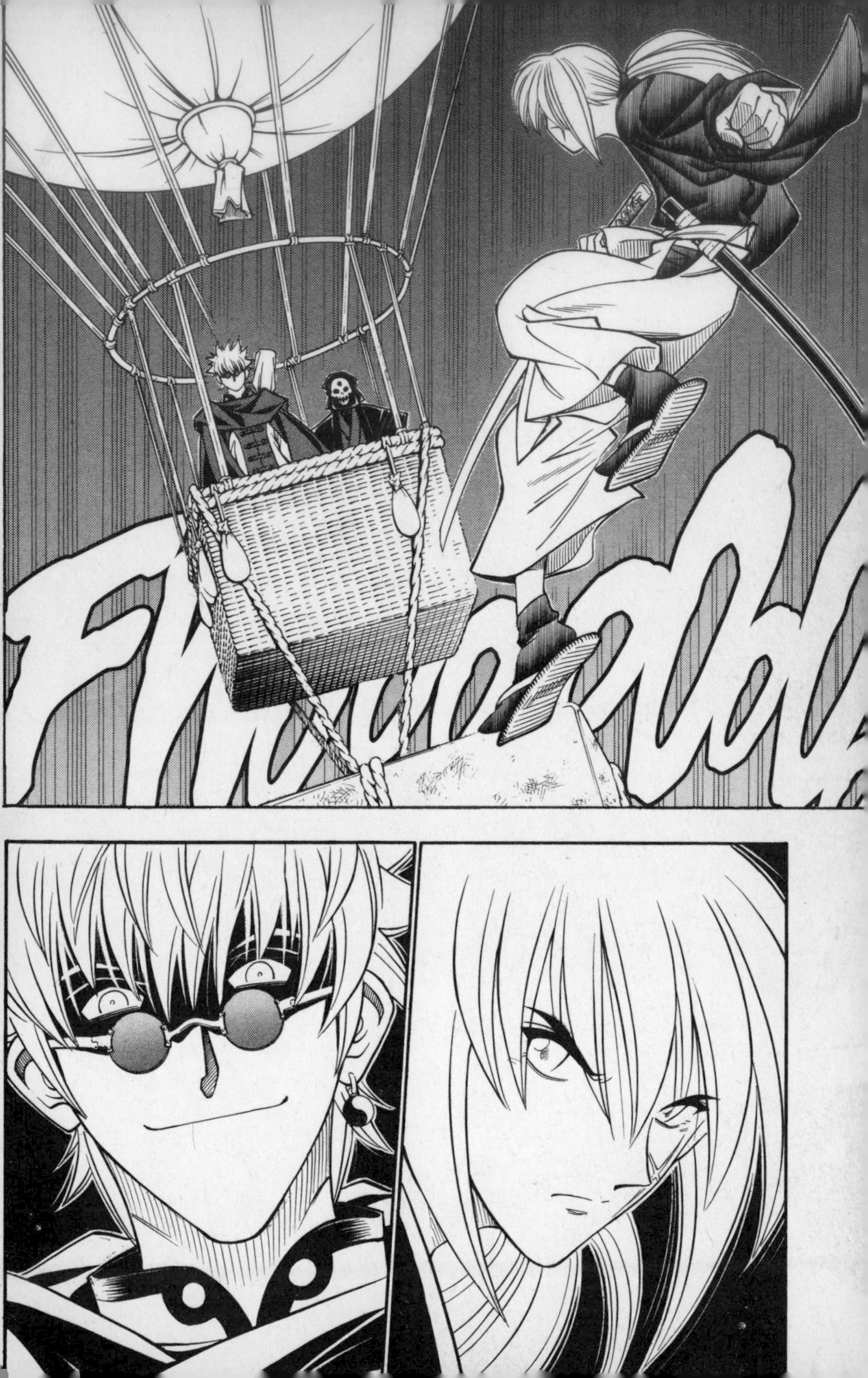

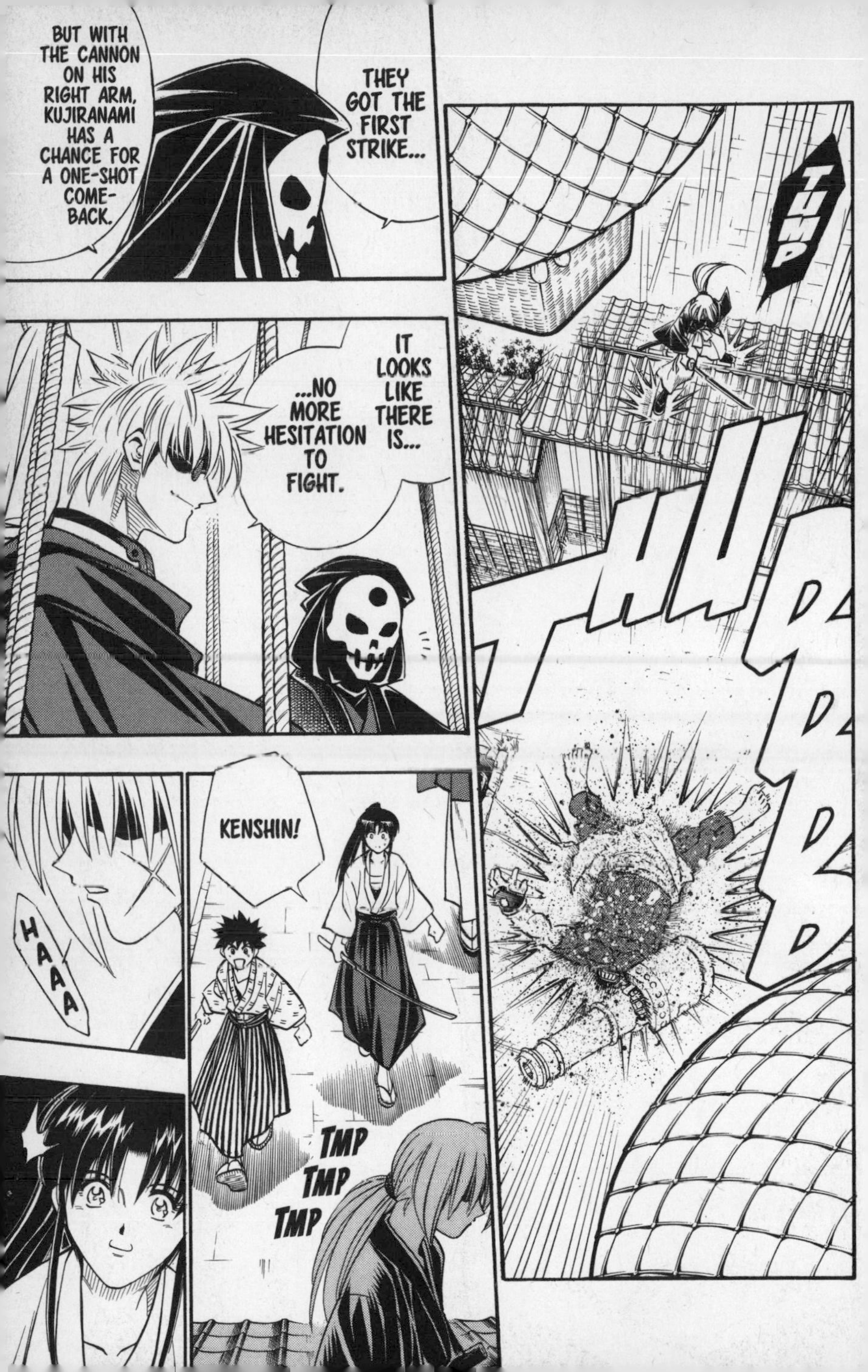
TUMP
THUD
THEY GOT THE FIRST STRIKE...
BUT WITH THE CANNON ON HIS RIGHT ARM, KUJIRANAMI HAS A CHANCE FOR A ONE-SHOT COME-BACK.
IT LOOKS LIKE THERE IS...
...NO MORE HESITATION TO FIGHT.
KENSHIN!
TMP TMP TMP
HAAA

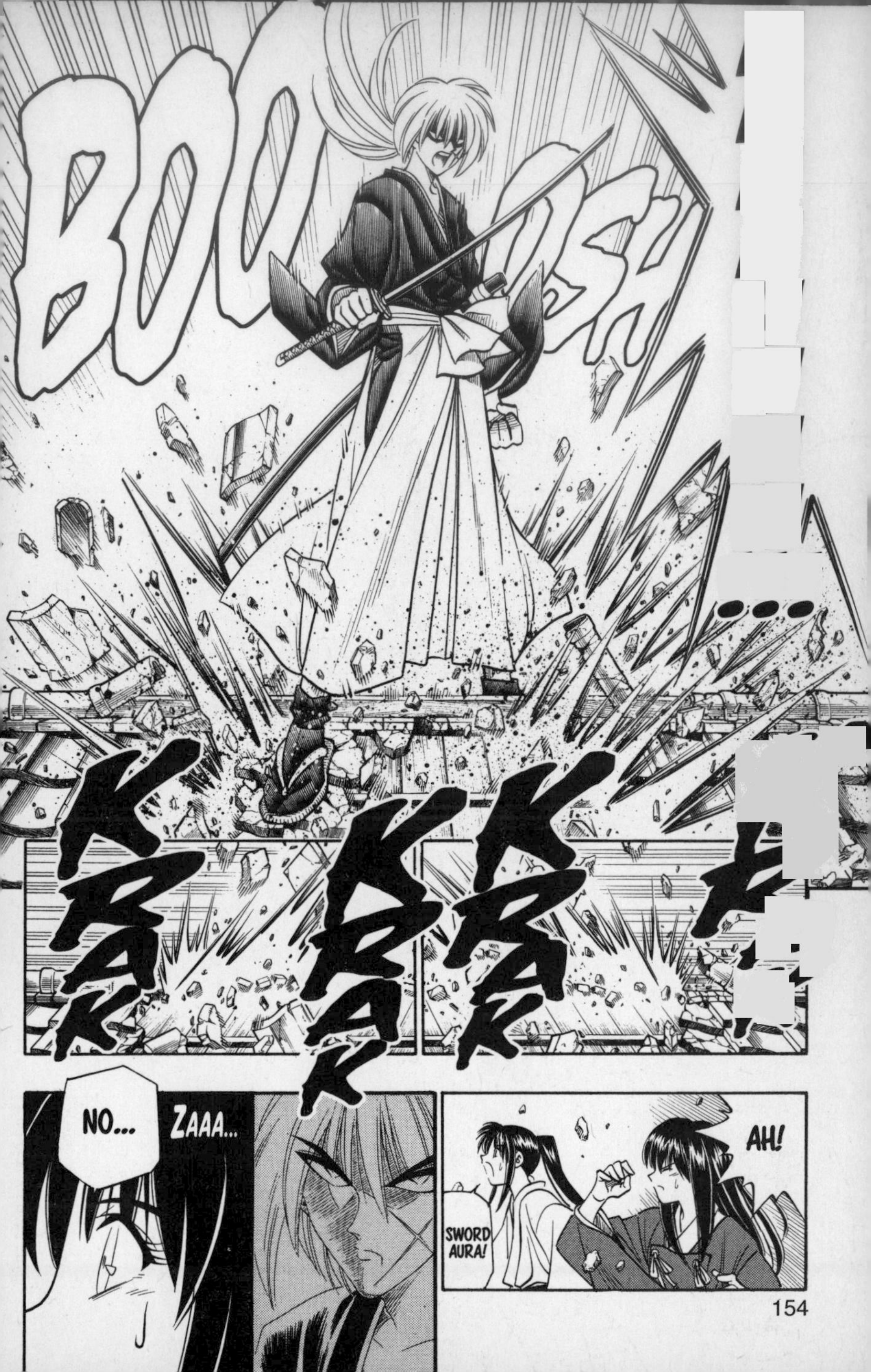
BOOOSH
AH!
SWORD AURA!
NO...
ZAAA...

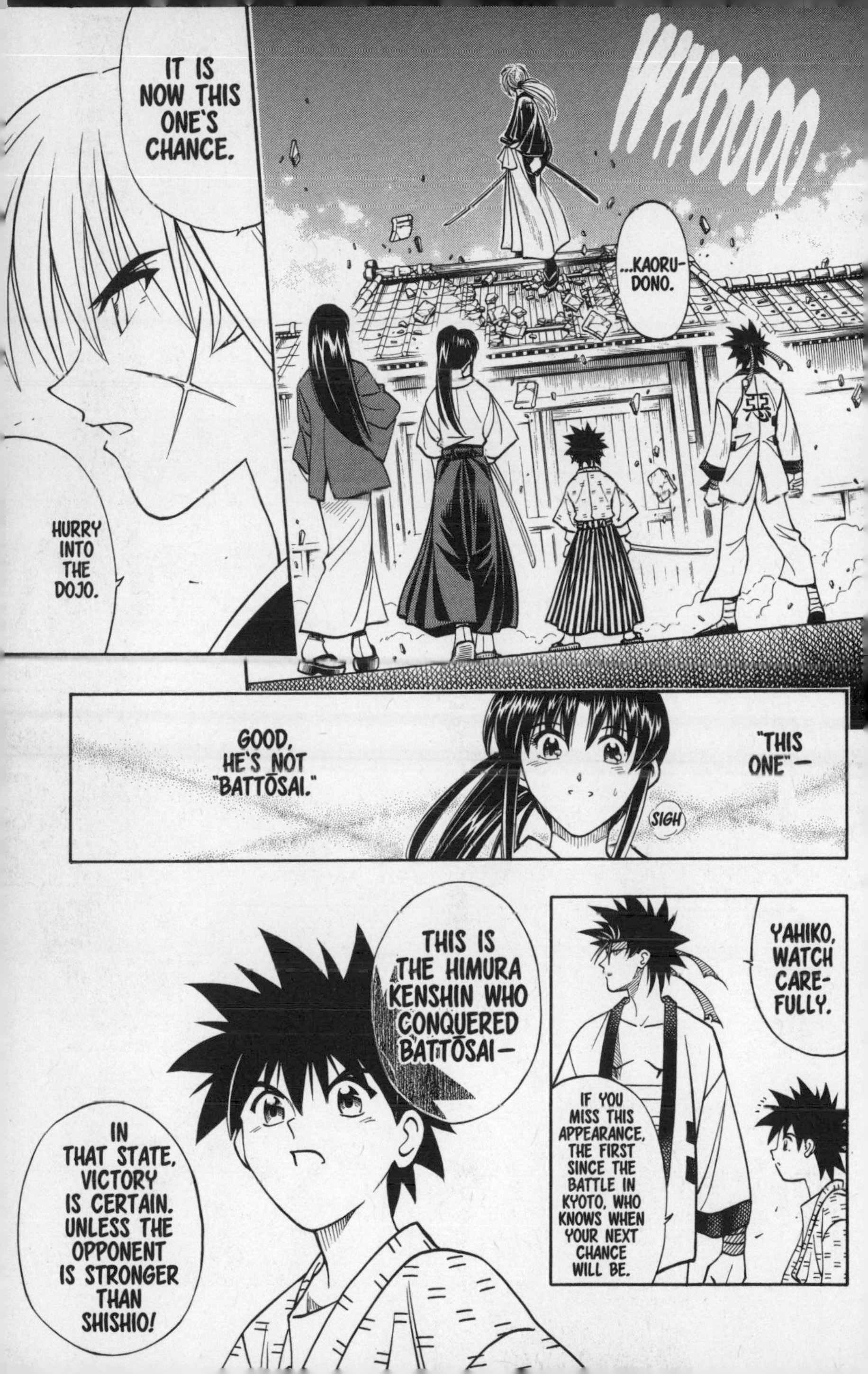
WHOOOO
...KAORU-DONO.
IT IS NOW THIS ONE'S CHANCE.
HURRY INTO THE DOJO.
"THIS ONE"—
SIGH
GOOD, HE'S NOT "BATTŌSAI."
YAHIKO, WATCH CAREFULLY.
IF YOU MISS THIS APPEARANCE, THE FIRST SINCE THE BATTLE IN KYOTO, WHO KNOWS WHEN YOUR NEXT CHANCE WILL BE.
THIS IS THE HIMURA KENSHIN WHO CONQUERED BATTŌSAI—
IN THAT STATE, VICTORY IS CERTAIN. UNLESS THE OPPONENT IS STRONGER THAN SHISHIO!

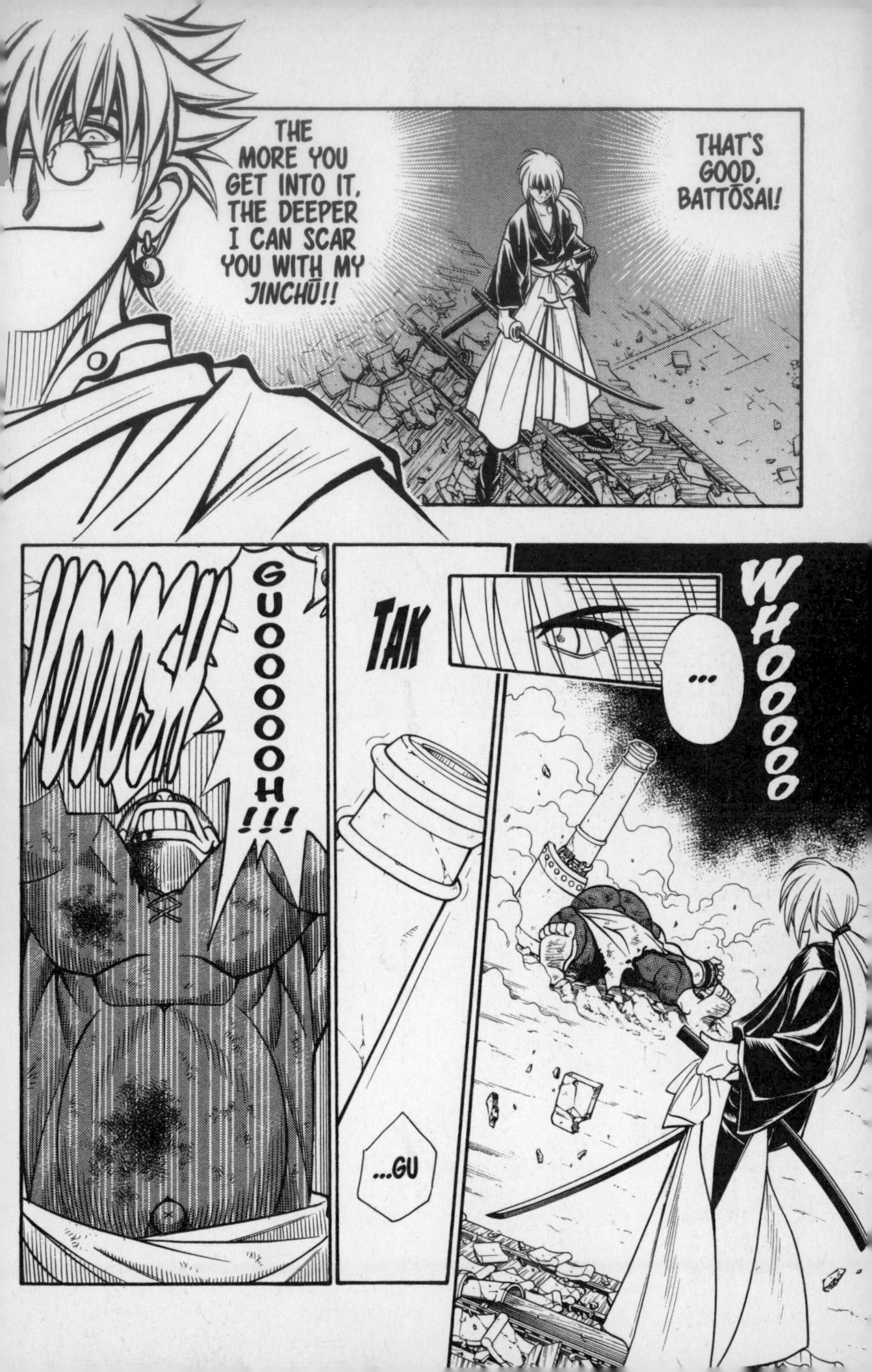
THAT'S GOOD, BATTŌSAI!
THE MORE YOU GET INTO IT, THE DEEPER I CAN SCAR YOU WITH MY JINCHŪ!!
WHOOOOOO
...
TAK
...GU
GUOOOOOOH!!!

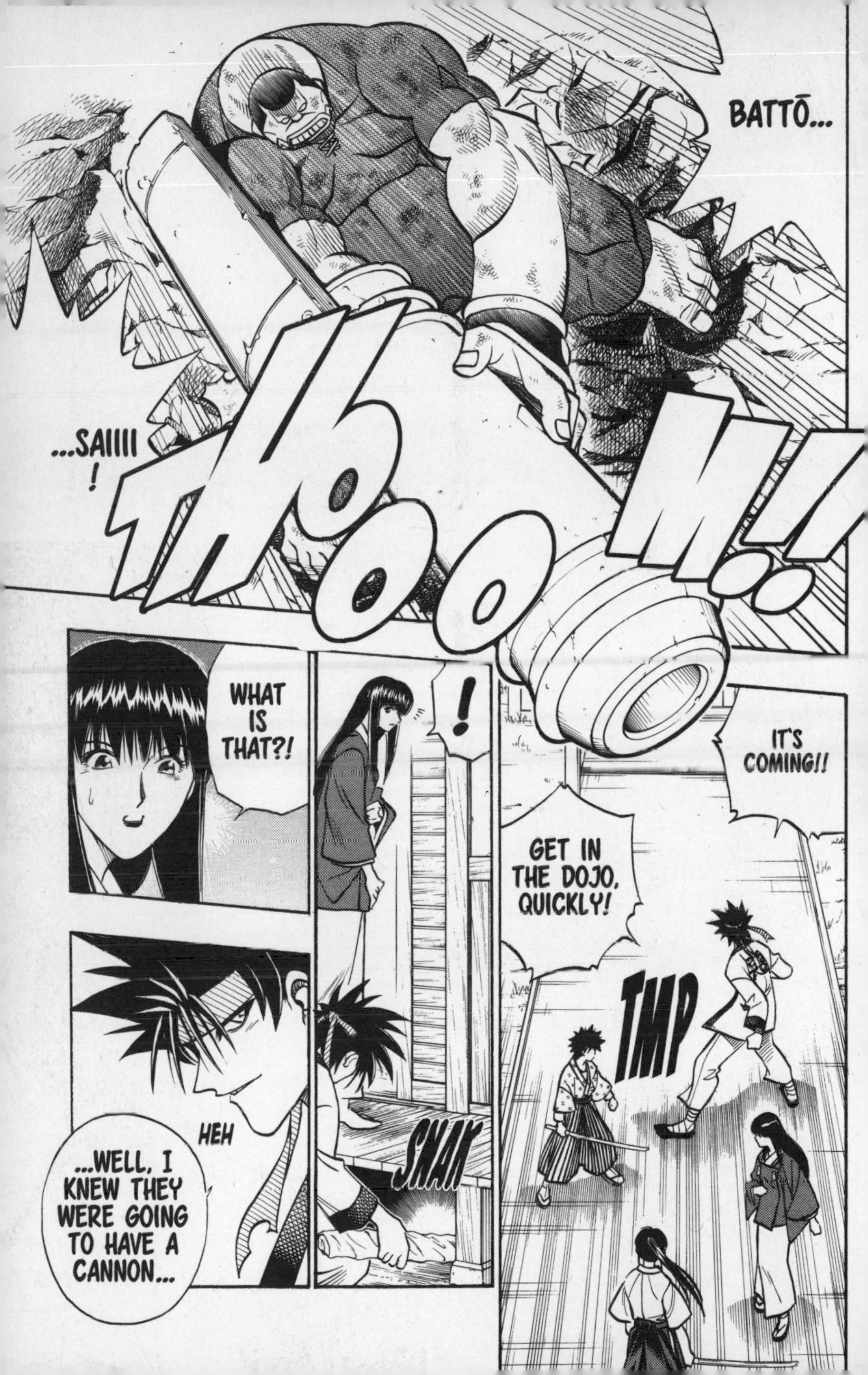
BATTŌ...
...SAIIII !
THOOM!!
IT'S COMING!!
GET IN THE DOJO, QUICKLY!
TMP
!
WHAT IS THAT?!
SHAK
HEH
...WELL, I KNEW THEY WERE GOING TO HAVE A CANNON...

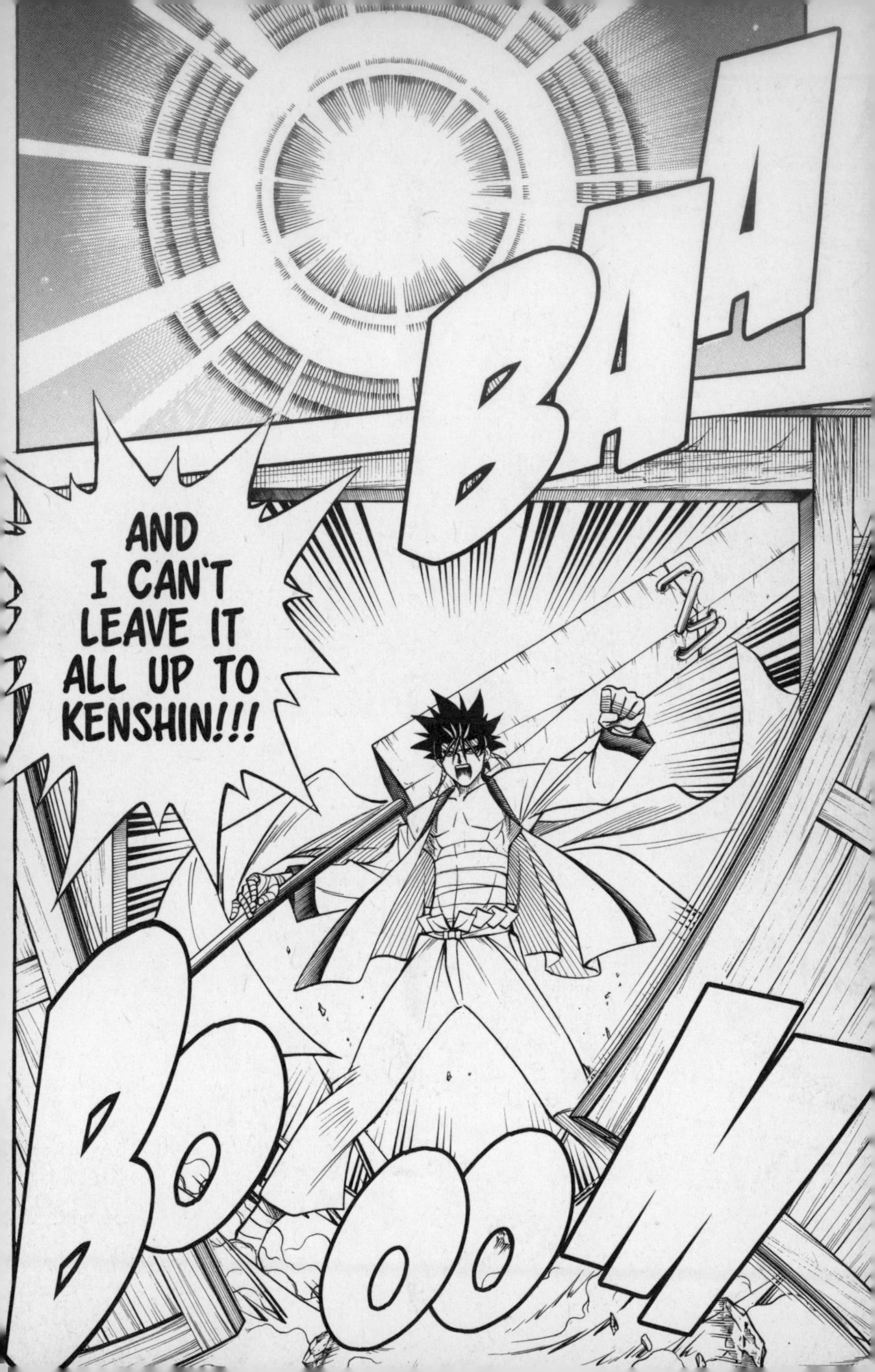
AND I CAN'T LEAVE IT ALL UP TO KENSHIN!!!

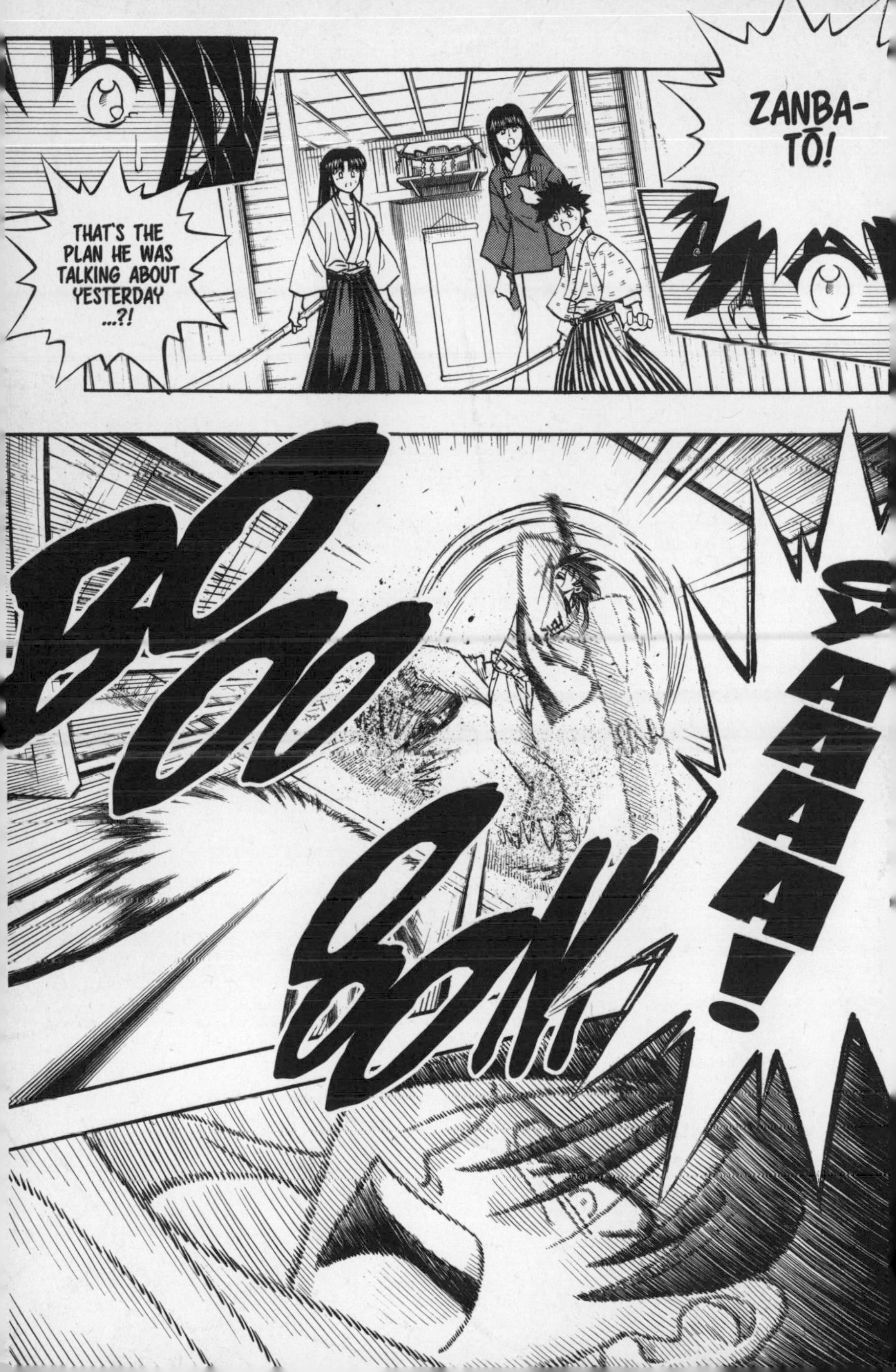

ZANBA-TŌ!
THAT'S THE PLAN HE WAS TALKING ABOUT YESTERDAY ...?!
GYAAAAA!

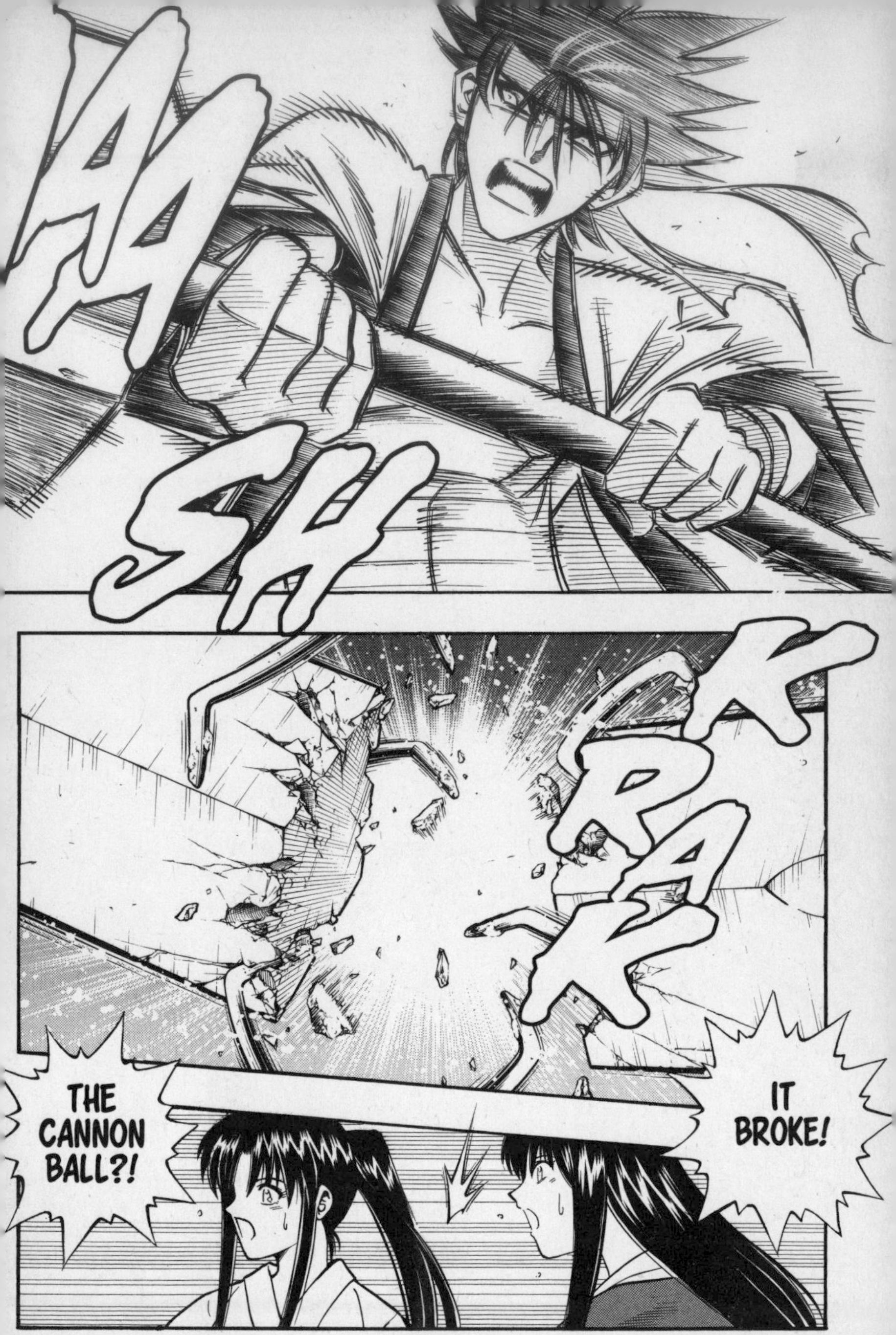
AASH
KRAK
IT BROKE!
THE CANNON BALL?!

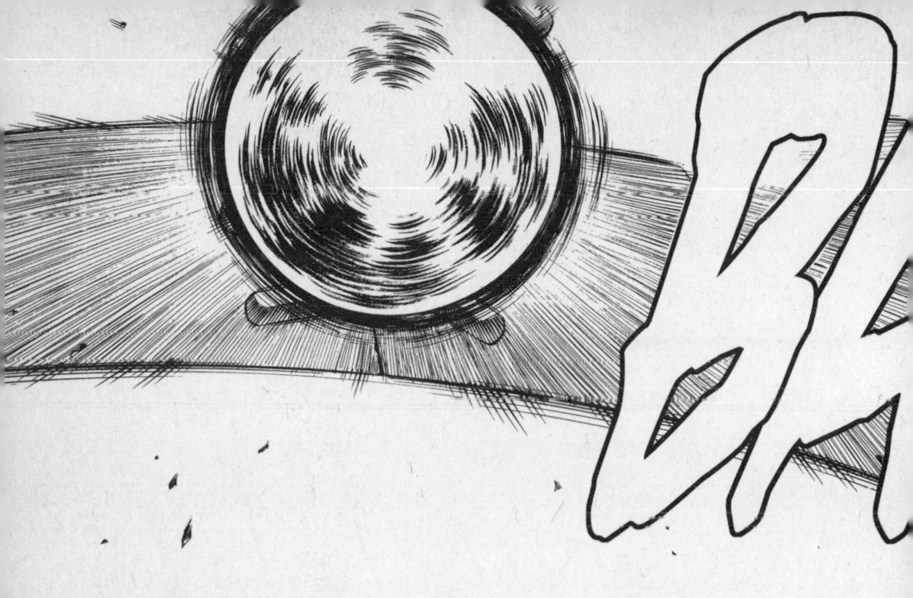
BA

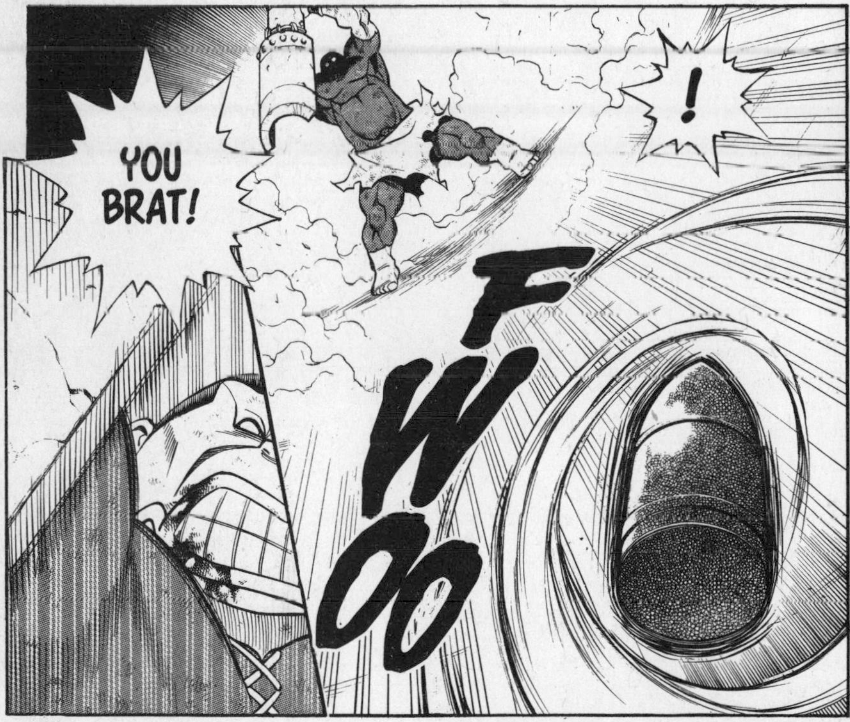
!
YOU BRAT!
FWOO

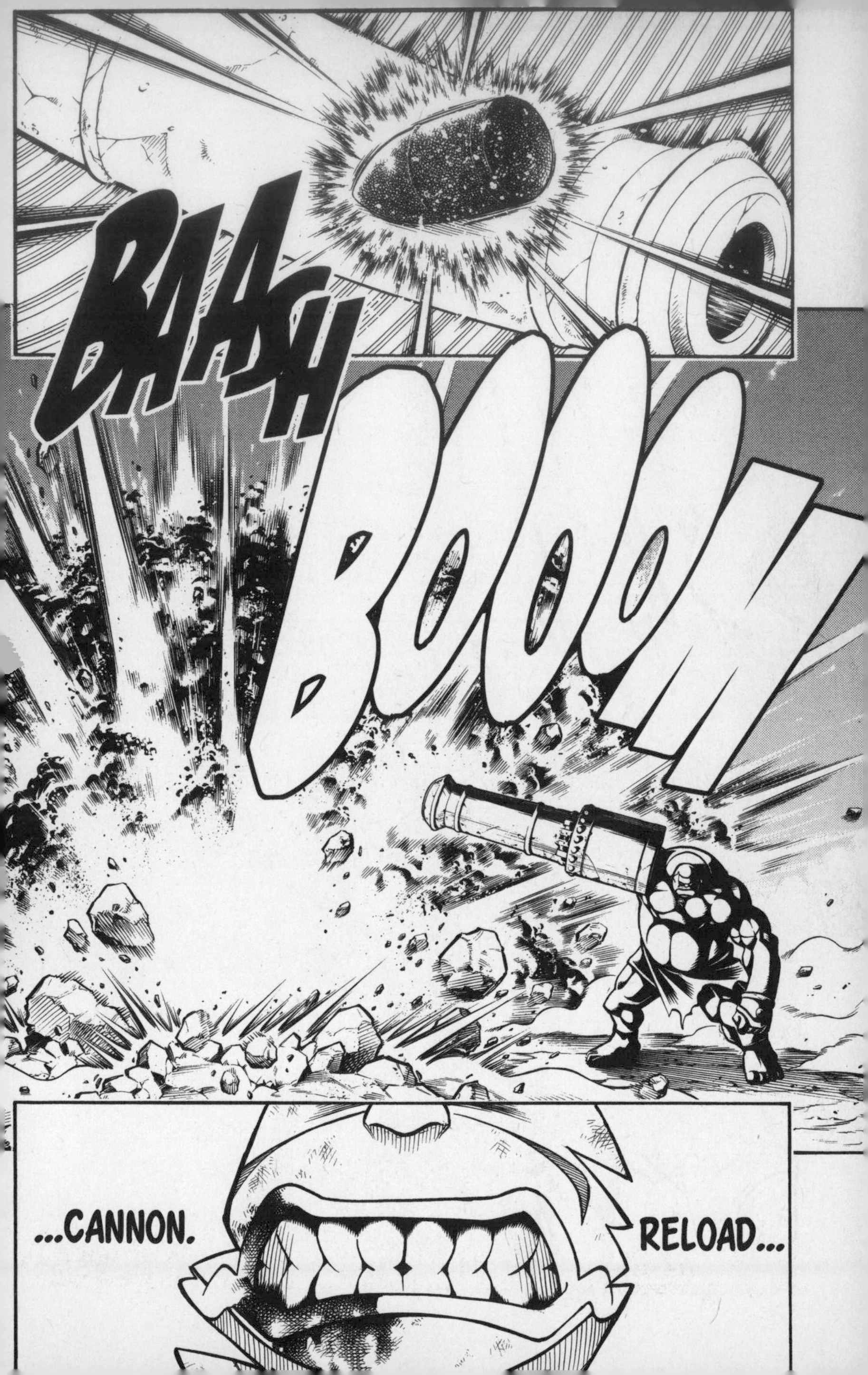
BAASH
BOOOM
RELOAD...
...CANNON.

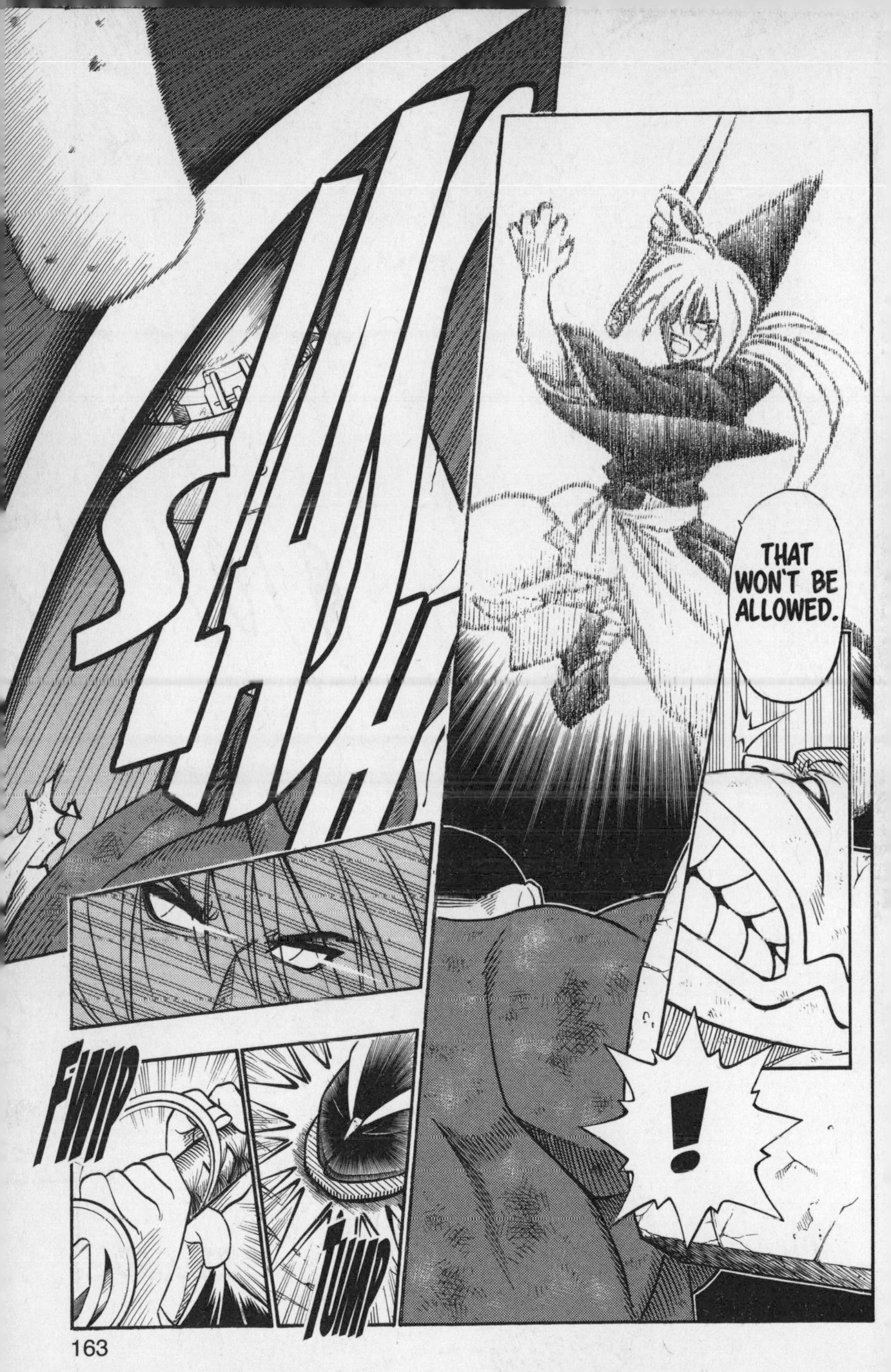
THAT WON'T BE ALLOWED.
!
FWIP
tump

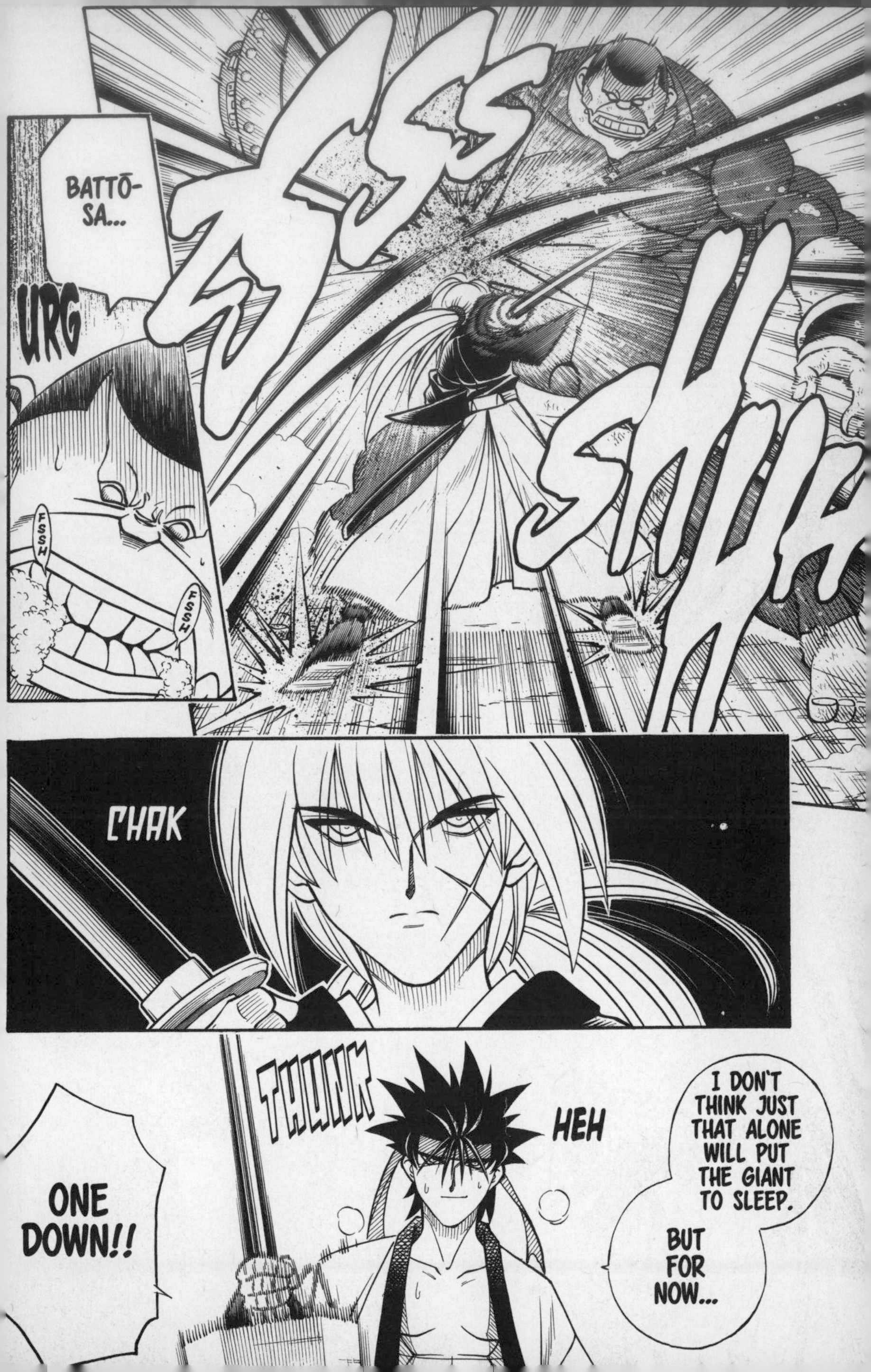
BATTŌ-SA...
URG
FSSH
FSSH
CHAK
I DON'T THINK JUST THAT ALONE WILL PUT THE GIANT TO SLEEP.
BUT FOR NOW...
HEH
THUNK
ONE DOWN!!

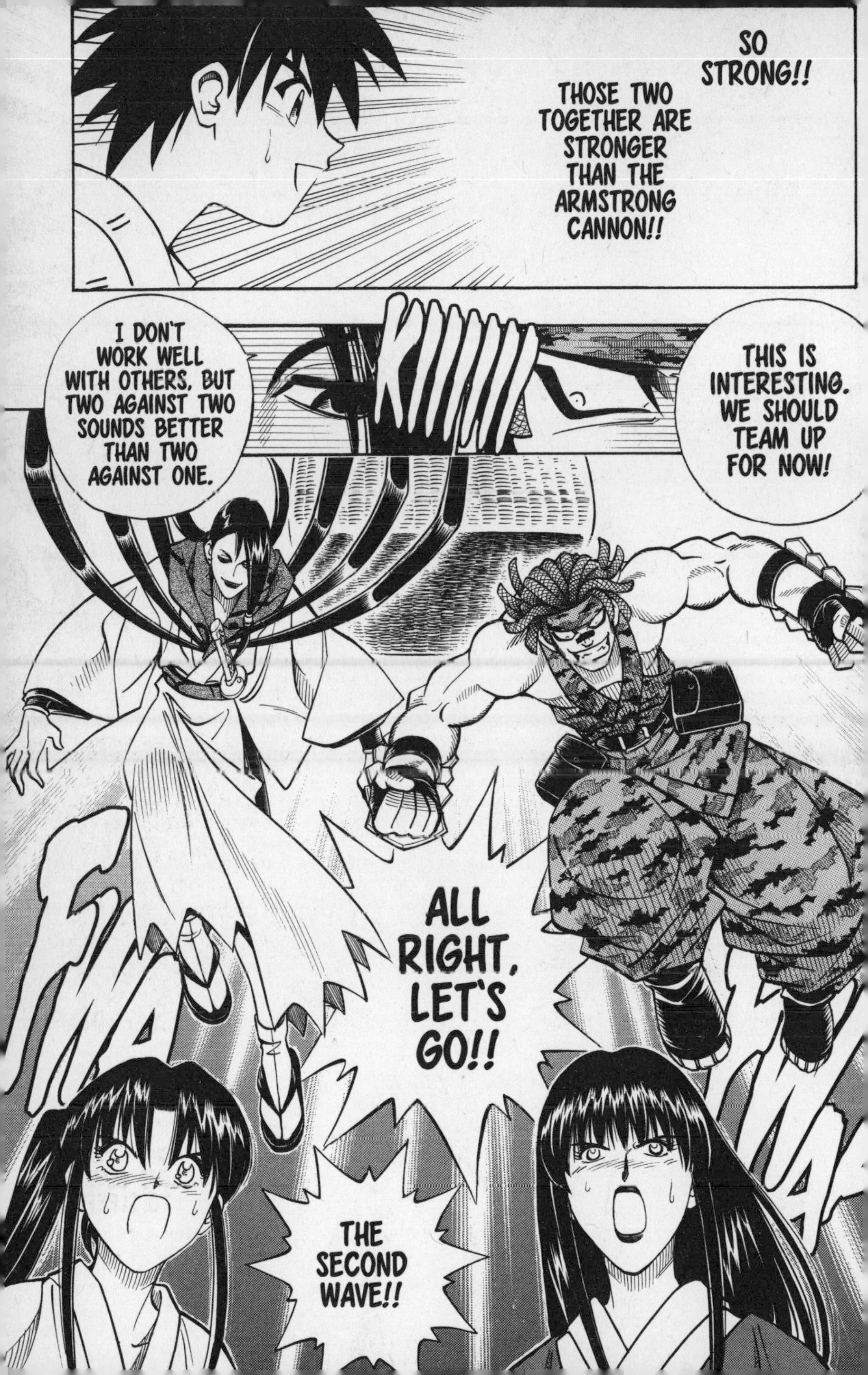
SO STRONG!!
THOSE TWO TOGETHER ARE STRONGER THAN THE ARMSTRONG CANNON!!
THIS IS INTERESTING. WE SHOULD TEAM UP FOR NOW!
I DON'T WORK WELL WITH OTHERS, BUT TWO AGAINST TWO SOUNDS BETTER THAN TWO AGAINST ONE.
ALL RIGHT, LET'S GO!!
THE SECOND WAVE!!

"FREE TALK"

Long time no see, this is Watsuki. We've finally found a place to move to, but now I can't make time to get ready, and I'm struggling. On top of that, perhaps due to the change in the seasons, or due to age, I've been falling into deeper sleeps. Even if I set six alarm clocks, or the phone keeps ringing, I can't wake up. If I force myself up, I get a bad headache for the rest of the day. I am so trapped.

But even so, I still make time for figures and games. The figures are in a dormant stage. I am waiting for "Manga Freak" and "Manga Cyber Violater" from "Manga Spawn 2," which are yet to be imported at the time I write this. I've said before, "Perhaps there will be figures with internal skeletons not showing the joints on the exterior," and according to the magazine I read the other day, they are coming up soon! There are no details yet, so I can't comment much. But the price of many millions of yen plus the blonde European look goes against Watsuki's...I LOVE black hair, which deters me from buying it. However, I would like to see it (of course, if it was Nakoruru, I would immediately buy it. How stupid). In terms of games, I am playing a little bit of Sega's "Virtual-On Oratorio Tangram." It's fun, but so many patterns of weapons make it complicated, confusing me. Once it comes out for the console, I will play more of it (I say this all the time now). Other than combat games, I would like to play RPGs, SLGs (simulation games), and ADVs (adventure games), but I can't do that while the series is ongoing. I have many things I want to do other than games, but the time is lacking. You can say "Time will never be available while you say there is no time," but I just really don't...Time passes so quickly that I feel like it flows differently just for me. This is a valuable experience, but I would like to be released soon.

However, there is a bit more until this work is completed, so I would like to keep working. I will see you in the next volume.

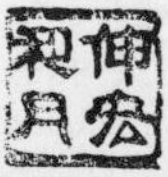
伸宏
和月

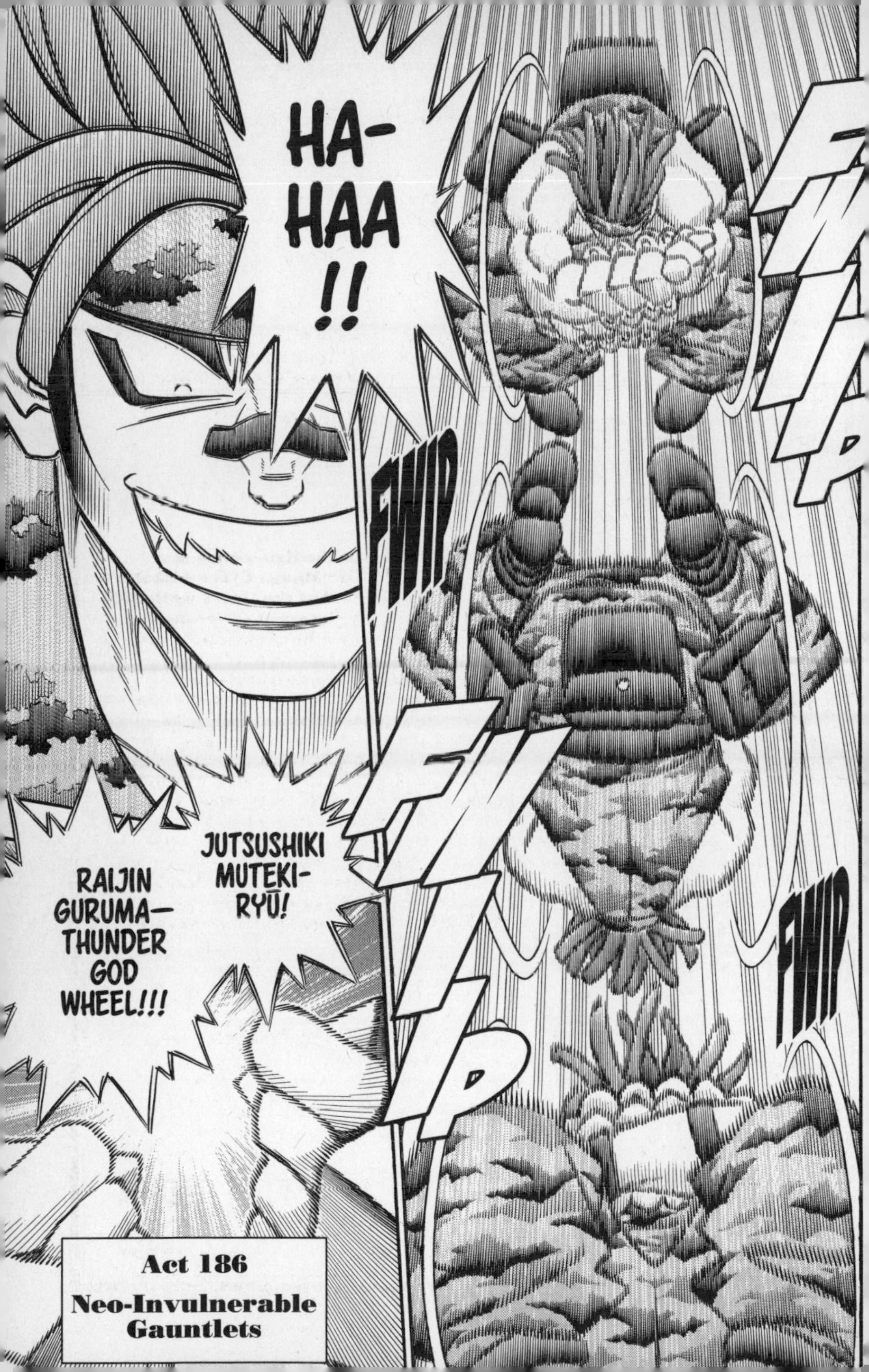
FWIP
FWIP
HA-HAA!!
FWIP
FWIP
JUTSUSHIKI MUTEKI-RYŪ!
RAIJIN GURUMA—THUNDER GOD WHEEL!!!

Act 186
Neo-Invulnerable Gauntlets

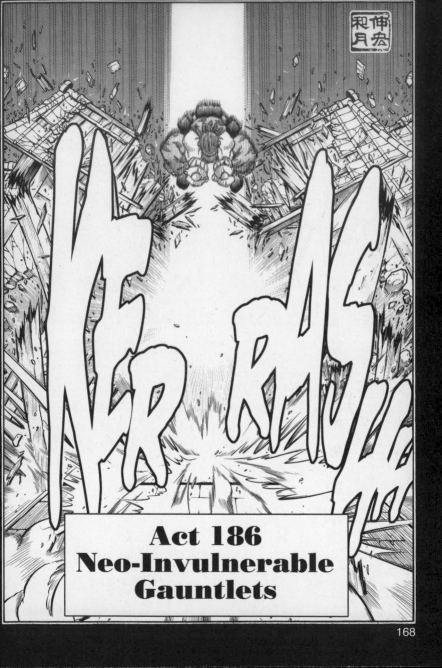

Act 186
Neo-Invulnerable
Gauntlets

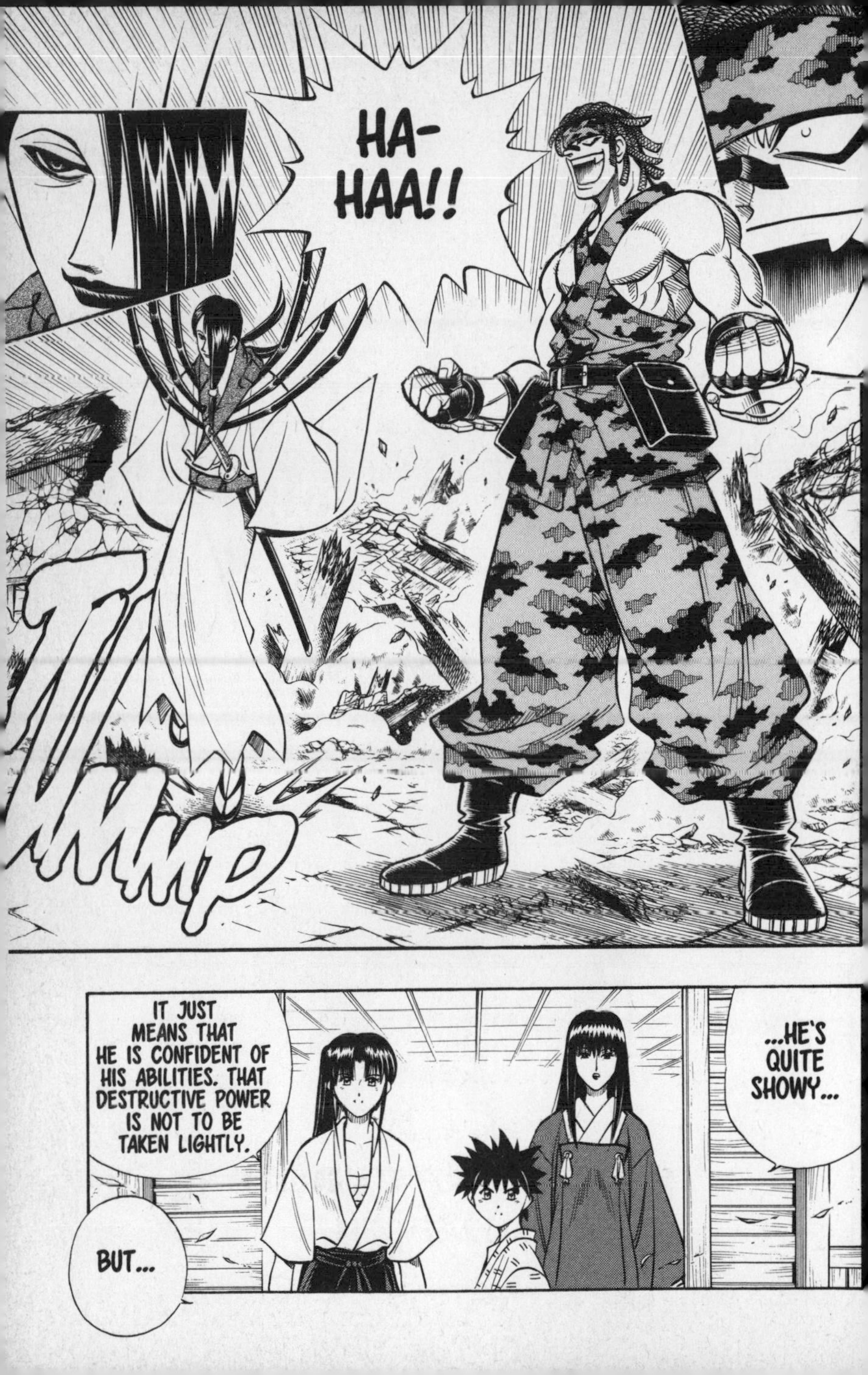
HA-HAA!!
...HE'S QUITE SHOWY...
IT JUST MEANS THAT HE IS CONFIDENT OF HIS ABILITIES. THAT DESTRUCTIVE POWER IS NOT TO BE TAKEN LIGHTLY.
BUT...

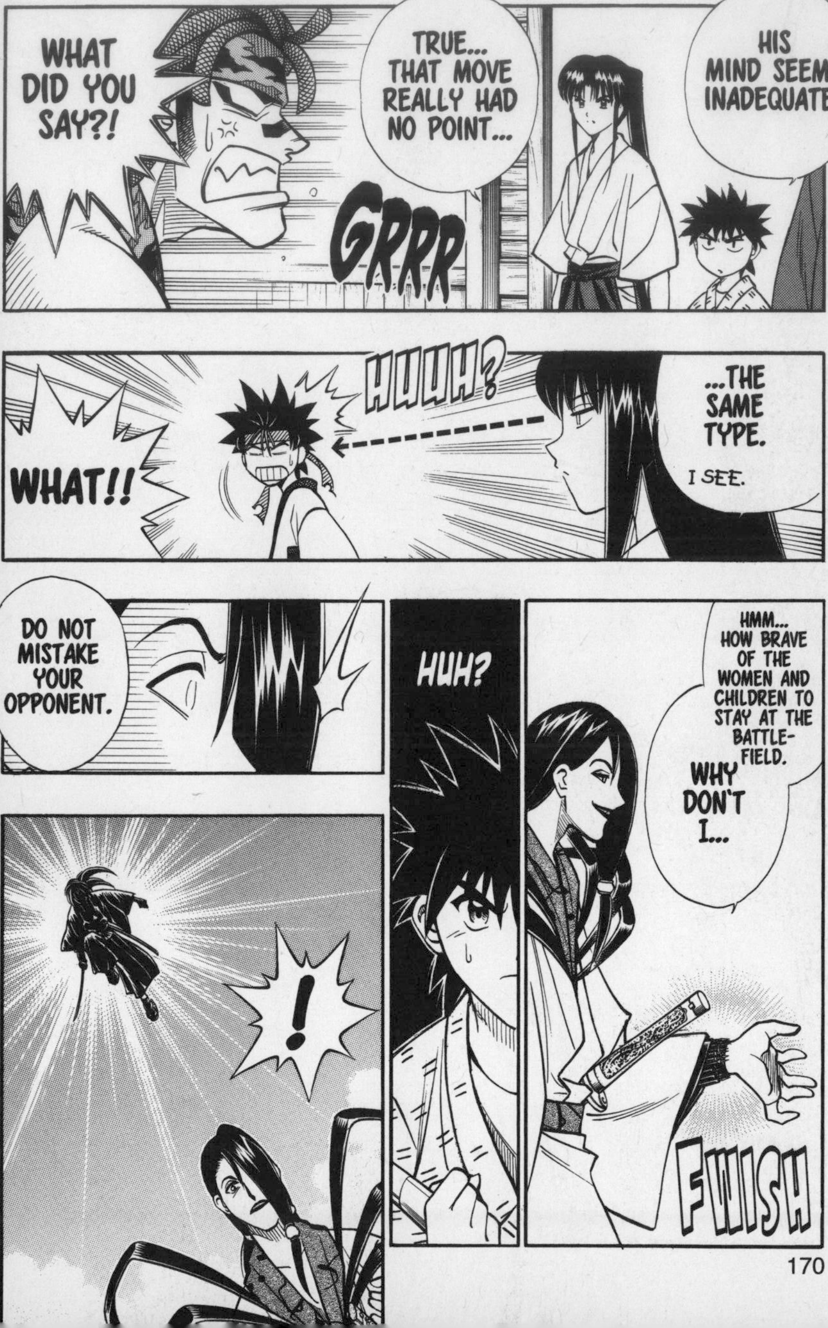
HIS MIND SEEMS INADEQUATE!
TRUE... THAT MOVE REALLY HAD NO POINT...
WHAT DID YOU SAY?!
GRRR
...THE SAME TYPE.
I SEE.
HUUH?
WHAT!!
HMM... HOW BRAVE OF THE WOMEN AND CHILDREN TO STAY AT THE BATTLE-FIELD.
WHY DON'T I...
FWISH
HUH?
DO NOT MISTAKE YOUR OPPONENT.
!

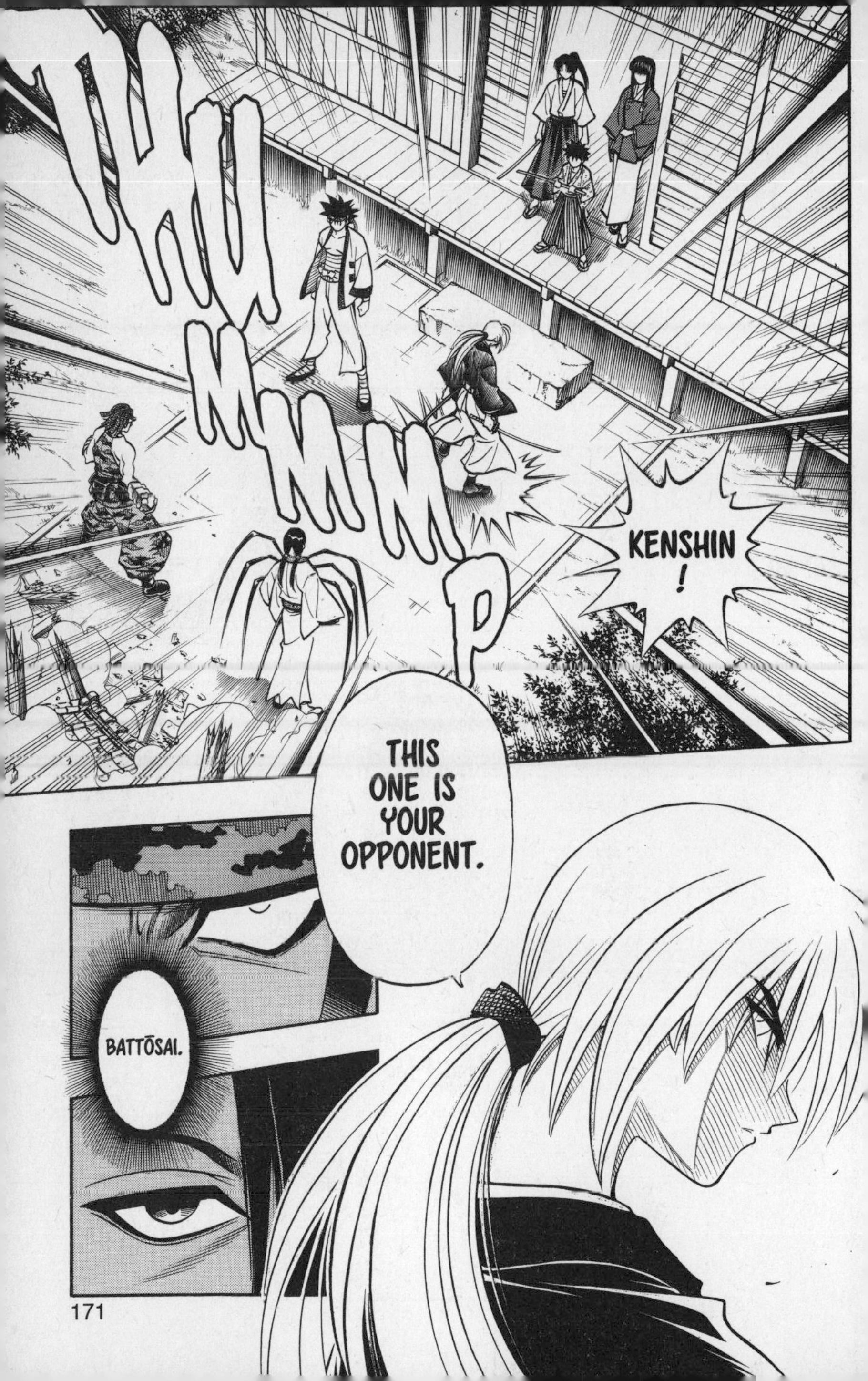
THUMMMMP
KENSHIN!
THIS ONE IS YOUR OPPONENT.
BATTŌSAI.

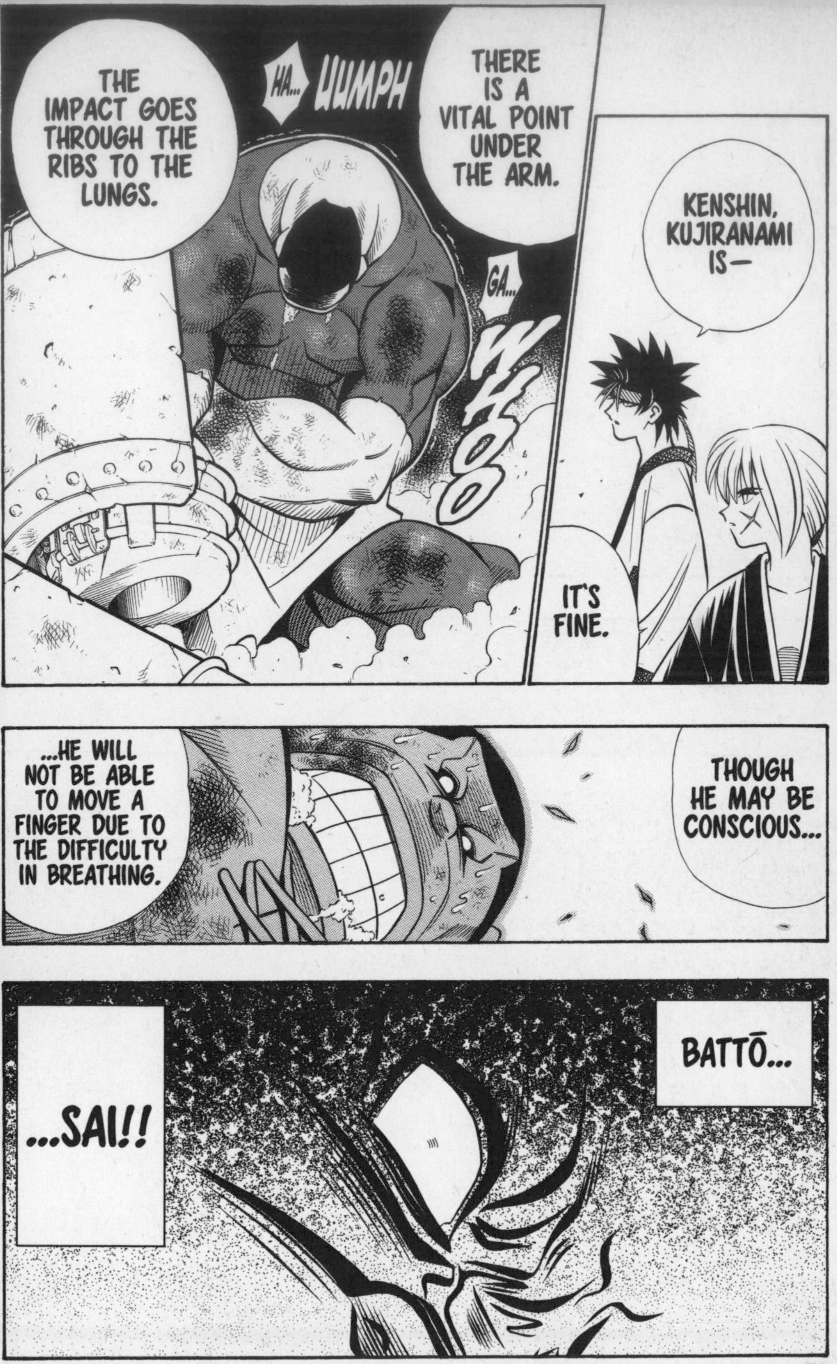
KENSHIN, KUJIRANAMI IS—
IT'S FINE.
THERE IS A VITAL POINT UNDER THE ARM.
HA... UUMPH
THE IMPACT GOES THROUGH THE RIBS TO THE LUNGS.
GA...
WHOOO
THOUGH HE MAY BE CONSCIOUS...
...HE WILL NOT BE ABLE TO MOVE A FINGER DUE TO THE DIFFICULTY IN BREATHING.
BATTŌ...
...SAI!!

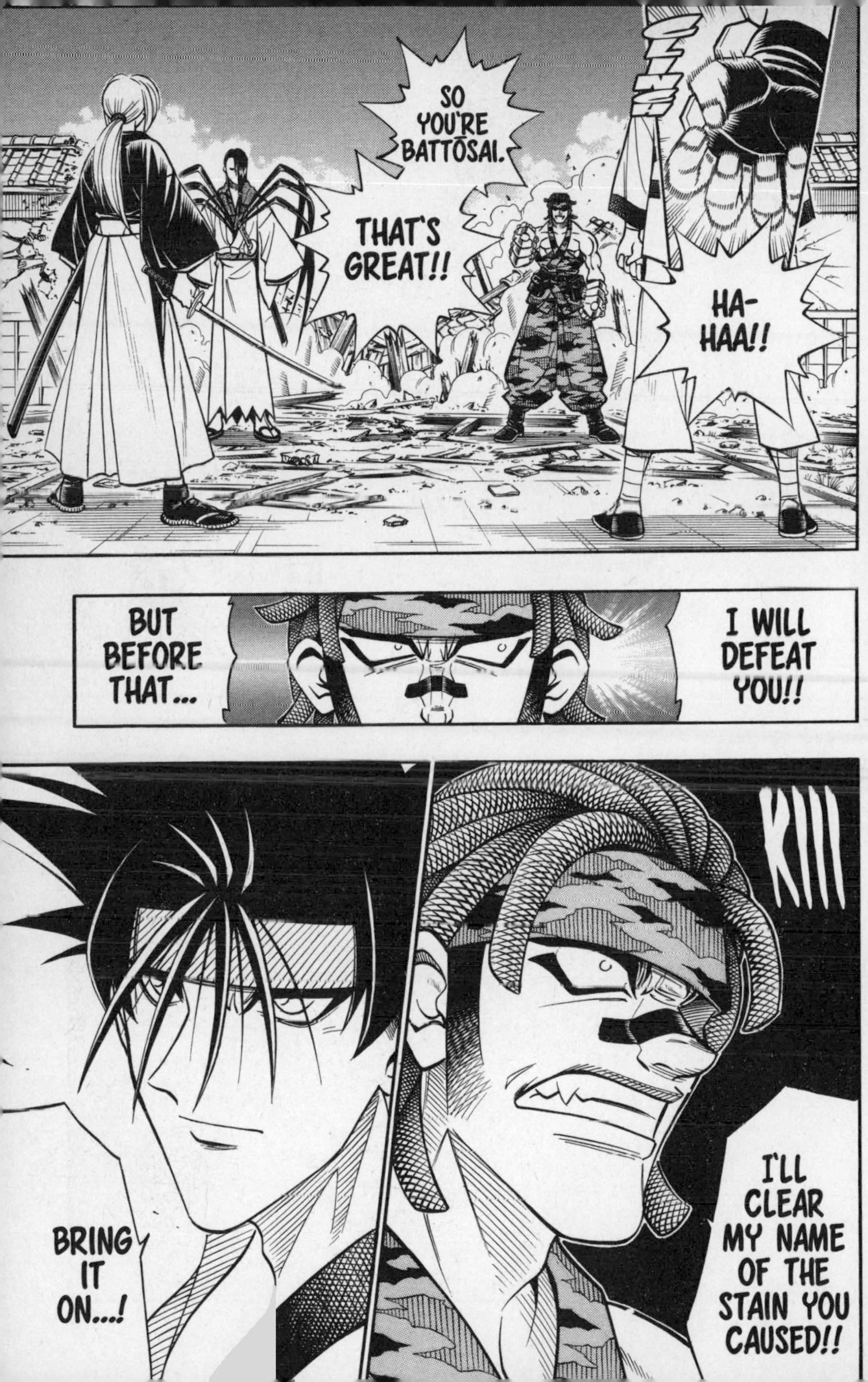
SO YOU'RE BATTŌSAI.
THAT'S GREAT!!
HA-HAA!!
I WILL DEFEAT YOU!!
BUT BEFORE THAT...
KIII
I'LL CLEAR MY NAME OF THE STAIN YOU CAUSED!!
BRING IT ON...!

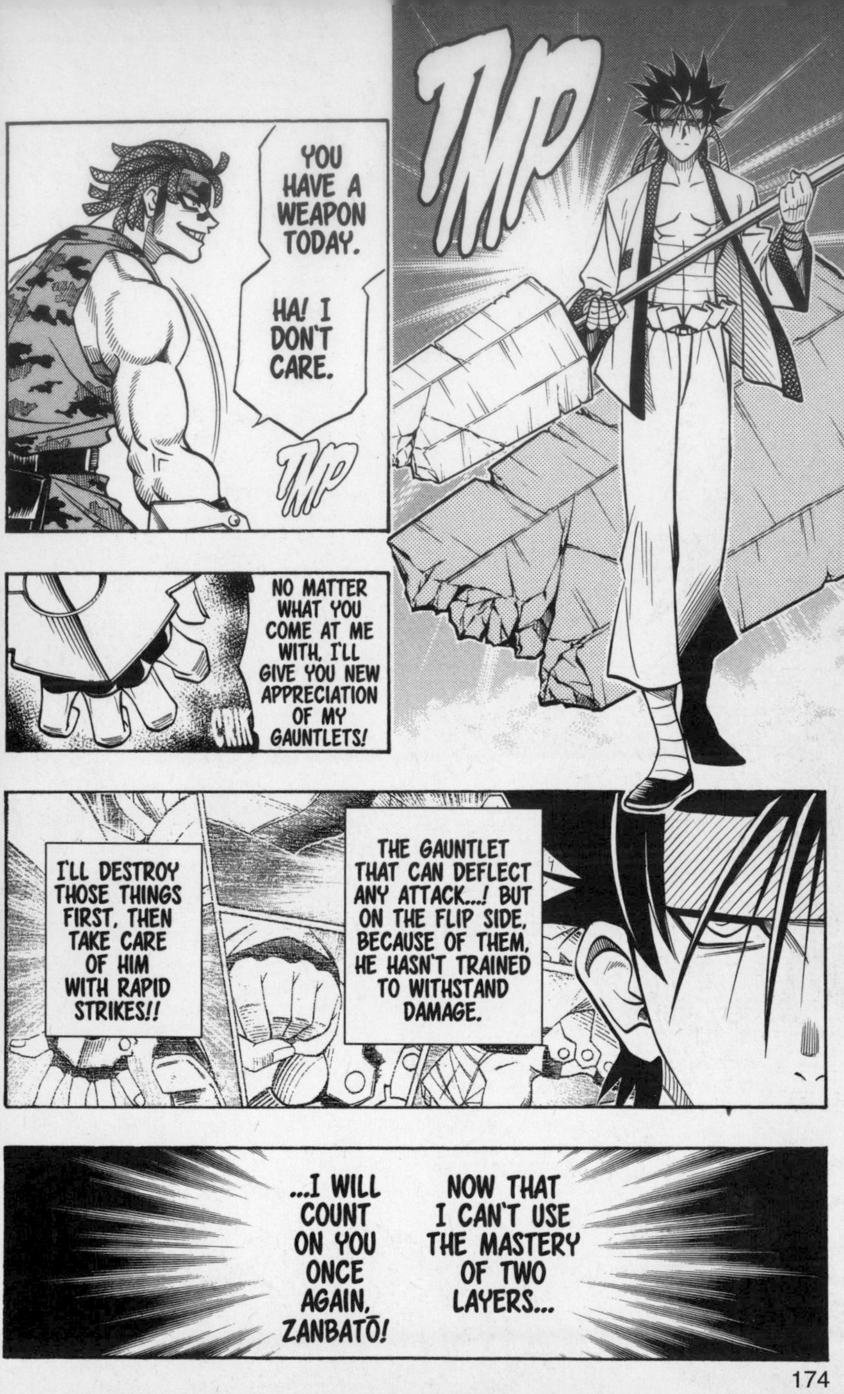
TMP
YOU HAVE A WEAPON TODAY.
HA! I DON'T CARE.
TMP
NO MATTER WHAT YOU COME AT ME WITH, I'LL GIVE YOU NEW APPRECIATION OF MY GAUNTLETS!
CRIK
THE GAUNTLET THAT CAN DEFLECT ANY ATTACK...! BUT ON THE FLIP SIDE, BECAUSE OF THEM, HE HASN'T TRAINED TO WITHSTAND DAMAGE.
I'LL DESTROY THOSE THINGS FIRST, THEN TAKE CARE OF HIM WITH RAPID STRIKES!!
NOW THAT I CAN'T USE THE MASTERY OF TWO LAYERS...
...I WILL COUNT ON YOU ONCE AGAIN, ZANBATŌ!

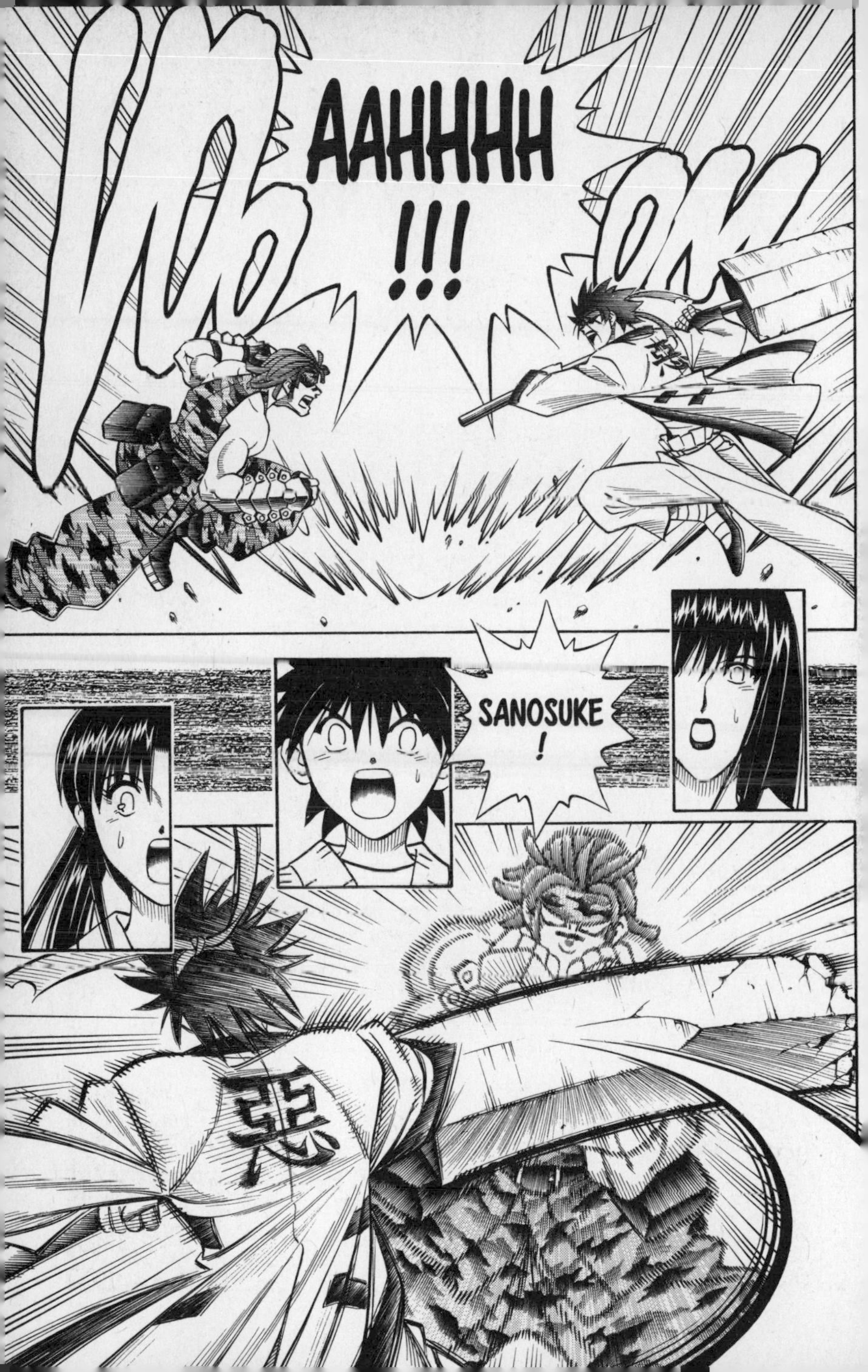
AAHHHH !!!
SANOSUKE !

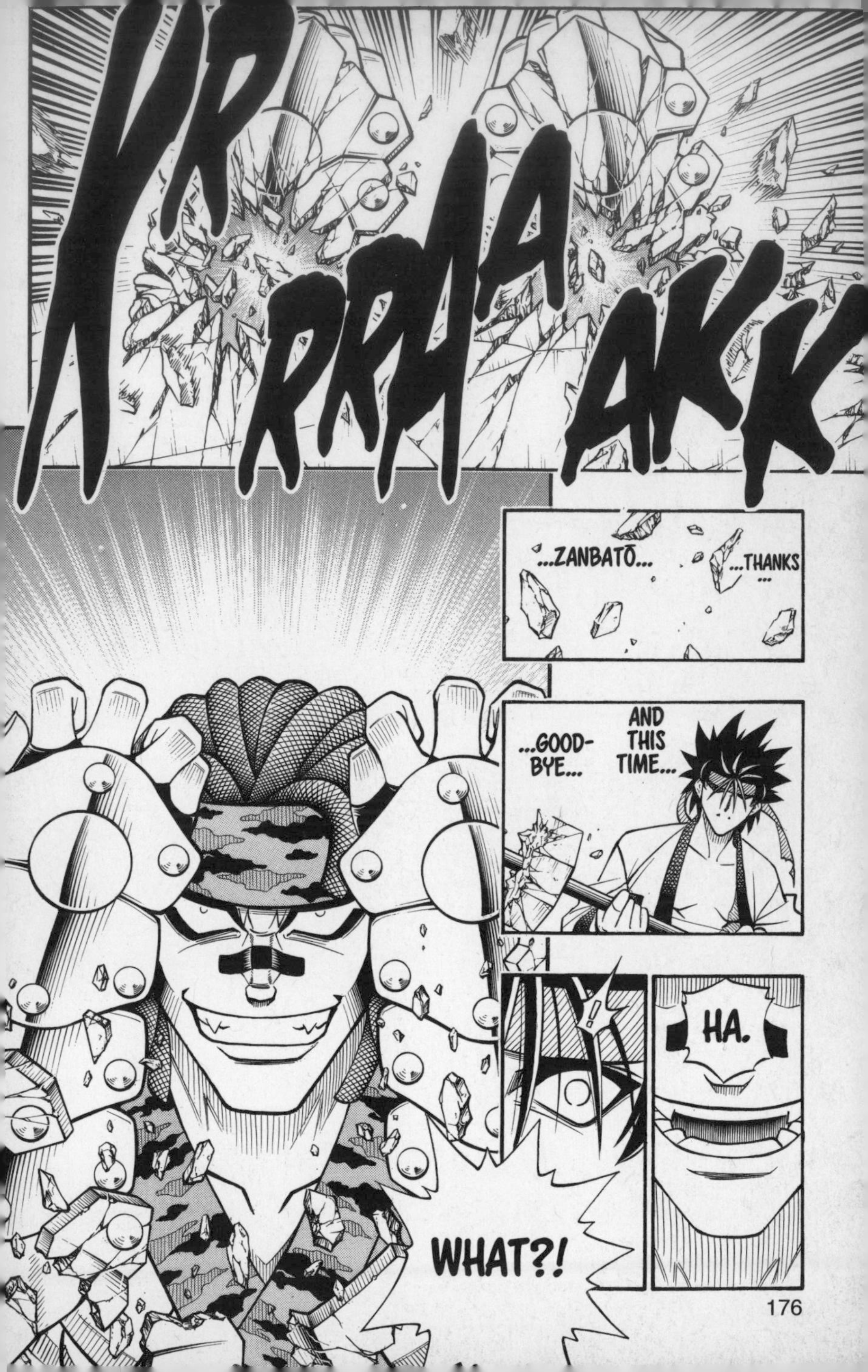
KRRAAAKK
...ZANBATŌ...
...THANKS...
AND THIS TIME...
...GOOD-BYE...
HA.
!
WHAT?!

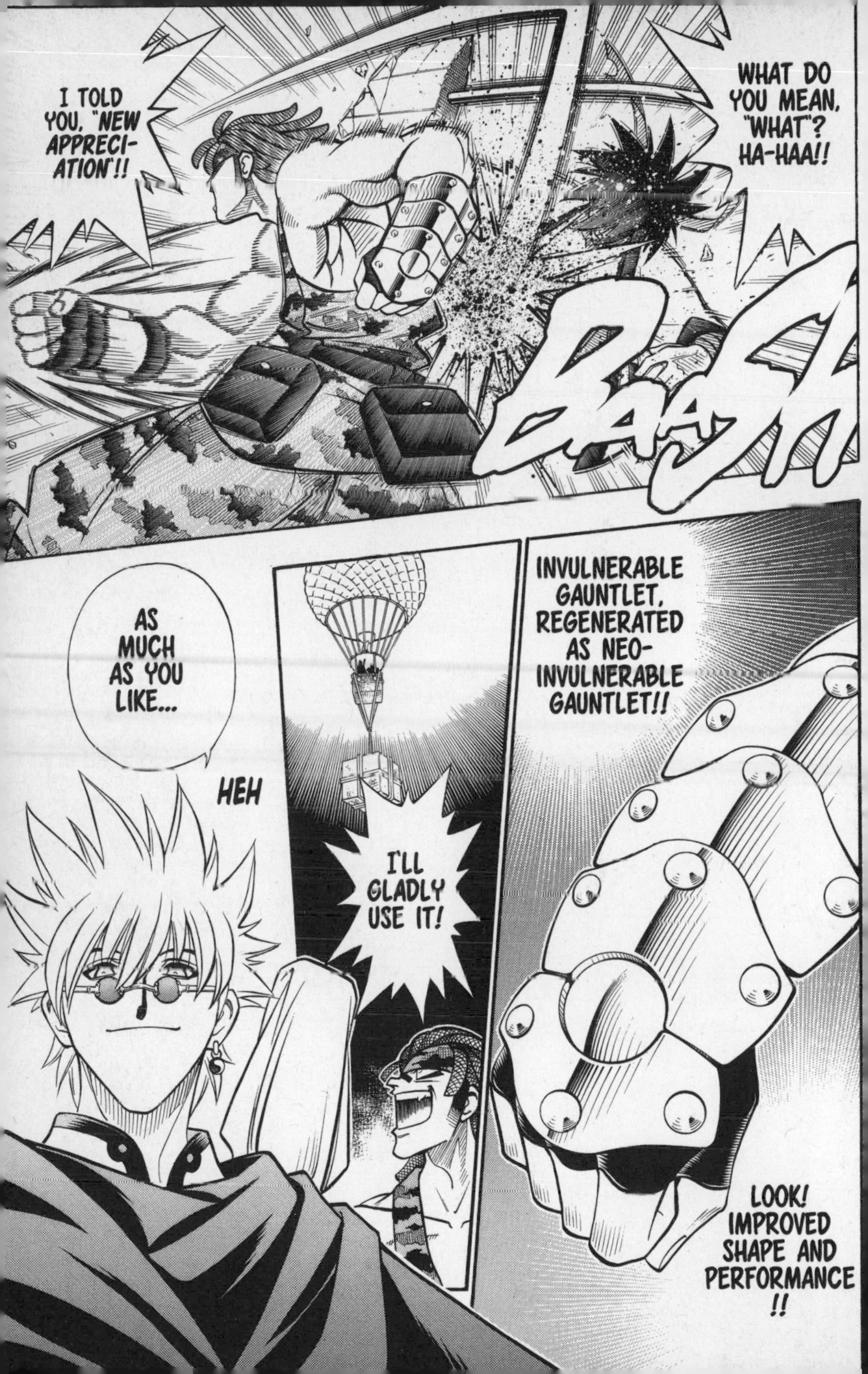
WHAT DO YOU MEAN, "WHAT"? HA-HAA!!
I TOLD YOU, "NEW APPRECIATION"!!
INVULNERABLE GAUNTLET, REGENERATED AS NEO-INVULNERABLE GAUNTLET!!
LOOK! IMPROVED SHAPE AND PERFORMANCE!!
I'LL GLADLY USE IT!
AS MUCH AS YOU LIKE...
HEH

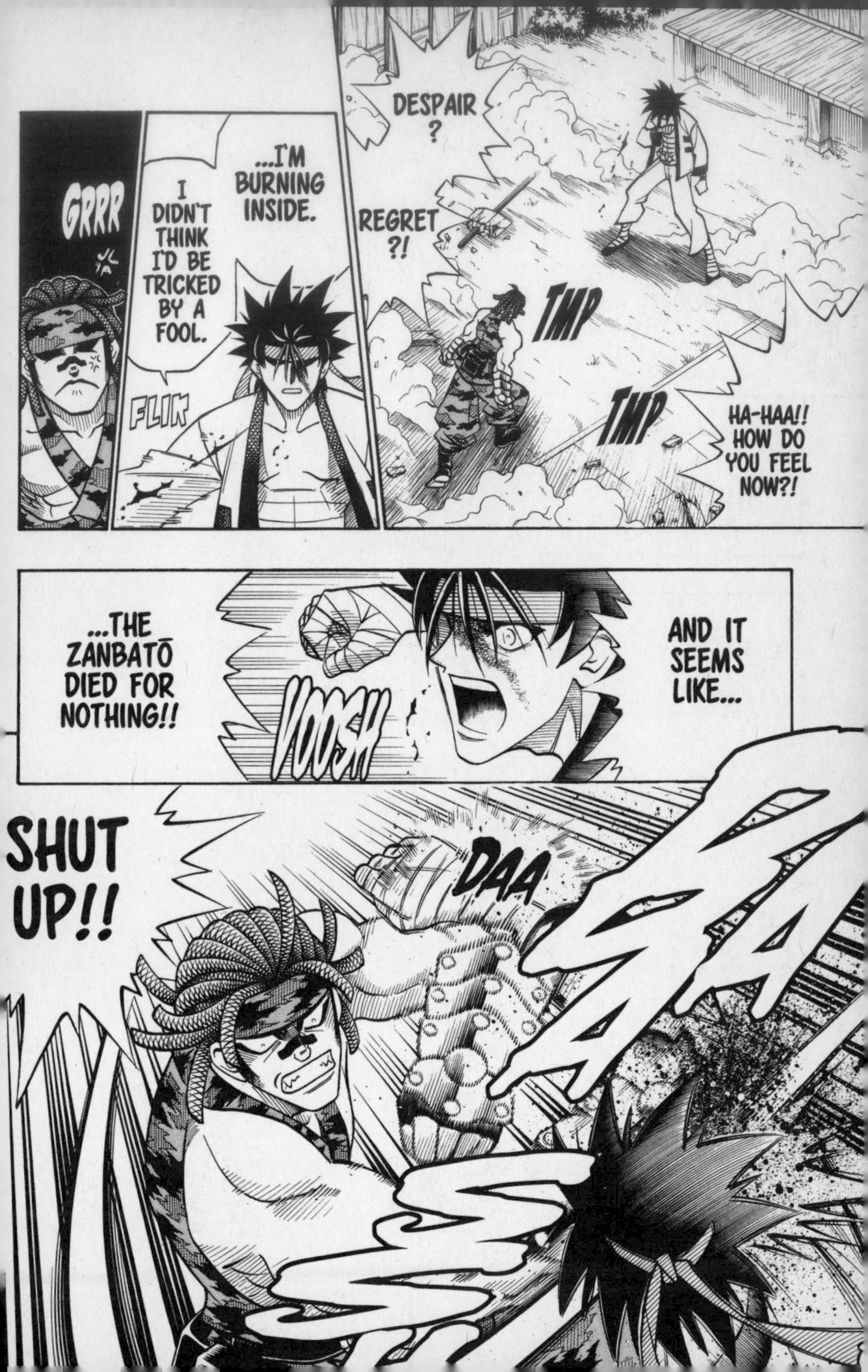
DESPAIR ?
REGRET ?!
TMP
TMP
HA-HAA!! HOW DO YOU FEEL NOW?!
...I'M BURNING INSIDE.
I DIDN'T THINK I'D BE TRICKED BY A FOOL.
FLIK
GRRR
AND IT SEEMS LIKE...
VOOSH
...THE ZANBATŌ DIED FOR NOTHING!!
DAA
SHUT UP!!

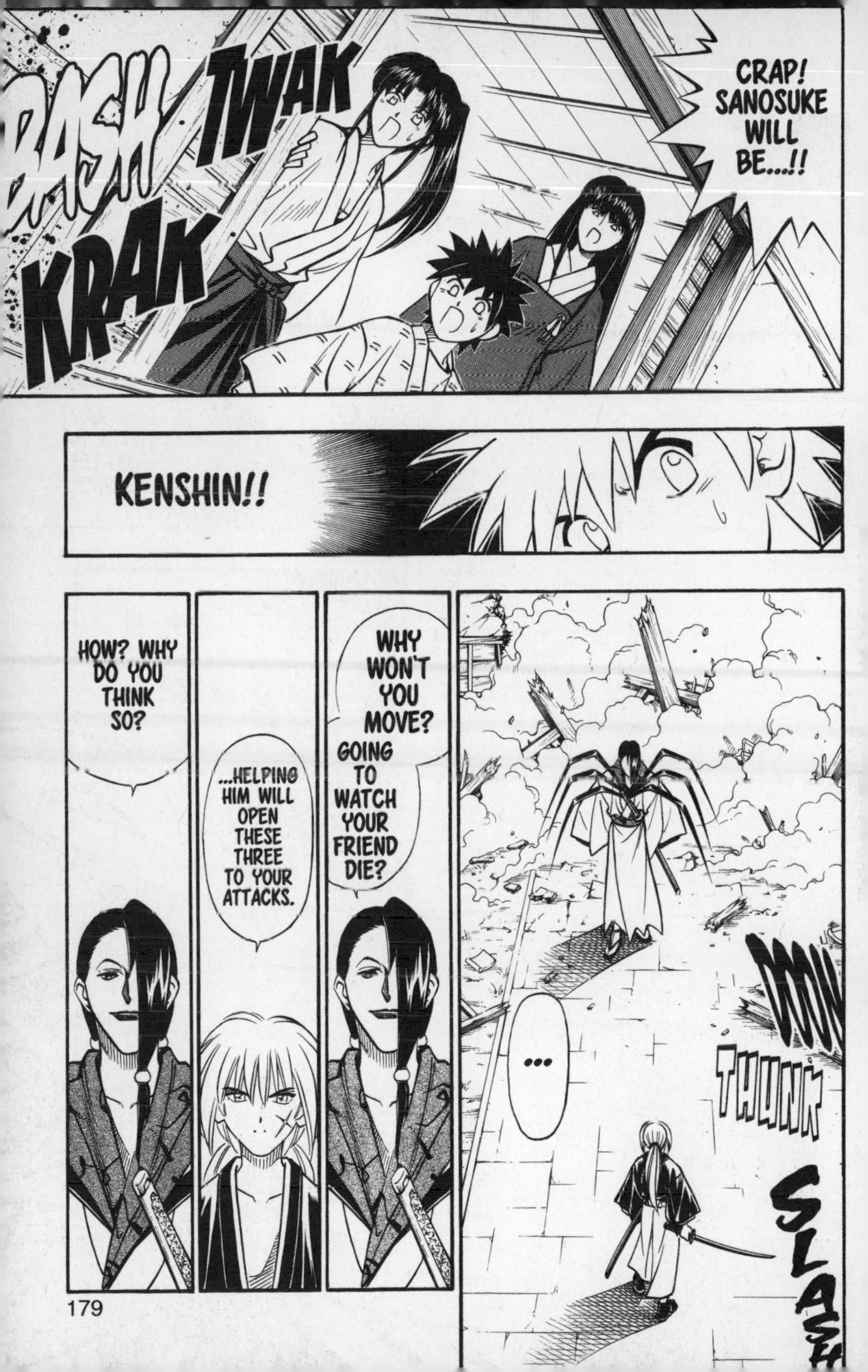
CRAP! SANOSUKE WILL BE...!!
TWAK
BACH
KRAK
KENSHIN!!
...
DOON
THUNK
SLASH
WHY WON'T YOU MOVE?
GOING TO WATCH YOUR FRIEND DIE?
...HELPING HIM WILL OPEN THESE THREE TO YOUR ATTACKS.
HOW? WHY DO YOU THINK SO?

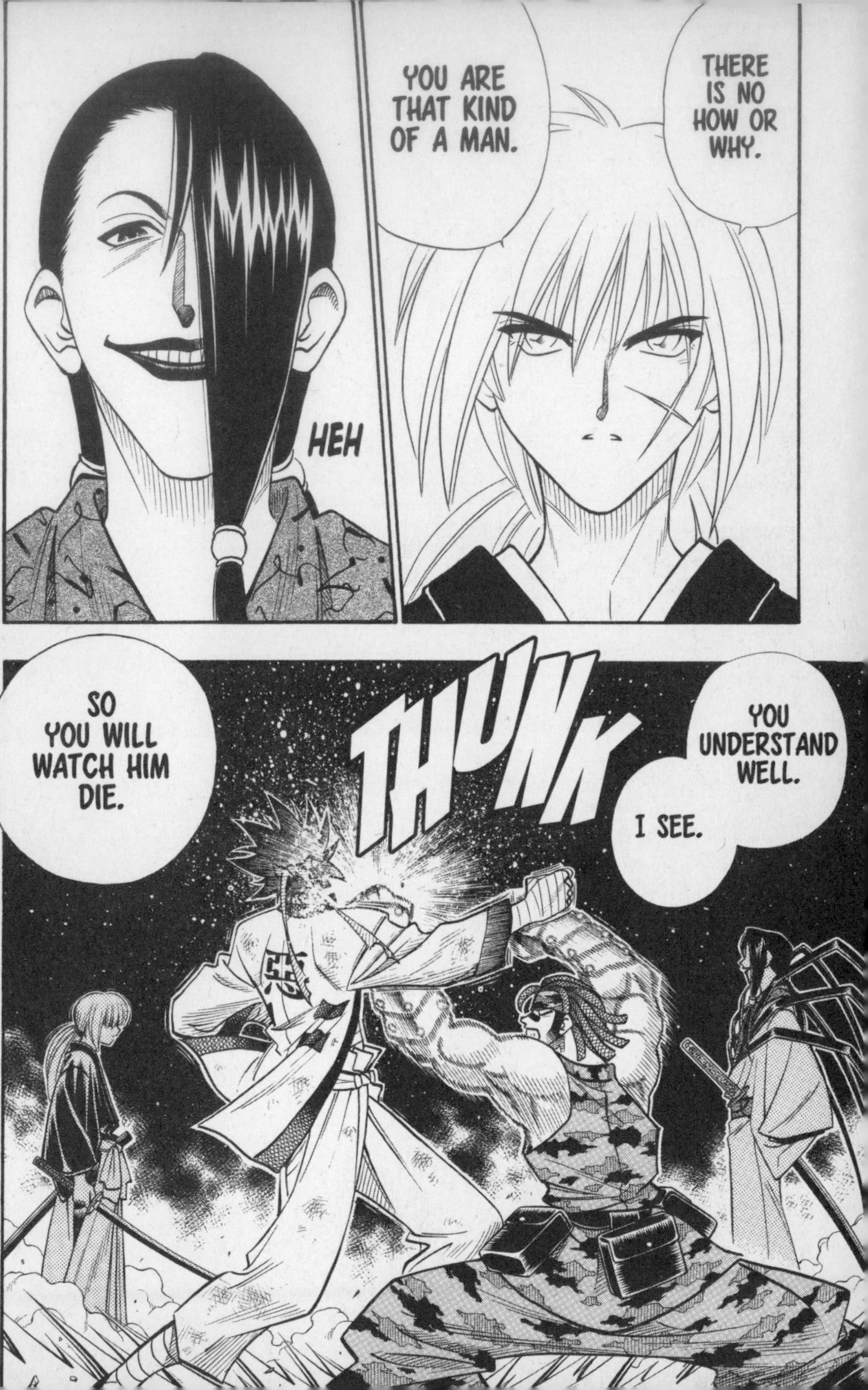
THERE IS NO HOW OR WHY.
YOU ARE THAT KIND OF A MAN.
HEH
YOU UNDERSTAND WELL.
I SEE.
THUNK
SO YOU WILL WATCH HIM DIE.

READ THIS WAY

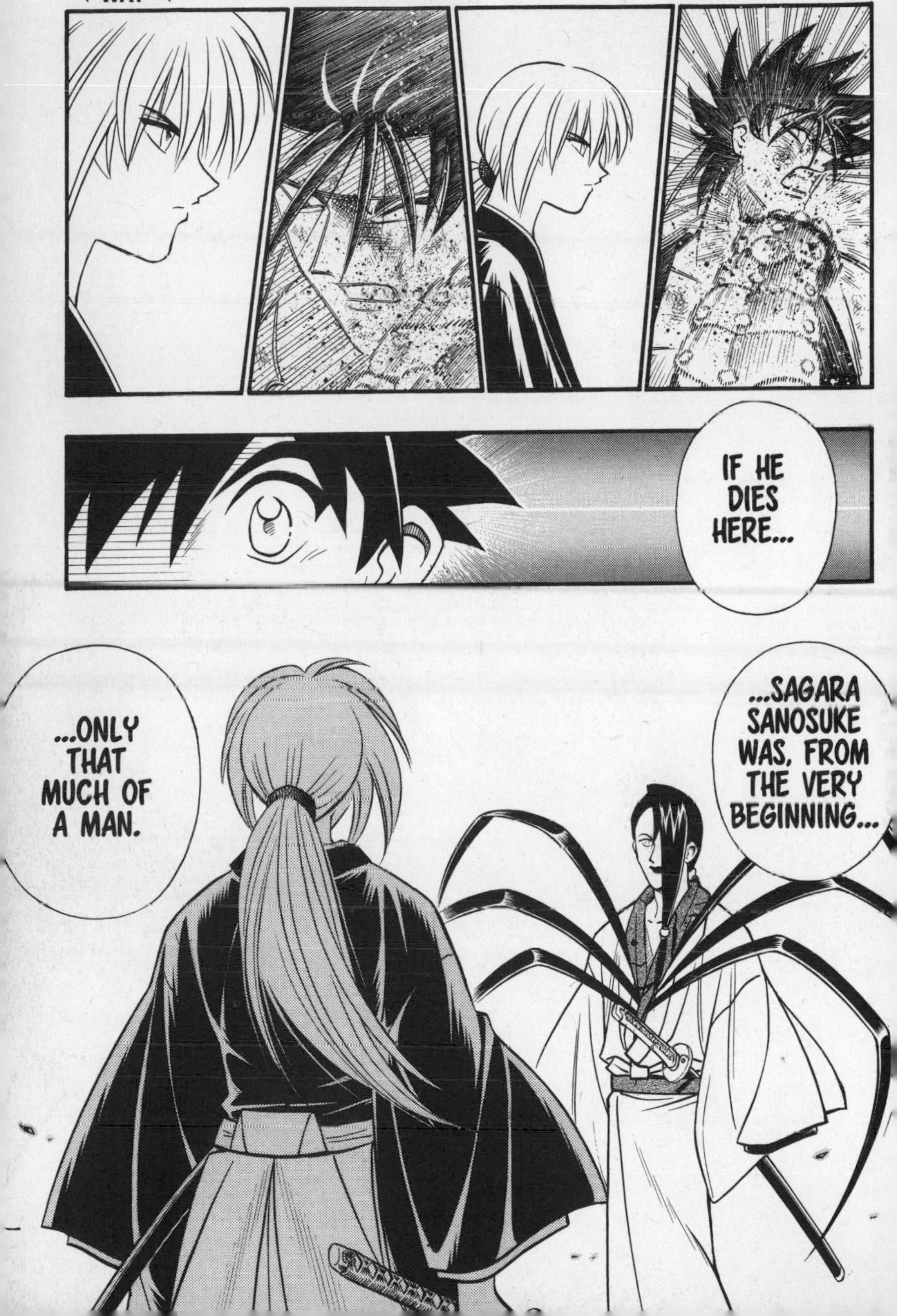
IF HE DIES HERE...
...SAGARA SANOSUKE WAS, FROM THE VERY BEGINNING...
...ONLY THAT MUCH OF A MAN.

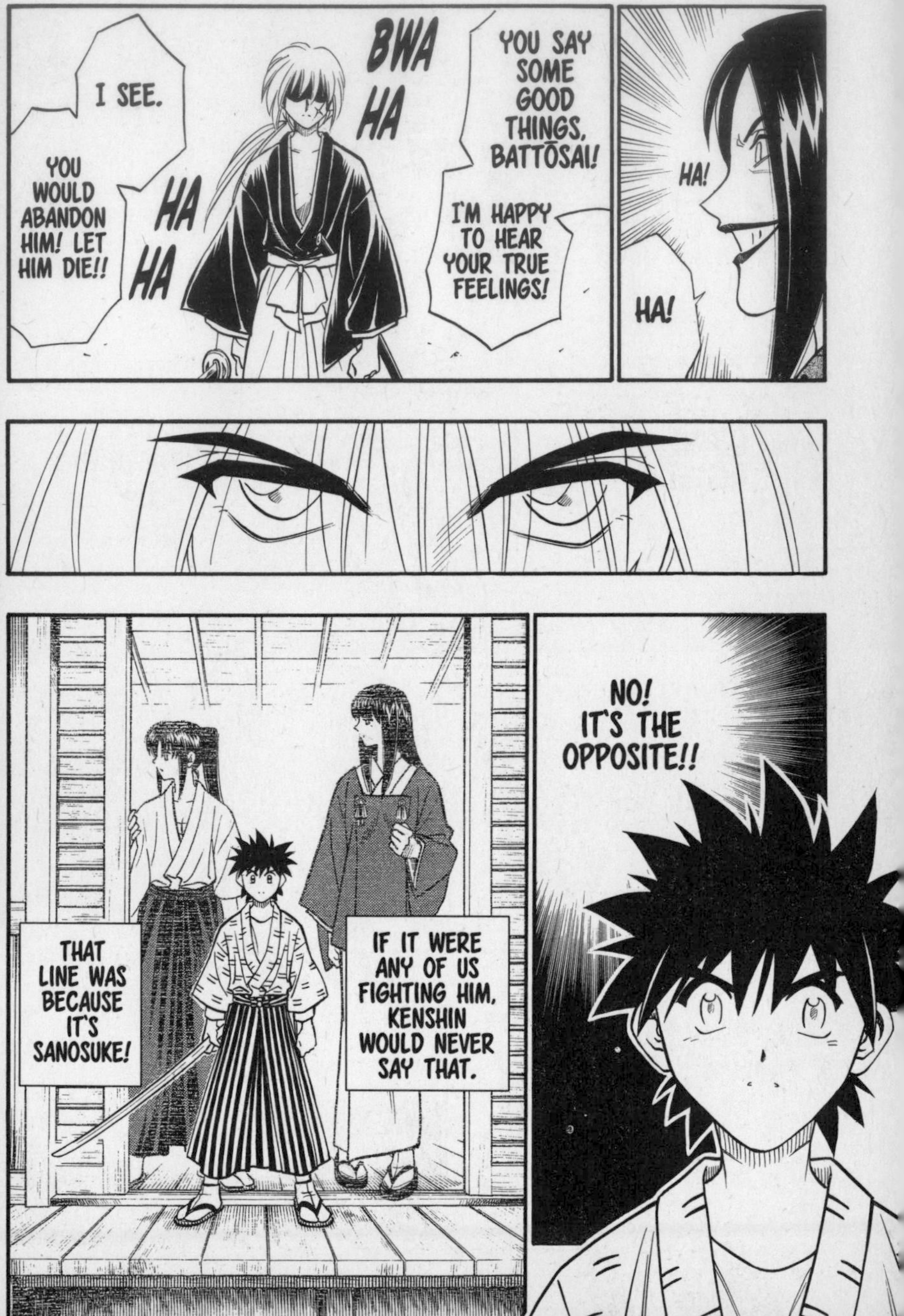
HA!
HA!
BWA HA
YOU SAY SOME GOOD THINGS, BATTŌSAI!
I'M HAPPY TO HEAR YOUR TRUE FEELINGS!
HA HA
I SEE.
YOU WOULD ABANDON HIM! LET HIM DIE!!
NO! IT'S THE OPPOSITE!!
IF IT WERE ANY OF US FIGHTING HIM, KENSHIN WOULD NEVER SAY THAT.
THAT LINE WAS BECAUSE IT'S SANOSUKE!

READ THIS WAY

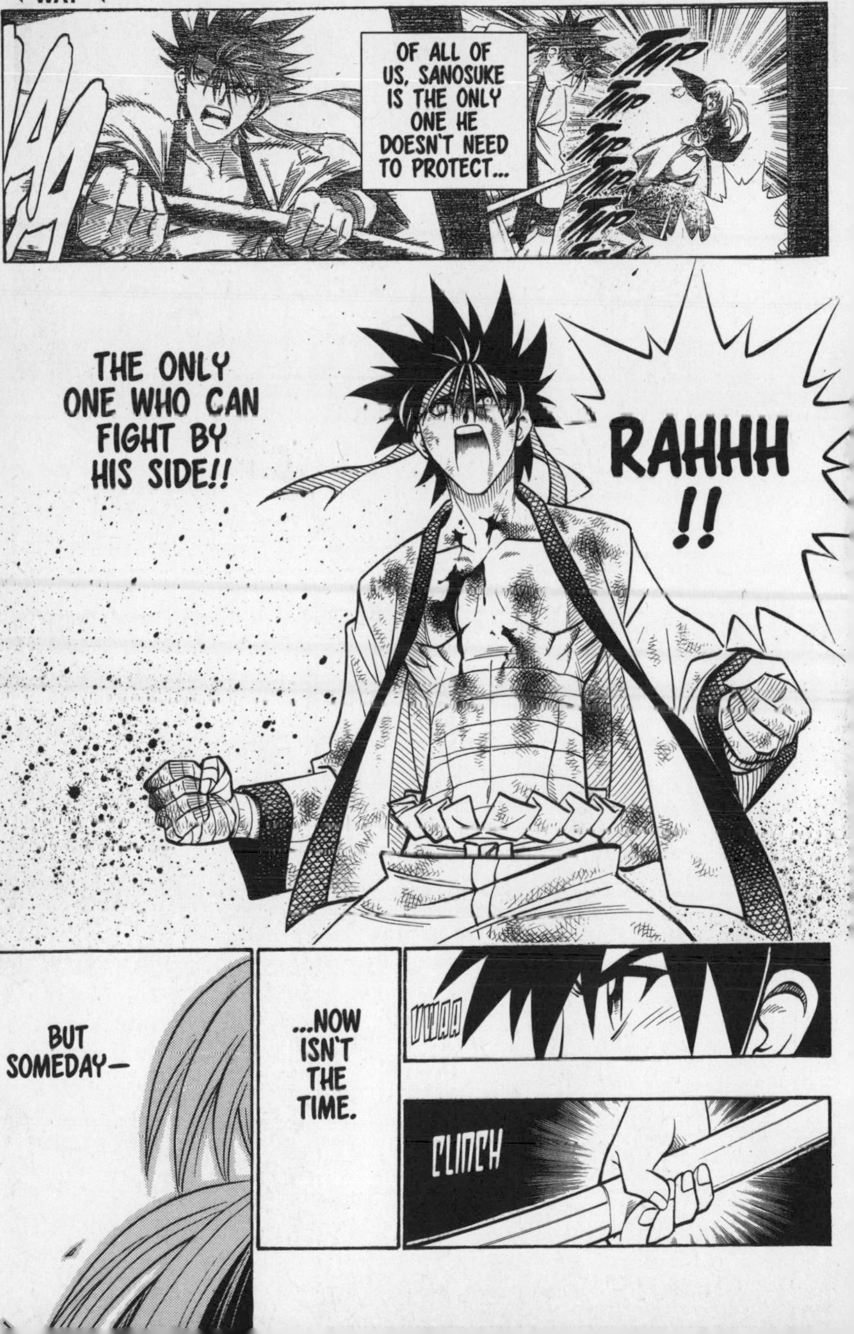
THP THP THP THP THP
OF ALL OF US, SANOSUKE IS THE ONLY ONE HE DOESN'T NEED TO PROTECT...
RAHHH!!
THE ONLY ONE WHO CAN FIGHT BY HIS SIDE!!
VWAA
CLINCH
...NOW ISN'T THE TIME.
BUT SOMEDAY—

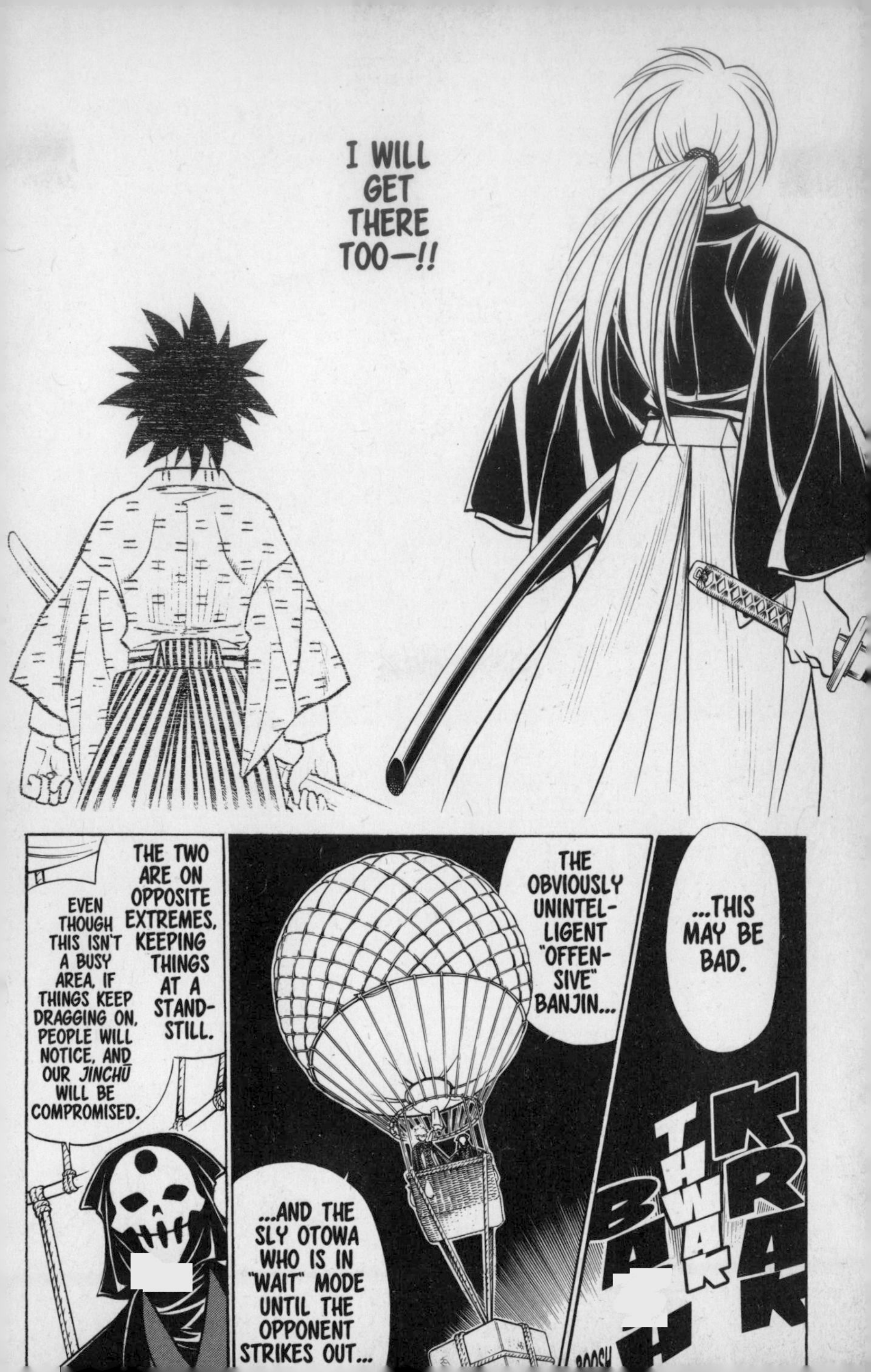
I WILL GET THERE TOO—!!
...THIS MAY BE BAD.
THWAK
KRAK
THE OBVIOUSLY UNINTEL-LIGENT "OFFEN-SIVE" BANJIN...
...AND THE SLY OTOWA WHO IS IN "WAIT" MODE UNTIL THE OPPONENT STRIKES OUT...
THE TWO ARE ON OPPOSITE EXTREMES, KEEPING THINGS AT A STAND-STILL.
EVEN THOUGH THIS ISN'T A BUSY AREA, IF THINGS KEEP DRAGGING ON, PEOPLE WILL NOTICE, AND OUR JINCHŪ WILL BE COMPROMISED.

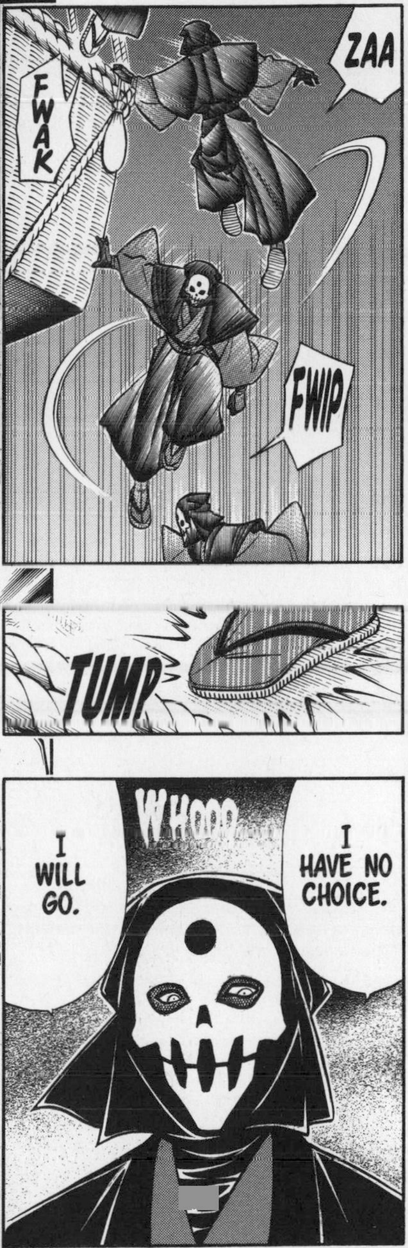
ZAA
FWAK
FWIP
TUMP
WHOOO
I HAVE NO CHOICE.
I WILL GO.

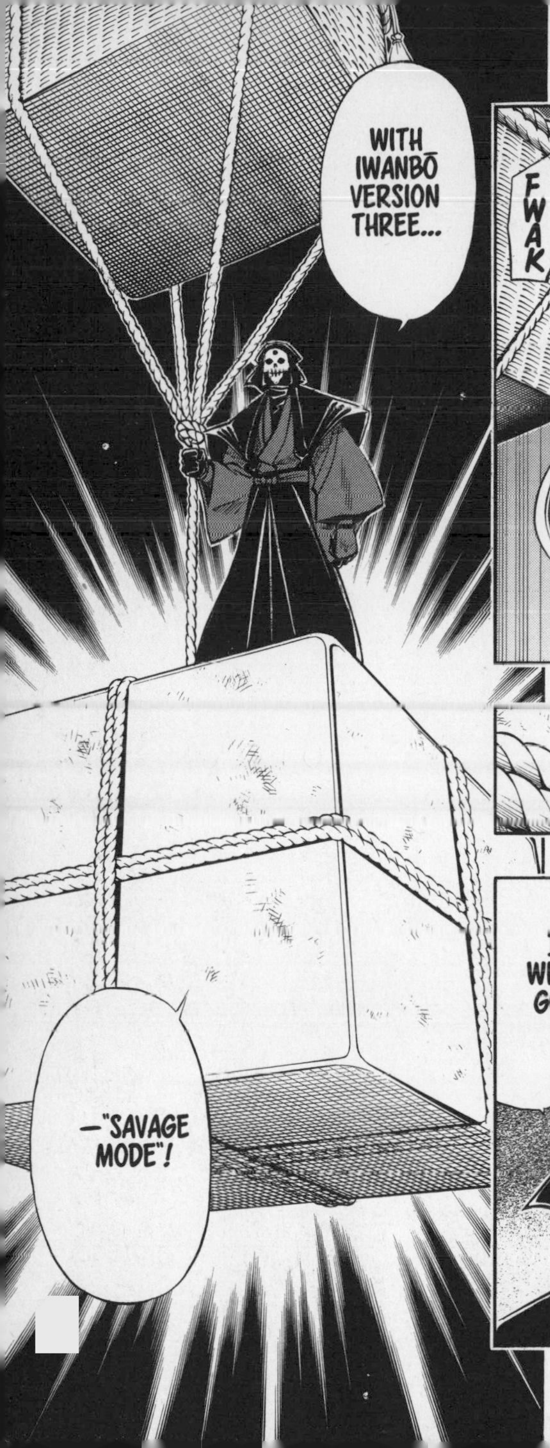
WITH IWANBŌ VERSION THREE...
—"SAVAGE MODE"!

To Be Continued in Vol. 22: Battle On Three Fronts

GLOSSARY of the RESTORATION

A brief guide to select Japanese terms used in **Rurouni Kenshin**. *Note that, both here and within the story itself, all names are Japanese style—i.e., last or "family" name first, with personal or "given" name following. This is both because* **Kenshin** *is a "period" story, as well as to decrease confusion—if we were to take the example of Kenshin's* sakabatô *and "reverse" the format of the historically established assassin-name "Hitokiri Battôsai," for example, it would make little sense to then call him "Battôsai Himura."*

Himura Kenshin
Kenshin's "real" name, revealed to Kaoru only at her urging

Hiten Mitsurugi-ryû
Kenshin's sword technique, used more for defense than offense. An "ancient style that pits one against many," it requires exceptional speed and agility to master.

hitokiri
An assassin. Famous swordsmen of the period were sometimes thus known to adopt "professional" names—**Kawakami Gensai**, for example, was also known as "Hitokiri Gensai."

Ikeda-ya Incident
A group of radical **Ishin Shishi** plot to burn Kyoto, assassinate government officials, and transfer the emperor to Chôshû, but an attack by the **Shinsengumi** derails the plan

Ishin Shishi
Loyalist or pro-Imperialist **patriots** who fought to restore the Emperor to his ancient seat of power

Kawakami Gensai
Real-life, historical inspiration for the character of **Himura Kenshin**

Kinmon Incident
A clash between the forces of Aizu and Chôshû

Bakumatsu
Final, chaotic days of the Tokugawa regime

Boshin War
Civil war of 1868-69 between the new government and the **Tokugawa Bakufu**. The anti-*Bakufu*, pro-Imperial side (the Imperial Army) won, easily defeating the Tokugawa supporters.

-chan
Honorific. Can be used either as a diminutive (e.g., with a small child—"Little Hanako or Kentarô"), or with those who are grown, to indicate affection ("My dear...").

dô
In *kendo*, this is a strike to the stomach

-dono
Honorific. Even more respectful than -**san**; the effect in modern-day Japanese conversation would be along the lines of "Milord So-and-So." As used by Kenshin, it indicates both respect and humility.

Edo
Capital city of the **Tokugawa Bakufu**; renamed **Tokyo** ("Eastern Capital") after the Meiji Restoration

hakubaikô
The fragrance of white plum blossoms

-san
Honorific. Carries the meaning of "Mr.," "Ms.," "Miss," etc., but used more extensively in Japanese than its English equivalent (note that even an enemy may be addressed as "-san").

Shinsengumi
Elite, notorious, government-sanctioned and exceptionally skilled swordsman-supporters of the military government (*Bakufu*) which had ruled Japan for nearly 250 years, the *Shinsengumi* ("newly selected corps") were established in 1863 to suppress the *loyalists* and to restore law and order to the blood-soaked streets of *Kyoto*

shôgun
Feudal military ruler of Japan

shôgunate
See *Tokugawa Bakufu*

Toba Fushimi, Battle at
Battle near *Kyoto* between the forces of the new, imperial government and the fallen *shôgunate*. Ending with an imperial victory, it was the first battle of the *Boshin War*.

Tokugawa Bakufu
Military feudal government which dominated Japan from 1603 to 1867

Tokyo
The renaming of "*Edo*" to "*Tokyo*" is a marker of the start of the *Meiji Restoration*

-kun
Honorific. Used in the modern day among male students, or those who grew up together, but another usage—the one you're more likely to find in *Rurouni Kenshin*—is the "superior-to-inferior" form, intended as a way to emphasize a difference in status or rank, as well as to indicate familiarity or affection.

Kyoto
Home of the Emperor and imperial court from A.D. 794 until shortly after the *Meiji Restoration* in 1868

loyalists
Those who supported the return of the Emperor to power; *Ishin Shishi*

Meiji Restoration
1853-1868; culminated in the collapse of the *Tokugawa Bakufu* and the restoration of imperial rule. So called after Emperor Meiji, whose chosen name was written with the characters for "culture and enlightenment."

patriots
Another term for *Ishin Shishi*...and, when used by Sano, not a flattering one

rurouni
Wanderer, vagabond

sakabatô
Reversed-edge sword (the dull edge on the side the sharp should be, and vice versa); carried by Kenshin as a symbol of his resolution never to kill again

-sama
Honorific. The respectful equivalent of *-san*, *-sama* is used primarily in addressing persons of much higher rank than one's self...or, in a romantic sense, in addressing those upon whom one is crushing, wicked hard.

IN THE NEXT VOLUME...

The time of Enishi and the Six Comrade's *Jinchû* is now at hand, and the fight has been brought straight to Kamiya Dojo. Yahiko squares off against a devious fighter who pulls no punches; Sano locks fists with a brawler whose lust for blood seems limitless; and Kenshin faces a familiar villain with a whole new appearance. Will the crucible of battle absolve Kenshin of his past sins?

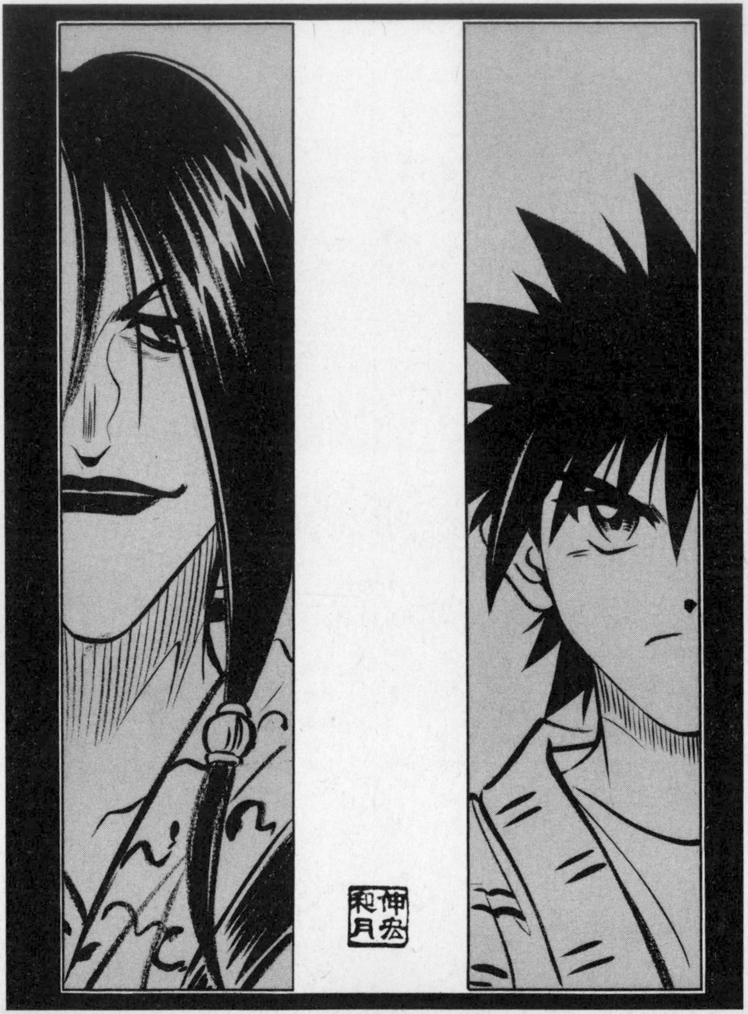

Available in January 2006

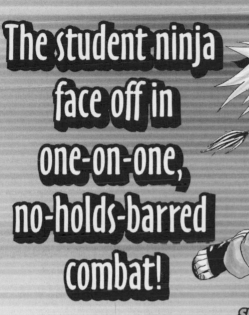

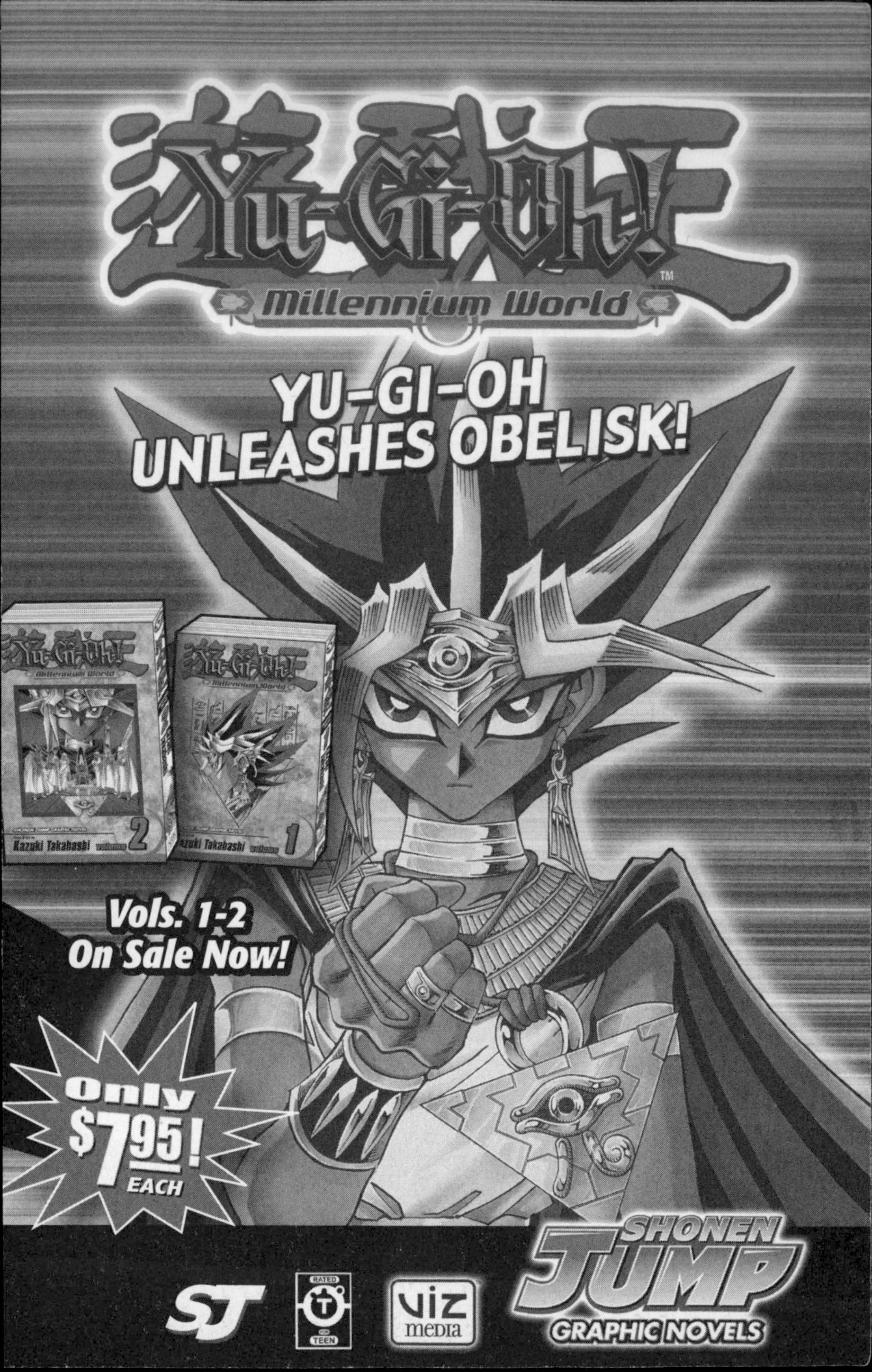
Yu-Gi-Oh!™
Millennium World
YU-GI-OH
UNLEASHES OBELISK!
Kazuki Takahashi volume 2
Kazuki Takahashi volume 1
Vols. 1-2
On Sale Now!
Only
$7.95!
EACH
SJ
RATED T TEEN
viz media
SHONEN JUMP
GRAPHIC NOVELS

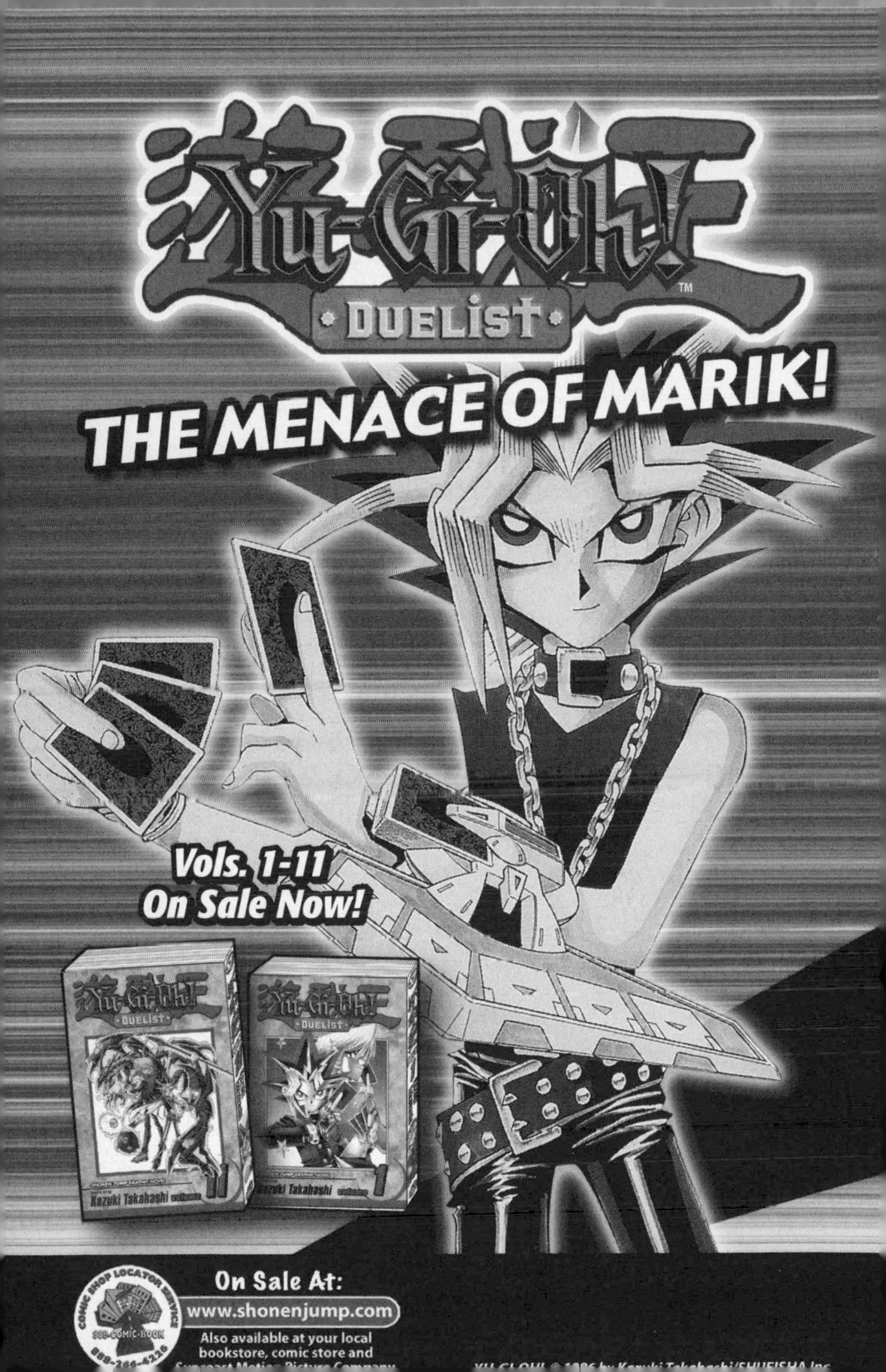

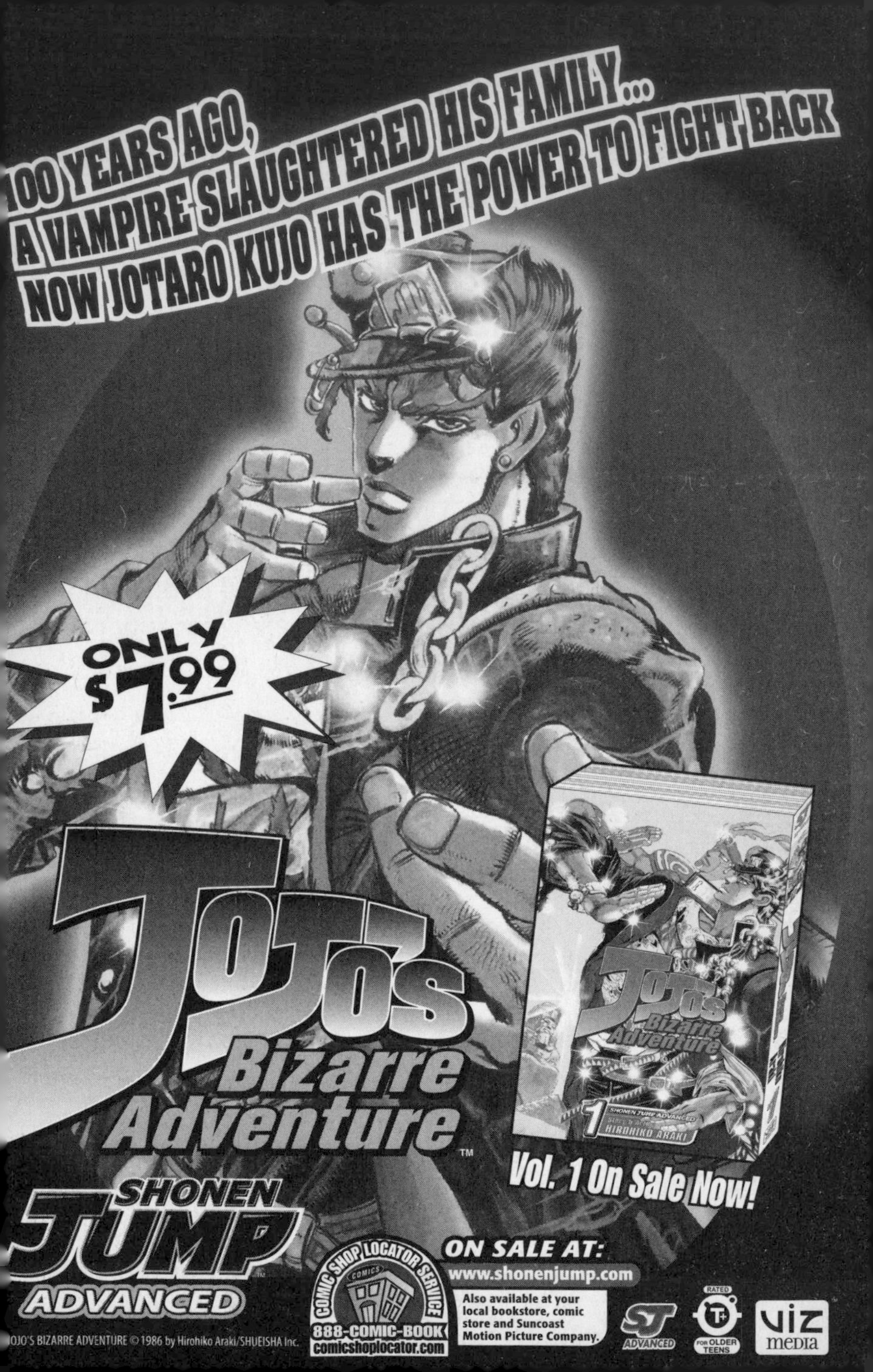

100 YEARS AGO,
A VAMPIRE SLAUGHTERED HIS FAMILY...
NOW JOTARO KUJO HAS THE POWER TO FIGHT BACK
ONLY $7.99
JoJo's Bizarre Adventure™
Vol. 1 On Sale Now!
SHONEN JUMP ADVANCED
ON SALE AT:
www.shonenjump.com
Also available at your local bookstore, comic store and Suncoast Motion Picture Company.
COMIC SHOP LOCATOR SERVICE
888-COMIC-BOOK
comicshoplocator.com
SJ ADVANCED
RATED T+ FOR OLDER TEENS
viz media
JOJO'S BIZARRE ADVENTURE © 1986 by Hirohiko Araki/SHUEISHA Inc.